*Brazil and the
Dialectic of
Colonization*

Brazil and the Dialectic of Colonization

ALFREDO BOSI

Translated by
Robert Patrick Newcomb

University of Illinois Press
URBANA, CHICAGO, AND SPRINGFIELD

Published in cooperation with the Lemann
Institute for Brazilian Studies, University of
Illinois at Urbana-Champaign

Funds for the publication of this translation
were provided by the Lemann Institute and
by the Ministério da Cultura do Brasil /
Fundação Biblioteca Nacional of Brazil

Obra publicada com o apoio do
Ministério da Cultura do Brasil /
Fundação Biblioteca Nacional

© 1992, Alfredo Bosi
Published in Brazil by Editora Companhia
das Letras, São Paulo

Translation © 2015 by the Board of Trustees
of the University of Illinois
All rights reserved
Manufactured in the United States of America
1 2 3 4 5 C P 5 4 3 2 1
♾ This book is printed on acid-free paper.

Library of Congress Control Number: 2015944265

ISBN 978-0-252-03930-0 (hardcover)
ISBN 978-0-252-08084-5 (paperback)
ISBN 978-0-252-09735-5 (e-book)

For
Celso Furtado
Jacob Gorender
Pedro Casaldáliga
thought made action

Contents

Acknowledgments ix
Author's Note to the North American Edition xi

1   Colony, Cult, and Culture 1
2   Anchieta, or the Crossed Arrows of the Sacred 48
3   From Our Former State to the Mercantile Machine 75
4   Vieira, or the Cross of Inequality 97
5   Antonil, or the Tears of Trade Goods 123
6   A Sacrificial Myth: Alencar's Indianism 146
7   Slavery between Two Liberalisms 163
8   Under the Sign of Ham 209
9   The Archeology of the Welfare State 235
10 Brazilian Culture and Brazilian Cultures 266
    Postscript to "Brazilian Culture and
    Brazilian Cultures" (1992) 299
    A Retrospective Glance 325
    Epilogue (2001) 333

    Notes 341
    Index 365

Acknowledgments

This book was written at different moments in time. Its point of departure is found in the courses on Brazilian literature I have taught at the University of São Paulo since 1970. Certain passages in the book were published previously and appear here after light or substantial revisions. The greater part of the text, however, has not been previously published. I would like to thank the Guggenheim Foundation, which in 1986 awarded me a grant that allowed me to conduct archival research in Rome and Lisbon. I am especially grateful to the following friends, who helped me access out-of-print or otherwise rare books: Helena Hirata, Jaime Ginzburg, José Sebastião Witter, Marcus Vinicius Mazzari, Almuth Grésillon, Sandra Teixeira Vasconcelos, and Eduardo Portella. I received thoughtful guidance in my research on visual culture from Maureen Bisilliat, Ruy Gama, Olivier Toni, Claúdio Veiga, Father Pedro Américo Maia, Aloysio de Oliveira Ribeiro, Emanoel Araújo, and Sérgio da Costa Franco. I benefited from the advice of the distinguished Latinist Ariovaldo Augusto Peterlini. I thank Dora and José Paulo Paes for their gift of a pair of lucky reading glasses; Viviana, for reading the initial drafts of this book; Hermínia Guedes Bernardi, for the dedication with which she prepared the original manuscript; and finally, Ecléa, for the unfailing generosity, the "puro orvaldo da alma" (pure dew from the soul), which she demonstrated throughout the process of writing this book.

A. B.

Author's Note to the North American Edition

In writing "Colony, Cult, and Culture" as the introduction to *Dialética da colonização*, the challenge I faced consisted in creating a space of convergence that would bring together some of the conceptual planes that are fundamental to the process of colonization. In this search for a common denominator capable of including the diversity of historical elements involved in this process without reducing them to the unity of an abstract term, I was aided by the very etymology of the words *colony* and *colonization*.

As the reader will perceive in the opening pages of the essay, both words have as their root the Latin verb *colo*, from which the terms *colony*, *cult*, and *culture* all derive. These are not mere lexical coincidences but actual historical dimensions that interact with one another throughout the colonial period and that may be recognized even today in postcolonial societies. The general idea that underlies these three dimensions is that of labor—physical, moral, and intellectual.

The colonizer is he who takes control of a foreign land and by means of force, technique, and skill, conquers it, exploits it, cultivates it, and dominates it politically; in sum, he exercises all the powers brought together in the verb *colo*, whose deverbal noun form is *colony*. In the interest of an accurate understanding of this process, economics and other social sciences may be called upon to research the material conditions that governed colonization. This has already been successfully accomplished by some of our best historians, among them Capistrano de Abreu, Caio Prado Jr., Celso Furtado, Raymundo Faoro, and Jacob Gorender. I used their work in my own as an indispensable reference for any study of our economic and political formation.

Of course, there can be no colonizing agent without a past or without memory. Conquerors did not spring forth from an atemporal zero-degree point. They brought with them in their caravels beliefs that conditioned their attitudes toward the native populations they came to dominate, when they did not destroy them altogether. Together with the sword and the blunderbuss came the cross and the Bible. The Iberian, English, and French colonies were populated by men who practiced either a popular and still medieval Catholicism or its counter-reformist version, or a puritanical Protestantism in revolt against Anglican hegemony. Monotheism brought them together as Christians opposed to "indigenous paganism," though they were divided into active or passive contemporaries of the Inquisition, the Reformation, or the Counter-Reformation, and by the religious wars fought during the sixteenth and seventeenth centuries. How can one understand José de Anchieta's Latin and Tupi plays or the sermons of Father Antônio Vieira (both missionaries and Jesuit writers whom I studied in individual chapters of *Brazilian Culture: A Dialectic of Colonization*) without examining in depth the peculiar quality of the medieval and later Baroque Catholic *cult*? How can one arbitrarily separate the missionary spirit from the project of colonization? How is it possible to separate colony-as-cultivation from colony-as-cult? How can their spaces of convergence and divergence be detected?

A parallel question may be directed to scholars of Anglo-Saxon colonization in the United States: how can this process be understood without exploring the religious and moral lives of the Puritans who established themselves there in the seventeenth and eighteenth centuries? In the Old as in the New World, and particularly during this period—prior to the Industrial Revolution and full-blown bourgeois hegemony—the relations between economic structures and religious ideas and practices were so interconnected that they can only be separated in the context of specialized (and, in truth, one-sided) academic studies.

The third dimension of the colonization process entails the development of a secular culture, heralded from the Renaissance forward and polemically advanced beginning in the Enlightenment. The word *culture* derives from the future participle of the verb *colo* and points toward the notion of a project—what must be cultivated, what must be built—that is, a set of virtual ideas and values that are a given in the minds and the wills of a certain social and intellectual group. This dimension became a fundamental component of the process of independence led by the New World's propertied classes and lettered elites, a component that shaped the model of political rupture with the colonizing metropolis. Liberal European culture was the ideological cement that bound together the emancipatory battles that broke out in all of Latin America during the first quarter of the nineteenth century. Later, with the republic proclaimed, positivist principles would inspire a politics of order and progress, which the leaders of the Revolution of 1930 in Brazil went on to translate into the forms of centralized government and state-led industrialization.

* * *

As the historian takes into consideration the multiple expressions of a given period's symbolic universe, his attention is drawn to the existence of diverging and, when taken to the extreme, contradictory tendencies of thought and of pathos. The conventional historicism that dominated the literary histories of the nineteenth century transformed those authors and works that departed from their period's standard style into exceptions or singular manifestations of backwardness or deviation (the *attardés* and *égarés* discussed by Gustave Lanson in his important history of French literature); in the best of cases, it celebrated the anticipatory qualities of some precursors.

In contrast to pure historicism, the dialectical vision of culture, adopting a Hegelian-Marxian approach, recognizes in the coexisting contradictions of every worldview the very dynamic of a history made up of tensions between dominant ideologies and the forces of resistance. Or, in Hegelian terms, it detects the tensions between the affirmative thrust of the thesis and the negative force of the antithesis. As long as this method is not automatized into a facile game of affirmations, negations, and sublations, it can offer a fruitful way for dealing with diversity and the conflicts inherent to each social formation in each of its historical moments. This is the most general meaning of the term "dialectic," as featured in the title of the book the English-language reader now has in hand.

In the chapter "Olhar em retrospecto" (A Retrospective Glance), which closes *Brazilian Culture: A Dialectic of Colonization*, I synthesized the results of my research and my reflections on the book's object of study in these terms:

> Colonization is a process that is at once material and symbolic. The economic practices of its agents are linked to their means of survival, to their memory, to their ways of representing themselves and others, and ultimately, to their desires and hopes. To put it another way: there is no colonial condition without a weaving together of labors, of cults, of ideologies, and of cultures. The relations between these fundamental dimensions of all civilizing processes (which Marxism summarized at the levels of infra- and superstructure) are modified, throughout time, by positive determinants of adjustment, reproduction, and continuity. Situations arise, however, in which it is the asymmetries and, in extreme cases, the ruptures that appear before the historian and anthropologist of colonial life.

The dialectical approach teaches us that we should pay just as much attention to moments of tension and change as to states of equilibrium and adjustment. Diachrony is only possible because synchrony is neither homogeneous nor static.

*　*　*

The corpus from which the examples considered in my book were taken belongs entirely to the history of Brazilian culture and, in several cases, to the history of the ideologies, counterideologies, and utopias constituted throughout the colonial and postcolonial periods. Insofar as each one of these complexes of symbols and values was of interest to the social groups that participated in the historical drama (here I draw on the strong meaning Habermas gives to the term *interest*), and given the extent to which retrospective ideologies and counterideologies played an effective role in this same drama, one may affirm that superstructural phenomena always occupy a place in the history of a people. It is the understanding of this place that draws the eye of the scholar of colonization.

I hope that my discussion is sufficiently clear, as well as instructive whenever possible, so that the text that follows may be understood by readers who are unfamiliar with Brazilian cultural and literary history.

Alfredo Bosi, Institute for Advanced Studies,
University of São Paulo
December 2007

Original version published in Alfredo Bosi, *Colony, Cult, and Culture*, ed. Pedro Meira Monteiro, trans. Robert Patrick Newcomb (Dartmouth: University of Massachusetts Dartmouth, 2008).

*Brazil and the
Dialectic of
Colonization*

1 Colony, Cult, and Culture

> O novo é para nós, contraditoriamente, a liberdade e a submissão. (For us the new represents, contradictorily, liberty and submission.)
> —Ferreira Gullar

Colo-Cultus-Cultura

It may not be in vain to begin with words. Relationships between phenomena leave marks on the body of language. The words *culture*, *cult*, and *colonization* all derive from the Latin verb *colo*, whose past participle is *cultus* and whose future participle is *culturus.*

In the language of Rome, *colo* signified *I live on, I occupy the land*, and by extension, *I work on and cultivate the land.*[1] *Incola*, or inhabitant, is an early descendent of *colo*. *Inquilinus*, one who resides in a foreign land, is another. *Agricola* belongs to a second semantic plane linked to the idea of work.

In the present tense, *colo* implies something incomplete or transitive, a movement that passes, or has been passing, from agent to agent. *Colo* is the root of *colonia* as a space in the process of being occupied, a land and people that can be worked on and subjected. For its part, "[c]olonus is he who cultivates a rural landholding in place of the owner, its administrator in the technical and legal sense of the word. This is found in Plautus and Cato as *colonia* . . .; the colony's inhabitant, in Greek the *ápoikos*, who establishes himself in the place of the *incolae*."[2]

It is not coincidental that whenever types of colonization are distinguished, so are two processes: that which attains to the populating of the colony and that which refers to the cultivation of the land. The idea of *colo* is present in both: I live in, I cultivate.

The Roman legal code is present in the verbal expression attached to the act of colonizing. What, then, distinguishes habitation and cultivation from colonization? In principle, it is the social agents' transplanting of their world onto another, where they will work the foreign land or have others do this for them. The *incola* who emigrates becomes a *colonus*.

Mechanisms of production and relations of power, and the economic and political spheres, are reproduced and reinforced—as if they were true universals in human societies—whenever a cycle of colonization begins.

But colonization is not limited to the rearticulation of these basic features: there is the structural plus of domination, an added concentration of forces around the figure of the conqueror that at times bestows on him epic connotations of risk and adventure. Colonization gives established cultures an air of rebirth and advancement.

The marked presence of domination is inherent to colonization in its various forms and almost always overdetermines them. To take care of, the basic meaning of *colo*, not only implies attentiveness but also ordering. It is true that the colonist does not always see himself exclusively as a conqueror; he will try to imprint on the minds of his descendants the image of a discoverer and settler, titles that legitimate him as a pioneer. In 1556, by which time the *leyenda negra* (black legend) of Spanish colonization was already spreading throughout Christian Europe, the use of the words *conquista* (conquest) and *conquistadores* (conquerors) was officially prohibited in Spain, and they were replaced by *descubrimiento* (discovery) and *pobladores* (settlers)—that is, colonists.

During antiquity, the rise of powerful political structures corresponded to the establishment of true imperial systems that followed wars of conquest. The Middle Eastern empires of Alexander and the Romans are among the oldest known concentrations of state power. In the case of Rome, the central organization of the state resisted disintegration until the barbarian invasions atomized Europe, which opened the way for the continent's eventual feudalization.

Multiple hypotheses purport to explain the genesis of these systems. The internal tensions that occur in a given social formation resolve themselves, whenever possible, in outward-looking movements of desire, of searching for, and conquest of, lands and peoples capable of being colonized. In this way, demographic imbalance may have been one of the causes of the ancient Greeks' colonization of the Mediterranean between the eighth and sixth centuries BCE. Likewise, Portugal's growing need for foreign commercial markets during the strenuous rise of the bourgeoisie served as an important factor in the kingdom's fifteenth-century expansion.[3] In neither case can colonization be treated as a simple migratory movement; instead, it represents the resolution of conflicts and the meeting of needs, as well as an attempt to reassert, under new conditions, one's dominion over nature and other people—an effort that invariably accompanies the so-called civilizing process.

As I pass, at this point, from the present tense of *colo*, with all its connotations of immediate activity and power, to the nominal forms of the verb, *cultus* and *cultura*, I must leave the here-and-now for the mediated realms of the past and future.

The past: as a deverbal adjective, *cultus* refers to the land that successive generations have cleared and planted. *Cultus* connotes not only the perpetually repeated action conveyed by *colo*, which implies cultivation over the centuries, but, especially, the qualities that result from this labor and that are incorporated into the worked land. When peasants from Latium referred to their cultivated land as *culta*, they sought to convey a cumulative meaning: both the act of cultivation itself and the countless hours of necessary labor it absorbed. This gives the participle *cultus*, a noun that is also a verb, a more dense and vivid signifying form than is implied by the simple naming of present labor. The Latin *ager cultus* and another deverbal, the Portuguese *roçado* (both meaning cultivated land), link the idea of systematic work to the quality obtained from that work, an association that becomes part of the speaker's emotional world. *Cultus* serves as a sign that a society that produces its own food is now possessed of a memory. The word contains the struggle between the subject and the object of collective bodily effort, and becomes a vehicle for indicating the presence of what *was* in what occurs *now*. Process and product coexist in the same linguistic sign.

As for the noun *cultus*, it was used to refer not only to working the land but also to the cult of the dead, a root form of religion-as-memory, as the conjuring and exorcising of those who have passed from the earth. Present-day anthropologists seem confident in their belief that sacred burial preceded the working of the soil: although the latter practice dates from the Neolithic period and the first Agricultural Revolution (beginning around 7000 BCE), the dead were already being buried some 80,000 years ago, during the time of the Neanderthals.

As Gordon Childe puts it:

> As to the magico-religious notions that held neolithic communities together, a few guesses may be hazarded. The tendance of the dead, going far back into the Old Stone Age, may have assumed a greater significance in the new. In the case of several neolithic groups, indeed, no burials have been discovered. But generally the dead were carefully interred in built or excavated graves, either grouped in cemeteries near the settlement or dug close to the individual dwellings. The dead are normally provided with utensils or weapons, vases of food and drink, and toilet articles. In pre-historic Egypt pictures of animals and objects are painted on the funerary vases. They presumably had the same magic significance as the cave

painting and rock-carvings of Old Stone Age hunters. In historical times they were transferred to the walls of the tomb, and then attached texts show that they were really designed to ensure to the dead the continued enjoyment of the services they depict.

Such tendance denotes an attitude to the ancestral spirits that goes back to far older periods. But now the earth in which the ancestors' remains lie buried is seen as the soil from which the community's food supply magically springs each year. The ancestral spirits must surely be regarded as assisting in the crops' germination.

Fertility cults, magic rites to assist or compel the forces of reproduction, may have become more prominent than ever in neolithic times. Small figurines of women, carved in stone or ivory, with the sexual characters well marked, have been noted in camps of the Old Stone Age. But similar figures, now generally modelled in clay, are very common in neolithic settlements and graves. They are often termed "mother goddesses." Was the earth from whose womb the young grain sprouts really conceived in the likeness of a woman with whose generative functions man is certainly familiar?[4]

At this point it will be useful to sum up the two linked meanings of the noun-verb that shows human beings chained to the land, digging holes that nurture them while they are alive and that shelter them when they are dead:

cultus (1): that which is worked *on* the land; cultivated;
cultus (2): that which is worked *in* the land; cult, burial of the dead; a ritual undertaken to honor one's ancestors.

A group's effort to root its present experience in the past is undertaken through symbolic mediation—through gestures, song, dance, ritual, prayer, verbal evocation, and verbal invocation. In the ancient world, this was all fundamentally religious and linked the present to the past-turned-present, tying a community to the forces that created it in another time and that sustained its identity.

The cult, with its continual reassertion of origins and ancestry, is another constant in human societies, along with the material struggle for survival and the relations of power that derive from it and that are implied, both literally and metaphorically, in the active form of *colo*.

In certain Greek colonies, the designs of the gods, as deciphered by the oracles, were often invoked as the causes of the settlement's foundation. In Delphi it was Apollo Archegetes who presided over the foundation of colonies. Portuguese colonizers in the Americas, in Asia, and in Africa were inspired by the project of spreading the faith, just as they sought to expand the empire: "dilatando / a Fé, o Império" (spreading / the faith, the empire) as Camões had it. And the Puritans who came ashore on the beaches of New England similarly declared themselves ready to perform the ways of God.

Colonization is a totalizing process the dynamic forces of which can always be found at the level of *colo*: in the occupation of new land, the exploitation of its resources, and the submission of its inhabitants. But the agents of this process are not merely physical supports for the operation of economic forces; they are also believers who in the arks of memory and language carry with them their still-present dead. The dead have two faces: they serve as a sword or shield in the ferocious conflicts of the everyday, but they can also make themselves heard in this theater of crime, with their pained voices conveying messages of censure and remorse. Santiago de Compostela (Saint James) rallies the *matamoros*, or Moor-slayers, in the battles of the Iberian *reconquista*, and then the Cross that has defeated the Crescent is planted in the land of Brazilwood to subjugate the Tupi. But the same cross is summoned by others to preserve the freedom of the Amerindians and urge mercy for black slaves. The same mass celebrated in the Jesuit missions of the Sete Povos is heard by the *bandeirantes* who, blessed by their chaplains, will mercilessly massacre the inhabitants of these settlements. Did the God of the missionaries and the prophets answer to the same name as the God of the warriors and Pharisees? The key question to ask is how each group read and interpreted scripture so as to adapt religion's universalizing discourses to its own particular practices.

What do religious symbols and rites, along with narratives of creation, the fall, and salvation, do if not reconstruct day-to-day experience, shot through as it is with economic divisions and oppressive hierarchies of power, as an idealized totality?

We can derive another participle from *cultum*, the supine of *colo*: this is the future *culturus*—what will be worked, what one wishes to cultivate.

In its substantive form, the word applies to the hard work of the soil, to *agri-culture*, as well as to all the work done to a human being since infancy; in this second sense, *culturus* became a Romanized form of the Greek *paideia*. Its more general meaning has been preserved to the present day, with culture understood as the sum of those practices, techniques, symbols, and values that must be transmitted to the next generation in order to guarantee the continuity of a given state of social coexistence. Education represents the institutional staging of this process.

The ending *-urus* in *culturus* communicates the idea of the future or of forward movement. In densely urbanized societies, culture also came to be understood as a more humane form of existence, which should be strived for as the end term of a civilizing process valued more or less consciously by all social classes and groups. Culture as an ideal of personal status, by then divorced from the religious connotations of a cult, was late in coming to

Rome. When it did arrive, it spread a program of *paideia* that became fixed from the fourth century BCE, as Werner Jaeger's and Henri Irénée Marrou's important studies demonstrate.[5] *Paideia*: an educational ideal oriented toward the formation of the adult in the polis and in the world.

The idea of culture presupposes a productive, laborious group consciousness that prizes out plans for the future from present circumstances. This projective dimension, implied in the myth of Prometheus, who stole fire from the heavens in order to change the material destiny of humanity, becomes more pronounced during periods in which there are social classes or strata capable of future hopes and projects, as in the Florentine Renaissance, the eighteenth-century Enlightenment, the various scientific and technical revolutions, or during the life cycle of socialist revolutions. The modern version of Titanism, which manifests itself in theories of social evolution, extends the certainties of the Enlightenment and conceptualizes culture in opposition to nature, generating a rationalized view of history as reducible to the development (technical and otherwise) of productive forces. Culture thereby approximates the idea of *colo* as labor and distances itself, at times antagonistically, from *cultus*. The present becomes a kind of spring, an instrument in the service of the future. As culture's productive function becomes accentuated, man is obliged to gain systematic dominance over the material world and over other men. In this context, to acculturate a people means subjecting them, or in the best of cases, adapting them technologically to a social arrangement held to be superior. In certain military-industrial regimes, this relationship is openly and unabashedly manifested. To produce is to control workers, consumers, and prospectively, citizens. Economics is politics in its brute form, and knowledge is power, to cite Francis Bacon's crude equation.

According to a certain reductive view, there is a strict connection between a society's superstructures and its economic and political sphere. It is important to recall, however, that some formative elements of modern culture (which become more apparent from the Enlightenment onward) grant science, the arts, and philosophy an inherent or virtual capacity to resist prevailing structural pressures. In the agonistic words of the historian Jacob Burckhardt, for whom power is in itself evil, the action of culture

> on the two constants [State and Church—Burckhardt was writing in the mid-nineteenth century] is one of perpetual modification and disintegration, and is limited only by the extent to which they have pressed it into their service and included it within their aims.
>
> Otherwise it is the critic of both, the clock which tells the hours at which their form and substance no longer coincide.[6]

This awareness of the capacity of culture to embody the consciousness of a present marked by sharp imbalances becomes a springboard for the creation of alternative ideas for a future that can be viewed as new in some way. Writing in another ideological context, Antonio Gramsci proposed, as prerequisites for a new cultural order, a critique of common sense and the consciousness of the historicity of one's own worldview.[7]

From the eighteenth century onward, the ideas of culture and progress have grown closer to one another, at times becoming one and the same. The fact that Enlightenment thinking was critically reflected in Hegelian-Marxian thought, in the sociology of knowledge, and in a certain phenomenology opposed to classical rationalism, did not mean that its original light was snuffed out.[8] And, if I may venture a comparison with what occurred to Neoplatonic idealism in its encounter with Christianity, I would say that just as Logos needed to be made flesh and dwell among us in order to reveal itself fully to humanity, so did contemporary reason seek to embody and socialize itself in its desire to transcend the dated project of the Enlightenment and protect itself from the risk of falling back on that static philosophy of reason of which even Karl Mannheim complained, or of irresponsibly placing itself in the service of capital and the bureaucratic machine. Formerly colonized peoples have more than enough motivation and accumulated experience to distrust a manifestly neo-Enlightenment language that complacently reproduces itself in the midst of the suffering and destruction wrought by a rationalized pseudomodernity that has no end other than enriching itself.

However, when the light of the Enlightenment illuminates itself and recognizes the source and the limits of its power, the contribution it makes to the human and material world carries the benefits of modestly limiting itself to saying only what it knows and promising nothing beyond what it can grant. The dialectic of Enlightenment, because it moves and while it remains in motion, does not exhaust itself in the perverse effects noted by the apocalyptic observers of the technocratic culture industry who have attempted to demystify the noncritical image of neocapitalism that those integrated into the system unceasingly describe and popularize. In any case, an embodied and socialized culture has an ever more central role to play in the elaboration of a future for poor nations.

Let us review the semantic areas occupied by the *colo-cultus* dyad, recalling that each element can convey material or symbolic meanings, depending on context:

1) The economic applications of the term *colo* represent the active, energetic capacities of a society in transition, which transplants itself into a new context. Cultivation of the land, after all, was a fundamental strategy for survival during the Roman period and in medieval Europe. Latin, an

eminently rural language, created the expression *colere vitam* (literally, "to cultivate life"), which is used in one of Plautus's comedies simply in the sense of "to live." *Egomet vix vitam colo*: I myself am barely cultivating life (*Rudens*, I, 5, 25). Or in Brazilian slang, *vou gramando* (I continue laying down grass, that is, working/suffering). How can one separate the social from its natural metaphor in this last expression? Here life is lived as the product of continual action by the cultivator who, as he labors, in fact cultivates himself.

2) In terms of the colo-cultus dyad's religious application, it remembers, it recovers the origins, it reestablishes the individual's connection to a spiritual or cosmic totality. The cult gives meaning to time, it redeems it from daily entropy and from the death to which each new moment of life consigns the moment that preceded it. O grave, where is thy victory? Paul's challenge to death, the great enemy in his address to the Corinthians, is the culmination and distillation of all human beliefs. The cult should not be confused with direct, instrumental manipulation of objects and persons (recall the universal distinction between magic and devotion); the cult, in and of itself, in its pure form and divorced from the powers that attempt to appropriate it for their own ends, signifies respect for the difference and transcendence of others, as well as the desire to break through the limits of one's self and use the power of the soul to overcome the anguish of finite, carnal existence. There are elements of renunciation and oblation in all religious activity and particularly in the spiritual and moral significance of the cult.

Reverence for ancestors, which is common to African and Amerindian religiosity and to popular Catholic veneration of saints, merits some specific discussion here. The deceased is simultaneously the absolute Other, closed off in immutable silence and removed from economic struggle, and a familiar image that stands in vigil over the homes of the living: when called upon by them, the deceased can give welcome comfort amid present-day suffering. The community makes use of a series of rituals and prayers (that consecrate, as opposed to substitute for, everyday practices) to access the power of the deceased. Far from being mutually exclusive, manual and religious labor complement each other in traditional societies. *Ora et labora* (pray and work) was the motto of the order of Saint Benedict, one of the first monastic communities of the Middle Ages.

Amplified Reflection and Contradiction in the Colonizing Process

Colonization refigures the three orders—cultivation, cult, and culture—within a dialectical structure.

The order of cultivation, first of all: the movements of migration and population reinforce the basic principle, common to all societies, of humanity's dominion over nature. New lands and resources are exposed to the invaders' greed. The predatory, mercantile impetus for economic development is reignited, leading to accelerated accumulation of wealth, generally with considerable implications for the system of international exchange. We can appreciate what relentless Latin American sugar cultivation and mineral extraction meant for the European bourgeoisie of the mercantile age. If we equate the increased circulation of goods with the idea of progress, then we cannot deny that New World colonization worked to modernize European commercial networks during the sixteenth, seventeenth, and eighteenth centuries. In this context, the colonial economy was a product of and stimulus for metropolitan markets during the long period between the last phase of feudalism and the beginning of the Industrial Revolution.

Karl Marx provides two obligatory citations for my discussion of this issue:

> The discovery of gold and silver in America, the extirpation, enslavement, and entombment in mines of the aboriginal population, the beginning of the conquest and looting of the East Indies, the turning of Africa into a warren for the commercial hunting of black-skins, signalised the rosy dawn of the era of capitalist production. These idyllic proceedings are the chief momenta of primitive accumulation. On their heels treads the commercial war of the European nations, with the globe for a theatre.[9]
>
> Merchants' capital in its supremacy everywhere stands for a system of robbery, and its development, among the trading nations of old and new times, is always connected with plundering, piracy, snatching of slaves, conquest of colonies. See Carthage, Rome, and later Venetians, Portuguese, Dutch, etc.[10]

Marx clearly saw that the colonizing process was not limited to its modernizing effect as an eventual stimulant of world capitalism. In fact, colonization promoted or reinvented archaic systems of labor, beginning with the extermination or enslavement of the native inhabitants of areas of greatest economic interest. Violent forms of social interaction are implanted in the colonized area as the result of an occupation oriented toward short-term resource extraction. The distinct models of the Mexican or Peruvian *encomienda*, the *engenho* of the Brazilian northeast, the Antillean plantation, and the hacienda of the River Plate region all played host to these forms of social relationships. Without entering into the difficult question of the conceptual nature of the colonial economy (was it feudal, semifeudal, capitalist?), we may safely note the continual state of coercion and strict dependence to which Amerindians,

Afro-Latins, and mestizos were subjected in the varied models of production implanted in Portuguese and Spanish America. The European conquerors tightened the mechanisms of exploitation and control in the name of more efficient and more secure resource extraction. This regressive deployment of tactical tools seems to have been a structural feature of colonization, with the European's dual role as New World colonizer and mercantile agent not exactly promoting the humanization of labor conditions.

The expansion of modern commercial capitalism, stimulated by the promise of conquering new lands, had the contradictory yet inevitable effect of brutalizing the day-to-day life of the colonized, of subjecting them to a bloody and primitive existence. The genocide of the Aztecs and of the Incas, the work of Cortés and Pizarro, was only the first act. There were many to follow—for instance, Argentina's murderous midcentury *conquista del desierto* (conquest of the desert) at the expense of Patagonian Amerindians and mestizos: "One could be paid in English currency for the ears *of an Indian*, but since it was quickly found that many of the Amerindians who had lost their ears were still alive, the more effective measure was taken of paying for a pair of an *Indian's testicles*. The authors of this genocide, many of whom were foreign adventurers, accumulated incredible fortunes. Others, finding themselves in the possession of stolen lands, rose into the ranks of the nobility."[11]

As the historian Manuel Galich comments:

> Why this desire for land? It was clearly in order to exponentially increase the number of cattle, since the value of cattle had grown exponentially in the English market. Cattle were no longer only good for leather, their hides, their horns, and their hooves. Beef had also become big business ever since the Frenchman Tellier had figured out how to preserve meat through refrigeration, and export companies like the River Plate Fresh Co. and La Negra had been formed as a result. It is notable and worthy of further reflection that the period of the *conquista del desierto* coincided with the opening of the international beef market and the invention of refrigeration (1876). This was a progressive move on capitalism's part, without a doubt.

Those who accompanied the cycle of the Iberian conquests did not ignore the extent of the crimes committed. The Dominican friar Bartolomé de Las Casas published his *Brevísima relación de la destrucción de las Indias* (A Very Brief Account of the Devastation of the Indies) in Seville in 1552, in which he put the number of Amerindians killed between 1492 and 1542 at fifteen million. And Michel de Montaigne, a probable reader of Las Casas and the first of the secular humanists, recorded these fiery words in Book III of his *Essais* (1588): "Whoever else has ever rated trade and commerce at such a price? So many cities razed to the ground, so many nations wiped out, so many millions of individuals put to the sword, and the most beautiful and the richest part of the world shattered, on behalf of the pearls-and-pepper business! Tradesmen's victories! At least ambition and political strife never led men against men to such acts of horrifying enmity and to such pitiable disasters."[12]

In Brazil, barbaric abuse of the environment and of people accompanied the march of colonization, both in the sugar-growing zone and in the backlands of the *bandeirantes*, bringing about the burning of forests and the murder or enslavement of native populations. Even Gilberto Freyre, an apologist for Portuguese colonization in Brazil and elsewhere, wrote that "sugar eliminated the Indian." Today we might add that cattle, soy, and sugarcane expel small and marginal landholders. The expansionist project of the 1970s and 1980s was, and continues to be, nothing more than an equally cruel extension of colonial-era military and economic incursions.

In his *Essai sur la colonisation* (1907), Carl Siger offers a curious defense of colonial methods, which he considers authentic "safety valves" (*soupapes de sûreté*) for the metropolises: "Young nations are a vast expanse open to violent individual activities that in the metropolis would clash with certain prejudices, and with a prudent and regulated view of life. However, in the colonies they can be developed more freely and can as a consequence better affirm their value. In this way colonies may to a certain extent serve as safety valves for modern society. This would be of immense value, even if it were the only benefit of colonization."[13]

To Marx, an economy subject to European capitalism but based on slave labor seemed an anomaly. He says as much in a revealing passage from his *Pre-Capitalist Economic Formations*: "If we now talk of plantation-owners in America as capitalists, if they *are* capitalists, this is due to the fact that they exist as anomalies within a world market based upon free labour."[14] To be exact, the term *anomaly*, which Marx applies to America's slave-based plantation economy, presupposes the existence of a norm (*nomos*) or an exemplary standard. In Marx's case, this standard was the mode of capitalist production in mid-nineteenth-century England, a mode conditioned precisely by the forced transition from agricultural servitude to salaried labor. At the beginning of the paragraph quoted above, Marx affirms categorically that "[t]he production of capitalists and wage-labourers is therefore a major product of the process by which capital turns itself into values."

The long duration of a system of nonsalaried labor on the Brazilian *fazendas*[15] and the plantations of the U.S. South appeared to the author of *Capital*, writing during the second half of the nineteenth century, as an aberration, a holdover from an earlier age doomed to disappear with the worldwide growth of openly capitalistic productive forces.

However, if our objective is to understand the peculiar internal workings of colonialism, the reality is that the anomaly of slave labor was long-lasting and represented a formative influence on colonial society's social and psychological existence. As Marx wrote in another context, "the civilized horrors of over-work are grafted onto the barbaric horrors of slavery."[16] Brazilian political practices were formed in the simultaneously modern and retrograde context of colonial Brazil's slave-based economy. If Marx was correct in his use of the term *anomaly*, then it falls to us to study the phenomenology of an anomalous situation.

In general terms, it is possible to describe colonial Brazil as a socioeconomic formation the basic characteristics of which were as follows:

1) The colony was dominated by a class of landowners whose interests were linked to groups of European merchants, particularly the traffickers of African slaves. Given this structural dependence on external forces, the prospect of an internally dynamic capitalist economy in the colonized zone became totally unrealistic. The expression *colonial capitalism* should be understood in terms of colonial-metropolitan commercial interaction.

2) The labor force was basically composed of slaves, and the economy of the time can therefore be characterized as a system of colonial slaveholding (*escravismo colonial*), the concept used by Jacob Gorender to describe the Brazilian, Antillean, and southern U.S. plantation economies.

3) The alternative to slavery was not the transition to salaried labor but the prospect of escaping to a *quilombo* (an Afro-Brazilian maroon settlement). Law, labor, and oppression were the interrelated guiding forces of colonial slavery. The slaves who were freed by their masters, which became more common after the peak of the colonial mines, faced the alternatives of a difficult life as subsistence farmers working marginal land or as subaltern *agregados* (subordinate, poorly remunerated plantation fixtures who outlived even the abolition of slavery). Regardless, the life of a free Afro-Brazilian amounted to a condition of dependence.

4) The political structure linked the interests of rural landowners to local representative chambers composed of the gentlemen of the community, that is, property holders. But the chambers' sphere of influence was limited, with the king nominating governors for four-year terms. The governor, invested with both military and administrative powers, presided over the local armed forces and the *Juntas da Fazenda e da Justiça* (Commerce and Justice Committees), following the criteria established by the Crown and expressed in royal decrees, letters, and directives. The *juntas* were composed of royal officials: *provedores* (administrators), *ouvidores* (judges), *procuradores* (attorneys), and during the period of the mines, *intendentes* (mine administrators). They were controlled from Lisbon and specifically, from 1642 onward,

by the *Conselho Ultramarino* (Overseas Council). From 1696, even municipal chambers were subject to metropolitan interference, with Portugal nominating *juízes de fora* (outside judges) whose powers superseded those of local, municipally elected judges. Historians have stressed the very limited sphere of action of local chambers under the Portuguese kingdom's statutes and laws; one of the results was tension between local oligarchies and an increasingly centralizing Crown, which would contribute to the political crisis that began in the late eighteenth century. With Brazilian independence in 1822, the authority and authoritarian tendencies of local oligarchies were able to assert themselves and were formally legitimized by the presence of *bacharéis* (elite men trained in law) in parliament and in the provincial assemblies.[17]

5) The exercise of citizenship was doubly limited: by an authoritarian state and by internal power dynamics. Throughout colonial Latin America, representative government was practically nonexistent, a situation that remained virtually unchanged (in quantitative terms, at least) after political independence in the first years of the nineteenth century. In imperial Brazil, an indirect, census-based electoral system proved ineffective to counter administrative centralization.

6) The lay clergy was tied both to large rural landowners and to the Crown, on which it depended economically and legally through the patronage system—hence, the prevalence of priests tied to specific *fazendas* or those who doubled as colonial functionaries. It is only when the colonial pact enters a crisis period, between the final years of the eighteenth and the first quarter of the nineteenth century, that liberal and radical priests begin to appear.

7) Religious orders, and especially the Jesuits, committed to the practices of a supranational Church, remained invested in the project of administering Amerindian missions. This possibility was opened at the onset of colonization, when the Portuguese colonizer's Christianizing role was a broadly accepted idea. Over time, the missions were limited to the margins and weak points of the system, and would in the long term succumb to the pressures of *bandeirantes* and the colonial army. The Jesuits would then be offered the alternative opportunity of ministering to the children of elite families as humanistic educators.

8) Intellectual culture was rigorously stratified, allowing for social mobility only in exceptional cases of educational patronage. These cases did not challenge the general rule. Mastery of the alphabet, which was reserved for the few, served as a dividing line between official culture and popular life. Day-to-day manifestations of colonial-era popular culture were organized and reproduced beyond the pale of writing.

9) The production of popular culture was able to take place either in enclaves seen today, retrospectively, as archaic or rustic or at the margins

of certain erudite or semi-erudite codes derived from the European arts: for example, in music, in popular festivals, and in religious imagery. The *romance de cordel*,[18] a form of marginal production, was late in making its appearance due to the barriers to literacy and printing that prevailed during the colonial period.

In a brief synthesis, it is possible to relate Brazil's formative colonial development as follows: economically, to the interests of slave traders and sugar and gold merchants; and politically, to absolutist metropolitan rule and to local authoritarianism, which engendered modes of social interaction that were patriarchal and stratified among the elites and based on slavery or dependency among the subaltern.

The Cult-Culture Dialectic within the Colonial Condition

The key factor for considering life in colonial Brazil as a network of values and meanings is precisely the complex alliance between an agricultural and mercantile system oriented toward the European economic machine and a domestic condition that was traditional, if not frankly archaic, in its mores and politics.

I distinguish between the terms *system* and *condition* so as to sound clearly the chords of this tune that some have perceived as rightful and harmonious and others as dissonant and discordant. I understand *system* as an objectively articulated totality. The *colonial system*, as a long-lasting historical reality, has been studied in the Brazilian context from a variety of structural perspectives by such eminent scholars as Caio Prado Jr., Nelson Werneck Sodré, Celso Furtado, Fernando Novais, Maria Sylvia Carvalho Franco, and Jacob Gorender.[19]

Economic life in Brazil during the first three centuries of Portuguese colonization depended on mechanisms that can be quantified because they are translatable into amounts of production and circulation, that is, into numbers that represent goods and labor. Long before the genesis of quantitative history, the poet Gregório de Matos, in a harsh sonnet dedicated to the city of Salvador da Bahia at the end of the seventeenth century, spoke of a *máquina mercante*, literally a ship of merchandise, an expression that can be extended metonymically to the entire machinery of colonial commerce.

The formation of the system required the reciprocal interaction of trade and slavery, monopoly and monoculture. At the international level, the back-and-forth flow of colonial merchandise was subject to market fluctuations and to economic competition among metropolitan states. In sum, the system as it was reproduced in Brazil, and as it was tied to the economies of the European center, occupied opposing sides of the same figurative coin.

The term *condition* comprehends a more diffuse set of experiences than the regular movements of production and trade described by *system*. To speak of a condition implies ways of living and surviving. It is not coincidental that we speak naturally of a human condition but never of a human system.

While the conditions of master and slave implied distinct roles to be played within the sugar economy (which we may uncover through a functional analysis of its system of production), they cannot be reduced to the actions those roles entailed. A person's condition comprehends multiple, concrete forms of interpersonal, subjective existence—memories, dreams, the daily marks made on the heart and mind, the manner of one's birth, physical sustenance, living and sleeping conditions, ways of loving, crying, praying, and singing, and the circumstances surrounding one's death and burial.

Earlier in this analysis I recalled some of the key studies that have contributed to our understanding of the colonial system. As for the colonial condition, Gilberto Freyre's and Sérgio Buarque de Holanda's classic studies are obligatory reading. In texts like *Casa-grande & senzala* (The Masters and the Slaves) and *Sobrados e mucambos* (The Mansions and the Shanties), Freyre dedicated himself to developing an existential anthropology of Brazil's northeastern sugar economy. Following his own synthesis of the process of colonization in *Raízes do Brasil* (Roots of Brazil), Buarque offered a detailed and elegant description of the daily life of the *sertanejos*, the "Luso-Tupi" inhabitants of Brazil's backlands, in *Caminhos e fronteiras* (Paths and Frontiers), a volume that provides a pioneering analysis of our material culture.

In their treatment of familial and clan behavior, Freyre's and Buarque's essays suggest a psychocultural interpretation of Brazil's past. This reading of our history is based on the general hypothesis that the Portuguese conqueror brought with him to Brazil certain recurring character traits that Buarque termed *psychological determinants*. They include individualism, which he qualifies as an extreme exaltation of the personality, an adventurer's spirit (hence the Luso-Brazilian ethic of adventure as opposed to an ethic of labor), our natural tendencies toward restlessness and disorder, cordiality, a sensual sentimentality exercised freely in what Freyre classified as polygamous patriarchalism, social plasticity, versatility, and finally, a tendency toward miscegenation that harkens back to the Portuguese interactions with the Moors and that was intensified by a lack of racial pride, a trait that appears in both scholars' analyses.

When the various patterns of so-called Luso-African and Luso-Tupi assimilation are seen through this psychocultural lens, the structural features of enslavement and violence become relegated to a subdued or implicit background, though they were in reality a constant of colonial history, as much a part of the northeastern *engenhos* and *quilombos* as of the *bandeirantes'* expeditions and the Jesuit missions of the South.[20]

Having fully acknowledged the value of these masterly texts, it may be helpful to offer a semantic correction to terms like *assimilation* (Freyre) and expressions such as the *process of successful acclimatization and cultural solidarity* (Buarque) when these are applied to contacts between the colonizers and the colonized. This vocabulary may lead less-informed readers to assume that the peoples who interacted during colonization became similar to one another and dealt with one another on friendly terms, as illustrated by their miscegenated daily routines, diets, sexual habits, production techniques, modes of transportation, and so forth. It is instructive to reread passages from *Casa-grande & senzala* and *Raízes do Brasil* that deal with how plantation owners and *bandeirantes* were compelled to adopt African and indigenous customs in response to the conditions of a new life in the tropics. The majority of these passages describe examples of the planter class's nutritional enjoyment of African cuisine and sexual enjoyment of African women as well as their culture, or the Portuguese in São Paulo's simple appropriation of Tupi-Guarani habits. The colonist literally incorporates African and indigenous material and cultural resources when, driven by self-interest and the pursuit of pleasure, he takes the bodies of their women, their well-tested methods of planting and cooking, and by extension, the general, indispensable know-how that allows them to survive in a rustic environment.

The use of the bodies of others and the appropriation of their bodily techniques, ably described by Marcel Mauss, do not make for properly reciprocal acculturation. The most we can say is that the colonizers took excellent advantage of their relationships with Amerindians and Africans.

In *Casa-grande & senzala*, Freyre insists on celebrating the northeastern plantation owner who, free from prejudice, mingled fruitfully and polygamously with female slaves, thereby providing the world with an example of racially democratic tolerance. For his part, Buarque attributes colonial-era miscegenation to the Portuguese colonizer's unique lack of racial pride. Even here we must qualify the argument so as to avoid sliding from a dubious social psychology into an ideology that ends up celebrating the European victor. The conqueror's libido, which nearly always exercised itself in an exclusively physical capacity, was more phallocentric than democratic: the female slaves impregnated by the plantation owners were not elevated ipso facto to the category of wife or *senhora de engenho* (lady of the plantation), nor were the children that resulted from these fleeting encounters treated as the equals of those considered legitimate heirs to the property. Rare, late exceptions to this rule can be cited, but the anecdotal material serves merely to confirm the larger truth. Intense sexual and reproductive activity does not necessarily equate to social generosity.

In Buarque's highly erudite texts, a subtle sublimation of *bandeirante* activity, presented as the natural outgrowth of the processes of Portuguese acclimatization to Brazil, downplays the aggression and conflict that objectively characterized the *paulista* incursions into the interior and the indigenous and Jesuit opposition they faced.[21] In arguing his position, the author of *Raízes do Brasil* subscribes to Júlio de Mesquita Filho's apology for Portuguese colonization in his *Ensaios sul-americanos* (South American Essays) and goes as far as to compare the plasticity of the Portuguese to St. John the Evangelist's figurative grain of wheat, which sacrifices itself in order to bear much fruit.[22] How could black slaves held prisoner in the country and the Amerindians hunted in the forests have imagined that the plantation masters and the *bandeirantes* were completing some sacrificial rite in which the ultimate victim was not black or Amerindian but white?

The elements of material culture that are cited ad nauseam as evidence of the colonizer's adaptation to the ways of the colonized should not be made to prove more than they are able. They illustrate the uses and abuses to which the Portuguese subjected Amerindians and Africans, both at the level of the global economy and in daily material and corporeal practice. Why should we idealize what occurred? Should Brazilian scholars compete with other colonized peoples to decide who was best colonized? I do not believe that this careless and often naïve game of comparisons, stacked to favor *our* colonizer, can lead to an adequate understanding of the process.

We must ask if, along with the most evident of the adaptations alluded to above, the forces of cult and culture (and the art that feeds on both), succeeded, through their capacity to grant meaning to life, in addressing that which routine left unfulfilled or untouched.

The reproduction of a certain set of habits certainly helped to prop up the colonial structure, but was the consuming, producing, and trading machine of colonization able to respond to the full range of values, ideals, dreams, and desires that issued from the past or that were projected, at least in potential form, into the future of both the colonizer and the colonized? In other words: was colonization a process defined by moments of fusion and construction, which ultimately balanced out material wants and symbolic forms, immediate needs, and imaginary worlds, or did colonization also produce, in addition to a machinery of interlocking parts, a dialectic of ruptures, differences, and contrasts?

Marx's words on the role of religion in oppressed societies help explain the tendencies of certain social groups toward the imaginary expression of their desires: religion is the "heart of a heartless world and the soul of soulless conditions."[23] A society's symbolic labor can reveal the dark consequences of forced labor and the search for new, freer forms of existence. This is much like the platonic Eros, who as a child of Wealth and Poverty, is in fact neither but is rather the will to free oneself from the yoke of the present and to ascend to the realm of imperishable values. Popular rituals, music, and religious imagery of the colonial era are signs of this desired state. In certain of these cultural manifestations we can detect the presence of both the weight of the past and the hope for the future within the links of the tightly binding chain of oppression. The colonial condition, like the colonial system, is reflexive and contradictory.

T. S. Eliot, addressing the broader dynamic between colony and metropolis, writes the following: "The culture which develops on the new soil must therefore be bafflingly alike and different from the parent culture: it will be complicated sometimes by whatever relations are established with some native race, and further by immigration from other than the original source. In this way, peculiar types of *culture-sympathy* and *culture-clash* appear, between the areas populated by colonisation and the countries of Europe from which the migrants came"[24] (my emphasis). There are cases of successful transplants, long-lasting grafts, and felicitous encounters; and there are sounds of dissonant chords that reveal poorly resolved contrasts and maladjusted overlappings. Colonial history is made from both empathy and antipathy.

In a typically perceptive passage, Alphonse Dupront alerts us to the limitations of a historiographical and ethnological language that makes use of acculturation, assimilation, and cultural encounter, broad terms that are able to express (or to conceal) opposing meanings: "There are encounters that kill. Should we say the same, with a kind of black humor, of cultural exchanges? Anthropologists would respond with assimilation. But isn't this too a form of black humor? Should we describe processes of death and processes of life using the same verbal sign, like the liars we are?"[25]

The transposition of European norms of behavior and language onto the New World yielded varied results. At first glance, colonial literate culture seems to reproduce the European model without exception; but when confronted with the figure of the Amerindian, it is inspired or even forced to invent. Let the first acculturating agent in colonial Brazil, the Jesuit friar José de Anchieta, serve as an example: when he composed his poem to the Virgin Mary while being held hostage by the Tamoios on the beach of Iperoígue, feeling the need to purify himself, he wrote in classical Latin. The same Anchieta learned the Tupi language and sang and prayed to the angels and saints of medieval Catholicism in Tupi in the plays he composed for the *curumins*. In the first case, Anchieta used the epic, an ancient literary form elevated by the Italian Renaissance, to give shape to the substance of a colonial situation. In the second, he changed codes in the interest of his evangelizing mission—not because his message had changed but rather his recipients. This new public, which was participating actively in a new, unique form of theater, required a language that could not be that and only that of the colonizer.

Further, Anchieta made use of a strangely syncretistic imagery, neither exclusively Catholic nor purely Tupi-Guarani, when he created mythical figures named *karaibebé*, literally flying prophets. His indigenous audience might see these as the heralds of the Land without Evil, while Christians would identify them as the angelic messengers of the Bible. And in Anchieta's plays Tupansy, the mother of Tupã, took on characteristics of Our Lady. Culture-as-reflection and culture-as-creation walked arm in arm.

The peculiar dynamism of the Jesuits in Brazil, who were compelled to faithfully observe the vows made by their order in Counter-Reformation-era Iberia, should be viewed up close. There would come a time when the cross and the sword, which had disembarked together from the caravels onto the shore, drifted apart, became hostile to one another, and ultimately waged battle for the shared good: the bodies and souls of the Amerindians.

The fight to the death between the *bandeirantes* of São Paulo and the Company of Jesus, which resulted in the Jesuits' final defeat in the mid-eighteenth century, speaks eloquently of how an unspoken opposition can explode into the open when missionary paternalism and the colonists' naked exploitation of the Amerindians could no longer be balanced.

Anchieta considered the Portuguese his primary opponents in catechizing the Amerindians, writing that "the Portuguese are the source of the greatest impediments, the first of which is their lack of dedication to saving the Indians. . . . Rather, they consider them savages."[26] Further, "What most frightens the Indians and causes them to flee from the Portuguese, and as a consequence from the churches, is the tyranny the Portuguese exercise over them. They force them to serve their entire lives as slaves, separating wives from husbands, parents from children, shackling them, selling them, etc. . . . These needless injustices caused the destruction of the churches that had been established, and are the cause of the great perdition of the Indians now in their power."[27]

Denouncing the *mamelucos* (children of whites and Amerindians) under the control of the patriarch João Ramalho, Anchieta wrote, "they most hatefully persecuted us, using all means and methods to do us harm, threatening us with death, but most especially working to nullify the doctrine we used to instruct the Indians, thereby causing them to hate us. If this deadly contagion is not eliminated, not only will the conversion of the unfaithful fail to progress, but it will weaken day by day and inevitably decline."[28]

Such was the first century of missionary activity in Brazil. Anchieta's fears were confirmed by the facts, as illustrated in his description of the flight of the Amerindians from São Tomé:

> Suddenly all the people of São Tomé rose up, rebelling such that the Devil seemed to be walking among them. In the streets they cried out: "Let us flee, let us flee from the Portuguese who are coming." Father Gaspar Lourenço, witnessing this upheaval, gathered them together and made them understand how grave it would be if they abandoned the church because of the lies told to them. Crying, they responded: "We flee neither from the church nor from you, and if you wish to go with us, we will live with you in the forest or the backlands. We see that God's law is good, but these Portuguese do not leave us in peace, and if you can see how the few of them that walk among us steal our brothers and sisters, what can be expected when the rest come and make slaves of us, our women, and our children?" With many tears and much emotion, some of them described the threats and showed the wounds they had received in the homes of the Portuguese.[29]

Anchieta's narrative foregrounds the sharp contrast between predatory colonization and the apostolic mission, which initially were linked of necessity. All the evidence indicates that these were distinct projects whose moments of reconciliation were invariably fleeting and diplomatic but whose inner dynamic forces were such as to lead them to open confrontation with each other.

The seventeenth century in Brazil is marked by conflicts between colonists and Jesuits, from Grão-Pará and Maranhão, where Antônio Vieira worked and served as a witness, to São Paulo and, most dramatically, to the Sete Povos do Uruguai (the Seven Missions of Uruguay). However, the tension between Church and state was not to be limited to the followers of Ignatius of Loyola.

Ecclesiastical power frequently entered into confrontation with civil interests and laws. Although the motives for conflict were varied, the tutelage of the Amerindians appeared as a causal factor on more than one occasion. See, for example, the problems faced by the prelates of Rio de Janeiro. The first occupant of the office, Father Bartolomeu Simões Pereira, died of poisoning in 1598; the second, Father João da Costa, was persecuted, expelled from the city, and removed from his position by a colonial court; the third, Father Mateus Aborim, was also the victim of poisoning; the fourth and fifth prelates made the prudent decision not to assume their office; the sixth, the Reverend Lourenço de Mendonça, was forced to flee to Portugal after escaping a fire that had engulfed his home, set by locals who had exploded a barrel of gunpowder in his yard; the seventh, Father Antônio de Mariz Loureiro (perhaps a relative of José de Alencar's Marizes), faced such opposition that he retreated to the captaincy of Espírito Santo, where he lost his mind after an attempted poisoning. I must pass over the story of the eighth prelate, the famous Dr. Manoel de Sousa e Almada, since the sources are intensely divided on the matter of his guilt or innocence: the fact remains that his palace was damaged by cannon fire. A Bahian court absolved the aggressors and, as if this were not enough, charged Almada with paying for the court case; Machado de Assis parodied the affair in his heroic-comic poem "Almada."[30]

This struggle is at once material and cultural, and is therefore political. If we are interested in tracing the development of ideas, not in and of themselves but in relation to the existential horizons of their authors, then we can identify two discourses at work in colonial writing: an organic discourse and an ecclesiastical or traditional discourse, to use Gramsci's felicitous distinction.

The organic discourse is produced in connection with the actions of the colonial enterprise and is often proffered by the colonial agents themselves. Witness, for instance, Pero Vaz de Caminha, the scribe attached to the armada that discovered Brazil; Gabriel Soares de Sousa, a plantation owner and New Christian who was a hands-on informant, as well as an accurate and precious one ("*étonnant*," in Alfred Métraux's judgment); Ambrósio Fernandes Brandão, the attentive and engaged chronicler who wrote the *Diálogos das grandezas do Brasil* (Dialogs on the Great Things of Brazil); and Antonil, an author who hid behind an anagram and discreetly called himself the Anonymous Tuscan, and who indiscreetly told of the whereabouts and the worth of the colony's natural resources in his *Cultura e opulência do Brasil* (Culture and Opulence of Brazil). Antonil had a modern, pragmatic mind and probed deeply into the quantifiable details of colonial production despite his Jesuit cassock. Finally there was Azeredo Coutinho, a bishop and Mason who, as the nineteenth century was dawning, called for maintaining slavery in the interest of Pernambuco's sugar economy and the well-being of the Portuguese Crown. In all these cases, and without regard to the individual's lay or ecclesiastical status, we find a frank and consistent dedication to exploring, organizing, and commanding in the colonial sphere.

The other discourse, which derives from a precapitalist ethic, resists the mercantile system even as it resides in its interstices. Though it lives off the system, issuing as it does from the quills of high officials, nobles, and religious figures, it shows little gratitude to the source from which it derives its privilege of leisure and relief from the cares of business, preferring to castigate the colonists for their hunger for profit and for their lack of Christian selflessness. This is the message of Gregório de Matos's moralizing satires against the foreign merchant (*o sagaz Brichote*) and the nouveau riche usurer who claims aristocratic roots (*o fidalgo caramuru*), and of Antônio Vieira's somber homilies, with their baroquely convoluted separation between a defense of good commercial practices and a condemnation of the abuses of slavery, which in fact were at the heart of that very commerce. The same sentiment can be seen vacillating in Basílio da Gama's *Uraguai* between, on the one hand, the author's glorification of colonial military force and Gomes Freire de Andrade's resetting of the overseas balance of power, and on the other, his poeticizing of the rebellious indigenous savages, ultimately the only people who are considered worthy of singing the song of freedom.

Colonial writing does not constitute an undifferentiated whole: it gestures toward practical knowledge, oriented toward the hard demands of the Western market system, while it also aspires toward its counterpoint, where obscure utopian dreams of a naturally Christian humanity fuse with the values of liberty and equality that were being very slowly advanced by the rising bourgeoisie. Whenever we are alerted to the presence of these counterideological gestures, we discover that the present either looks back to the past and is linked to the *cult*, or that it looks toward an ideal future and responds to *culture*.

Ghosts of this old, intermittently appearing dream haunt Vieira's millenarian tirades, the missionaries' idealized descriptions of the Sete Povos, Aleijadinho's statues of suffering but indomitable prophets, and the escapist landscapes of the Arcadian poets of Minas Gerais. Of course there are many types of utopia, and it is only by analyzing each given context that we can see how they came into being, and toward and against whom they were addressed.

But where do the varied fantasies of utopia put down roots in the rocky soil of colonial culture? The Neapolitan philosopher Giambattista Vico characterized collective human fantasies in terms of "extended or compounded memory."[31] A people's shared past is freely reconfigured by each succeeding generation, taking on new meanings. Memory gleans countless themes and images from a more or less remote spiritual history, but the conflicts of the here-and-now compel it to give a defined form to the open, polyvalent legacy provided by cult and culture.

In Vieira's messianic words, the Bible was made to defend the Jews. The same Bible defended the Jesuit himself against the forces of the Inquisition, which also drew on the holy scripture to make their case against him. Rabbis, Jesuits, Dominicans: all were experts in scriptural exegesis. The prophets Isaiah, Daniel, and Jeremiah supplied the missionary Vieira with the words to castigate the slaveholders of Maranhão for their greed, even as Vieira endorsed Paul's oft-abused argument for servants to remains loyal to their masters in advising the Portuguese king against a mediated solution to the conflict with the revolting *quilombolas* of Palmares. The great rhetorician drew on the treasury of shared memory, whether to argue for the slaves or to defend capital. The past helps compose the forms of the present, but it is the present that draws old or new garments from the chest of the past.

What a strange religion—half baroque and half mercantile—a religion that denounces the victors and then leaves the victims to their fate, and that abandons a fragile, defenseless Holy Word to the scheming designs of the powerful, who plunder it for all they want!

Art, whether sacred or profane, redraws the profile of tradition. The profusion of tortured devotional images hammered out by the Iberian Counter-Reformation inspired the mature Aleijadinho's prophetic figures at Congonhas do Campo, whose appearance, according to some, foreshadows the *mineiros'* rebellion and its bloody suppression by the Crown. During the same turn-of-the-century period, our Arcadian poets would draw on Virgil and Horace to fill with woodland flowers the tropical plain surrounding the Ribeirão do Carmo (Carmo Creek), which they sang of with a classical lyre. And in the Vila Rica clinging to the hillside, Virgilian shadows fell broadly from the golden hills.

Fantasy amounts to memory, either expanded upon or compounded. To try to understand colonial culture in its symbolic forms is to deal with the coexistence of a culture of the day-to-day, born of and developed from the practices of migrants and natives alike, with another culture that confronts the machinery of daily routine with the ever-changing faces of the past and future, sometimes juxtaposed and sometimes transforming each other.

Vieira denounced the cruelties of slavery in the northeastern *engenhos* using a universalizing, prophetic, and evangelical discourse (it would be anachronistic, when referring to his time, to speak of the liberal or, especially, democratic principles of later centuries). Christianity's basic message, that all men are children of the same God and are therefore brothers, contradicts, in principle, pseudo-arguments that have been marshaled to defend colonial particularity. These arguments have been presented in a utilitarian, fatalistic, and even racist language: the self-interested speech of the oppressor rooted in the organic reasons driving conquest, which reasserted itself on a planetary scale, with little variation, until the last phase of colonial imperialism that began at the end of the nineteenth century.[32]

In Brazil, heaping praise on plantation owners, *bandeirantes*, captains, and governors-general—in short, the Crown and its collection of servants and bureaucrats—was the vulgar but inexhaustible rhetorical strategy of the Bahian academies, the *Esquecidos* (Forgotten) and the *Renascidos* (Reborn), as well as the favored theme of the genealogists of São Paulo and Pernambuco, centers of the Brazilian nobility since the eighteenth century. This discourse also drove epic texts composed in various periods: Bento Teixeira's *Prosopopéia*, a Camonian pastiche written at the beginning of the seventeenth century and dedicated to the hereditary captain of Pernambuco, Jorge de Albuquerque Coelho; Brother Manuel Calado's *O valoroso Lucideno*, which celebrates in verse and prose the achievements of João Fernandes Vieira, a Portuguese magnate who owned five sugar plantations and mills and helped lead the resistance against the Dutch in northeastern Brazil; Brother José de Santa Rita Durão's *Caramuru*, written in honor of Diogo Álvares Correia, the patriarch of Bahia; and finally, Cláudio Manuel da Costa's *Vila Rica*, a poem written to celebrate the civil order imposed by Antônio Dias in Minas Gerais. The last two texts belong to the neoclassical Luso-Brazilian literary corpus read (and in part, misread) during the Second Empire by the Brazilian Romantics who were in search of prototypical examples of the official nationalism they were working to construct. Theirs was a misinterpretation: despite neoclassicism's celebration of the landscape and its chronicling of local life, the eighteenth-century epos cannot be dislodged from the colonial context. Its tendency toward localism, which was quite visible in Pernambuco after the expulsion of the Dutch and in post-*bandeirista* São Paulo, was tied to elite families' self-fashioning as local nobilities. These same families would eventually constitute the ruling class of the future Brazilian nation-state.

To recapitulate: two rhetorical tendencies were present in colonial letters, which generally ran parallel but were sometimes in tangential contact with one another. These were a humanistic-Christian rhetoric and that of the intellectual spokesmen for the agro-mercantile system. While the first sought to join together culture and cult, utopia and tradition, the second firmly placed writing in the service of the efficient operation of the colonial economic machine, articulating culture and *colo*. Placed side by side, these two languages, one grounded in humanism and the other in economic concerns, seem to contradict each other. However, if we examine them closely and in their respective contexts, we can find more than one instance of mutual approximation.

Vox Populi vs. Colonial Epos: A Camonian Parenthesis

> Modern colonialism started with the fifteenth-century voyages of the Portuguese along the west coast of Africa, which in 1498 brought Vasco da Gama to India.
> —*International Encyclopedia of the Social Sciences*, 1968, vol. 3, s.v. "colonialism."

Ezra Pound once described poets as antennas. In as rich and dense a text as Luís de Camões's epic poem *Os Lusíadas* we can detect the first signs of an ideological contrast that foreshadows the dialectic of colonization. In his poem, Camões does more than simply play host to different perspectives;

he conceives of the Portuguese campaign of maritime exploration and conquest as an act of violent dismemberment. As an observer and participant, as an author and actor in the colonizing adventure, Camões constructs his epic presentation of Vasco da Gama's voyage from a variety of materials, incorporating premonitory visions, exemplary myths, accounts of Atlantic maritime voyages and disasters, and elements of contemporary drama into the text, sometimes embodying these elements in hieratic figures who verge on the allegorical.

Camões's narrator was able to mold the epic substance of his chosen topic into a dialectical opposition at the exact moment of the Portuguese's greatest glorification. Glory, after all, is at the heart of *Os Lusíadas*: the glory of Dom Manuel, the glory of da Gama, the glory of the heroes of Portugal's maritime explorations of Africa, and the glory of Portugal.

Let us take a close look at the steps that lead up to the crucial hour of the crew's departure for India. Vasco da Gama's speech to the king of Melinde begins in Canto III. The captain narrates the history of Portugal as one of incessant and ultimately victorious armed struggle against the Moors and the Castilian nobility. The House of Aviz emerges from these centuries of combat, and it is precisely Dom João I's alliance with the bourgeoisie, or the "people," as described in Canto IV, that allows for a policy of maritime exploration: "To touch the rosy fingers of the dawn, / The very quest to which I myself was born" (IV, 60).[33]

In trying to reach a climax in his apotheotic treatment of da Gama, Camões accelerates the pace of the narrative, bringing the African cycle of the poem to a quick close. The poem's thesis, which is the affirmation of the kingdom's expansionist project, gains the irresistible force of myth. The king Dom Manuel, "whose constant / Passion was to enlarge the kingdom," does not deviate "[from] his unique / Inheritance"; he neither rests in daytime nor in night, with his thoughtful vigil leading to allegorical dreaming, "where imaginings can be so vivid."

Of what does Manuel *o Venturoso* (the Fortunate) dream? "Morpheus, in various guises, rose before him." In his dreams the king rises to a great height, from where he can see other worlds and faraway nations. He sees that two great rivers spring from the Far East, flowing through a wild, verdant land, as yet untrodden by human feet. From their waters majestically rise two old men, "of venerable appearance." The descriptive beauty of this dreamtime transformation is admirable: the streams of water become the men's hair and beards. Their dark skin indicates that they come from a tropical region, and the "chaplets of grass and nameless fronds" adorning their heads, along with the grave expressions on their faces, point to royal status. Their words to Dom Manuel answer the riddle of their mysterious identity: they are the

The Prophet Ezekiel. "Aleijadinho's prophets are not Baroque, they are biblical" (Giuseppe Ungaretti).

Ganges and the Indus, the sacred rivers of Asia, which flow from Heaven to Earth to offer their "tributos grandes" (tributes) to the Portuguese sovereign.

This episode is revealing of certain ideas that are dear to Camões: the size and strangeness of a hostile world, "whose necks were never before yoked," and the fatal power of the Portuguese Crown, to which nature and men from the remotest regions anxiously and even insistently give themselves over.

Dom Manuel's dream must be seen as foretelling good fortune, insofar as it participates in the ideological economy of the poem. It is a dream where imaginings can be so vivid, a phrase that illustrates the role of allegory as a figure fulfilled in the text's conceptual apparatus and ultimate resolution. Indeed, the episode's connection to the telos of the poem becomes apparent immediately after the ghosts of the night vanish. Dom Manuel awakens and calls upon his loyal counselors (there are always counselors available to determine royal wishes), who dutifully decipher "the figures of his dream."

Roman soldier, Aleijadinho's workshop. Caricatural figures of the Stations of the Cross: art at the frontier between the erudite and the popular.

From this moment on there is no time for hesitation, only continuous action: the wise men "resolve at once to equip / A fleet and an intrepid crew" and the *Venturoso* charges Vasco da Gama with leading the expedition.

Once the fog of the dream has lifted, the narrative proceeds in lively and cheerful fashion to the scene of the fleet's departure, in which all the pipes and trumpets of the Camonian muse will sound. A period of celebration, of "noble bustle" and "youthful spirits" begins, with soldiers dressed in many-colored outfits and flags flying high in the wind.

Although this is a joyful scene, the emotional climate of the episode is, to the reader's surprise, marked by sadness and foreboding. The sailors' ritual prayer speaks of "prepar[ing] our souls to meet death." Divine favor is petitioned, but God's response is uncertain. The narrative turns to the interior life of the hero, up to this point known only as the monolithic *forte Capitão* (stalwart commander) dedicated to the glory of the kingdom:

> O King, I tell you, when I reflect
> On how I parted from that shore
> Tormented by so many doubts and fears,
> Even now it is hard to restrain my tears. (IV, 87)

With this mention of doubt and fear, the narrative has taken its first steps toward the antithetical climax of the episode. In effect, Vasco da Gama does not undertake his spiritual labor in isolation but is accompanied by a true tragic chorus composed of those staying behind—the elderly, the invalid, children, and especially women—whose anticipated feelings of longing for their loved ones give way to mourning and finally to open revolt. Da Gama's feelings are in harmony with the concrete collective anguish that surrounds him. His doubts and regrets are joined to the doubts and regrets of all those not participating in the overseas adventure, but who, staying behind in Portugal, will suffer the consequences of the voyage in their daily lives. Indecision, an antiheroic trait par excellence, informs both da Gama's subjective existence and the objective insecurity of the journey.

> The people considered us already lost
> On so long and uncertain a journey,
> The women with piteous wailing,
> The men with agonizing sighs;
> Mothers, sweethearts, and sisters, made
> Fretful by their love, heightened
> The desolation and the arctic fear
> We should not return for many a long year. (IV, 89)

There is a clear opposition to be observed between the certainty and expressions of confidence Dom Manuel's dream inspired in the royal counselors and the emphasis placed here on the word *dúvida* (doubt) and its adjective *duvidoso* (doubtful, uncertain, dubious), which appear three times over a short stretch of five stanzas:

> Tormented by so many doubts and fears; (IV, 87)
> On so long and uncertain a journey; (IV, 89)
> Why, for so dubious a voyage. (IV, 91)

The idea of doubt gives effective expression to the uncertainty of all voyages whose protagonists give themselves over to chance.

The women intone the most pathetic strains of the chorus sung to the sailors upon their departure. The mothers' voices utter the mournful sobs of those who fear the death of their children at sea,

> bloated fish your only burial.

The wives' voices sharply and compassionately deny, in the name of "us," their husbands' right to make the journey:

> Why do you risk on the angry seas
> That which belongs to me, not you?
> Why, for so dubious a voyage, do you
> Forget our so sweet affection?
> Is our passion, our happiness so frail
> As to scatter in the wind swelling the sail? (IV, 91)

Is this epic, lyrical, dramatic? What is epic is the choral historicity that serves as background staging for the expression of feelings, as well as the journey through the angry seas, the shadowy, risk-laden path of the explorers, and the wind that blows the Portuguese ships whichever way it pleases. What is lyrical is the voice of the eternal feminine, which remains sweet even as it makes the bitterest complaints (the most moving among them that which invokes the idea of forgetting: "Why . . . do you / Forget our so sweet affection?"). Also lyrical are love, frail happiness, and the intuition that the waves of the sea can undo fragile human ties in an instant. Finally, what is dramatic is the woman's interpellation of the man, her silent interlocutor caught between the contrary passions of love and glory. Dramatic is also the conflict to be seen within these divided families, as well as the deepening division between the ways in which those who depart and those who stay behind interpret existence. The text as a whole is epic, lyrical, and dramatic—truly poetic—in its overcoming of rhetorical boundaries and its relativizing of individual genres, each of which, after all, uses multiple strategies to describe human relationships and appeal to the emotions in a variety of affective tones. The chorus attains cosmic dimensions when the mountains echo in response to the voices of the women, the elderly, and the children.

But the anticlimax is still to come. Collective lamentation is not enough: as a classical poet, Camões must present us with a whole, eloquent discourse in which he expresses truth in an irrefutable succession of reasoned arguments. Camões will excavate this Logos, which runs counter to the voyage as a manifestation of national glory, from the repressed history of Portugal, the history of its people, and will present it in the speech of the *Velho do Restelo* (the Old Man of Restelo).

The Old Man, one of the many spectators on the shore, a man of the people speaking from "among the people," rejects unequivocally the maritime undertaking at the exact moment of the ship's departure.[34]

Point by point, his speech undermines the organic purpose of *Os Lusíadas*, which is to glorify da Gama's deeds, as well as the Aviz dynasty, Portugal's noble warriors, and the country's mercantile machine involved in the project.

The Old Man leaves nothing untouched. He calls the noble motivating force of Fame, a much-invoked Renaissance topos, by its true name—the will to power: "O pride of power! O futile lust / For that vanity known as fame!"

The feudal valorization of honor, still very much alive in the sixteenth century, is demystified as a "hollow conceit which puffs itself up / And which popular cant calls honour," and the Old Man launches an exemplary attack on the demagoguery the powerful employ in order to excite popular fanaticism to support the war machine: "They call distinction, they call honour What deserves ridicule and contempt" (IV, 96). He sarcastically adds:

> To what new catastrophes do you plan
> To drag this kingdom and these people?
> What perils, what deaths have you in store
> Under what magniloquent title?
> What visions of kingdoms and gold-mines
> Will you guide them to infallibly?
> What fame do you promise them? What stories?
> What conquests and processions? What glories?

The voyage and all that it entails are presented as a disaster for Portuguese society, leading to a depopulated countryside, humiliating poverty and begging, the dispersal and death of able-bodied men, and ever-present adultery and the orphaning of the young. As Sá de Miranda had written before the publication of *Os Lusíadas*, "The kingdom disperses / at the smell of cinnamon."

The radical shift in the poem's perspective, from da Gama to the Old Man, gives us an idea of the spiritual force of a Camões who is both ideological and counterideological, a contradictory, living writer. His Old Man moves from condemnation to malediction, the final outcry of an impotent soul that refuses to surrender. He categorically damns ambition, which since the collapse of the peace that reigned in Eden or in the Golden Age has consigned humanity to an iron age of labor and war. He casts a harsh light on the mythical figures of Prometheus, Daedalus, and Icarus, civilizing heroes of ancient Greece, revealing them as victims of pride and *hybris*. Finally, he goes as far as to denounce progress and technical knowledge, implying that all Titanic adventures end in the ruin of their protagonists. The *nau* (ship) and *fogo* (fire), great inventions of a remote past that are about to guarantee the success of the colonial enterprise, are presented as signs of a grievous fate:

> The devil take the man who first put
> Dry wood on the waves with a sail!

> Hell's fires are too good for him
> If the laws I live by are righteous!
> . . .
> Prometheus stole the fire from heaven
> Which rages in every human heart,
> Setting the world ablaze with arms,
> With death and dishonour, and all for nothing!
> How much better for us, Prometheus,
> How much less harmful for the world,
> Had you not breathed into your famous statue
> The restlessness that goads mankind to match you! (IV, 102–3)

At the outset of Portugal's maritime and colonial adventure, the enterprise's greatest writer voices a perplexed conscience: "Mísera sorte! Estranha condição!" (What miserable luck! What a strange condition!) (IV, 104).

This somber moment quickly passes, however, at least on the poem's factual surface. The navigators absorb the Old Man's harsh words, though they continue nonetheless, since as Camões put it,

> As the honourable old man was uttering
> These words, we spread our wings
> To the serene and tranquil breezes
> And departed from the loved harbour;
> And, as is now the custom at sea,
> The sails unfurled, we bellowed:
> "God speed!," and the north winds as usual
> Heard and responded, shifting the great hull. (V, 1)

Dom Manuel's allegorical dream has cleared the way, in tactical terms, for the conqueror's voyage: India's sacred rivers would flow to a sea dominated by the Portuguese. Those who stay behind tearfully denounce the brutality of events and, through the figure of the Old Man, recall the myths of humankind's youth, casting a negative light on the heroes who worked in the interest of material progress. But history moves forward, "shifting the great hull," and its winners and losers continue to confront one another.[35]

Beyond the Pale of Writing

The Old Man of Restelo and the populace who witnessed Vasco da Gama's departure were likely to become those migrants who, a half-century later, destitute and uprooted, would seek out land and work in India, Africa, and Brazil—though by this time they would no longer find a poet of Camões's stature to hear their voices and transmit them onto the page.

Since the sixteenth century, a culture has come into formation beyond the pale of writing and in the context of a poor and oppressed people. Its language, the product of a diversity of racial and ethnic encounters, became as miscegenated as its speakers, such that today it borders on an anachronism to speak of a purely black, indigenous, or even rustic culture.

In the first years of colonization, the degree of ethnic difference was naturally quite high. The chroniclers of the sixteenth century, writers like Jean de Léry, Hans Staden, and Fernão Cardim, were still able to witness the ceremonies of the Tupi inhabitants of coastal Brazil. And the rituals of Bahia's Afro-Brazilian population, which received scholarly documentation in the nineteenth century, had clearly originated in earlier centuries. In time, however, cultural symbiosis, whether *caboclo*, *mulato*, or *cafuzo* (i.e., indigenous-white, black-white, or indigenous-black), would come to dominate all aspects of symbolic and material production: cuisine, clothing, domestic life, speech, prayer, festivals, and so on. Without a doubt, acculturation is the paradigmatic theme of colonial anthropology.

Here we should make a preliminary conceptual distinction between markedly *primitive* or *archaic expressions*, that is, forms of material and spiritual culture peculiar to those who have always lived beyond the pale of writing, and *frontier expressions* that are the products of contact between popular culture and the erudite conventions introduced during the process of colonization. There is an evident difference between a cannibalistic ceremony witnessed by Staden while he was a captive of the Tupinambás and the representation of war as it appears in a play written by Anchieta in Tupi and performed by the same Tupinambás, now exposed to Christianity and possibly even taught the Roman alphabet. To cite another contrasting pair, a religious rite performed by African slaves at the beginning of the eighteenth century, and described as *calundu*, in horrified terms, by Nuno Marques Pereira in his *Peregrino da América* (American Pilgrim), is not the same as a funeral procession led by the Confraternity of Our Lady of the Rosary of the Black Men of Vila Rica a few short years later. Once more, the image of Exu (a Yoruba deity) or a geometric form designed by a Guarani weaver are not equivalent to a religious image created by a mulatto *santeiro* (carver of saints), modeled on Portuguese sacred art, and destined to be placed in a plantation chapel. And finally, the refrain sung in a *candomblé* ceremony among the *nagô* (Yoruba-origin) population of Salvador is far from identical to the hymn sung to the Virgin by the members of the Brotherhood of São José of the Black Men in a rural town somewhere in Minas Gerais.

All these, however, may with equal legitimacy be termed popular creations, regardless of their ethnic affiliations and remote origins. What is certain is that it was the poor who transmitted and sometimes were the direct producers of these expressions, whether primitive or frontier, pure or mixed, whether prohibited, tolerated, or actively promoted. They have equal anthropological value. It is the role of formal analysis to determine the stylistic components (or traces, as they are often termed) of these rites, narratives, and figures; and it is the task of sociohistorical interpretation to locate the meanings and values around which these symbolic creations are organized.

The majority of the expressions of nonliterary culture can be described as complexes of signifying forms grounded in religious cult and devotion, and as institutions ordered so that through them the community may articulate its sense of existence and identity.

All that is necessary necessarily returns.

The repetition of formulas, the reiteration of rhythms, the abstract markings of Amerindian design, the fixed expressiveness retained in African masks, the rituals that are performed identically each time and everywhere, the precisely regular parts played by the participants in a chorus or dance: all of these reflect a desire to summon—by means of a reduced number of formulas, each pregnant with meaning—a simultaneously feared and adored transcendence (of the dead, of the gods, of the Other) that holds the personal and group destiny in its hand.

Nonetheless, as the process of acculturation continues and new influences are received from the colonizing matrix, a will toward stylization (already affected by erudite culture) emerges from the religious-popular base that gave rise to these expressions. The distinct Baroque style of seventeenth-century Minas Gerais (the *barroco mineiro*) is lighter and more stylized than the religious architecture of sixteenth-century Bahia. This is due to the veritable urban recolonization of Minas that brought wave upon wave of Portuguese settlers to the recently discovered gold-producing zone. The *mineiro* style seems late or anachronistic when compared in linear terms to European artistic development; however, the *barroco mineiro* was not an art produced by simple imitation or an offshoot of a displaced and derivative culture, but rather the result of an original merger of new, internal expressive needs with still-prestigious artistic models imported from Portugal and Italy.

In this frontier art form, the lived emotions of daily life in the colony—veneration, fear, love—are communicated through an economy of forms that, though they originated in remote spaces and times, are nonetheless flexible and capable enough to create strong, coherent images. The *mestiço* sensibility of colonial urban life and the models of sixteenth- and seventeenth-century Portuguese art converge in the figures carved by Aleijadinho through a synthesis in which the high style manifestly plays the orchestrating role. Yet what is important here is not the mathematical sum of the verifiable stylistic factors (so much of the cult, so much of the popular) but the need to determine, in each case, the perspective and meaning of the forms employed.

The relation between intervening forces is inverted once we take into consideration, for example, anonymous religious images, Carnaval street songs or dances, processional hymns, or orally transmitted narratives from the Iberian romance storytelling tradition. In all of these frontier expressions, colonial popular inspiration manipulates, in its own way, materials of remotely European and lettered origin.

A *Caboclo* Prayer in Greater São Paulo

I'd like to recall, in this context, a religious ceremony I attended on the night of Saint Anthony in 1975, during a celebration dedicated to the saint. The small chapel, which still stands, is located about a hundred meters from the Raposo Tavares highway, near where it rises from Vargem Grande. Or, more exactly, it is located in Vila Camargo, in the yard of Nhá-Leonor's house. Neither the physical appearance of the neighborhood nor the occupations of its inhabitants justify referring to it as rural. No one plants crops, whether to eat or to sell, and everyone works in the city or at the construction sites on its outskirts. For many years now they have been working for wages, shopping in supermarkets, and watching television.

On that day, Nhá-Leonor had a barbeque and we ate beef from a freshly slaughtered animal (she had a cow killed once a year to fulfill a promise made to the saint). At ten the chaplain arrived. He was not a priest (the hostess had fallen out some time earlier with the Irish priests from Cotia, who were too modern for her taste) but a round man in his fifties with a pink face and smiling eyes who arrived from São Roque with two boys and a thin, middle-aged black woman.

The chaplain and his acolytes stood before the small blue altar adorned with stars made of glitter and began praying the rosary in a loud, strong voice. The faithful, almost all mulatto men who were drunk and stumbling back and forth, as well as some women, less poorly dressed than the men, responded to the prayer in equal tone and volume. This simple, pretty routine continued until all the Hail Marys and Pater Nosters were completed. A song to the Virgin Mary followed, with the chaplain intoning the hymn in Latin ("Salve regina, mater misericordiae"); to my surprise, the congregation joined in immediately and without hesitation. And then came the truly astonishing moment for me: the recital of the entire long litany of Our Lady, also in Latin. I could not believe what I was witnessing: the same neighborhood *caboclos* whom I had seen slaving away every day as lowly construction workers were putting a beautiful *caipira* (folk) spin on the medieval call-and-response prayer:

"Espéco justiça"—ora pro nobis
(Speculum justitiae)
"Sedi sapiença"—ora pro nobis
(Sedes sapientiae)
"Rosa mistia"—ora pro nobis
(Rosa mística)
"Domus aura"—ora pro nobis
(Domus aurea)

Mirror of justice, seat of wisdom, mystical rose, house of gold, morning star, ark of the covenant, refuge of sinners, comforter of the afflicted, queen of angels, queen of prophets, queen of peace—singing in his deep voice, the chaplain enumerated all the attributes ascribed to the motherly figure of Mary by the faithful down through the centuries. The tall black woman followed him, improvising a melody on a *caipira* guitar and complementing the music with at once ecstatic and controlled gestures of adoration. And the boys and the congregation added a chorus of astounding beauty.

After leaving the chapel I asked the chaplain about who had apprenticed him in his role. He responded that it was his father, who served as a chaplain in the small rural landholdings of Sorocaba and Araçariguama. The night was cool, the moon shone high above, but the freight-moving trucks were still running heavily over the nearby asphalt.

What should we think of this fusion of the medieval Latin liturgy with *caipira* intonation and musical accompaniment, and of its resistance to the Catholic Church's dogged insistence since Vatican II that the vernacular be used in all religious celebrations?

The existence of this uniquely anachronistic chaplain says a good deal about the autonomy of popular religious practice in relation to official Church hierarchy. The old synthesis of Luso-colonial and rustic practices seems to have retained its inner dynamism in the ceremonies of these *caipiras*, quite urbanized in economic and quotidian terms. They passively resist the innovations promoted by the ecclesiastical establishment, which in recent decades has turned to an openly politicized pastoral language and which during the 1970s and 80s joined in the opposition to the dominant political regime.

Religious devotion, perhaps more than any other aspect of social life, is conducive to manifestations of symbolic persistence, which at some critical moments of reaction to the despotism of the modernizing state take shape as an obstinate re-archaization of the community. This was the case with certain millenarian movements, like Canudos and the Condestado, which were both regressive and prophetic, traditionalist and rebellious.[36]

All seems to indicate that the colonial encounters of conquering, lettered cultures and conquered, nonlettered cultures represent a coexistence of extremes, with Western capitalism's most aggressive projects situating themselves among ancient and in certain aspects resistant patterns of life. New fieldwork and textual analyses must confirm the hypothesis that this cohabitation of the archaic with the modernizing does not represent a circumstantial paradox but rather a recurrent feature of the history of colonization.

If we make a synchronic incision through those moments from the history of popular culture in which the force of colonization renews itself, we will find cases in which the new interrupts or disorders the old and the primitive, or in which the antiquated adopts, with barely a sign of distress, a few traces of the modern wherever traditional culture has put down roots and remains capable of surviving.

Oswaldo Elias Xidieh, one of the most perceptive scholars of Brazilian folklore, makes the following theoretical proposition: where there is a people—that is, where there is reasonably articulated and stable (or rooted, as Simone Weil would say) popular life—there will always be a traditional material and symbolic culture with a minimum of spontaneity, coherence, and a feeling for (if not awareness of) its identity. In its own way and within certain limits, this basically oral culture will absorb ideas and values from other sectors of society, be it, since colonial times, through the church and the state, be it through schooling, propaganda, and the multiple institutions of the culture industry. This absorption does not imply, however, a definitive self-destruction of popular culture, as the traditionalists fear and the modernizers hope: it merely allows for a change in the appearance of certain objects and symbols.[37]

There is no doubt that in situations of social trauma and forced migration, the agents of popular culture suffer great material and spiritual shocks, and are only able to stay afloat if they attach themselves to the life raft of certain dominant economic structures. However, this sort of survival does not (and cannot) have positive results in terms of cultural creation, since it blindly follows the system's exploitative mandate. The migrant who reaches the city or a foreign land is a mutilated, deprived being. Fabiano, the protagonist of Graciliano Ramos's novel *Vidas Secas* (Barren Lives), is not a mythological figure invented by the author. His conduct will oscillate between the most humiliated subservience and flashes of violence until, one day, his working conditions or the circumstances of his community or family allow for the reconstruction of that web of signs and practices known as "popular culture."

Every instance of relief or improvement will seem to him a product of fortune. And he will still almost always turn to cult, to religious faith of the type now found in the *seitas* (sects)—the collective term for the evangelical (normally Pentecostal and millenarian) churches that have proliferated in Brazil since the 1960s—as the weaver capable of spinning together the strands of his fate. If you live for a while in a poor neighborhood on the outskirts of São Paulo, Rio de Janeiro, Buenos Aires, or Lima, you will see the results of the migrant's peculiar condition. The migrant is no longer the figure of folklore, but neither is he fully absorbed into the culture industry that produces infinitely more than the people are capable of consuming. Capitalism has always both uprooted and reused (and only to the precise extent of its interests) the labor of migrants from traditional or marginal areas. And from what source do they derive the energy to lift themselves, albeit on rare occasions, a small step above the hard floor of reality? In the majority of cases, it is only from that "heart of a heartless world" that gives form to beliefs and rituals, to words and songs, to prayer and trance, and that only communitarian devotion is able to express.

The Meaning of Forms in Popular Art

To return to the question posed by colonization, that of cultural encounter, we should keep in mind that it is not always easy to determine precisely where the erudite ends and the popular begins in frontier symbolic forms.

In an anonymously carved religious image, for example, the piece's remote stylistic model may reside in the late Gothic period or in the Iberian Baroque, but the intense, concentrated, and fixed, almost mask-like expressiveness of the face betrays an archaic-popular way of sculpting the human soul in wood or clay. As Leonardo da Vinci advised, "Learn the secrets of expressive gestures from the deaf."

It would not be sufficient if, in the search for formal constants, we were to state that redundancy is an intrinsic feature of popular art. In fact, popular artistic expression plays host to numerous recurring marks, lines, colors, dance steps, rhythms, melodic phrases and hooks, echoes, refrains and entire verses, and opening and closing motifs. When we look through the traditional ballads and poems collected by Sílvio Romero in his *Cantos populares do Brasil* (Popular Songs of Brazil) and by Amadeu Amaral in his *Tradições populares* (Popular Traditions), the presence of repetition is more than apparent. I cannot help quoting one of many possible examples, a children's rhyme that has been recited in northeastern Brazil since the beginning of the nineteenth century:

Amanhã é domingo,
pé de cachimbo,
Galo monteiro
Pisou na areia;
A areia é fina
Que dá no sino;
O sino é de ouro
Que dá no besouro;
O besouro é de prata
Que dá na mata;
A mata é valente
Que dá no tenente;
O tenente é mofino;
Que dá no menino;
Menino é valente
Que dá em toda gente.[38]

Tomorrow is Sunday,
a pipe's foot,
A mountain rooster
Stepped on the sand;
The sand is fine
It hits the bell;
The bell is gold
It hits the beetle;
The beetle is silver
It hits the forest;
The forest is brave
It hits the sergeant;
The sergeant's a sad sack,
He hits the boy;
The boy is brave
He hits all of us.

The sound repetition we note in the pairings *domingo-cachimbo* and *monteiro-areia* is established from the first couplet, with rhymes and medieval *leixa-pren* intermingling.[39] Sound and meaning go hand in hand until the appearance of the choral image in which the smallest element of the piece, the boy, because he is brave, "hits" all of us. The boy closes the circle opened by another sign of smallness: the fine grains of sand, which "hit" the bell. The need for repetition is so great that the rhyme's global meaning ends up absorbing internal couplings (the bell that "hits" the beetle, the brave forest, etc.) in the interest of preserving sonic and syntactic reiteration.

As is well known, repetition is present in high art as well, though there it is a concealed feature due to the requirements of the modernizing ideology inaugurated by the Romantic revolution, which valued the originality of a creative subject liberated from strict formal constraints. At times, literary analysis does not progress beyond the task of identifying a text's recurrent and nonrecurrent elements, its symmetrical and asymmetrical features, and so on. It falls to interpretation to locate the cultural meaning of an expressive movement and to determine what perspective an artist reveals and what values he or she espouses when repeating a trace or a word.

The social explanation for repetition may be a community's desire to preserve collective harmony on the basis of a shared set of emotions and ideas. Repetition's psychological weight comes from memory, which more easily recalls symmetrical or at least recurrent elements.

Think of the consistency with which the figure of Christ, or *Bom Jesus* (Good Jesus), is represented in Luso-Brazilian religious imagery. He is and is not a human being like us. There is an austerity in his features, whether we refer to the examples found in Iguape, Pirapora, or Perdões, and his position is invariably frontal, severe, and dignified. But within the confines of this hieratic posture, proper to a god, the Passion has marked the body of Jesus, the Christ of the *Ecce Homo*. His arms are limp, his hands tied, his forehead cut by thorns, his eyes are hollow, and he is marked by the five wounds: he is a creature given over to destiny's fury. His scepter, which in Brazil may be made of sugar cane (some call him *Bom Jesus da Cana Verde*, or "Good Jesus of the Green Cane"), is the sign of degraded, ridiculed royalty.

In this case, to invariably reproduce the same set of features of face and body is to conform to internal needs of social perception. The Good Jesus, the man who can pardon us because he is divine, the deity that suffers because he is human, must always appear identical to himself, to the artist who sculpts him, and to the devotee who contemplates and venerates him.

Although the material used (wood, plaster, and most recently cardboard), the size, and the execution may vary, reflecting differences in time period and technique, this in no way alters the image, which is reproduced in the name of its religious identity. It is identity that commands reiteration, in the first instance, and not vice versa. The saints represented in the *paulistinhas*, fired clay pieces that have been produced in São Paulo since the eighteenth century, are identifiable through certain invariable features or objects: Saint Benedict is identified by his dark beard and by the snake coiled around his cassock; Saint Gertrude, by the heart of Jesus inscribed on her chest; Saint Joseph, by his boots, book, and lyre; Saint Gonçalo of Amarante, by a *caipira* guitar or book; and Saint Anthony, by his Franciscan habit and the Child Jesus in his arms.[40]

The repetition of certain features serves to reinforce the image's basic expressive aim. Sometimes it only takes one repeated element to identify the deity: this is the case of an image of the Child Jesus from Pernambuco, which Luís Saia recognized as Xangô (the Afro-Brazilian lord of storms and thunder), due to the red stripe painted across his stomach by followers of *candomblé*. This sign, motivated though nonfigurative, expressive, and abstract, encompassing both color and trace, half-symbol and half-index, told the faithful that the figure, while not necessarily appearing as such, was in fact Xangô.[41] The figure's sacred character was guaranteed by a single distinctive feature, the color red that always accompanies representations of Xangô. That which returns signifies, and only returns because it signifies.

The high visual arts from the Renaissance through the neoclassical period likewise flee from the dangers of undifferentiation. But the artist's are other methods. The academic sculptor engages in the *rifinitura* (refinement) of the material as much as possible, creating meticulous, unique surface features in pursuit of a desired individualization in form and detail. The sculptor's tools mold the marble to produce a realistic representation of folds, rendering even the fringe of a robe an iconic feature. It is true that urban European craftsmanship also took pleasure in such masterful detailing (I am thinking of certain eighteenth-century Neapolitan crèches, of which the Museum of Sacred Art in São Paulo has a superb example), but we must recognize this as a case of Mannerist and Baroque erudite styles that subtly made their way into the semipopular Catholic imagination, which in Italy was particularly cognizant of the techniques of high art.

What we should take from this discussion is an awareness of popular art's dual character in the context of the Brazilian colonial condition: on the one hand, the almost schematic rigidity of general composition, which leads many to contrast archaic abstraction with the urban, cultured artist's figurative or realistic style and, on the other hand, a form of expressiveness that is ontological rather than psychological. Rigidity and expressiveness transform the anonymous sacred piece into a mysterious object, an enigma simultaneously rough and solemn.

In formal terms, hieratic style reproduces and preserves postures and lines. By its nature, what is solemn cannot vary; it tends toward a self-perpetuating *Gestalt*, or good form. This holds true for all artistic expression identified as typical, whether high or low, sublime or grotesque.

Within this rather spacious and flexible internal model, which in itself contains all the virtual potential of art, given that it fuses the abstract and the expressive, popular culture remains open to a host of influences and impulses not screened for color, class, or nationality. Moreover, popular culture does not discriminate based on historical time, a fact that is rich in consequences. The culture of the people is local by force of its environment, but in its humble dialectical movement it becomes practically universal: it rejects nothing on principle, assimilating and refashioning everything by necessity. The Brazilian folkloric manifestations known as *cheganças* and *congos*, which since the eighteenth century have depicted the battles between Christians and Moors during the time of Charlemagne, are notable examples of popular synchronicity. As for sacred imagery, detailed stylistic analyses have revealed Byzantine, Gothic, and Baroque elements in devotional pieces from nineteenth-century São Paulo.[42]

It is precisely this democratic syncretism that was sometimes lacking in the artistic styles favored by erudite culture, particularly when they were codified by closed and self-perpetuating institutions. Much of what appears to be unchanging in popular art, and is therefore described as typical, is actually the product of a subjectively lived faithfulness to good form, whereas academic artists were instructed, over many generations, in a kind of forced repetition that resulted in imitation for imitation's sake, in an *etichetta* (*piccola etica* . . .), or, in other words, in the repetition of a formula merely because of its social and political prestige. It is one thing to spontaneously experience and dedicate oneself to a tradition; it is quite another to demonstrate one's familiarity with it in an affected, pedantic, and snobbish manner. In English institutions of centuries past, *snob*, short for *sine nobilitate* (without nobility), was applied to students of uncertain noble origin.

As for expressiveness, in archaic popular art it is customarily all-encompassing, whereas in high art details tend to multiply for their own sake, with the artist delighting in the sophistication of the copy of the model.

It is worth asking what is occurring in anonymous sacred imagery when a particular anatomical detail is isolated or enlarged. This is a case of the part signifying for the whole, as in the ex-votos found at the base of crosses erected in northeastern Brazil, which Luís Saia examined in his fine study: enlarged hands and feet, sculpted with great care, speak to the amount of grace in the cure. Here the part does not stand for itself, as in Mannerism; rather, it is the individual's overall well-being that gives thanks in plastic form. The basic scheme at work remains one of total expressiveness.

The ex-votos placed at the base of *cruzeiros de acontecido* (literally, "crossing for something that happened," erected at sites of tragic deaths), which are at the same time representations of promises made to Catholic saints and sculptures of remote African origin, challenge the observer to confront the problem of different ages operating simultaneously.

During its colonial acculturation, at least two time periods were present in Brazilian popular art: the time of Christian catechization and the time of black religiosity. The catechism, temporally located between the late medieval and Baroque periods, is merely traditional, whereas African religiosity is manifestly archaic. Catholicism, a key component of Western history, has exchanged its visual signs with successive Western artistic styles—hence the tendency of Catholic art to shift from the purely allegorical to realistic figuration, and its acceptance during the Renaissance of classical ideas of perspective and representation. In contrast, the Bantu or Sudanese ritual art brought to Brazil by African slaves did not undergo this process of stylistic updating but preserved its symbolic and animistic heritage. In a way, colonial acculturation managed to fuse these two artistic traditions in the popular sacred object: it shaped the Catholic ethos of the promise, as depicted in the ex-voto, into the archaic mold of the African mask.

While the catechization of the Brazilian people was not exactly an illusion, as Nina Rodrigues[43] understood it, it was certainly incomplete, operating as it did within a complex religious system that was older and more diffuse than official Catholicism. The ex-voto, located between two universes, serves as an example of a frontier cultural product. It may also be understood in terms of formal acculturation (Roger Bastide's term) or, following Melville Herskovits, as the reinterpretation of one culture by another.

The Prophets and the *Calundu*

Art that operates beyond the pale of writing preserves in an unchanging form certain traditional patterns and seems to survive outside of history, or at least outside of the rhythm of the ideological history of Western Europe, which in turn is faithfully reproduced in the mental life of dominant colonial classes.

In reality, frontier culture exhibits a certain permeability with regard to symbolic forms from other eras, however remote, which is indicative of a different historical consciousness, a broad, knowing synchrony that makes the most of its particular circumstances. "Aleijadinho's prophets are not Baroque, they are biblical," exclaimed Giuseppe Ungaretti after inspecting them during a 1968 trip to Minas Gerais with the photographer Sérgio Frederico. Since a properly biblical statuary does not exist, what the poet saw with his eagle eye was the expression in stone of a religiosity more majestic and choral and, at the same time, more intrepid and freer than that allowed for by the Mannerist models of eighteenth-century sculpture.

The art of colonial Brazil could only be fully appreciated when bourgeois academic taste began its period of terminal decline at the end of the belle époque.[44] The modernists, who were drawn both to the primitive and to the new in their desire to rediscover Brazil, redeemed the *barroco mineiro* from the disdainful evaluation it had received at the hands of the neoclassicists of the French Artistic Mission of 1816. An enthusiastic historian celebrated the 1816 mission in the following terms:

> In architecture, colonial institutions, feelings, and ideas upheld during the Baroque, the Jesuit, the Plateresque, and the Churrigueresque periods were replaced by neoclassical feelings and actions.
>
> In painting, the ancient world, mythology, and history replaced the almost exclusively religious work of the *santeiro* artists of the colony and of the last years of the viceroyalty.[45]

Note the twice reiterated idea of the substitution performed by the new artistic school that accompanied Dom João VI to Brazil and replaced the religious and popular Baroque of the *santeiros* with the secular and modernizing neoclassical style. As is well known, much of our civil architecture, particularly in nineteenth-century Rio de Janeiro, conformed to neoclassical standards. Our so-called national painting would likewise follow French academic standards, beginning in the Regency period (1831–1840) and to a greater extent during the Second Empire (1840–1889). Gonçalves de Magalhães, the *romantic arrependido* (regretful Romantic), and Araújo Porto Alegre were both disciples of Debret. Thus it is not surprising that Bernardo Guimarães, a Romantic and a regionalist born and raised in Ouro Preto, wrote of Aleijadinho's statues of the prophets at Congonhas do Campo with a total lack of aesthetic understanding yet with awe at the artist's exceptional energy:

> We know that these statues are the work of a sculptor with a missing or deformed right hand, who needed to attach his tools to his wrists in order to work.
>
> It is doubtless for this reason that his artistic execution is far from perfect. One need not be an expert to recognize the errors in design, the lack of harmony and proportion in certain forms. Deformed heads, inexact proportions, too-heavy and shortened bodies, and many other major and minor errors reveal these prophets to be the products of a rough, uninstructed chisel. That said, their postures in general are characteristic, imposing and majestic, they are artfully assembled, and at times the uneducated sculptor's tools managed to give their faces expressions worthy of the prophets.
>
> The sublime Isaiah, the terrible, somber Habakkuk, and the melancholy Jeremiah are especially notable for the beauty and solemnity of their expression and posture. If we do not look at them with the minute and scrutinizing eye of an artist, an initial glance is sure to result in a strong impression of respect and wonder. These statues seem to be rough, incorrect copies of fine artistic models, which the artist had in front of him or imprinted on his imagination.[46]

What Bernardo Guimarães, with his Romantic sensibility, could not help but admire was precisely Aleijadinho's totalizing expressiveness: he writes of that which is sublime, terrible, somber, melancholy, of their postures in general, worthy of the prophets, the beauty and solemnity of their expression, and his strong impression of respect and wonder. Yet what Guimarães's academic criteria made him reject was the very artistic approach that granted the figures their expressive force. Aleijadinho's creative impulse prevented him from applying (nor did he need) correct anatomical proportion, the perspective of a Donatello, the virtuosity of mimetic detail, or the sweet harmony of spiraling curves; his approach required other symbolic forms and strategies of execution. The last sentence of Guimarães's commentary, which takes for granted the existence of "fine artistic models" of which the sculptures in question are "rough, incorrect copies," betrays the aesthetic distortion of a gaze hardened by neoclassical formulas.

This seems to be a case of structurally inevitable misunderstanding. Learned aesthetic criteria have their own history, marked by European cultural battles, between the opposition between the neoclassical standards of the Enlightenment and the devout, semipopular Baroque "obscurantism," which is seem summarily as an obstacle to be overcome. When the spirit of this struggle makes its way into the ideology of the colonized country's ruling elite, it manifests itself in critical judgments against the cultural expressions of other segments of society, not only those situated at the purely popular level but also on the frontier between the illiterate and the educated. In this way, elitism becomes an inescapable feature of Latin American ideological development, insofar as the general ideas of evolution, progress, and civilization remain divorced from the values of social and cultural democracy.

Through the division of labor and power, official taste during the nineteenth and early twentieth centuries differentiated the values of the colonizer and the colonized, reducing the latter to nonvalues. As a result, the colonized always experienced their symbolic universe ambiguously, as both positive (in itself) and negative (for the external Other and for the interiorized Other in oneself).

One of the aims of this book is to suggest that the cultural schism that accompanied modernization as it was experienced by elites manifested itself in other ways, and with apparently harsher consequences, within the colonial context. It is well known that the first Jesuits in Brazil effectively demonized Tupi religious practices, with the exception of Tupã, arbitrarily identified with the God of the Bible. Nonacceptance was even more pronounced with regard to African rites.

Reading Nuno Marques Pereira's Baroque allegory *Compêndio narrativo do Peregrino da América* (The American Pilgrim's Narrative Compendium), published in 1718, I find an episode that illustrates how religious differences were resolved in pure and simple exorcism. The Pilgrim is staying in the house of a generous plantation owner. However, he cannot sleep at night because of the noises made by the slaves during their religious dances. Here is what happens next:

> He asked me how I had passed the night. I responded: "Comfortably, but awake. I couldn't fall asleep the whole night." Concerned, he asked me why. I told him that I had been tormented by the noise of *atabaques, pandeiros, canzás, botijas,* and *castanhetas*; the cacophony was so horrendous that it seemed like the very chaos of Hell.... "Now I remember what I wanted to ask," I said to him. "What are *Calundus*?" "They're dances, divinations," he said to me, "that these blacks say are customary in their land, and which they perform here whenever they get together, in order to find out the causes of sicknesses they're suffering from, or where to find things they've lost, or so as to have good fortune in their hunts and in the harvest, and for many other purposes besides.

The landowner's explanation, which in fact serves as a good anthropological lesson, describes in simple terms the integrating functions of a ritual that, transplanted from Africa, managed to survive in the harsh conditions of the fields and slave quarters.[47] But the Pilgrim is neither convinced nor calmed. On the contrary, he condemns his host's tolerance to the point of calling both him and the slaves *excomungados* (ex-communicates) for violating the first commandment, against the sins of idolatry and devil worship, just as the poet Gregório de Matos had done a generation earlier in his condemnation of Afro-Brazilian customs, written from the perspective of the city of Salvador da Bahia:

> I have *quilombos*
> with great masters,
> where at night they teach
> *calundus* and spells!
> . . .
> What I know is that Satan
> is involved in those dances,
> for only this master priest
> could teach such errors.
>
> ("Bahia protests, through its advocate, that the faults attributed to it are not its own, but those of the wicked persons who find shelter in it.")

Meanwhile, in *Peregrino da América*, our inquisitorial Pilgrim moves from words to action. He calls for the "Master of the *Calundus*," probably a *babalaô*, asks him what he does, and gives him a bizarre etymological lecture in order to demonstrate the demonic character of his art:

> "Tell me, son (who should more properly be called father of wickedness), what are *Calundus*?" He responded with great reticence and shame that they were a custom from his land, feasts of entertainment and divination. "Don't you know," I asked him, "what the word *Calundus* means in Portuguese?" The black man told me he didn't. "Well I'd like to tell you," I said, "what the etymology of the name means. In Portuguese and Latin, it means this: they are both silent. *Calo duo*. Do you know who these two are who keep silent? They are you and the devil. The devil keeps silent, and so do you, about the great sinful pact you've made with the devil, and which you're teaching to the others, causing them also to sin, so that you'll take them with you to Hell when they die for what they did here in your company."[48]

The landowner, the *pai-de-santo*, and the slaves were all terrified, and the Pilgrim asked them to

> bring [to him] all the instruments they used in those diabolical dances. They did this and the instruments were brought to the *terreiro*, where a great bonfire was lit and they threw everything in. My clearest memory is of smelling the horrible stench and hearing the noises made by the *tabaques, botijas, canzás, castanhetas,* and *pés de cabras*. There was smoke so black that no one could bear it. It had been a clear day, but it soon darkened with a fog so dark that night seemed to be falling. So then I, who trusted entirely in His Divine Majesty, prayed the Creed, and right away a fresh gust of wind blew and everything dissipated.

This is followed by a long narrative, filled with other examples of idolatrous and libidinal dealings with the devil, acts in which many souls had been damned for all eternity.

What is most striking about this episode of the *Peregrino da América* is the war without mercy waged by official religion against the rites of African origin, a war that culminates in a true auto-da-fé in which the slaves' sacred instruments are destroyed. And it is worth noting how the Pilgrim removes the fetid cloud that blocks out the sun: he recites the Creed, just as someone might recite a magic spell against an enemy, "and right away a fresh gust of wind blew and everything dissipated."

In the process of colonial acculturation, the more modern protagonist will at times regress to the arcane ethos of past eras.

We can extract a common and more general meaning from these (mis) encounters in the form of a dialectical complex composed of distinct social periods, the simultaneity of which is structural, just as both the meeting together and the opposition of the dominating and the dominated are structural. The eye of the colonizer did not forgive, or barely tolerated, the articulation and survival of difference. The rigid orthodoxy enshrined by the Council of Trent was violently opposed to Afro-Brazilian dances and songs. Later, French-modeled academic taste would malign the archaic-popular style of the *barroco mineiro*, still alive in the religious architecture of the nineteenth century. Cultures (or cults) invariably draw on their dominant position in passing judgment on the cultures and cults of others. Colonization delays democratization in the world of symbols.

In order to be received sympathetically, the symbolic formations of the colonized had to wait until the first quarter of the twentieth century, a period in which the European intelligentsia, then in the midst of a profoundly self-critical examination of Western imperialism, began reconsidering popular art, the American Baroque style, and African cultures. Franz Boas's antiracist anthropology, which was brought to Brazil by Gilberto Freyre, the Parisian avant-garde in the visual arts and its valorization of *art nègre*, and shortly thereafter the reconsiderations of Baroque aesthetics by German and Spanish stylistics: these are some of the disparate critical strands that contributed to a new attitude among the intellectual elites of Latin America. Although this sentiment might be confused in certain respects with the nationalism then surging through the ex-colonial nations, it transcended this framework of militant ideology as it turned to the universalizing potentialities of art and religion—hence the propitious convergence of cosmopolitism and rooted localism in the avant-garde manifestations of those years of Latin American and Afro-Antillean renaissance.

2 Anchieta, or the Crossed Arrows of the Sacred

In reading the poetry of José de Anchieta, immersed as it is in Catholic devotion, we run the risk of understanding it as an undifferentiated whole. In fact, when examined closely it reveals internal differences of form and meaning that are worth examining in greater detail.

Allegory and Catechism

When Anchieta wrote for a native audience, or for colonists who understood the *língua geral* spoken along the Brazilian coast, he almost always wrote in the Tupi language.[1] The linguistic acculturation visible in these texts is the deeply inscribed mark of a historically original situation. The poet seeks, using Tupi cultural codes, to craft a poetic form that is quite close to the poetry of the medieval troubadours in its popular Iberian variants: using *redondilho*, Anchieta forges four- and five-syllable lines in which he constructs a series of rhymes that now alternate, and now are opposed to one another.

Redondilhos, five-syllable lines, end consonance: here we are at the heart of peninsular poetic practice, which has now been transplanted onto a very different public and cultural context:

> Jandé, rubeté, Iesu,
> Jandé, rekobé, meengára,
> oimomboreausukatú,
> Jandé amotareymbára.
>
> Jesus, our true Father,
> Lord of our existence, you vanquished
> our enemy.[2]

The words are Tupi (with the exception of *Iesú*), as is the syntax: but the rhythm, which with its accents and pauses is typical of the period, is not indigenous but rather Portuguese. The rhythm, though not the entire music of the poem, is Portuguese, yet the sounds that appear in the poem are derived from Tupi.

Acculturation is synonymous with translation.

The project of communicating the message of Catholicism in the language spoken by the Amerindians entailed an effort to penetrate the worldview of the Other, and this was the task of the first apostle to Brazil. In the movement from one symbolic sphere to another, Anchieta encountered obstacles that at times were insuperable. How, for example, to speak to the Tupi of sin, if they lacked the very notion of sin, at least in the sense that the word took on during the European Middle Ages? Anchieta, in this as in other cases, prefers to graft the Portuguese term onto the trunk of the native language; he does this, for this and for more pressing reasons, with the word *mass* and in the invocation of Our Lady:

Ejorí, Santa Maria,
xe anáma rausubá!

Come, Holy Mary,
protector of mine own!

These cases, however, are atypical. More commonly, Anchieta looks for a homology between the two languages, with uneven results:

Bishop becomes *Pai-guaçu*, that is, great priest. Our Lady sometimes appears under the name *Tupansy*, or mother of Tupã. God's kingdom is *Tupãretama*, or land of Tupã. Church, logically, becomes *tupãóka*, or the house of Tupã. Soul is *anga*, which means both a shadow and an ancestor's spirit. Demon is *anhanga*, which is an errant or dangerous spirit. For the angels of the biblical and Christian tradition, Anchieta coins the term *karaibebê*, or flying prophet.

This new representation of the sacred amounted neither to Christian theology nor to Tupi belief but constituted a third symbolic sphere, a kind of parallel mythology only possible in the colonial context.

Beginning with the arbitrary equation of Tupã with the Judeo-Christian God, the entire system of correspondences created by Anchieta operates by way of uncertain shortcuts. Tupã was the perhaps onomatopoeic name for a cosmic force identified with thunder, a celestial phenomenon that occurred for the first time when the head of the mythological figure Maira-Monã was split open.[3] In any case, what could it have meant, for the Tupi, to join the name of Tupã to the notion of a God that is both one and a trinity, both an all-powerful being and the vulnerable Son of Man of the Gospels?

The Christian paradox appears in naked form in verses such as these:

Pitanginamo ereikó,
Tupánamo eikóbo bé.

You are a little child,
though also a God.

Here the homology between the Judeo-Christian God and Tupã reveals itself to be wholly inadequate. Anchieta created a similar problem for himself in the very word that, as discussed above, he created in order to convey the notion of "angel" in his plays. The term *karaibebê* lends itself to two divergent meanings: *Karaí* may describe either a white man (even today in Paraguay, *karaí* is used as a term of respect, meaning *sir*) or a Guarani singer-prophet, that is, a holy man who travels from tribe to tribe heralding the Land without Evil. But what would the Amerindians have thought of, once they made the association between *karaí* and the idea of flight expressed by *bebê*? Of their own nomadic, seeing shamans, who now possessed wings? Or perhaps of winged Portuguese? In his *Auto de São Sebastião* Anchieta enchants himself with the fantasy of a kingdom of angels: *karaibebê rupape*!

This Catholic-Tupi acculturation was marked by solutions that were strange and sometimes violent as well. The Amerindians' sacred circle of being, which was once strongly articulated and which preserved the tribe and was shared by its members, lost its unity and was divided into opposing and irreconcilable zones: on the one side, Evil, the kingdom of Anhanga, who takes on the role of a threatening Anti-God, much like the hypertrophied Demon of medieval fantasy; on the other side, the kingdom of Good, in which Tupã is invested with creative and saving powers, in open contradiction to the original myth of Tupã, which attributed to him the annihilating power of the lightning bolt.

Anchieta narrates the conversion of a very old Amerindian, "who I believe is older than one hundred thirty years," who lived in the village of Itanhaém:

> we told him that we wanted to baptize him so that his soul would not be lost, but that we could not teach him the things he needed to know for lack of time, and we told him to prepare for our return. He reacted to this news as if it had come down from Heaven, and it made such a strong impression on him that when we saw him again and asked if he wanted to be a Christian, he said with great happiness that he did, and that he had been waiting for us. . . . What truly made an impression on him was the mystery of the Resurrection, which he spoke of many times, saying: "The true God is Jesus, who left His grave and went up to Heaven, and one day will return, wrathful, to burn everything". . . . Reaching the church doorway

we sat him down on a bench where his godparents and other Christians were waiting for him. There I turned to him and told him to say what he had to say before the crowd; and he responded with great feeling that he wanted to be baptized, and that he had spent the whole of the previous night thinking about God's wrath, with which He would destroy the world, and burn everything, and that we would all be brought back to life.

After his baptism the old Amerindian supposed "that he would be raised up to Heaven, but having instead returned to his home he began to weep, as did his children and grandchildren."[4]

This narrative provides us with an example of the fusion of the Christ who provides individual resurrection and Tupã as a cosmic destroyer. This is a singular Tupã who enters into the humanized economy of the story of the Christian Incarnation: he has a mother, Tupansy, who is also his daughter, Tupã rajyra (let us recall Dante, "Vergine Madre Figlia del tuo Figlio," from Canto XXXIII of *Paradiso*); he also has a home and a kingdom.

Wicked habits are associated with Anhanga's dark kingdom. They include cannibalism, polygamy, drunkenness from consuming *cauim* (an alcoholic beverage made from manioc or corn), and the effects of tobacco inhaled during indigenous ceremonies. Speaking of the first of these, the devouring of one's enemy was, in the life of the indigenous community, an important practice, a sacred act that granted to those who participated in it a new identity and a new name. But Anchieta the catechist exorcised cannibalism's sacramental function. He saw the work of the Devil in it, and considered it a nefarious vice that the Amerindians should renounce entirely. In order to differentiate this from other rituals, Anchieta coined the term *angaipaba*, comprised, as per Maria de Lourdes de Paula Martins's analysis, of *ang* (soul), *aíb* (evil), and the nominal suffix *aba*, and whose meaning approximated the notion of *things of a deviant soul*. With this term Anchieta reified the idea of sin and rendered more visible that which he execrated.

With the objective of converting the native, Anchieta created poetic and dramatic works that describe a Manichean world torn between forces in perpetual struggle: Tupã-God, with his familiar constellation of angels and saints, and Anhanga-Devil, with his cohort of evil spirits that announce themselves in Tupi ceremonies. An ontological dualism presides over this totalizing conception of indigenous life: one of its most powerful effects, in terms of acculturation, follows from the missionary having linked the ethos of the tribe to powers that are external to and superior to the Amerindian's will.

Clearly, this demonization of Tupi rites would not produce a religious practice that would in turn give rise to the figure of the moral human being as the subject of his actions. The catechist was seen (and saw himself) as a being possessed by unearthly forces, who would be delivered by a deus ex machina preached by the *abarê*, or priest, and distributed throughout the sacraments with the aid of supernatural beings like the angels and the souls of saints.

In Anchieta's plays we witness the dramatization of a process that impacted tribal life from the outside inward. I have already described its dualistic structure, which was long-lived and carried forward by later works of acculturation.

Here we should insist on a point made previously: the missionaries made a strategic distinction with regard to the natives' symbolic expressions. They collected and retained from the indigenous narratives only those mythical passages in which there appeared either cosmic entities (Tupã) or civilizing heroes (Sumé) that could be at least partially identified with the biblical figures of the God who creates or the Son who saves. Since, at least as far as is known, the Tupi did not worship gods and heroes in an organized sense, it was relatively easy for the Jesuits to infer that they had no religion whatsoever and to fill this theological void with the fixed notions of Catholicism, specifically creation and redemption.

This characterization is broadly applicable, appearing not only in Jesuit texts but in non-Jesuit sources as well: Hans Staden, Jean de Léry, André Thevet, Gabriel Soares de Sousa, Gândavo. To cite an exemplary passage from Anchieta's *Informação do Brasil e de suas capitanias* (Report on Brazil and Its Captaincies, 1584):

> They worship no creature as a God, and only believe that thunder is God, though not even for this reason do they honor thunder in any particular way. They neither have idols, nor fetishes, nor do they communicate with the Devil, and indeed they are afraid of him, because he sometimes kills them by blows in the woods or in the rivers, and when he does not harm them in places that are frightful or in which this is said to occur, when they pass by that place, they leave an arrow, feather, or some other thing as an offering.

Some lines later, referring to shamans (*pajés*), the missionary affirms that yes, the Amerindians do treat with the Devil.[5]

The observations made by the missionaries and secular chroniclers alike are generally ordered as follows:

a) they roundly reject the notion that the Tupi have a religion;
b) they refer to their fear of thunder, understood to be a manifestation of a divinity known as Tupã;

c) they tell of cases of persecution and death of Amerindians at the hands of evil spirits, Anhanga and Juripari, which they identify as demons;
d) finally, they make mention of the influence of the *pajés* and *caraíbas* (shamans).

As the missionaries became more knowledgeable of indigenous life, they came to perceive that the absolute absence of rituals honoring Tupã or Sumé, which they had previously noted, indicated that they would need to seek out the center of Tupi religiosity within another symbolic locus. The living, meaning-making core of this religiosity would be found neither in liturgy, nor in divine beings, nor in myth, but in the cult of the dead, in the conjuring of good spirits and the banishing of evil ones. This was the function of the ceremonies of song and dance, of *cauim*, of tobacco, and of the trances over which the *pajé* presided.

These practices were truly rich with meaning. These rites bound the Amerindian to a communal past at the same time as they confirmed his identity within the group. Cannibalism had no meaning unless understood in terms of the belief that he who consumed would gain life force through the absorption of the bodies and souls of enemies killed in honorable combat.

It was this that was the true target the Jesuits sought to destroy through their preaching. It did not take long to find the most effective method of attack: generalize the Amerindian's vivid fear or horror of evil spirits and extend this fear to all those beings conjured in trances. In other words, the Jesuits sought to demonize all of those ceremonies that fostered contact with the dead.

Official Catholic doctrine sought during this age of Renaissance and Reformation, at the edge of lay or heterodox modernity, to wipe away any vestiges of animism and mediumship from religious activity. This was a period in which magic was implacably persecuted, a time in which witches and sorcerers were hunted down, and not only in Spain and Portugal. In this context, Anchieta's choice of the Devil as the protagonist of so many of his plays becomes comprehensible. And moreover, we may understand how the Angel of Evil appears as such a familiar figure in the grotesque or humorous scenes in which sins are described and in the scenes in which justice is meted out in these cobbled-together Tupi–medieval mystery plays.

It was necessary in these plays that Evil be circumscribed, surrounded, defeated, and subordinated by the forces of Good. The speech of Guaixará, the king of the evil spirits in the play entitled *Na Festa de São Lourenço* (At the Feast of Saint Lawrence), is exemplary in this regard. And the choice of the name Guaixará was not coincidental, as a Tamoio hero with this name had attacked the Portuguese twice, at São Sabastião de Rio de Janeiro (1566) and São Lourenço (1567). Another Tamoio chief, Aimbirê, is represented as Satan:

> The virtuous disturb me,
> their new ways
> irritate me.
> Who has brought them
> to befoul our land?

> I am
> in this village
> as its guardian,
> forcing it to follow my laws
> From here I travel far
> visiting other villages.

> Who am I?
> I am the notorious,
> the great, fiery devil
> called Guaixará,
> and am known to all.

> My ways are pleasant
> I do not wish them challenged,
> or abolished.

> I will
> stir up all the villages.

> It is good to drink *cauim*,
> until you vomit.
> This is very good.
> This I'd recommend,
> This is something to be admired!

> Here the *moçaracas*, the drinkers
> are acclaimed.
> Those who drink until the *cauim* is gone
> they are brave,
> they are ready to fight.

> It is good to dance,
> to adorn yourself, to paint yourself red,
> cover yourself with feathers, paint your legs,
> make yourself black, smoke,
> practice witchcraft . . .

> The Indian should not
> restrain his fury, stop killing,
> eating others, capturing Tapuias,
> carrying on, being dishonest,
> being an adulterous spy.
>
> So I
> live with the Indians,
> so that they believe in me.
> Those priests who have now come,
> preaching God's law,
> try uselessly to drive me away.[6]

This translation, which is meant to be strictly literal, tends at times toward the prosaic. But what a dramatic *cordel* this list of the Devil's boasts would make in the hands of a northeastern popular poet!

What do the things Guaixará names in his speech as his work—ingestion of alcohol, nightlong dancing, personal adornment, red and black body paint, tattoos, feathers, tobacco, consultations with the oracular *pajé*, cannibalism—represent if not the system of Tupi rituals?

Here the conflict between cultures is placed into relief. Religions that affirm a unitary personal consciousness, such as Judaism and Christianity, fear magical rituals, whether these are naturalistic or shamanistic, and suspect these of fetishism and idolatry—hence their rejection of phenomena that recall mediumship or possession and their horrified reaction to acts in which one's personal identity is submerged in a trance. There is a centuries-old tradition within Judaism and Christianity (and Islam as well) toward the purification of the imagination, a tradition that remits to the Law of Moses, to the prophets, to the Pauline letters. And this fear of a resurgent polytheism led to the extreme actions of the iconoclasts. The European Christian liturgy, in its more modern, Protestant manifestation from the sixteenth century forward, tended toward an ascetic Calvinism that was hostile to figures and gestures, and in its most severe form was opposed to any symbol that was not the unadorned word of the scriptures. In this context one's relationship with the transcendent was almost entirely textual, mediated through the naked word of the Bible, only interrupted at very occasional, well-defined moments by the sober intonation of a sacred hymn—nothing more.

It was at this historical moment, in which European religion became more intellectualized, that European Christians entered into contact with animistic practices from Africa and the Americas. The arrows of the sacred crossed. Unhappily for the native peoples, the religion of the discoverers came armed with horses and soldiers, arquebuses and cannons. This conflict was not merely one of competing theodicies but of tragically unequal technologies. The result was either a massacre, pure and simple, or a situation of degradation in which the victor was free to stamp out the religious practices of the defeated.

In the Luso-Brazilian case, the distance between the symbolic lives of the Tupi and Christianity could be bridged because of the more sensible, flexible, and earthly character of Portuguese Catholicism in comparison to the English or Dutch Puritanism that prevailed in the colonies of New England. Iberian popular religious devotion did not dispense with images; rather, it multiplied the number of images in use. Moreover, this form of Catholicism made extensive use of figures that could mediate between the faithful and the divine, such as angels and saints, who indeed amounted to the souls of the dead interceding on behalf of the living.

In regard to these tangible mediations, the catechism in Brazil made use, when possible, of the sacraments, which were corporeal signs of the relationship between humankind and God. And alongside the symbolic language of the bread and wine (the Eucharist), water (Baptism), oil (Confirmation or Chrism), and bodies (Marriage), a modest set of so-called sacramental objects came into circulation. These included incense and holy water, relics, medallions, rosaries, figurines of saints, scapulars, candles, ex-votos, and a seemingly infinite number of signs that made the doctrine accessible to those Amerindians and blacks to whom it was taught in colonial Brazil.

Reinforced by the common fear of evil spirits among the Amerindians, the Jesuits attacked at their core those rituals in which the dead were summoned and which cemented the relationships that existed between members of the tribe. They replaced the Tupi-Guarani ceremonies with a choral and picturesque liturgy that drew extensively on processions and the Stations of the Cross, and with a popular devotional practice in which legions of angels and souls in Heaven could be invoked, as intermediaries within the Church hierarchy, to respond to the needs of the faithful.

The general principle of mediation, made manifest by spiritual entities (some diurnal and nocturnal, such as guardian angels), in practice permitted Iberian Catholicism, which in the sixteenth century was still medieval, to bridge the divide between the religious practices, or cults, of the colonizers and the worldviews of the colonized. However, this contact, allowed for by a common belief in the existence of spirits, could not be described as a fraternal union between people that destiny sought fit to bring into contact at a particular moment. Since this encounter was one premised on domination, indigenous ceremonies that brought the living into contact with the dead were viewed by European travelers and missionaries alike as symptoms of barbarism and frequently were considered manifestations of demonic possession. The colonial process prevented symbolic acculturation from taking place freely, easily, and horizontally, without disjunctions and fracturings of meaning and value.

In the eyes of the colonizer, the gestures and rhythms of the Tupis as they danced and sang no longer represented the movements of worshippers participating in a collective, sacral action (the very meaning of the idea of liturgy) but instead appeared as the product of the violent powers of evil spirits who surrounded and continually tempted the members of the tribe. At any moment Anhanga, the wandering shadow and clandestine observer of men and a perpetual threat, might arrive on the scene. In Anchieta's plays, Evil comes from outside the self, and can inhabit and possess the individual, forcing him to commit perverse acts, that is, *angaipaba*.

The age-old appeal in Anchieta's plays to the bestiary illustrates the regressive quality of the entire process being described. The figure of the Devil is described as an animal on more than one occasion. Elements of nature that cannot be controlled are considered dangerous. In *Na festa de São Lourenço*, evil spirits are described as *boiuçu* (king cobra), *mboitininguçu* ("whistling snake," that is, rattlesnake), *andiraguaçu* (vampire bat), *jaguara* (jaguar or hunting dog), *jibóia* (boa), *socó* (heron), *sukuriju* (anaconda, or "snake that strangles"), *taguató* (kite), *atyrabebó* (anteater), *guabiru* (common rat), *guaikuíka* (opossum, or "forest rat"), *kururu* (toad), *sariguéia* (opossum), *mboraborá* (black bee), *miaratakaka* (skunk), *sebói* (leech), *tamarutaka* (lobster), *tajassuguaia* (pig).

Everything in the animal kingdom that frightened or disgusted the Europeans was transformed into a menacing sign of dark powers, both natural and supernatural. Evil ranged through the forests or hid in caves and swamps, from which it emerged at night in the form of snakes, rats, bats, and leeches. But mortal danger occurred when these external forces penetrated into a man's soul. Here the inquisitor's eye saw forms of mass possession in tribal practices that brought the body into a state of spastic trance. The *cauim* that old Amerindian women spat out boiled the blood, moved up to the head, and tempted the Amerindian toward luxury and brutality. The smoke blown from the sacred pipes, gourds where the ancestors live and from which they speak, led to similar excesses. To alcohol and tobacco we must add the most potent of drugs, the raw flesh of heroes killed in battle. For the missionary, cannibalism tied together in an unholy knot the capital sins of anger, gluttony, and unrepentant pride. Catechism would describe these and other indigenous rituals as the acts of Anhanga.

An additional relation of exteriority makes itself quite evident in the alternately comic and serious poem "O pelote domingueiro" (The Sunday Cloak), which probably functioned as the dramatic nucleus of the *Auto da pregação universal* (*Auto of Universal Judgment*), which of Anchieta's plays was the most frequently staged during his travels between the settlements of the Brazilian coast.

The allegorical meaning of the poem points to the divine grace received by Adam from on high. The *pelote*—that is, the fine cloak worn on Sundays—represents the grace with which the first man was "cloaked" while in Eden but which he lost when he allowed the Angel of Evil to take it from him.

Take note of this sequence: good, which occupies a position of exteriority in relation to the individual, just as clothing stands in relation to the body, is taken from the individual by external forces, in the case of the poem the Devil's rapaciousness and cunning ("the snake, jealous of the miller / hissed and maligned him / and took from him the Sunday cloak"). Later, with the coming of Jesus Christ, the new Adam is compensated for his original loss: it is only then that he is once again granted the honor of wearing the cloak.

Man first receives the gift of eternal life, then he is tricked into having it stolen from him, and in the end he recovers it, but not as the result of his own initiative. Here "grace" and "divine gifts" are synonymous with the notion of gratuity:

> They gave it to him without charge,
> because it was called "Grace"
> and he wore it,
> with great gallantry, through the square.
> But they stole,
> from the poor miller,
> the Sunday cloak.
>
> The poor little children
> fell deathly cold,
> when the father, mad with rage,
> was shoved face-first into the dirt.
> The thief, with his pack of animals,
> blocked all the escape paths,
> and tore off the cloak.
>
> It was taken from him without charge,
> but it cost a pretty penny
> to the grandson, the third,
> who would recoup the loss.
> Your Sunday cloak,
> was recovered with great cost.
> (Lucky you, oh miller!)[7]

It was not the sinner but "the miller's grandson," Jesus Christ, descended from Adam, who paid the price to recover the cloak. Here the soul is, as always, the staging ground for a duel between the powers of evil and good, which transcend and objectify the soul.

The play *Na vila de Vitória* (In the Town of Vitória) is, perhaps, the most coherent example of the allegorical process as described by Anchieta. In the play there are no dramatic characters in the traditional sense: rather, there are voices, or mouthpieces for political, moral, and religious entities. There is the Town, the Government, Ingratitude, Fear, and Love of God, along with the ever-present Angels of Evil, Lucifer and Satan, who take to insulting each other before suffering a resounding defeat at the hands of the celestial hosts of Saint Maurice and the Archangel Michael.

If we understand allegory as a form of thinking and expression that is fixated on general abstract notions (and that obscures the rich differences of lived experience), the emblematic figures that populate this play effectively illustrate this process. The moralizing speeches of the Government and Fear obscure and, at the same time attempt to resolve from above, some of the sharp political tensions that, in the final years of the century, cut through the captaincy of Espírito Santo.

At this time, the town of Vitória was in the ambiguous and uncomfortable position of being, simultaneously, the seat of a Portuguese captaincy that in 1589 had been left vacant (due to the death of its donatory, Vasco Fernandes Coutinho) and a city that since 1580 had been legally Castilian as a result of the union of the Iberian states under Philip II. Dona Luísa Grimaldi, a Monegasque noblewoman and Fernandes Coutinho's widow, was governing the captaincy when a pro-Castilian movement appeared that called for placing the administration of Espírito Santo under direct royal control. The opposing, pro-Portuguese faction aimed to secure the regency of Vitória for one of the close relatives of the deceased Fernandes Coutinho and, as such, called for a special governing statute for the town, "a new title / with a new administration."

In the midst of all of this discord, the Jesuits gave discreet but firm support to the party of Philip II, and along with Dona Luísa made diplomatic overtures designed to keep Dona Luísa in power in the captaincy, which would remain formally subject to Spanish central power.

Anchieta's play evokes this historical moment but through the lens of a political and religious allegory. The city speaks as a grave matronly woman (a clear allusion to the widowed Grimaldi), confused and internally divided between the *bom zelo*, the good though indiscrete zeal of her husband's inheritors, and her obedience to the authority of Castile; in the end what wins out is obedience, represented by a wise counselor known simply as Government, and an adherent to the doctrine of the divine right of kings, "because true faith / is peaceful government" (vv. 712–13).

Discord and anything that smacks of disloyalty are portrayed as inspired by Evil, and more specifically, by the cardinal figure of the play, Ingratitude, a sinister old woman and former concubine of both Lucifer and Adam who tempted both toward revolt against God.

At the opening of the play, Lucifer credits his own scheming with bringing about the schism that occurs in the hour of secession. The topos here is that of a world turned upside down:

> who but I could,
> coming from Hell below,
> turn summer to winter?
> Everything has turned upside down
> in law and government . . .
>
> Do you not see
> my trickery, my deceitfulness?
> How I seek to suddenly
> turn everything upside down
> the head now the feet,
> and the feet now the head? (vv. 92–102)

The Devil plays the role of subversive par excellence. At the climax of the play, Ingratitude, who is obviously in league with demonic forces, and the Jesuit ambassador, who is pro-Castilian and has been sent from Paraguay to retrieve from Vitória the relics of Saint Maurice that the rebellious city has proved unworthy of safeguarding, exchange words in speeches that are alternately comic and serious.

Since the scene is presented in figurative terms and populated with emblematic figures, the viewer is not given access to the real historical drama behind the events portrayed, nor the political acts of the groups apparently manipulated by the cruel Inquisition. The Inquisition's external manifestations are presented as alternately frightening and laughable, in line with an established comic and rhetorical practice of mimicking socially reproachable attitudes in exaggerated form, in speech and gestures. This was designed to appeal to an illiterate audience: morality and the ludic intertwined in the service of political interests.

Ingratitude enters the scene carrying an old bowl (*tacho*) that she spins continually, an image of the intrigues she continually provokes: "I am who

I've always been / a sower of confusion" (vv. 951–52). Her speech is insolent and injurious; upon seeing the Castilian ambassador, she immediately rains insults down on him: "Oh blathering Castilian, / Andalusian braggart" (vv. 862–63). The ambassador's wounded pride compels him to respond in kind:

> Oh, Saint Francis, protect me!
> I thought you were a dragon,
> or that fearsome cannon,
> they call a basilisk,
> or the wild *tarracón*![8] (vv. 877–81)

Ingratitude is a fat-bellied old woman who takes pride in having been impregnated by the Angel of Evil and by the first man, though (and here from the grotesque we move over to the monstrous) her pregnancy does not end at the moment of delivery: "Do you not know that every day / I, with a happiness that is quite strange, / give birth, without ever giving birth?" (vv. 1019–21). Every act of betrayal committed by the rebellious inhabitants of Vitória is a new birthing by Ingratitude, whose habitual state of pregnancy she herself describes:

> Yes, I will always be pregnant,
> and never finish giving birth,
> because mankind will always sin
> one way or another,
> as long as men exist (vv. 1069–73)

The inspiration for the motifs and their sequencing obeys the logic of mythical thought, though it is also subject to an allegorical and political perspective that is deeply rooted in a dynamic of interests and power.

What comes to mind here is Dante's allegory of the she-wolf (Lupa), the last and most ferocious of the beasts that bar the poet's way to the mountain of Paradise; critics interpret the Lupa as signifying deceit, greed, or the even worse sin of betrayal committed in cold blood against a friend or benefactor. Certain common characteristics can be found in both Anchieta and Dante. Anchieta's figure is described paradoxically, like the Lupa of the *Inferno*, as both empty and full, a bottomless sack, with a large and voracious orifice, impregnated by her own endless and always resurgent desires:

> You appear as an enchanted Mooress
> just arrived from Algiers,
> your womb like a tunnel,
> and your face gaunt
> and dry like paper!

Ingratitude explains:

> This is
> because Ingratitude
> is such
> that, full of hatred,
> she exhausts the reserves and blessings
> of divine piety (vv. 1028–38)

In Dante: "And then a she-wolf showed herself; she seemed / to carry every crawling in her leanness" (Inf., I, 49–50).[9] And further along: "her nature is so squalid, so malicious / that she can never sate her greedy will; / when she has fed, she's hungrier than ever" (Inf., 97–99).

Both the pot-bellied old woman and the she-wolf breed often, and the products of these unions are new sources of evil:

> Ingratidão
> Tu não sabes que emprenhei
> do formoso Lucifer
> quando quis tamanho ser
> como Deus, eterno rei,
> e ter supremo poder?
> Depois foi meu barregão
> e me tomou por amiga
> o ingrato padre Adão.
> Não vês se tenho razão
> de ter tamanha barriga? (vv. 1001–10)

> Ingratitude
> Do you not know that I was impregnated
> by Lucifer
> when he so much wanted to be
> like God, eternal king,
> and have supreme power?
> Later I was the concubine
> I was the friend
> of the ungrateful father Adam.
> Do you not see why I should
> have such a large belly?

Note the skill with which Anchieta makes a grotesque association between *barregão* (common-law husband) and *barriga* (belly).

And in Dante: "She mates with many living souls and shall / yet mate with many more" (Inf., I, 100–101).

Ingratitude and betrayal appear as complementary vices, tied together by the lust that leads them to place acts of unfaithfulness in the hearts of men. Once again, in the allegory, the day-to-day lives of social groups and their desires and conflicts are reduced to extreme, exemplary cases: these groups either degrade themselves and become bestial, or they sublimate themselves by way of the ideological mechanism that transforms them into figures, a "speech about one thing meant to be understood as about something else."

To the modern consciousness, and especially for modern aesthetic theory, which runs from the humanism of Goethe to Croce and to the young Lukács, the use of allegory is the residual trace of an older subordination of art to other ends, whether religious, political, or moral; and as such, allegory becomes a negation of poetic autonomy. Allegorization, to this way of thinking, is the rule of the abstract over the subject's concrete, free expression. This drastic judgment came in for revision beginning with Walter Benjamin[10]: it is with his essays on Baroque drama that contemporary literary criticism grants to allegory the ideologically complex title of the revelatory (and not necessarily mystifying) form of the dehumanization to which the oppressed have for centuries been subjected. There is, in the semantics of allegorical images, a radical judgment of Power, that specter of the Other, which devalues men as individuals and sweeps them under the rug of overarching abstractions. Benjamin aims to identify the denunciatory potential of allegory in Baudelaire's modern verse, in Kafka's naked prose, in Brecht's didactic theater, in Paul Klee's *Angelus Novus*.

It is problematic to apply Benjamin's critical intuition in reconsidering Anchieta's plays, in which allegory is a cipher for a legitimist vision of power. For the Jesuit's theater, Lukács's affirmation might be more apt: "The old allegory, which acknowledged religious transcendence, sought to reduce earthly reality to the status of nullity by comparing it to otherworldly or celestial existence."[11]

In speaking to Amerindians and colonists, Anchieta appears to have tied himself to the most hieratic expressions of archaic or popular culture: those beliefs and rites that he does not condone, he condemns because he cannot clearly control the consciousness of the free moral individual. Deep within the colonial condition, a rhetoric was designed for the masses that could only express the doctrine that the acculturating agent sought to popularize in grand allegorical terms.

Allegory exercises a singular persuasive power, not infrequently terrible for the simplicity of its images and for the uniformity of its collective reception—hence its use as a tool of acculturation and its presence from the first moment of our spiritual life. Its use was cemented during the Counter-Reformation, a period during which the final years of the Middle Ages and the early Baroque overlapped.

The force of the allegorical image is not directed toward people as subjects of a process of knowledge; rather, it moves from a center of power that is both distant and omnipresent. And anonymous and generally passive spectators absorb it not as a sign to be thought through and interpreted but as if the image were the origin of its own meaning.

More than a simple "other discourse," as implied by the Greek etymology of the word, allegory is the discourse of the other, that Other which speaks and silences us, which prompts us to fear and obey, even as the grotesque puppets of its representations (the Devil or the fat-bellied old woman) make us laugh.

Allegory was the first tool of an art created for the masses by organic, acculturating intellectuals.

Symbol and Effusion

Upon reading Anchieta's theater, the modern reader of his lyric poetry may be surprised by certain moments of intense personalization and an ardent subjective note that the poet succeeds in granting to his discourse when, instead of preaching to the Tupi or the colonists, he expresses his own spiritual tensions through a relation of I–you that the soul maintains with Jesus Christ.

Pure exteriority, confined to the sacred sublime or the demonic grotesque in Anchieta's plays, gives way in some of the lyric poetry Anchieta wrote in Spanish or Portuguese to a living interjection of the transcendent. Faith comes to occupy the same plane as experience.

Two lines of poetic expression come together in granting meaning to intimacy with the divine: (a) the use of symbols taken from daily life, and (b) the proliferation of a mystical and effusive language.

The first of these lines is the path by which the transcendent is revealed through the granting of an aura to the immanent—the sacramental mode par excellence. God is made perceptible and nameable through multiple bodily signs and in a discourse of food, drink, warmth, and amorous ecstasy. God is *pão* (bread), *vianda* (food), *fogaça* (a soft Portuguese loaf), *divino bocado* (divine meal), *fonte que embebeda* (water that quenches the thirst), *deleite de namorados* (lovers' delight), and *fogo gastador* (the fire that burns). What is more, parentage—whether affective or carnal—becomes a convenient way to describe the relation between the human and the divine, as we see in the terms brought together in this passage from "Ao Santíssimo Sacramento" (To the Most Holy Sacrament):

> My dear, my love,
> my husband, my master,

> my friend, my brother,
> the center of my heart,
> God and father!
> As with a mother's substance,
> you wish me to consume you,
> take all that I am,
> for yourself!

Christ is simultaneously father, mother, brother and husband, friend and master! Here we are evidently confronted by an attempt at approximation that superimposes and fuses together forms of relation that are quite distinct, and even, in formal terms, mutually exclusive, beyond all dogma and within a logic of the heart capable of guarding within it opposing tendencies and paradoxical movement. It is not insignificant that the last line in the poem reads: "take all that I am, / for yourself."

In the attempt to give a name or singular form to the beloved, all corporeal life is made metaphorical, all relations are sublimated. The heat and energy produced by the believers' physical contact with each other is transposed onto the ideal plane of contact between man and God. Realism and mysticism converge in the space of the sacramental rite. It is also true that this process by which the body is universally assimilated by the lover's soul requires, in the Jesuit's ascetic mind, an accompanying control over instinct, which maintains the opacity of blood and sex, and for this reason must be presented as an impure fire that another, mystical fire will combat: "This food / serves to eliminate vices."

All that was condemned as the work of the Devil in the lives of Tupi communities—the use in tribal celebrations of food and drink, dance and song, prayer and trance—is referred back, in a positive sense, to the Eucharist as an expression of an interpersonal religious practice that makes use of food in order to sanctify it.

This is the body-bread, the wine-blood of a fraternal, saving God-man.

In terms of historical psychology, are we confronted here with a collision between two forms of mysticism that are distinguished by degrees? A Christian religious consciousness, for which the sacred is markedly personal, would view as satanic (that is, backward) certain archaic religious practices in which the human subject's character as a unified, conscious being grounded in selfhood appears to be challenged. The ideal of *visio intellectualis*, which Christian theology inherited from the Neoplatonists, recoils at the spectacle of the intoxicated, decentered, and plural trance of the Tupi-Guarani *pajés*. The Eucharistic union rejects in horror the crude consumption of cannibalism. The matrimonial bond denies polygamy. Monotheism, which was so dearly achieved, looks with suspicion on the old cult of the spirits found in the winds, waters, and forests.

The tumultuous movement of the Tupi dances leads to a multitude of visions, whereas Christian prayer and liturgy are based on the contemplation of a single God: the unity of the "I," which corresponds to the unity of the divine being that is contemplated.

The notion of the demonic rests on its connotations of polymorphic idolatry ("my name is Legion," says the Gospel), which divides the believer's soul against itself, dulls the light of his mind, robs him of his identity, and lowers him to the blindness and anomie of naked flesh and unchecked instincts.

There is surely more to say about the aversion that certain indigenous (and, mutatis mutandis, African) practices inspired in the Christian priests. Perhaps it was the terror of falling back into a deep, dark prehistorical hole that had with time been submerged within but not expelled from the boundaries of the individual conscience? *Sacer* also means, in the old Latin, terrifying and execrable (*auri sacra fames*), that which must not be named.

This said, pious Catholics during this same century of Counter-Reformation embarked on an intense exploration of the material imagination of Heaven and Hell, causing feelings to be reignited that bordered on mystical transport. Anchieta and the Jesuits of his time were the direct disciples of Ignatius of Loyola, the founder of the company, whose *Spiritual Exercises* induce the believer's soul toward methodically terrifying visions of the Beyond, just as they prepare him to experience the ecstasy of contrition and adoration.

In any case, the processes of Christian sublimation strongly demarcate themselves from Tupi ritual. If the spirits that populate the forest come down and inhabit the tribe that invokes them, inspiring visions as violent and fast-moving as a lightning bolt, the Christian God, "who art in Heaven," prayed to in solitary *oratorio* and in composed *meditatio*, comes to the mind of the believer in the entirely human form of Christ. If in Tupi ceremonies the sacred circulates through the loss of prior identity (each cannibalistic ritual is followed by the renaming of its participants), orthodox Christian practice seeks the fullest realization of the individual soul. The medieval theologians who were Ignatius of Loyola's teachers called this *visio beatifica*. Contemplation is, in principle, a trial undertaken in desert-like solitude, a conquest made possible by the ascesis of the emotions and the imagination, an arduous struggle that prepares one for the encounter with a Thou that is as alone and solicitous as the I: *beata solitudo sola beatitudo*.

In reading the poem, "To the Most Holy Sacrament," one perceives that for the poetic I, the ultimate goal of the symbolic operations that transmute the bread, the wine, the human warmth, and the kiss is always to see God. Physical contact with consecrated substances allows for sight, "the most spiritual sense" (Saint Augustine), which is the corporeal means through which contemplation is achieved.

The eating of the bread, the communal act par excellence, is the penultimate step of the mystical journey, a provisional mediator of faith, a necessary stage for the believer who has not yet been given, in life, immediate proof of the sacred:

> while I wait for the presence
> of your divine face,
> let the satisfying and sweet taste
> of this bread
> be my repast
> and let all of my appetite
> be my soul's
> kind invitation,
> a fresh air to calm me,
> a fire to warm me,
> fresh, clean water to drink,
> a sweet kiss
> that satisfies the desire
> with which I breathe and wail for you,
> a hope I fear
> to lose.

The ultimate goal is direct knowledge of the divine, to see God face to face:

> I eat it to ensure,
> that part of me lies within it,
> and that I am satisfied in you,
> by seeing you!

The state of plenitude described above, as in all theology grounded in Augustine, amounts to awestruck contemplation of the ever-living.

Why is this road built with symbols and not allegory? Because, as Goethe insightfully put it, "The Idea in the image remains eternally valid."[12] There will always be new ways to express the idea of supreme happiness in concrete form and in images, in which, nonetheless, some residual element always remains. The symbol, for Goethe, increases our capacity to form ideas, whereas allegory closes off certain meanings and can reduce figures to fetishes. In the case of allegory, representation focuses on an enigmatic, unchanging human destiny before which the individual may humbly yield or scrutinize this destiny in order to try to locate a meaning that has been fixed for all time.

The work of the soul that generates new symbols and new analogies may suffer from the opaqueness imposed by human limitations, though it increases the prospects for loosening the resistance of the sign and for ultimately gaining intuitive knowledge of the ever-living light. This is the goal of Saint Bonaventure's *itinerarium mentis in Deum*, the wandering believer's journey that precedes Dante's poetic journey through the black circles of Hell and the gray shadows of Purgatory. The light of dawn will come later. "For now we see through a glass, darkly; but then face to face: now I know in part; but then shall I know even as also I am known," said Paul to the Corinthians.

The second line of poetic expression utilized by Anchieta as a lyric poet builds not on the trajectory charted between figure and face, but rather seeks to overcome as quickly as possible the distances that separate the means of signification from their objectives and makes impatient use of emotion.

Anchieta composed some poetic passages in this language, which we might call effusive, and in Spanish, which was quite probably the language he spoke in childhood. We can only speak in terms of probability because there are some who affirm that he first learned to speak Basque, the language of his father.

These are poems that dispense with the use of symbolic correlations (fire, food, drink) and engage in a dialogical operation in which the I of the enunciated is identified as the impetus of the emotions. In these texts, the mediating veil of the figurative plays a secondary role, if it is not altogether absent.

This phenomenon, which at first glance appears entirely psychological, is better understood in light of cultural history. An old gothic piety, fashioned into allegorical series and illustrative emblems that even today may be seen in church bas reliefs, progressively gave way to a more modern expression of the I, to a forceful, individual way of speaking. As early as the *Spiritual Exercises* of the founder of the Company of Jesus, seeing in order to know, which is unquestionably of Thomistic extraction, is crossed with feeling in order to know oneself, which marks the intimate prose of the *Imitatio Christi* and the piety of the senses that typified the "autumn of the Middle Ages."

The poem, rather than a syntax of images, flows in the manner of animated speech and resonates with the *devotio moderna* of the Flemish mystics, which in the meditations of Thomas à Kempis wet the hard earth of Ignatius of Loyola's ascetic texts.

Christ speaks to the poet, and the poet responds in a closed dialogue that in its structure allows the first person to oscillate between the two speakers, with the core of the discourse never distancing itself from the subject:

I was born because you die,
because you live I die,
because you laugh I cry,
I hope because you hope,
because you gain I lose.
("The Child born to the Sinner")

In formal terms, this is an example of *encadenado* (chained) verse, to use the Spanish poet Juan de Encina's term, taking from his *Arte de poesía castellana* (Art of Castilian Poetry), a text that bridges the Middle Ages and the Renaissance. The rhetorical figures utilized join words to actions and utilize pairs of antithetical concepts, and are designed to relativize the distance separating the human believer and his redeemer, and to tighten the bonds that tie the two together:

You are born, and I do not die!
I live, and you will die,
Child, prince of peace!
I tell you that I want to be yours . . .
I do not know what more to say to you!

This dialogue lays bare how dramatic the act of redemption can be. And how far we are here from the magical and external relation through which the Devil took the Sunday cloak from the miller and God restored it to him. Here, Christ's sacrifice ("because you live I die") is not matched by the sinner ("you are born, and I do not die!"). Though admitting this moral distance, the desire for mystical union imposes itself and expresses itself once again: "I tell you that I want to be yours. . . ."

In the *redondillas de arte mayor* of "Jesus e o Pecador" (Jesus and the Sinner), an original tendency reflecting a new spirituality makes itself known: the tense declaration of distance is followed by a vigorous confession of verbal impotence. The expressive phrase *no sé que* (I know not what) is indicative of how the modern subject, less certain than the medieval subject, recognizes the limits of his language and suspects that poetry may not have words suitable for the Other. Baroque and Romantic poets, along with the expressionistic poets of our time, grant distinct auras to this shared sense of impotence:

Digo que eres todo bueno,
digo que eres creador,
digo que eres redentor,
digo que eres amor lleno,
digo que eres todo amor,
digo que eres mi Señor,

> ARTE
> DE GRAMMA-
> TICA DA LINGVA MAIS
> VSADA NA COSTA
> DO BRASIL.
>
> *Feita pelo P. Ioseph de Anchieta Theologo & Prouincial que foy da Companhia de* IESV, *nas partes do Brasil.*
>
> Das letras.   Cap. I.
>
> ESTA lingoa do Brasil não ha f. l. s. z. rr. dobrado nem muta com liquida, vt cra, pra, &c. Em lugar do s. in principio, ou medio dictionis ferue, ç. com zeura, vt *Açô, çatâ.*
> ¶ Algũas partes da oração se acabão em til, o qual não he, m. nem, n. ainda q̃ na pronũciação diffirão pouco, vt, *Tĩ, Ainupã, ruã.*
> ¶ Não ha hũa consoante continuada com outra na mesma dição: excepto, mb. nd. ng. vt *Aimombôr, Aimondô, Aimeẽng.*
> ¶ Acrecentandose algũa particula depois da vltima
>   A   con-

Facsimile of the frontispiece of the first chapter of Anchieta's *Arte de Gramática* (Art of Grammar).

digo que muerto serás,
digo que das vida y paz.
digo que es sin fin tu honor . . .
¡No sé qué te diga más!

I say that you are wholly good,
I say that you are the creator,
I say that you are the redeemer,
I say that you are love in full,
I say that you are all love,

A rare image: Anchieta smiling. Seventeenth-century oil painting, Museu Padre Anchieta, São Paulo.

> I say that you are my Lord!
> I say that you will die,
> I say that you grant life and peace,
> I say that your honor is without end ...
> I do not know what more to say to you!

In his poem, Anchieta recognizes his inability to say who God is, after having used nine times in a row the verb "to say," which precedes each verse at the culmination of his praise to God. The logic of mystical discourse leads necessarily to an acknowledgment of the ineffability of its object.

In other texts we see a discourse designed to maintain the intimate relationship between the believer and his God, a melodious poetry composed of expressions of pain and protest that allows the human soul to share the agony of Christ on the cross. We also see manifestations of a paraverbal or transverbal language, in which questioning, exclamation, and expressions of reticence are mixed, and in which "whispers," "blood," "tears," "cares," "pleasure," "wounds," and "cries" announce themselves.[13] The impatient cry "Venid!" (Come!) presides over everything:

> Venid a suspirar con Jesu amado,
> los que quereis gozar de sus amores,
> pues muere por dar vida a los pecadores.
>
> Tendido está la cruz, corriendo sangre
> sus santas hechas limpios baños,
> con que se dar remedio a nuestros daños.
>
> Venid, que el buen pastor yo dió su vida,
> con que libró de muerte su ganado,
> y dale de beber a su costado.
>
> Come, and whisper to the beloved Jesus,
> all those who wish to receive his love,
> for he dies to give life to sinners.
>
> The cross has been erected, blood runs down,
> his holy deeds are purifying waters
> that wash away our pains.
>
> Come, the good shepherd has given his life,
> has freed his flock from death,
> and has given it his blood to drink.

This new lyrical and religious style reaches its highest point in its employment of paradox, of obligatory use in the expression of the ineffable. This figure draws on the rhetoric of the *Cancioneiro geral* and anticipates the Mannerist games of the early Baroque poets. That which is incapable of being said, because it is infinite, tends to be suggested in the sequence of opposites (death/life), imposing a new meaning built on paradox. The drama of the Calvary (death), which is identified with the salvation of mankind (life), presents us with a fundamental contradiction.

Another pair of opposing terms, infinite/finite, which appears at first glance to be irreconcilable, is resolved in a paean to the Eucharist in which the absolute is contained in the smallest crumb of bread:

> Oh! Infinite God,
> made human for us,
> I see you in so small a form
> that I am shocked
> . . .
> For this reason I struggle
> against my senses,
> because I do not see
> God in what I eat.
>
> The flesh in which I clothed myself
> will have a cold death
> because I want you
> always alive for me, I want
> to be shackled by a great love.

"I struggle against my senses." Struggle presupposes the freedom to accept or refuse the love of the other, even if this other is an omnipotent God. Anchieta's Spanish verse likewise allows for the individual to dare to say "no" to a friend's invitation:

>   No!
> He who died to give us life,
> called to me many times,
> but I told him no,
> no, no, no, no!
> He told me not to sin,
> that he had died to save me,
> but I told him no,
> no, no, no, no!

In reading this passage, with its heatedly personal refusal, the differences in style and in cultural context between this poem and the grotesque allegory of Ingratitude that Anchieta included in his play "In the Town of Vitória" become apparent.

Reconnecting the Strands

The missionary who traveled among the Amerindians, preached to them in Tupi, and composed devotional (and at times, comic) plays for the purpose of converting them, helped spread an Iberian-origin understanding of salvation according to which the savage was immersed in barbarism and according to which his practices were directly inspired by demons.

The indigenous ceremonies amounted, in the final instance, to examples of the victory of temptation. Like a cobra, evil struck those who participated in the songs, dances, drinking of *cauim*, and the cannibalistic rites. The exterior dominating the interior, pure exteriority, the most brutal of meals: this is the image the Jesuits invented for the Tupi rituals and which they handed down to us. It is no wonder, then, that the foundational, original messages of Christianity, such as the equality of all men and the commandment of universal love, have suffered a high degree of entropy in the process of catechism. The pedagogy of conversion erased any potentially progressive elements of the Gospel, causing them to descend to the status of substitutes for Tupi magic. However, the poetry of the Anchieta who wrote devotional verses looked toward a new historical and psychological time, the time of one who chooses to accept or refuse the love of a personal and profoundly human God.

We are so resigned to think "realistically" (if this is the case, then it is because it had to be so) that we do not ask ourselves if, in reality, what occurred may, frankly speaking, have been a regression of the cultured European consciousness in the context of the praxis of conquest and colonization. As in the crusades and holy wars, religion and collective morality degenerate rapidly and violently, become pure tools of power; what is gained in tactical efficacy is lost in the quality of the humanizing process.

The case of Anchieta seems exemplary because he is our first militant intellectual. The fact that he lived his life continually inspired by what is undeniably the faith of an apostle only renders more dramatic the truth of the almost necessary divide between the colonizing man of letters who used a certain code for his own use (and for his peers) and reserved another code for the people. There we have symbolism and an effusion of subjectivity; here, a rigid, authoritarian, allegoric didacticism. There we have the mysticism of the *devotio moderna*; here, the missions' morality of terror. And later, we will find the Enlightenment joined to the dictatorship of the second colonization, and liberalism married to slavery.

Anchieta not only spoke a variety of languages but spoke distinctly depending on his audience. Christian universalism, which is unique to the evangelical message of the first centuries after Christ's death, requires special historical conditions to maintain its coherence and purity. In the process of cultural transplantation, the alliance of Christianity with dominant social and political strata proves lethal for the maintenance of its integrity.

Perhaps the break, which this essay observes, between the exteriority of the theater of catechism and a lyricism of religious feeling might prompt us to rethink the internal contrasts of the intellectual "who lives in the colonies."

3 From Our Former State to the Mercantile Machine

A troca torna supérflua a gregariedade e a dissolve.
—Marx, *Fundamentos da crítica da economia política*

Let us begin with "À Bahia" (To Bahia), a sonnet written by Gregório de Matos during the last twenty-five years of the seventeenth century:

Triste Bahia! ó quão dessemelhante
Estás e estou do nosso antigo estado!
Pobre te vejo a ti, tu a mi empenhado,
Rica te vi eu já, tu a mi abundante.

A ti trocou-te a máquina mercante,
que em tua larga barra tem entrado,
A mim foi-me trocando e tem trocado
Tanto negócio e tanto negociante.

Deste em dar tanto açúcar excelente
Pelas drogas inúteis, que abelhuda
Simples aceitas do sagaz Brichote.

Oh se quisera Deus que de repente
Um dia amanheceras tão sisuda
Que foras de algodão o teu capote!

Sad Bahia! Oh, how changed
Are you and I from our former state!
Poor I see you now, pawned you see me,
Rich I saw you then, abundant you saw me.

The mercantile machine traded you,
Entered into your wide bay,
It has been trading me and has traded
So many goods and so many sellers.

You exchange so much excellent sugar
For useless drugs, enraptured,
You buy potions from the clever Brichote.

God willing that suddenly, one day
You might wake up so wise
That your cloak would be of cotton!

An initial, open-ended reading of this text uncovers two opposing tendencies. First, the lyrical *I* enters into a relationship of sympathy with the *you*, that is, the city of Bahia, which is given living, personified form. Second, we find a separation: the *I*, playing the role of judge, castigates the other, and calls for the intervention of a third party, God, a powerful mediator able to execute the deserved sentence. The first tendency animates the sonnet's quatrains, the second, its tercets.

In stylistic terms, how is the empathy we initially witness between Gregório and his city constructed? This occurs in a variety of ways, beginning with the opening notes of the sonnet: *Triste Bahia!* (Sad Bahia). This expression is both nominal and exclamatory. The city's proper name, when expressed in isolation and without any connection to a larger phrase, tends to concentrate within itself all of the pathos invested in it by the poetic subject. Consider the arcane Indo-European derivation of nomem from numem. Bahia is named in this way, as a living space, neither cut off from nor unfamiliar to the voice of the poet, but rather animated by the force of his passions; not the name in itself, in the abstract, but the name-for-the-self, the name that suffers, the name that the poet's exclamatory tone grants the quality of song; the name qualified by the word *triste* (sad). This adjective is, in truth, ambiguous: it denotes a depressive and melancholy state of being; but it also connotes—if considered in light of the sonnet as a whole—the idea of infelicity, over which, along with other terms from our language such as *desgraçado* (disgraced, damned) and *miserável* (miserable, poor), looms a shadow of guilt. Not only has Bahia been wounded, it is also a pitiable example of change for the worse, whose responsibility Bahia cannot deny. Yes, Bahia is sad in the manner of someone who has lost his *antigo estado* (former state), but it is also "sad" like a clever, badly behaved boy who inspires his mother to exclaim: "That boy is a *sad* case!" The full meaning of the adjective *triste* becomes known only upon concluding one's reading of the poem.

The same aura of affliction surrounds the period described in the poem's initial apostrophe: "ó quão dessemelhante / Estás e estou do nosso antigo estado!" (Oh, how changed / Are you and I from our former state!)

Sealing this contrast, which separates the past from the present, we have this central idea: *quão dessemelhante* (how changed). The difference is tem-

```
rich                                              pawned
          you                    I



          you                    I
poor                                             abundant
```

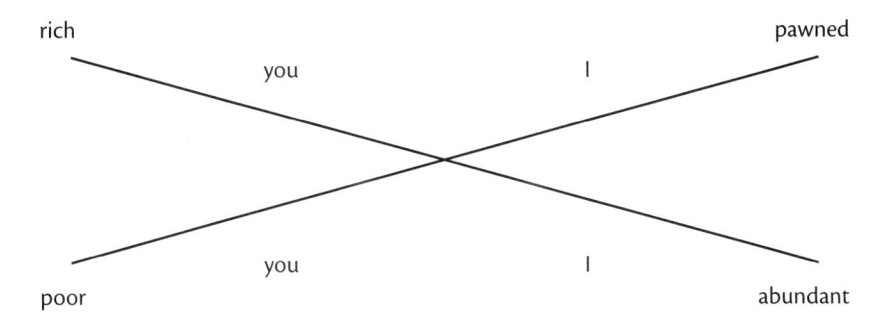

poral: there was an *antigo estado* (former state), the loss of which is the motive force for the whole of the poem's discourse. In this first quatrain, it is important to note that the force of change has impacted both Bahia and Gregório. It is in this profound identification between subject and object that the lyricism of the poem is to be found: the contradictions of social history speak here through an individual's voice.

The poet's empathy toward his land is magnified through repetition—*estás, estou, estado* (you are, I am, state)—syntagmas the poet utilizes to affirm a sameness that persists despite transformations.

The individual's self must confront time's other. This provokes a chiastic, Baroque game of mutual mirroring (figure 5). The poet sees the city, and the city sees the poet. What occurs here in the present occurs just as it did in the past: I see you, you see me, I saw you then, you saw me. The quality of being, reflected in each one's eyes, is what has changed with the passage of time: old prosperity has given way to the poverty of today.[1]

In the lamentation centered on the pair *eu–tu* (I–you), terms that are closely tied together in the first four verses, the poet moves from the act of identifying the forces that have dislodged both him and Bahia from the state of happy abundance in which they once lived. The second quatrain is relentless in its denunciation of the agent responsible for this shared disaster. The words that refer to this disaster comprise a precisely described set of references, which the expression *máquina mercante* (mercantile machine) ties together in exemplary fashion.

What is this mercantile machine?

In a literal sense, it comprises the merchant ships, many of them British, French, and Dutch, that brought luxury goods, principally from India and Europe, to Bahia. They docked in the Bay of All Saints, described by the poet, not without sarcasm, as *larga* (wide). Here he plays with the double meaning (physical and moral) of the term and suggests the dangerous ease with which the port received traders from abroad.

Figuratively, "mercantile machine" rings, to our contemporary ears, as an ingenious metonym for the entire mercantile system. I will discuss this second interpretive possibility during my later historical analysis.

But what is it that creates the mercantile machine? Gregório utilizes the most appropriate verb, *trocar* (to trade, exchange), whose protean application conforms to various verb tenses and situations. The machine traded (*trocou*), has been trading (*foi trocando*), and has traded (*tem trocado*), because it has acted not only in a remote, well-defined past but has also remained active over time, and its effects, multiplied by *tanto negócio e tanto negociante* (so many goods and so many sellers), remain operative in the present. The marketplace is a shared, noisy space in which no one can remain quiet or risk losing his place. The verb *trocar* possesses, in this context, the precise—and today, somewhat archaic—meaning of "to change" or "alter," complemented here by the direct object: the mercantile machine *trocou-te*, that is, it transformed the city of Bahia and its inhabitants.

We have already seen who is implied in this metamorphosis: Bahia and the poet, which from a state of former prosperity have become debtors (a parenthesis for those who believe in the subliminal enchantment of sounds: the consonant cluster /tr/, which features in so many words from the second quatrain, in the various conjugations of *trocar* and the verb *entrar*, also begins the word *triste*, which features in the title of the poem and communicates the poem's essential pathos).

It was the cleverness of the mercantile machine, that harmful object, that thing par excellence, that led Bahia to surrender itself. And here we see the transition from suffering lyricism (*Triste Bahia!*) to harsh satire. Sympathy is withdrawn and the moralizing gaze returns to sit in severe judgment over the prodigal, negligent, and careless Madame Bahia described in an equally famous poem by Gregório. In its dealings with the merchant, the city did not figure out how to successfully trade its white gold for those things gold coins might purchase: "You exchange so much excellent sugar / For useless drugs."

For the producers of tropical goods, this was a harmful bargain in a colonial sense. The only thing that came from abroad was the false gold of disastrous luxury. The colony acted stupidly, whereas the British merchant, *o Brichote* (might this be a peculiarly Portuguese pejorative term for *British*?), was *sagaz* (clever, wise). Bahia's ineptitude does not bear full responsibility here. Its vain and pointless curiosity, which the epithet *abelhuda* (enraptured) denounces, is also to blame, not to mention the sweet taste of the honey produced by the implied term *abelha* (bee).

In the poem's closing tercet, the victim is turned on its head. Sad Bahia should be punished and, as is proper, should repent, replacing rapture with wisdom, fatuousness with seriousness, prodigality with austerity. The conversion will be marked by the subject's simplicity of dress, with clothing being a visible sign of modesty or vanity in women. Let Bahia no longer clothe herself in silks and velvets but rather content herself with a simple cotton cloak, a cheap garment woven by slaves and which only the poorest of the poor would deign to wear: "God willing that suddenly, one day / You might wake up so wise / That your cloak would be of cotton!"

Gregório in Context: Class, Race, Sex

Gregório is so disconsolate in his lamentation of change that it falls to historians of colonial society to determine what should be understood by the *antigo estado* (former state), which Bahia apparently experienced and which the mercantile machine brutally cut short.

The fluctuations in trade experienced during the seventeenth century are relatively well understood. Thanks to studies by Roberto Simonsen, Magalhães Godinho, and Frédéric Mauro[2] on the rise and fall of the economy of the Brazilian northeast during the colonial period, we know that the ongoing crisis in sugar prices entered a new, more difficult phase by midcentury, by which time Caribbean plantations were outcompeting Portuguese enterprises. According to Mauro, "in Lisbon the price [for sugar] fell from 3,000 *réis* per *arroba* in 1650, to 2,400 in 1688."[3] Gregório, an observer *in loco*, says it better:

> The Sugar is all gone? It fell.
> And the money is no more? It rose.
> And did it then recover? It died.
> What happens to a sick man
> happened to Bahia,
> he collapsed onto his bed, went from bad to worse,
> fell, rose, and died.
> > ("Anatomical explanation of the ills that afflict the body of
> > the Republic, in all of its parts, and which wholly define
> > Bahia for all time.")

The first half of the seventeenth century (when the poet was a young man) saw the growth of the sugar plantations and the rise of the Luso-Bahian lower nobility. This group benefited from the support of metropolitan laws, which reached the extreme of impeding the collection of debts when the debtors in question were sugar producers. It was as if the Crown had thought: "For the plantation owners, everything!"

But this protectionist policy entered into rapid decline during the second half of the century, as the Portuguese economy entered into the orbit of England and progressively lost its independence, with the final blow coming from the Treaty of Methuen in 1703—hence the historian Alan K. Manchester's statement: "Portugal virtually became England's vassal."[4]

The transformation from the former state to the mercantile machine was marked by the effective opening of the port of Salvador to foreign ships, after a period of more than a half century during which Portuguese ships alone enjoyed legal entry. Following the Restoration of 1640, King João IV, following the lead of King Sebastião (1571) and King Filipe II (1605), relaxed tax laws, which previously had prohibited Dutch, English, and French merchants from trading along the Brazilian coast. João IV's anti-Spanish policy amounted, in effect, to an alliance with Great Britain.

Gregório de Matos directly experienced the effects of this shift. His family, members of the old Portuguese nobility and owners of a plantation of medium size in the Recôncavo, the fertile sugar-growing region surrounding the city of Salvador, lost—like so many other families—the unrestricted official support they had received during the first few decades of the seventeenth century. The dramatic drop in sugar prices created a new situation that benefitted three economic groups: first, foreign corporations; second, certain owners of large plantations who survived the crisis through increased production and continued use of slave labor (these are probably the native-born, mestizo, or *camamuru* nobility to which a resentful Gregório satirically referred); and third, and to a partial extent, a solid class of Portuguese-born merchants who had by this time rooted themselves in Bahia and Recife, and whom colonial privileges still protected.[5]

As an intellectual and *clerc*, Gregório's movements were not strictly limited to the social spheres in which material goods were produced and in which they circulated. A place was reserved for him in the administrative apparatus—specifically, in the colonial bureaucracy and the Church. It was here that the circumstances into which he was born and the title he earned at the University of Coimbra of doctor *in utroque jure*, along with his luster as a successful literary man, contributed to his professional success. He was vicar-general of the Archdiocese of Bahia and its chief treasurer beginning in 1681, by which time he was already benefiting from the patronage of Dom Gaspar Barata, the archdiocese's highest-ranking official.

However, Gregório's liberal habits and acid tongue caused him setbacks and made him enemies. If we are to believe the poet's first biographer, the *licenciado* Manuel Pereira Barreto, he lost his two positions and supported himself for a time as a lawyer, ultimately frittering away his familial inheritance: "In need of money, he sold a piece of land for three thousand *cruzados*, and having received his money in a sack, he ordered that it be dumped out in a corner of the house, where it was divided, with neither method nor care, to pay for expenses."[6]

Nobility of birth and a prestigious liberal profession conspired to form Gregório's quite peculiar perspective that, nonetheless, does not entire divorce him from the figure of the traditional intellectual as described by Antonio Gramsci.[7]

The Italian Marxist thinker described the two fundamental ideological groups that coexist in societies in which the capitalistic, bourgeois mode of thought engages in hand-to-hand combat with institutions and values inherited from the old regime. In these historical formations, the ecclesiastical intellectual (as opposed to the organic intellectual, who is tied to the system of production) resists, culturally and emotionally, the values of mercantilism and impersonal functionalism, and holds fast to old rights of blood and name and to the honors and privileges of the closed orders such as the nobility, the Church, the tribunals, the arms, the Inquisition, and the university.

The tendency of the traditional man of letters during the Baroque period was toward existential division: his relationship with social structures was marked by both self-identification with an idealized human type (the *nobre*, the chevalier, the gentleman, the *honnête homme*, the hidalgo, the *discreto*, the *cortigiano* or *galantuomo*, and our own colonial-era *homem bom*, or "good man") and by repulsion before the low personal circumstances of other men whose necessities and conditions he described with the crudest sort of naturalism and that he almost always identified with barbarism.

Observing this venal, competitive struggle from outside and from above, the cultured man who occupies a certain position within the hierarchy constitutes himself in ideal terms. This is Gramscian *autoposizione*, which distances itself from the dirty war for personal enrichment and, therefore, from entire social groups involved in trade and manual labor, both of which were activities maligned by the seventeenth-century nobleman. To this distain, which is corporative in nature, we must add the corollary of racial prejudice against the Jew, who is identified as a merchant, and in the colony, against the *mestiço*, who has the blood of slaves.

The knot of prejudice becomes inextricably tangled when inequality produced by social division is combined with racial and religious discrimination. In the colony, both the oppressors and the oppressed were thus doubly marked.

Gramsci connected the cleric's pretensions toward autonomy with the survival of traditional groups still valued and favored by the state. By all indications, in the case of seventeenth-century Brazil, this relationship was reinforced during periods in which the agro-mercantile economy suffered reverses. The honorable solution for an educated heir was to join the bureaucracy or the clergy, which was firmly tied to the Crown through patronage.

The nineteenth-century Brazilian literary critic Araripe Jr., who viewed Gregório through the lens of Taine and who was perpetually in search of the dominant faculties of the writers he analyzed, very clearly saw Gregório's deep resentment toward the disorders suffered by Bahia at the end of the century. However, the critic also attributed singularities of character to Gregório. Araripe Jr.'s interpretation, which is diffuse and psychologizing, does not entirely grasp the system of social relations that comes into view when we account for the various strata that fell victim to the poet's elegant criticism. This was not a case of blind rage, of *atra bilis* projected, indirectly or directly, onto individuals dissimilar from each other. It only appears that the groups stung by the satirist's pen had nothing in common: what, at first glance, binds together the foreign magnate and the mulatto vicar of the town of São Sebastião do Passé, in Bahia, or the landowner proud of his ancestry and the New Christian merchant who has recently come into money? These targets of Gregório's arrows appear to the reader, removed from the context to which they refer, merely as individuals whose faults attracted Gregório's sarcasm and barbed verse. This explains the strong pull of the moral register, as we see in Araripe Jr., and on the other hand, of a sort of formalism oriented toward the structures of Gregório's satirical discourse in and of themselves and for which the social types lambasted by the poet are topoi taken from a long literary tradition rather than spatially and temporally circumscribed historical and social formations.

Once again, it is historical knowledge of the writer's point of view that prevents us from entering into the labyrinth of arbitrary hypotheses. The *filho d'algo* in financial straits does not tolerate foreign or successful New Christian merchants. What is at play here is not an irritated form of national or Bahian consciousness but rather a rigid structural opposition between a nobility in decline and an ascending merchant class. This antagonism dates from the Middle Ages, during which the businessman and the moneylender were slandered as villains and usurers, though the antagonism became more pronounced and was formalized during the seventeenth century, during which the aristocracy continued to wage its long war against other classes. More than ever before, the nobility and bourgeoisie struggled for political power; more than ever before, tradition confronted and clashed with modernity. As Amador Arrais, a Discalced Carmelite and anti-Semite who died in 1600, said: "The Prince should not be a merchant, for this low behavior has a foul odor."[8]

If the sonnet "À Bahia" (To Bahia) denounces the clever Brichote, Gregório's gloss on the theme "Efeitos são do cometa" (The effects of the comet are) spares neither "o Holandês muito ufano" (the very prideful Dutchman) nor "os Franchinotes" (the Frenchies) who subject us to "sly trickery / to take our money / in exchange for trinkets."

On the other hand, monopolizing traders (the *Arte de Furtar*, or "Art of Stealing," mentions "atravessadores," or middlemen) and immigrants of dubious bloodlines were working their way into the interstices of the colonial system. They knew how to save and invest, and as a result became creditors and holders of hard currency, in a city in which the decline in the price of "sweet gold"—that is, sugar—led to increased indebtedness and the need to pawn one's possessions:

> Stupendous usury in the markets:
> All those who do not steal, very poor:
> Here we have the city of Bahia.
>   ("To the Good Sirs Who Govern the World . . .")

The rapid ascent of a New Christian cloth-seller is described in the verses of "À cidade da Bahia" (To the City of Bahia). Here Gregório tells the tale of a poor but daring seller of common cloth who, aided by his parents but most of all by his own desire for gain, "entra pela barra dentro" (once again we have an audacious intruder who "enters the bay" of Bahia), disembarks, opens a store and warehouse, deceives, avoids censure, marries a rich heiress, and ends up a *vereador do pelouro* (a sort of councilman), "que é notável dignidade" (which is a distinguished honor):

> Here we have Canasteiro
> who still smells of cheap cloth,
> transformed into a great man:
> this is a real figure.

What befouls Gregório's good humor more than anything else is witnessing the (ultimately satisfied) pretensions of merchants who wish to occupy honorary positions that for centuries had been reserved for *homens bons* (good men). So have differences of birth been eliminated? Can money achieve or buy anything?

> I speak not of Nobility,
> Which is as a blank slate.
> For the Nobleman, is, in the end, noble:
> he who is honored, honors in return:
> and rogues act roguishly;
> and give nothing back.
> . . .

In Brazil, Nobility,
never lies in good blood;
or in right action:
in what then, does it reside?

It consists in piles of money,
and in hoarding it:
each one guards it well
so as to spend it badly.
>   ("The author bids farewell to the City of Bahia,
>   having been forcibly banished to Angola by the
>   Governor D. João de Alencastre.")

That the overarching opposition for Gregório consists of the pairing of noble and ignoble (and not Brazilian and foreign) becomes clear in the poet's hilarious satire of the "Fidalgo da terra" (local nobleman), the "Adão de massapê" (Adam of the loam), a symbol of the small but powerful class of Bahian landowners who bore a significant amount of indigenous blood. The poet does not forgive the air of triumphalism that, as a result of their wealth and victory against the Dutch, surrounded this group, which would come to dominate national life and whose interests would over time distance them from the *reinóis* (native-born Portuguese). The following poems provide some notable examples of Gregório's satire: "A fidalguia do Brasil" (The Brazilian Nobility), which closes with a decasyllable in intentionally broken speech, "Cobé pá, aricobé, cobé, paí"; "A fidalguia ou enfidalgados do Brasil" (The Nobility or Self-Made Nobles of Brazil); and the sonnet, "A Cosme Moura Rolim insigne mordaz contra os filhos de Portugal" (To Cosme Moura Rolim, Celebrated and Fierce Critic of the Sons of Portugal).

The theme is consistent: the former savage, an "alarve sem razão, bruto sem fé" (ignoramus without reason, brute without faith), claims for himself the right to a title. The immediate humor of the passage resides in the contrast between haughty pretension and low origins, which Gregório denounces through the former savage's bizarre lexicon.

Even more delicate, or thorny, is the question of the black, and as a corollary to this question, that of the mulatto. The antipathy that the latter inspires in Gregório speaks of a society in which miscegenation was sufficiently common so that free men of color would constitute a visible portion of the population.

Racial and color prejudice announce themselves, cruelly, when there is the threat of competition in the struggle for money and prestige. What was once latent and diffuse becomes patent and localized. In our poet, the *punctum dolens* is always the question of honor, a privilege that, according to the code

HÆC MAXIMA DONA VIGESCUNT.

S. Salvator
in Brasilien.

Corporis, Ingenii donis, Sortisq; coruscat   Si quis; hæc tria sunt maxima dona Dei.

"The mercantile machine traded you,
Entered into your wide bay,
It has been trading me and has traded
So many goods and so many sellers."
—Gregório de Matos, "À Bahia" (To Bahia)

of the old regime, could be enjoyed only by men of proper ancestry.[9] Now then, differences in color are the most visible and most "natural" sign of the inequality the reigns between men. And within the colonial slaveholding structure, this mark is inherent to the separation of social strata and functions. For the social order assailed by crisis from which Gregório sprang, the world has been turned upside down by the *Brichotes*, the Jews, and the grandchildren of Caramuru (that is, persons of partial indigenous ancestry) who displaced the men of old stock who could trace their ancestors back to the Crusades. But the height of the absurdity in this unfortunate city occurs when free *mestiços*, having married into wealthy families or having acquired positions in the Forum or the Cathedral, receive considerations that Gregório, white, noble, and educated, has been refused!

I know not for what purpose
in this pestilent Brazil

> an honorable white man
> marked by no other blood is born.
>
> A land so gross and crass,
> that respect is shown to no one,
> save those who show themselves
> to be Mulatto.
>
> Here the dog strikes the cat,
> not because he is the braver,
> but because others always defer
> to the dog.

The following verses are particularly ferocious, attacking the Relação, that is, the tribunals of justice charged with prosecuting and fining white masters who killed their slaves, who are once again called *cães* (dogs).

> Here white men can do nothing
> but suffer and keep quiet,
> and if they kill a black man,
> expenses rain down on them.
>
> The audacity of the dog
> does not work as a defense,
> because the tribunals
> are always hungry.

The former state, remembered nostalgically, is not always humane. Trade goods, black skin, miscegenation, Jewish blood: everything that is not "noble" and "pure" becomes the target of Gregório's implacable disdain.

A Fragmented Eros

As an aside, it is worth examining Gregório's so-called burlesque poetry, in which black and *mestiço* women are simultaneously objects of lust and of derision.

Here the prejudice that is so directly expressed in the verses discussed above takes on a more complicated form, as it lowers itself to the subterranean plane of an erotic practice that produces, intimately and simultaneously, physical attraction, repulsion, and sadism.

Gilberto Freyre's valuable observations in *Casa-grande & senzala* (The Masters and the Slaves) on sexual license in northeastern plantation life attempt to lend coherence to this terrible ambivalence. And while the sociologist's conclusions are optimistic, in that they affirm the existence of a

Luso-Brazilian racial democracy, we need only read Gregório's obscene verses to remind ourselves of the basic question: did this fusion of skin and flesh imply a social union as well?[10]

We find something of an answer when we look at the sexually explicit and amorous verses written by this apparently cultured and idealizing poet. Dedicated to white women of good birth, this poetry decants, refines, and sublimates erotic impulses. It reinscribes formulas taken from an erudite poetic tradition, which has its origins in the Provençals, in the "stilnovo," with its vision of the "donna angelo," and in Petrarch, and which crystallizes in Camões before taking on a more mannered form in the Spanish poets of the seventeenth century, in whose footsteps the virtuoso Gregório follows.

The waters do not mix.

On one side, there are the distant beloved women, worthy of "a thousand good qualities," women who are "rigorosas," "tiranas," and "cruéis" (exacting, tyrannical, and cruel), and whose names are the products of centuries of refined poetic tradition: Dona Ângela, "an angel in name, with an angelic face"; Dona Teresa, "a star of the meadow, a pearly star"; Dona Victória, "a rose in the flesh"; Dona Francelina, "a hidden enigma," "a miracle of snow fired by blood"; and Dona Maria dos Povos, his future wife, "discrete and most beautiful Maria," referred to as Sílvia after their nuptials, "because of her honesty"; not to mention the maidens with Arcadian names, like Clóris, Fílis, and Marfida, who jump from Guarini's eclogues to make their home in our Bahian's languid verses.

In writing of the hurt, pain, suffering, and torment occasioned by these passions, the "mágoas," "penas," "pesares," and "tormentos" that for being so terrible are all the more beautiful, Gregório utilizes a flexible rhetoric that makes use of the resources of *coincidentia oppositorum*. Opposed values are joined together to form ideas that suggest sudden transformations: "Hours in Hell, moments of happiness"; "pleasure is fleeting, pain merely marks time"; "thoughts with little hope / but constant ill fortune"; "death is the color of my happiness"; "amorous disdain, zealous suffering"; "I am the prey of the one who has triumphed over me."

Guided by the power of physical distance, this is a poetry of loss and not of possession, of renunciation, not of pleasure. "These stars of love, many and beautiful, / To see them once is to admire them, / To see them again, would be to offend them."

And the other side?

Here we see displayed the many black and mulatto women, raised in the slave quarters, for whom freedom led to a life of prostitution. These are Maria Viegas, whom the poet deconstructs and reprimands in grotesque *décimas* titled "Anatomia horrorosa que faz de uma negra Maria Viegas" (Horrifying Anatomy of the Black Woman Maria Viegas); Babu, Macotinha, Inácia, Antonica, Luisa Çapata, "a famished mulatto woman," Chica, "a graceless black woman," Vivência, and so many others who blend together in a gallery of lascivious fantasies in which we never see the women's faces but only scatological displays of genitals and anuses.

How should these contrary and extreme figurations be interpreted?

In the case of Gregório's obscene verses, it is not enough to refer to a tradition of graphic naturalism, as does Russian philologist Mikhail Bakhtin in his reading of Rabelais, whom he interprets in light of popular medieval and Renaissance-era sources.[11] Latin American critics have, at times, abused—that is, made mechanical use of—the concept of "carnivalization," which Bakhtin situates within a fixed system of relationships between text and context. In Gregório de Matos, elevated discourse and gross impropriety are not two sides of the same coin, just as they are not the serious and comic sides of the same erotic phenomenon. Rather, they represent distinct and opposed intentions, because their objects are opposed.

In Gregório, a poet rooted in our colonial life and slaveholding past, the elevation and vilification of women is a function of color and class. The use of terms considered vulgar occurs precisely in situations in which the woman in question belongs to a socially despised *gentalha* or *canalha* (rabble), or, in a case that demands historical research, in the world (now foreign to us) of girls hidden away in convents, supposedly in order to hide some "mau passo" (bad turn) on their part but in reality so that their greedy siblings could take their portion of the family inheritance.

The woman who would never be taken as a wife is, then, objectively disqualified. Blackness fuels this disqualification, which in Gregório's poetry is expressed with an unparalleled violence of tone and lexicon—in sum, of style.

M. Bakhtin uses topographical terms to describe certain peculiarly grotesque processes of demystification that occur in the language of Gargantua. Rabelais reverses positions, overthrows the elevated, and turns the world upside down. The sublime is ground down by verbal disdain in a play of divergent views of the same object—that is, the aesthetic and moral obverse and reverse of individuals normally spared from criticism due to political or clerical censorship. Prohibited names for human body parts and terms that refer to vital functions serve Rabelais, just as they did the buffoons of the medieval courts, as escape valves that allow for criticism of weighty, ritualistic conventions.

This does not occur in Gregório, who marks a sharp distinction between two separate areas of experience and meaning. Unlike Rabelais, the profane register does not feature in all of the Bahian poet's works. Rather, the profane is a particular way in which Gregório uses language to brand those who fall under his disdainful gaze.

Gregório's are other sources that, while textually remote, are accessible and familiar to us in their colloquial use. The recourse to obscene speech for the purpose of mockery was common in the comic genres of the so-called low style, which traces its roots beyond the Middle Ages as far back as antiquity. Armando Plebe, an erudite scholar of the hierogamic rituals and the Hymenaios of ancient Greece, demonstrated in *La nascita del comico*[12] how the Mediterranean peoples evolved away from a frank practice of sexual union, which was considered an augury of bountiful harvests, to the malicious laughter of secret nuptial rites, and finally to the foul-mouthed mocking invective of classical and Alexandrine satire and comedy. Sexual organs and acts, when named, become symbols of aggression.

Not everything, however, tends toward the extremes. Curiously, we find within Gregório's lascivious body of verse certain moments in which the absolute opposition he draws between white and black women gives way to a hesitant ambiguity that presents us with felicitous moments of self-analysis.

Let us recall the rondel "À mesma Custódia mostra a diferença entre amar e querer" (Custódia Is Taught the Difference between Loving and Desiring). Custódia was a "graciosa" (pretty, beautiful) mulatto woman in love with Gregório's son, the young Gonçalo de Matos. The troubadour, divided between desire and respect for a woman who has presented herself as a potential daughter-in-law rather than a lover, composes a subtle defensive argument that attempts to prove to himself and to the girl that his feelings for her are purer and more elevated than any lowly desire to possess her. Conceptual distinctions constructed for the purpose of undertaking a moral analysis of the movements of the soul were frequent in Baroque literature and tended almost always toward the specious. We must not forget that this line of thinking finds its logical structure in the classificatory formalism of the old Scholasticism, which education during the Counter-Reformation re-enshrined within Iberian letters:

> For a generous love,
> the higher aim is love,
> without desire of favor,
> without fear of disdain.
>
> Love loves, love suffers
> without seeking any reward,
> and in hoping to be worthy,
> does not think how it is worthy.

> Custódia, if I consider
> that to want is to desire,
> and love is to love perfectly,
> then I love you, but do not want you.

This is elegantly defined and uses proper diction and an internally consistent argument. "Love" here, "desire" there, "eu vos amo" (I love you), "não vos quero" (I do not want you). The poet's moral conscience and personal virtue seem secure. But in the twentieth and final quatrain, concepts that, once fully expressed and distinguished from one another, now mix, and what we have is the expression of a muddied coexistence:

> In coming to the end
> since nothing has been left out
> I say that he who adores you,
> may also desire you.

We may compare this dubious conclusion to the poet's musings on Custódia with the cycle of poems Gregório wrote as consolation for his difficulties in loving Brites, a haughty white woman who, in the end, would cast him aside for a younger suitor with more proper customs. The topos of these *décimas* is found once again in the Provençal tradition. The poet sings the praises of love, which is all the more perfect for being unreciprocated:

> All lovers who wish
> to be successful in love,
> seek the beautiful,
> rather than love beauty:
> he who worships the pure light
> of an exacting love,
> loves with generous correctness,
> and is always despised,
> because my disgrace
> does not rob you of your beauty.

There is a platonic vein within this poem that severs Eros from body and soul. One may desire sensually or adore. These options are weighed and measured differently. The libido, a roaring current that has the potential to place the objects of desire on the same plane and to democratize the universal relationship between man and woman, here flows through someone who is mentally imprisoned within the experience of colonization and slaveholding, and who experiences, in the flesh, prejudices that are tattooed onto women's bodies:

I am unclean and a brute,
I am wicked, and so my actions are wicked,
and if I spend a coin
it is only on black women from Angola,
a wild satyr,
who the University
could not improve,
and if, by chance, I studied something there,
it was disorder and tomfoolery.

God Read Backwards and Forwards

Gregório de Matos's so-called sacred poetry also suffers from an internal division, in this case between a moralizing conscience and mysticism, with the former predominating over the latter.

The basis for Gregório's most celebrated religious sonnets is found in a confession of disobedience against a superior Being, a transgression that takes the form of sins against biblical commandments. A set of moral doctrines, rigorous in appearance and in the classification of perverse acts, reifies the relationships between men and within man, and runs the risk of paralyzing the inner life of the faithful individual, who oscillates between feelings of specific guilt and the anguish of remorse.

The cathartic experience of loving a God made flesh, which animates and frees great religious lyrical poetry, is stultified and ultimately poisoned when the full weight of the conscience is placed upon the dark terrain of past actions. The practice of confessional absolution, which the Council of Trent elevated and ritualized, presents itself as a way out.

The fear of eternal death, which is alleviated and in a certain way controlled by the ecclesiastical mechanism of formalized penance, reveals the substance of the religiosity that ran through the Jesuit Baroque. In the colony there was no Pascal who, in the name of a freer and more personal relationship between man and God, could reveal the irony in the skillful casuistry produced by the trinity of sinner, sin, and repentance. There is a lively quality, which would delight the historian of ideas, in the intersection of social satire and a Counter-Reformation moral code in the long romance entitled "Queixa-se a Bahia por seu bastante procurador, confessando que as culpas, que lhe increpam, não são suas, mas sim dos viciosos moradores que em si alberga" (Bahia's Lament to Her Zealous Inquisitor, Confessing That the Sins Attributed to Her Are Not Hers, but Those of the Vicious People Who Are Sheltered by Her), a poem organized according to the Ten Commandments of the law of Moses. Each sin is represented by one or more actions, situated within the space and time of the poet's Bahia: *calundus* and spells, which give hope to the people, are forms of idolatry that violate the first commandment; false testimony, the second; men's impious gestures during mass and women's use of personal adornment, the third; the wicked habits of children, the fourth; sharp tongues, the fifth; lascivious dances and touches, the sixth; robberies committed by the newly enriched, the seventh; and so on.

In these minute calculations, each sin adds to the sinner's sum total and worsens his condition. The sinner's salvation depends upon the presence of an infinite grace, or rather, that this grace be conjured through a prayer that is more solicitous than pious: "I, Lord, am the sheep who has strayed. / Receive it, for you, divine Shepherd, do not wish, / For your glory to be lost to your sheep."

Here forgiveness depends on a shift in which the gesture of pardon, which should be an act of absolute giving (*per-donare*), becomes God's gain, while the act of condemnation would constitute a loss for God's glory. God is asked, in sum, not to make a bad deal. This same idea is present, albeit in more nuanced form, in Quevedo, who closes his Psalm XIII from the series *Las tres musas* (The Three Muses) as follows:

> I confess that I have offended
> the God of the armies of destiny
> that His alone will be the vengeance
> and the recompense upon my death;
> but, as I was born
> in His living image
> I hope for his mercy when I reflect
> that God loses what is His if I am lost.

But at the feet of these superficial transactions and games of conscience, learned from the Roman treatises of Moral Cases, there appears the shadow of damnation, which is patent in the Baroque era's terrible images of a cosmic final judgment, and its certainty of a human destiny reduced "to dirt, to smoke, to dust, to shadows, to nothing." Gregório grants his apocalyptic poetry the tone of the sermonizers of the time, who developed the menacing theme of the final stages of human destiny, death, judgment, Hell or Heaven.

The tercet and sonnet transcribed below appeal to two sources of the Baroque imagination, the *memento homo* and the *dies irae*:

> Let all of the mortal wood of this human ship,
> If it seeks salvation, come ashore now,
> For this land is a sovereign port.
>   ("On Ash Wednesday")

* * *

The joyous day made mournful,
The silence of the night disturbed,
The light of the sun eclipsed,
And the shining of the moon obscured.

Let all that was created be destroyed with a moan.
What of you, world? What has become of you?
If everything ends in this instant,
To not be is the same as to have been.

The trumpet's blast from on high,
Brings to the living and dead the news
Of damnation for some, salvation for others.

Let the world end, because it is time,
Let the dead rise from the grave,
For the Day of Judgment has come.
    ("On the Day of Judgment")

Calculation of merits and demerits and the attempt to favorably influence the coming judgment cannot quash a renewed terror before death and universal punishment. Indeed, one can see the fractious terrain underlying the traditional morality of the seventeenth century, subject to a time of extreme darkness and anguish, "for the Day of Judgment has come."

But in order to leave behind these grand metahistorical abstractions, we must ask, what world is this that must end in catastrophe?

The man of letters educated in the *forma mentis* of the Counter-Reformation is confronting a rising flood of international commerce, which would only crest with the ascent of the bourgeoisie in the eighteenth and nineteenth centuries.

The vision of a well-ordered social body,[13] which Gregório absorbed from the world of the Iberian corporative orders while a student of law and divinity at Coimbra, could not accommodate itself harmoniously to the brutal pace of change brought to an uncultured colony by transformations in fortune and condition. Even the "natural" opposition between black and white was blurred in a *mestiça* Bahia in which educated mulattos who were the recipients of special favors became clerics. In sum, the sharpness of the divide between honor and commerce was blunted by the rapacious activity of the mercantile machine. And what remained of the reduced and mismanaged inheritance of the nobleman in crisis would fall into the hands of the moneylender. How can one resist such an evil as this, which has penetrated the body of the system and the subject?

The only way to resist is to denounce, to moralize, to repeat to everyone that they are dust and to dust shall they return, to bring the Day of Judgment to the here-and-now. Death, judgment, Hell or Heaven. In this movement in which the entire universe trembles, if the sinner is not perfectly contrite, he might yet save himself through imperfect attrition, through repentance motivated not so much by love of God as by fear of the torments of Hell—imperfect, but as the clever casuists would say, sufficient to receive divine pardon.

Now as long as fear of punishment is stronger than the will toward the Good, the path of affective mysticism is blocked, and all that remains is moralism or terror. The code of behavior becomes more rigid in light of the idea of transgression, which like a ghost, obsessively circles the sinner's soul:

> God calls to me with forgiveness
> through help and counsel,
> I fall on my knees,
> and I show myself repentant:
> but as it is all a lie,
> my deceit fails me.

> Whenever I confess,
> I say that I have put sin aside,
> before returning to the wickedness,
> that is certain to be my damnation;
> there lies one who will receive payment for my ways:
> I will pay for my repeated sins
> against He who gave me life,
> with the roaring flames
> of my repeated torments.

Vigilance against sin draws sin toward it, and the movements approach each other, moving toward an impossible embrace. In this conflict, which vexes and oppresses the conscience, the death drive awaits its turn. The desires for negation and unhappy repression, which are frustrated with and resentful of one another, await the hour in which the living body becomes a cadaver and in which creation is rent apart in cries of agony: "Let the world end, because it is time."

This said, if this tone—which lies somewhere between legalistic and catastrophic, and which dominates Gregório's religious poetry—were his only available means of expression, there would not be that internal division announced at the beginning of this discussion. Thankfully, there is another way of writing poetry *a lo divino*, which we see in the quite distinct context of Anchieta's Spanish-language verse. This tone is neither original to Anchieta nor to Gregório, and curiously, in the latter's glossing we find the most surprising exercises in osmosis—for instance, in the female narrative voice that dictates the long and subtle "Solilóquio de madre Violante do Céu ao Diviníssimo Sacramento: glosado pelo poeta para testemunho de sua devoção, e crédito da Venerável Religiosa" (Soliloquy of Mother Violante do Céu to the Most Holy Sacrament: Glossed by the Poet as Testimony of His Devotion, and in Honor of the Venerable Holy Woman).

Here the inspiration for the text is found not in the anguish of repeated failings nor in the fear of eternal suffering but in the story of Christ's Passion, recreated through the sacrament as an act of freely given love and without any relation to the merit of the faithful individual. Gregório, like his contemporary Baltasar Gracián, momentarily lifts the veil of pessimistic satire and gives himself over to mystical certainty. Or as that ardent writer of the Baroque wrote in the *Comulgatorio*: "There can be no horror where there is love."[14]

The freely given quality and spontaneity of the "Solilóquio" work to humanize religion, change the quality of feeling, and set images free. Metaphors that were morbid and darkly earthen become finely wrought and joyful. Air and light mix in buoyant expressions like "*arrebol*" (the redness of a sunrise or sunset), "*cândido Oriente*" (clear Eastern sky), "*cândidos lírios*" (white lilies), "*fonte clara*" (clear well), "*epiciclos de neve*" (epicycles of snow), "*sol nascente*" (rising sun), "*cristal puro e fino*" (crystal pure and fine), "*divina neve*" (divine snow), "*gala*" (gala), and "*bizarria*" (exquisiteness).

Significantly, one of the forms of poetic logic that runs most strongly through the text consists of the counterposing of the sky's darkness after Jesus's death with the sun's brightness, which is recovered by the bread of the Eucharist. Light is contained in the sacrament as if by an opaque shroud, which we might term in the language of *culturanismo* an "emblem" or "enigma":

> And suppose that thought
> wonders at the dark enigma,
> and the sublime mystery
> of seeing you in the Sacrament:
> here my understanding
> knowing you so well,
> sees more and more of your brightness contained,
> the better it understands
> this rarest Enigma of love.
>
> That you are wholly, and in all divinity
> in the Sacrament,
> I know to be true,
> though you hide it:

> why do you conceal yourself
> in this strangest of mysteries,
> if, marveled, I see you,
> closely watching you, so that
> you are clearer to my understanding,
> than you are to my eyes?
>   (Text 3—Gloss)

In giving such radiant inner form (which the veiled description "*sanguinosamente escuro*," or "bloodily dark," had earlier obscured), the pregnant metaphors used are "*fogo ativo*" (roaring fire) and "*infinito ardor*" (infinite heat), mystical and erotic images par excellence, here drawn to the focal point of the subject and its body, its "*peito amante*" (loving breast):

> My chest burns in the heat,
> I desire
> as I burn,
> in this great fire of love,
> would you censure a loving breast,
> that did not ask
> for such love,
> but to which the flames of the burning fire
> have always given a home?
>   (Texto 19—Glosa) (I, 94–95)

> Come to my breast, o Lord,
> make the divine human
> . . .
> and as a sign of your power
> make the human divine.
>   (Text 19—Gloss)

The presupposition of a transcendence contained in the immanence of a God-Man who, "transformed each and every one / making the divine human," underlies the notion of universal brotherhood, to the extent that it postulates that all men were created and saved by the same God.

But this movement of the ideal, toward the dignifying of the individual in and of himself, was unable to transcend Gregório's religious poetry and penetrate his satires of day-to-day life in a colony composed of landowners, dishonest traders, and slaves.

4 Vieira, or the Cross of Inequality

True nobility lies in action.
You are what you do, nothing more.

—Vieira, *Sermão da Terceira Dominga do Advento*
  (Sermon for the Third Sunday of Advent)

Gregório de Matos and Antônio Vieira were contemporaries. There is evidence that they knew and admired each other when both were living in Bahia, a period that coincided with the end of their lives: the poet died in 1696, the preacher the following year.

Vieira's world was larger than the *piccolo mondo* of Gregório, the satirist and chronicler of Bahia's ills. A Jesuit, advisor to kings, confessor to queens, tutor of princes, a diplomat to the courts of Europe, a man who defended the New Christians, and with equal zeal, evangelized in Maranhão and Pará, Vieira was a man of stature and international dimensions. The interest that Vieira's extensive and varied oeuvre (207 sermons, exegetic texts, prophecies, letters, political reports, etc.) continues to generate can only increase if we grant it greater coherence by interpreting it in light of its rich contradictions, which are the contradictions of the colonial system as a whole and which the Brazilian experience per se cannot explain.

As a reader and devotee of Vieira for at least thirty years, I will attempt in these pages to provide a brief sketch of some of his strongest visual features. His lively, dark eyes, ringed by the circles of one who has suffered, looked toward the future: each element of his weathered face seems to indicate a struggle, always lost, which he would substitute for another struggle, without rest and without losing heart. This helps explain his declaration, which he made while attempting in vain to convince noblemen and the clergy to pay a heavy tax levied for the reconstruction of the kingdom, that "true nobility lies in action."

Unlike the poet Gregório, who was nostalgic for the *antigo estado* (former state), Vieira knew that the irreversible, inexorable mercantile machine was here to stay. Given the uselessness of lamenting its intrusion into the colony's ports, what was needed was to master it, to imitate its mechanisms and create, within the structure of the Portuguese monarchy, a similar structure that could defeat it in the international competition between empires.

This project places Vieira at the nerve center of colonial politics during his time. As Dom João IV's favorite and advisor, Vieira inspired the king to found a Companhia das Índias Ocidentais (West Indies Company), financed primarily by Jewish capital. The company was created in spite of the Inquisition and began its activities in November 1649, when its first fleet left Lisbon harbor. Regular voyages between Lisbon and the ports of Bahia and Rio de Janeiro began, and the company was granted a monopoly on certain foodstuffs that were heavily consumed in the colony: wine, olive oil, flour, and salt cod. Further, this new venture was compelled to provide escort ships for the fleets transporting sugar and tobacco, which ran the risk of being attacked when they embarked for Portugal.

Vieira's plan in all respects followed the strategic model adopted by Portugal's rivals, England and Holland—specifically, the East India Company founded by Elizabeth I in 1599, which provided the nucleus for the first British Empire, and an institution of the same name founded by the Dutch, who followed with the West India Company that was so active in the invasion of Brazil's northeast.[1]

However, Iberian society during the seventeenth century was not subject to the full hegemony of bourgeois thought, which had by then imposed itself upon the economic practice and culture of Protestant England and Holland. Vieira preached in a climate of hostility and suspicion, and had to convince his listeners (Dom João IV, the nobility, the theologians, the men of letters of Coimbra, the Holy Office) of the orthodoxy and correctness of a company that would in large part be financed by New Christian bankers and merchants. The result, in terms of Vieira's Baroque rhetoric, was a unique symbiosis of biblical-Christian allegory and mercantile thought, which snakes its way through the strange *Sermão de São Roque* (Sermon for Saint Roch), delivered in the Royal Chapel in 1644, on the occasion of the prince Dom Afonso's first birthday.

Initially, the sermon's line of argumentation follows the topos of false appearances. What appears to some as risky will be in truth the source of salvation for all. The paradox of the dangerous remedy is illustrated with stories and examples taken from scripture and the *Flos Sanctorum*.

Saint Roch, a French nobleman, returns home after having traveled in Italy, which at the time was at war with France. His family does not recognize him and, suspecting that he is a spy, they detain him. Though appearances incriminate him, the facts find in favor of Roch, who then provides his family with the best possible support in their fight. What we fear most is what will save us.

That is:

The apostles were in Saint Peter's little boat struggling against the waves: Christ left the shore to help them, and they began to tremble, thinking that He was a ghost. *A ghost?* How could this be? Wasn't this Christ, here to help them? Wasn't this Christ who would free them from danger? How could they think that He was a ghost? *Because just as there are ghosts that appear to be remedies, so are there remedies that appear to be ghosts.* It bears noting that the same thing that frightened them as a source of danger was the remedy that freed them from the storm.[2]

The net of analogies is woven together and then cast. Now all that remains is to weave in the final term, which appears as a new strand, but one already prepared for by the work of narration: "The remedy that is feared, or that is called dangerous, lies in the two mercantile Companies, one for the East, and the other for the West, whose powerful fleets, armed against Holland, will safely bring us the goods of India and Brazil."

And in addition to this external conflict, we should recall the struggle between the two peninsular nations: "And Portugal with these same goods will have, year after year, the necessary capital to continue the internal war against Castile, which will doubtless last for some years."

Put in these terms, what would impede the Portuguese nation from undertaking such a prudent plan, to create these companies? Perhaps prejudice of blood or religious scruples?

In the end, what is asked of the New Christian bankers is a neutral and universal mediator, without race, or country, or religion: money. And Vieira borrows from the language of political realism the pragmatic idea that reason of state always justifies the means: "This remedy, which is appropriate to the circumstances, is not only approved of, but admired by the most politic nations of Europe, except for Portugal, in which the fact that some of its businessmen are of dubious reputation in matters of faith, and specifically as concerns the mixture of less Christian money with Catholic money, as opposed to the mixture of individuals, causes the same remedy to appear suspicious, and therefore dangerous."

Portugal is alone in obstinately ignoring the example of the "most politic nations of Europe." Only Portugal misguidedly seeks to distinguish between money that is faithful and unfaithful, pious and impious, noble and ignoble.

Vieira's rationale now embarks on a path in which dangers are frankly subordinated to the remedy. He concedes to a powerful and feared interlocutor—in this case, the Inquisition—that the purveyors of capital, the New Christians, might be perverse, but he affirms that it is most wise to send against evil the very arms that are proper to that evil, and in so doing, render them innocuous or tactically useful. To do the opposite—that is, to deport Portugal's Jewish merchants to Holland—would send reinforcements to the Dutch heretics that were at this time hungrily surrounding the plantations of Pernambuco.

Vieira draws a quite scholastic *distinguo*: the sanctity of God's designs bears no relation to the imperfect and contingent means that are the fruit of human frailty. He recalls the story of the prophet Elias, who received bread not only from angels' hands but also from crows' talons: "To serve the faith with the arms of the infidel, oh what a Christian politics! To win victories for faith, at the expense of the infidel, oh what a politic form of Christianity!"

And the money of Judas, the supreme traitor, was it not well spent in purchasing a tomb from the pilgrims to the Holy City? According to the medieval legend, Christ asked that Dom Afonso Henriques engrave on Portugal's seal his five wounds and the thirty coins, "so that we would understand that Judas's money, applied in a Christian manner, neither defaces Christ's wounds nor the arms of Portugal. Rather, combined, they can be displayed on our flags, as they wave to commemorate our victories in the conquest and restoration of the faith, as they always have in both worlds."

From this distinction between ends and means, which operate independently in terms of values, there follows a quite modern separation between ethical-religious principles and political action in the present. Vieira does not recoil when confronted with this profane space, opened by the founder of the bourgeois science of power, the Florentine secretary: "The reason is that the goodness of works lies in their ends, not in the instruments for their achievement. God's works are all good; the instruments utilized may be good or bad."

Vieira, advisor to a modern merchant-prince; Vieira, advisor to an absolute head of state.

The Argument for Action, between Politics and Theology

As the Court preacher, our Jesuit had access to privilege. But his oratorical weaponry took aim, in paradoxical and risky fashion, precisely at the privileges and exemptions enjoyed by noblemen and clergymen during this phase of the reconstruction, in which the empire was doubly threatened: by Spain, on the European chessboard, and by Holland, in the Atlantic and colonial strategic theater.

His fundamental rhetorical problem was this: how to compose a persuasive argument—that is, one sufficiently universal so as to move, in particular, the nobility and the clergy to contribute to the reconstruction of the kingdom, which up to that point had been supported principally by the bourgeoisie and New Christians.

In ideological terms: how could Vieira check the antimercantile and anti-Semitic ideas that, as is well known, flourished in the friar Amador Arrais's model dialogues and were present, among us, in Gregório de Matos's satires?

We must consider the obvious and recall that Vieira's actions took place during the Portuguese ancien régime, before Enlightenment criticism began to eat away at the social metaphysics that had encrusted itself onto the old social rankings. Vieira was speaking to an audience for which the nobleman was, ontologically speaking, noble, just as a clergyman was a clergyman *in aeternum*, a commoner common, a Christian Christian, a Jew Jewish. This was as the divine will had ordained, as the natural order had established.

Vieira's political goals obliged him to move his listeners toward a dialectically unsettling conceptual restructuring of their values (What is noble? What is not?), and toward a reclassification of persons and groups (Who is a nobleman? Who is not?)—hence the strange modernity of certain of his texts, which may seem at odds with the hierarchical universe of seventeenth century, Counter-Reformation-era Iberia. His agonized and tortuous discourse would lead one to believe that the culture of his time was far from homogeneous and static.

In the following paragraphs, I follow Vieira's argument from his *Sermão da Primeira Dominga do Advento* (Sermon for the Third Sunday of Advent), which he delivered in the Royal Chapel in 1650.

The sermon's theme, as demanded by the fact that it would be given during Advent, was man's second birth, a topic with messianic resonances but which Vieira develops here in the context of an exhortation to fashion a new individual within the arena of social struggles.

The Christian's second birth depends on his will and his effort. Each man has within himself the power to correct the inequalities that reign in a world ruled by chance: "Humble, lowly men of the people, good news! If nature or fortune was uncharitable with you at birth, know that you will be born again, and to as honorable a condition as you desire: you will then amend nature, you will triumph over fortune."[3]

If through ill luck one has not received an honorable station by blood, then one must achieve it through one's efforts, from which honest action springs: "If we are to be born again, why should we not toil mightily so that we might be born with honor? To be born without honor the first time carries with it the excuse that God made us. *Ipse fecit nos* (S1 XCIX, 3). There is no excuse for being born without honor the second time: ours is the glory of having made ourselves. *Ipse nos*."

The natural order, though understood as definitive, is in reality only the *primum mobile* of our individual existence. Advent proposes a "second time," a rebirth that can be taken in hand by our will and intentions. It is in this other time, fashioned by the conscience at work, in which value is asserted. Vieira gives traditional medieval-Baroque terms such as *honor*, *aristocracy*, and *nobility* new semantic meanings; by situating them within the sphere of labor, he liberates them from the bonds of familial inheritance and inherited station.

"Action" is situated on the positive side of this axiological operation, with its most negative countervalue being "omission." Vieira's eulogizing of the *vita activa* occurs within a syntactical chain in which his discourse highlights the worth of the conscientious man and the failings of those who have relapsed:

> Let us refer to more public examples.
> Through an omission one misses the tide, through a missed tide one loses a voyage, through a lost voyage one loses an armada, through a lost armada one loses a state: thus God takes away an India, thus God takes away a Brazil through an omission. Through an omission one loses notification, through lost notification one loses an opportunity, through a lost opportunity one loses a kingdom: thus God takes away so many things, thus God takes away so many lives, thus God takes away so much wealth, thus God takes away so many honors, through an omission.[4]

How many internal symmetries, parallelisms, and figures are brought from the *leixa-pren* of the medieval lyric to this paraenetic prose! These are all elements of emphasis applied toward the speaker's ultimate goal: to persuade, and by persuading, to move the nobleman, who occupies a preeminent position within the state, to sacrifice his leisure time and to truly share in rebuilding the kingdom's economy. What the old authors of treatises on rhetoric, beginning with Quintilian, called *inventio*—that is, the open search for topics and motifs—is granted a wide range of possibilities in Vieira. Such is the speed with which he conjures from the depths of his memory sounds and images to give life to his proposed theme. Biblical passages, fables, anecdotes, proverbs, episodes taken from the lives of the saints: Vieira makes use of all of these to wrap his argument in the splendor of the concrete:

> A bandit in the woods kills a man with one shot; the prince and minister with one omission kill a monarchy in one blow. These are the hesitations of one without scruples; it is for this reason that sins of omission are the gravest of all.
> Omission is a sin of what one commits by doing nothing. . . . The prophet Elijah was living in a cave in the desert, and God appeared to him and

said to him: *Quid hic agis, Elijah?* You here, Elijah? Here, my Lord! So where am I? Am I not living in a cave? Have I not removed myself from the world? Am I not dead in life? *Quid hic agis?* And what am I doing? Am I not disciplined, am I not fasting, am I not contemplating and praying to God? So if Elijah was making his penance in a cave, how could God reprimand him and be so surprised at him? The answer is that though Elijah's works were good, those that he did not do were greater. What he did was a matter of devotion, what he did not do was a matter of obligation. God had made Elijah prophet of the people of Israel, he had given him a public role; Elijah was in the desert, when he should have been at court; Elijah was living in a cave, when he should have been in the public square; Elijah was contemplating the Heavens, when he should have been improving the Earth; this was a great fault.[5]

The time we have is the right time, *kairós*, pregnant with potential action. An irreversible moment, this is what is meant by the terrible phrase "Time can in no way be recovered."

Here is the same idea, presented in a series of tightly bound phrases: "Ministers' sins of time should be noted and severely castigated. Because they do next month what they should have already done; because they do tomorrow what they should do today; because they do later what they should do now; because they do soon what they should do immediately."[6]

Everything that the friar Amador Arrais, Tomé de Jesus, Heitor Pinto, and the Portuguese mystics whose writings flowed into Manuel Bernandes's *Nova Floresta* (New Forest) exalt (contemplation of the eternal, removing and distancing oneself from worldly things, a life of solitude) can, according to Vieira, be described as examples of blameworthy inertia. The defense of action over inaction inverts the meaning of the idea of nobility, a guiding category of the ancien régime, with inherited value giving way to virtue won through labor.

In the *Sermão da Terceira Dominga do Advento*, human actions come to take precedence over titles and determine the value of these titles. What defines a man is what he determines to do, not the substance that lies inert in things. Within this new ontology, Vieira understands that things—that is, the nonhuman—are known by their *essência* (essence), whereas human beings are known by *ação* (action): "because each is determined by what he does, and by nothing else. Things are defined by their essence; John the Baptist was defined by his actions; because one's actions are one's essence."[7] Here Vieira describes the active or self-actuating manner in which John the Baptist addresses himself when asked of his identity: "I am the voice of one crying in the wilderness." As we see from the biblical text, John defines himself through the verbal declaration of action that signals his act of crying out or preaching. This passage from Vieira can be compared to certain other passages from the *Sermão da Sexagésima* (Sermon for the Sixtieth), in which the speaker minimizes the importance of the category of the name when divorced from speech: the only preachers who are worthy are those who preach, not those who are preachers in name only. From the perspective of the Jesuit will to action, action is the essence of the rational and free soul. During the second half of the seventeenth century, the Church of Rome, directly inspired by the activist and pragmatic theology of the Company of Jesus, condemned various propositions advanced by the Spanish mystic Miguel de Molinos, whose *Guía espiritual* (Spiritual Guide) can be considered the fundamental text of Catholic Quietism. At the same time, in France the Jansenists faced trials impelled by the Jesuits, who accused them of preaching a subjective doctrine in which a believer's faith was sufficient even when not accompanied by works or public displays of piety.

Vieira is severe: "One is his actions, and nothing else."

The sermon, which was given to the nobility, gives priority to doing and not to substance, though it spends little time on the sort of metaphysical speculations that, during that part of the century, had divided theologians into irreconcilable camps, into the voluntarists (defenders of a greater range of worldly action, to be understood in light of free will) and the Quietists, for whom the power of grace was far removed from man's strivings.

Our speaker's perspective was pragmatic. Vieira moved quickly from the enunciation of universal maxims to particular applications that were of immediate interest to him: "Oh what a grand doctrine for where we are now! When you ask yourselves who you are, look not to your grandfathers' noble titles, look to the record of your actions. You are what you do, nothing more." And to repeat: "True nobility lies in action."[8]

In his *Sermão de Santo Antônio* (Sermon for Saint Anthony), which he delivered in Chagas Church in Lisbon in 1642, Vieira tightens the cords of his rhetorical instrument in order to disabuse the nobility of their confidence in the unjust system of tributary exemptions, which was as noxious to the Crown's finances as it was onerous to the Third Estate, here termed the *povo* (people). This sermon, which is perhaps the fieriest of all those Vieira delivered to the privileged, leads us to the limits of what was possible at the time in terms of an equitable contribution by the three estates to the maintenance of the kingdom.

Universalism, which is necessary to make Vieira's case, is grounded here in two historically disparate realities: the national-mercantile system, on the one hand, and the proposals for fraternity among men contained in the Gospels, on the other.

Seeing these two currents mixed together, our first reaction might be one of puzzlement, if not anger. The history of worldviews should not, however, be subject to such impatience. In an ardent essay from his youth, Engels speaks of a "Catholic candour" that was capable of bridging the greatest of contradictions, and ingenuously bringing them to light, though this was being displaced during the eighteenth and nineteenth centuries by "Protestant hypocrisy," as when North American utilitarianists set out to prove, with Bible and Calvin in hand, the purity of profit and the sanctity of liberal industrialism.[9]

Understood in these terms, Vieira's argument appears progressive and morally impeccable. He asks that all contribute so that those already contributing may be relieved: "Let the remedies be universal, not partial; let the burden fall on all, not merely on some."[10] "Christ's law is a law that applies to all, in like terms—to the great and to the small, to the tall and to the short, to the rich and to the poor. It measures everyone by the same standard."

But this is not all. The revealed law of Christ does not negate the natural law, which is present in the consciences of all men. Both call for strict equity, both teach that goods, distributed to all men by God, should be universally enjoyed by the three estates, who find their common home in the state. Vieira gives natural law an anti-aristocratic interpretation, that is, one that benefits the alliance between the Crown and bourgeoisie.

In any case, privilege sins against the divine laws, both those inscribed in the sacred text and those inscribed in the nature of things and of men.

The analogy with cosmic phenomena—a rain that falls on the just and unjust alike—leads Vieira to a singular expansion upon his example. From its celestial position, the rain looks without distinction upon men. But in falling onto the *elemento grosseiro* (low thing) that is the Earth, the water distributes itself unequally: flowing down the mountains, it leaves the summits dry, whereas in pouring into the valleys, it places the inhabitants of the lowlands at grave risk of floods and drowning. Likewise, all laws issued from on high (from the supernatural or natural heavens) are just and beyond objection. The firmament is unified and internally consistent, as benefits the smooth, incorruptible spheres of Ptolemaic astronomy. The Earth, in contrast, is uneven and pockmarked. It is the Earth's mountains and swamps, its dry soil and its wetlands that produce disparities: "If the sun rises, all are warmed. If rain falls from the sky, all are soaked. If all the light were to fall onto one part and all of the storms onto another, then who would suffer? But I don't understand the unjust condition of this low thing on which we live, in which that which issues from the sky in equal terms, upon reaching the Earth, is made unequal."

Rain falls from the sky with the truly equal distribution we observe; but when the water reaches Earth, the mountains remain dry as the valleys drown: the mountains throw off the weight of the water, and the entire force of the current flows downhill to drown the valleys; and so that the valleys do not become a source of diversion for those watching from above, God wills that they see the shepherds' cabins swimming against the ruinous deluge. Let us be spared a universal flood, for when God makes the unequal equal even the tallest mountains are flooded and drown.

The final sentence contains a severe warning, almost a threat to the great men of this world: "What matters most is that the mountains be made equal with the valleys, for it is the mountains that are for the most part threatened by lightning. The burden should be divided equally, so that it will be a light burden for all."[11]

It is the inventive character of Vieira's analogical production that drives his argument forward. Again and again, the speaker finds principles of equity in nature, the same nature that would later provide the rhetoric of pure liberal capitalism with symmetrically opposed arguments. Rui Barbosa, for example, seems to have legitimated social inequality with reference to the biological differences between plant and animal species, as well as his irrefutable analogy to the five fingers of one's hand.

Vieira, in comparing justice from above with justice from below, not only affirms that the law of equality prevails over arbitrary inequalities but also exhorts men to change the world in which they live, to abandon "who they are so as to become who they should be."

The sermon uses ethnical norms to strike at the heart of privilege, as it was experienced on a day-to-day basis throughout Portuguese history. And as his manifest intention was to change these quotidian relations, Vieira places the principle of what should be, the ideal of the *res publica*, above the contingency and imperfection of these relations: "If the kingdom's three estates are unequal, in terms of their preeminence, then let us attend to our interests, and not permit them to be" and "Let them no longer be what they are, in order to be what they must be, and let necessity make equal what fortune has made unequal."

He asks that the clergyman "forfeit his exemptions and pay the Crown liberally."

To the nobleman he declares: "It is right that those sustained by the wealth of the Crown do not fail to sustain that same Crown with their own wealth."[12]

And what does he say of the Third Estate? Vieira makes this cutting observation: "Ordinarily those forced to pay are those in the professions, those least able; I do not know if by law, or if through bad luck. It is best not to know why."

Vieira veils his critique of power through ironic suspension of the phrase "I do not know.... It is best not to know why," but he is suggestive enough to make his point apparent to all of his listeners. In his *Sermão XVI do Rosário* (Sixteenth Sermon on the Rosary), his tone is more direct and vibrant, and achieves a note of prophecy: "God has merely to appear in the world, as small as a lamb such that I can measure Him with my finger, and the mountains and hills will fall, crumble on their own, and fill the valleys, such that there will no longer be heights and valleys on Earth, such that everything will be equal. And what mountains and hills are these? The mountains are the upper nobility, the most powerful; the hills are the lower nobility."[13]

In order to interpret this passage with philological exactitude, we must first of all ask what Vieira meant by the term *povo* (people), or more specifically, by the *Terceiro Estado* (Third Estate).

In consulting other sermons Vieira delivered in Portugal, we receive a helpful response regarding the extension of the concept, though a less helpful one regarding its meaning. The Third Estate includes all those excluded from the two privileged classes—first, the nobility, both upper and lower, with the latter group also including some men of arms and high-ranking magistrates, and second, the clergy. The heterogeneous character of all those excluded from these groups is striking, particular for us today, living as we do under industrial capitalism and prone to distinguish sharply between the bourgeoisie and the working class. Vieira's personal criterion, and that of his age, was evidently distinct from our own and more attuned to a social order that allowed for traditional—or rather, semifeudal—ways of life, and for which the economy was frankly mercantile in orientation. As such, the most obvious differentiation to make was between privileged groups, formed into a strict hierarchy, and all the rest, that is, the "people."

But who are these others? Our speaker brings together all those treated unjustly or oppressed by the first two groups: merchants, peasants, tradesmen, journeymen (salaried men), and servants and housekeepers. He unites the "bourgeoisie," represented by merchants and small landowners, and "workers," that is, all urban and rural laborers, as well as artisans and those involved in physical labor. This is the Third Estate.

The *Sermão da Quinta Dominga da Quaresma* (Sermon for the Fifth Sunday of Easter) is required reading for all who want to understand the social conditions of Portugal during Vieira's time. Vieira adopts an enumerative method of composition. He inventories his signs and distributes them in a polarized fashion: objects of luxury on one side and exploited human beings on the other. Broadly speaking, this process seeks to achieve a theatrical effect. We are clearly in the domain of Baroque *evidentia*.

From the first, Vieira's form of elocution is gestural. The speaker imagines that he, along with his invited listeners, is entering a palace belonging to wealthy nobles whose crest, displayed over the doorway, includes lions and eagles, allegories of the family's "most Christian Catholic faith."

> Let us enter and examine what we see step-by-step. First of all I see horses, litters, and carriages: I see servants of all types, some uniformed and some not: I see fine clothes, I see jewels, I see tableware. I see the walls covered in rich tapestries: through the windows I see gardens in the foreground, and farmland in the background; in sum, I see the palace and the oratory as well, *but what I do not see is faith*. And why does faith not appear in this house? I will tell its owner. If your horses eat thanks to the peasant, if the bits they bite down on and the wheels and carriages they pull are made by poor tradesmen, and they work but did not cost a cent, how can one see faith in your stables? If your lackeys' and pages' uniforms, and the support for armies of servants, both male and female, depend on monthly payments to your merchant, and if at the beginning of the year you pay him with hope and at year's end pay him with a desperate fear of going bankrupt, then how can one see faith in your family? If the fine clothes, jewels, and tableware were acquired either within or outside the kingdom with so much injustice and cruelty that if the gold and silver were melted down, or if the silks were wrung out, then blood would pour out from them, then how can one see faith in this false wealth? If your walls are adorned in rich tapestries, and the poor souls you strip bare to adorn your walls are naked and dying of cold, how can one see faith, if it is not even painted on your walls? If Spring laughs in the gardens and in the farmland, but the water is in the eyes of the mournful widow and orphaned children, whom you do not support either from obligation or from charity, and you likewise fail to thank those who served your parents, how can one see faith in these flowers and pathways? If the stones of the very house in which you live, from the rooftop to the foundation, pour with the sweat of laborers to whom you never give a day of rest, and who, if they wish to make their living somewhere else, you forcefully detain and oblige to stay, how can one see faith, or even the shadow of it, in your house?[14]

Vieira registers similar protests against priests who adorn churches in Lisbon with gold, silver, and precious stones when, both within and outside these theaters of pomp, life does not accord with belief but rather denounces its hypocrisy and destroys it:

> The gold and the brocades that adorn the walls are vulgar objects to behold. The harmony of the choruses pricks the ears. The amber and musk, and other aromatic incenses burning in the censers can be smelled from the street, and bring in the public through olfaction. Is this Earth, or Heaven? It is Heaven, but with much that is earthly mixed in. Because this celestial

worship, which is exterior and sensory, is likewise undone and contradicted through the senses. I refer not only to the many offenses that are committed outside of these temples, but moreover to the public displays of irreverence that take place within them, and which result in loss of respect for the faith and even for God Himself.

Would you like me, dear Lisbon, to speak the truth to you quite sincerely, without flattery, even if I discover that you have erred against the piety of which you are so proud? Your faith, which is so liberal, so rich, so adorned and so pleasing of scent, is not a living faith, but what is it? It is a dead, embalmed faith.

The Baroque allegories of the glory of God, which the monarchy and Church alike promoted in all of their magnificence, are deprived of any religious meaning when they merely represent unjust wealth and not the faith that these powers claim to exalt.[15]

The style of the seventeenth century, one that leaned heavily on spectacle—erecting buildings made up of "marvels," with false doors, false windows, and polychrome ceilings that utilized trompe l'oeil, employing a post-Tridentine liturgy that sought to convert souls through the senses, through figures and ornaments, through solemn music played during masses and in oratories, and even by appeal to the sense of smell through the scent of incense and musk that wafted through church naves—in sum, the spirit of the time, which frenetically multiplied images and sounds, is turned back upon itself in Antônio Vieira. He ascetically condemns the "culto exterior e sensível" (external and sensory worship), and finds, amid all the finery, death and a mummified religiosity that this plethora of signifiers should represent: "Your faith, which is so liberal, so rich, so adorned and so pleasing of scent, is not a living faith, but what is it? It is a dead, embalmed faith."

Through a dialectical movement, the great Jesuit's rhetoric builds up and tears down, brick by brick, the *gran teatro del mundo*. And behind its monumental façade, the listener hears, with a mixture of indignation and sadness, the hungry worker, the penniless, unpaid artisan, and the defrauded merchant. Meanwhile, the decorations on the walls are coated with the sweat and blood of laborers who died from the cold.

The Italian-style stage on which the nobility stride fails to maintain the distance between the machine and its illusions. Vieira recognizes and denounces the deceptive effects of perspective: "If we were to give painted form to this enigma, we would see that from different perspectives, things in the background would be depicted with dark colors, while things in the foreground would be depicted with light colors. But if we were to touch this same picture with our hand, we would discover that this variety, concocted through color, is nothing more than an optical illusion, a waking dream, and that while we appear to be far from the background and close to the foreground, in reality, we maintain the same distance from everything."[16]

He who is trained in the art of fiction becomes a master of *desengaño*. It is logical that in periods saturated with Mannerism, individuals would explore the full potential of classical styles to unmask the most fully concealed lies. The fiery voice of this highly intellectual preacher (intelligent enough to avoid the pitfalls of empty erudition) lays bare the powerful and reveals, far in the background and in all of their pathetic deprivation, the workers on whose backs rests this ornate, cruel civilization.

In uncovering the miseries of an opulent Lisbon, in exposing the abuses committed by the First and Second Estates, Vieira's discourse achieved a biblical, Christian universality (here I refer to the Bible of the prophets). Here the old scholastic notion of distributive justice is used to tacitly support the struggles of the mercantile class (Jewish or otherwise) and to alert the privileged that manual labor was becoming so exploitative as to approximate slavery.

Vieira's political project in Portugal, which favored an alliance between the Crown and the Third Estate, appears progressive from our vantage point, when it is compared to the reaction of the Inquisition and a good part of the nobility.

Now we must ask how Vieira's defense of a life of action and of the producers of wealth appears when confronted with the thorny questions (which to a certain extent were new to Europeans) of Amerindian and black labor within colonial society.

Amerindians

The defense of the Amerindians from colonists in Maranhão is the topic of Vieira's *Sermão da Epifania* (Sermon for Epiphany), given in the Royal Chapel in 1662 and in the presence of the widowed Queen Luísa, who ruled while Dom Alfonso VI was a minor.

It is useful to recall the circumstances surrounding Vieira's sermon. He and other missionaries had returned to Lisbon after being expelled by colonists following a series of disagreements relating to the question of Amerindian slavery. The speaker, taking advantage of the presence of the regent and her son, the future king, asked that the Jesuits be permitted to return to Maranhão in order to found missions that would be autonomous from the slave-owning colonists.

The sermon is exemplary in its depiction of a veritable chessboard of social conflicts, which, given the interests in play, obliged Vieira in his discourse to alternately defend extreme positions and to utilize a language of compromise.

Fundamentally, Vieira found himself divided between a greater universalistic and egalitarian logic, and a lesser ad hoc, particularistic, and self-interested rhetoric. The effect is a mix of ardor and diplomacy, of vehemence and indirectness, which defines our Jesuit's greatness and limitations.

The contrast becomes increasingly sharp the more definitively Vieira asserts his basic doctrine of equality between all peoples, which at a certain stage, is brought to the forefront of his sermon. In making his argument, Vieira cites *razões da natureza* (reasons from nature), which have evidentiary authority, and *razões das Escrituras* (reasons from scripture), which carry the authority of revelation.

First, the natural truths: "Of the nations, some are whiter and some are blacker, because some are closer and others are farther from the sun. And could there be a greater error of understanding, or a greater error of judgment among men, than to believe that I should be your master, because I was born farther from the sun, and that you should be my slave, because you were born closer to it?!"[17]

And next, the argument from Christian tradition, according to which one of the Three Kings, Melchior, was black, while the other two were white. All three were saved by God from Herod's fury, "since men of all colors are equal by nature, and even more so through faith."

The common and universal parentage of men, all of whom were created by a single God, is the guarantor of their brotherhood: "Between Christians there is no difference in nobility, nor are their differences of color. There is no difference in nobility because all are the children of God, nor are there differences of color because all are white." This last sentence, which is naturally off-putting, can be explained by the doctrine through which baptism spiritually cleanses all, without distinction.

With Vieira's argument understood in these terms, what would follow from it, if we were to preserve its degree of internal coherence? His pure and simple condemnation of customs in Brazil would survive; that is, his repudiation of all forms of slavery would take on a logical form. The thrust of Vieira's ethical arguments moves in this direction. Moving in this direction are the similes that speak of the double movement of the star of Bethlehem, which first led the magi to Christ (a figure for the conversion of the natives) and then led them away from the path by which Herod would have killed them (a figure for the liberation of these same Amerindians from the colonists' clutches). In an analogous sense, the dual mission of the Jesuits was to bring the good news to the souls of the Tupinambás and to defend their bodies from falling into the hands of the whites.

In terms of orthodoxy, Vieira knew that he was supported by documents written by various popes that were favorable to the liberation of the Amerindians. The first of these was papal bull *Sublimis Deus*, which is cited below and which Paul III released in 1537, a year in which a theological polemic was raging in Spain concerning the true nature of the Amerindians: "Through the present Letters we declare, drawing on our apostolic authority, that these Indians and all other peoples that from this day forward become known to Christians, though they lack faith in Christ, are endowed with liberty of which they should not be deprived, and should not be deprived of dominion over that which is theirs. Moreover, they shall be free to use, possess, and freely enjoy this liberty and this dominion, they should not be reduced to slavery, and all that occurs contrary to this, at any time and in any fashion, is null and void."[18]

However, this ideal, specific and absolute though it was in terms of *jus naturale* and as an article of faith, had already been abandoned through the political compromise (to which Vieira confessed) made by the priests, who had "descended" with the Portuguese to the Brazilian backlands, captured and bent the natives to their will, and brought them to Belém do Pará and São Luís to work for half the year on the colonists' lands. In practice, the rise in production created a need for more laborers and longer periods of service. The Jesuits resisted these terms as abusive and, indeed, they reserved the other half of the year for catechizing the Amerindians in their own villages. As a result, they were expelled from Pará and Maranhão, and this expulsion was the primary motivation for Vieira's protestations to the regent Dona Luísa.

Vieira's homily does not conceal the *punctum dolens* of the overarching question: using the pretext of a just war, the Church had permitted the capture of Amerindians. In this way the very shepherds charged with caring for their flock had placed their sheep in the jaws of the wolves:

> However, I cannot deny that all of us here, and myself above all, are quite guilty. And why? Because though we were obliged to defend the natives which we had brought to Christ, as Christ defended the Magi, we reconciled ourselves to our weak position and to the power of outsiders, and we abandoned justice, and we failed to come to their defense. . . . Christ did not permit that the Magi be deprived of their homeland, because *reversi sunt in regionem suam* (Matthew 2:12). We, however, not only permitted that these natives be deprived of their homeland, but through persuasion and promises (which we have not honored), we uprooted them from their lands, and brought entire villages to live and die alongside us. Christ did not permit that the Magi lose their sovereignty, because they arrived as kings and they would return home as kings. We, however, not only permitted that these natives lose the natural sovereignty with which they were born, and which allowed them to live free of any subjugation, but in

placing them under the spiritual yoke of the Church, we also placed them under the temporal authority of the Crown, and forced them to pledge themselves as vassals. Christ did not permit that the Magi be deprived of their liberty, because he freed them from Herod's power and tyranny. We, however, not only have not defended their liberty, but we negotiate with them and for them, as their keepers, and the result is that they are semi-captives, obligated to work half the year.[19]

The contradiction running through the colonial Church, of which Vieira was quite conscious and which prompted his remorse, illustrates the ambiguous condition of this same church.

How could an institution, which was a part of the monarchical state and which survived thanks to the state's largesse, advance a cohesive social project that would not be subject to the dominant forces within the system?

This tension could be resolved in two ways, neither of which was beneficial to the Jesuits. The options were compromise or resistance. The first option was employed in Maranhão, and the result was instability, due to the distance between the model of slow-paced subsistence agriculture that was practiced in the mission villages and the agro-mercantile model practiced in the mills and in the cotton and tobacco plantations. Inevitably, the latter would progressively require more and more labor power from the former, and in so doing, the precariousness of the pact between the colonists and Jesuits would be revealed, leading to conflict that would be fundamentally asymmetrical in terms of power.

In São Paulo de Piratininga, resistance led to an outcome that is well known: conflict and expulsion in 1640, following a series of skirmishes with the *bandeirantes*. The missions in the south came to a tragic end in the mid-seventeenth century.

In the south, despite Dom João IV's initial support for Vieira, the fathers were unable to pursue their plan for villages in the backlands, because the *capitão-mor* had ordered that they restrict their activities "ao ensino de Doutrina e Latim" (to the teaching of Doctrine and Latin), and had asserted his authority over the question of Amerindian labor (1653–1655). Undaunted, Vieira appealed to the Crown and received orders that were supportive of the missionaries, though the truce was short-lived.[20] After a series of conflicts, the colonists summarily expelled the missionaries from Belém and São Luís (1661). When Vieira returned to Lisbon in 1662 and preached before the regent, he did not receive the same favorable reception as he had during the time of Dom João IV. A law decreed on September 12, 1663, rigidly separated temporal and spiritual activities, allowing clergymen to exercise the latter only. As Vieira's sermon declares: "They want the ministers of the Gospel to limit themselves to the care of souls, and that the enslavement and captivity of bodies be the domain of the ministers of state. This is what Herod wanted."[21]

Vieira would be disgraced that same year, when the Inquisition prohibited him from preaching in Portuguese territory because of his messianic writings.[22]

But let us return to the defense of compromise, which Vieira would come to regret at a certain point but which he defended and justified on other occasions. How does the speaker manage to marry his universalistic arguments with a particularistic discourse that seeks a basic compromise with the colonists? In truth, he limits himself to juxtaposing those basic truths that occur to him with pretexts taken from then-current ideology, to which he was compelled to reconcile himself: "It is not my argument that there should be no slaves. Rather, as I have advocated in this court, and as can be clearly seen in my proposal, there should be a meeting of the most learned men concerning this subject, that they should define the causes of legitimate captivity, and the law should register this decision."

Vieira's argument recalls earlier facts that asserted a suspect distinction between legitimate and illegitimate captivity.

There was a period (and this is the object of the mea culpa cited above) of good relations between the fathers and the colonists, an accommodation by the less powerful or "weaker" (the missionaries) to the strength of the more powerful (the landowners). This pact implied subjective guilt (specifically, cowardice), though at the same time it was the condition of possibility for objective political survival. The logic of natural law and Christian *kerygma* required the freedom of fellow men, while a rhetoric concerned with interests sought to distinguish between legitimate and illegitimate captivity.

Although the sermon's internal structure is significant, so is the terrain it describes and on which both the speaker and his listeners maneuvered. The sermon alternately ascends with the high tide of a universalizing reason and descends to concessions in the interest of various pressure groups. Here the universal falls back upon itself—is deflated, if you like—and this is what prompts Vieira's ashamed reaction to the pact he had earlier made with those in power.

The same occurs in the *Sermão da Primeira Dominga da Quaresma* (Sermon for the First Sunday of Easter), delivered in Maranhão shortly before the incidents described above. Here too Vieira denounces slavery, describing it as a pact with the Devil: "All the Devil needs is a thatched hut and two Tapuias and they will fall to their knees and worship him." In this way he threatens the Amerindians' masters with the torments of Hell: "You have all committed a mortal sin. You all will live and die in a state of damnation, and you will all go directly to Hell." It is on these grounds that Vieira formulates general abolitionist principles: "Any man who owns the labor or freedom of another, and who is capable of restoring these but does not, will certainly be damned. All or almost all men in Maranhão own the labor or freedom of others and are capable of restoring these but do not. Therefore all or almost all are damned." Despite his indignation ("Go to Turkey, go to Hell, for there is no Turk in Turkey so Turkish, nor is there a Demon in Hell so demonic, as one who says that a free man can be a slave. Are there any among you who possess the natural flame who would deny it?"), there comes a moment in Vieira's sermon in which he offers a conciliatory proposal to the stubborn colonists.

In sum, according to Vieira's proposal, there are three types of Amerindian in Maranhão: those slaves who are already in the cities, those who live in the king's villages as free men, and those who live in the wilderness.

1) *The slaves in the cities.* These are in the direct service of the colonists. Since they were inherited or captured in bad faith, they should have the right to choose between ending their captivity and continuing the work they are doing. The idea is to give them the option of going to *as aldeias de El-Rei* (the King's villages), which are the Jesuit missions to which the Crown gave moral support.

2) *The slaves in the king's villages.* The preacher views them as free. Therefore, nothing more need be said.

3) *Those who live in the wilderness.* Of these, who were the targets of the *bandeiras* and colonists, the only ones who could be enslaved were those who had already been captured by an enemy tribe or who were in imminent danger of death. The colonists would, therefore, free them by bringing them to the city as slaves. This was referred to as an *operação de resgate* (rescue operation) in which the Portuguese would return with the *índios de corda* (tied-up Indians).

The often arbitrary character of this "rescue" is signaled by the sarcastic way it is described by Vieira: "This buying or rescuing (as they say) gives the pious name of 'rescue' to a sale that is so forced and violent that it is perhaps effected with a pistol pointed at one's chest."[23]

Further, Vieira concedes that Amerindians may be taken from the backlands who have been "sold as slaves by their enemies, or taken in a just war, of which the judges will be the governor of the whole of the state, the high judge [*ouvidor-geral*], the ranking priest [*vigário*] of Maranhão or Pará, and the prelates of the four orders, the Carmelites, Franciscans, Mercedarians, and the Company of Jesus." According to the judgment of these authorities, those captured in so-called just wars would go to the city, and the rest would go to the villages. The latter group would live in the villages for six months of the year, alternating with others so that they could attend to cultivation and to their families.

Antonio Vieira. Oil painting by an unknown artist, eighteenth century.

"The expansive sky is starred with blue
He, who had both fame and glory,
Emperor of the Portuguese language,
Was also our sky."

—Fernando Pessoa, "Antonio Vieira" (*Mensagem*)

From this we can infer that those rigorously considered as slaves would be the "tied-up Indians" and those captured in a "just war," along with those who preferred to remain subject to the Portuguese in Maranhão.

In the case of rescue, Vieira is so specific that he names a price: two *varas* (or 2.2 meters) of cotton, which are worth two *tostões* (or 200 *reis*). The agreement should be signed by all parties and submitted to the king.

Detail of an unfinished likeness of Saint Catherine, two meters in height, produced by the inhabitants of the Mission of São Lourenço.

Vieira seems to have tried to achieve something positive and certain (the liberation of the Amerindians in the city and the safety of the Amerindians in the mission villages) by way of something negative but uncertain, that is, the purchase of Amerindians in a "just war," a purchase that must always be judged by the colonial authorities and representatives of the religious orders that he believed he could influence.

The concession he promised going forward was the bait with which he tried to persuade the colonists to undue the *ataduras da injustiça* (bonds of injustice), which was a way around the fundamental problem of the justice, or lack thereof, of captivity, a question that the maxims of natural law and the Gospels had resoundingly resolved in the negative.

At the close of the homily, after having attempted mediation with his interlocutors, Vieira returns to the severe distinction between good and evil, with conscience on one side and self-interest on the other. His indignation is more than apparent: "Let the world know that conscience still exists, and that contrary to opinion, self-interest is not the absolute, universal ruler of all."[24]

And with "death!" to the Devil and to ambition, and acclamations of God and of conscience, Vieira concludes this sermon in which logic and rhetoric duel with one another in order to exercise control over a difficult triangular operation, in which the least powerful among the powerful (the Jesuit) attempts to convince the strongest (the colonist) to spare the weakest of the three, the Amerindian.[25]

Blacks

An even wider gap between evangelical doctrine and colonial practice is found in the case of slaves who are not Amerindians but Africans.

The corpus, in this case, is comprised of certain sermons given by Vieira on devotion to the rosary. As is well known, many of the lay brotherhoods organized around devotion to Our Lady of the Rosary, both in Bahia and Pernambuco, were comprised exclusively of blacks. This distinguished these brotherhoods from those devoted to the Most Holy Sacrament, which accepted whites only, and others devoted to Our Lady of Mercy, whose members were mulattos.

The specific theme of black slavery appears in Vieira's fourteenth, sixteenth, twentieth, and twenty-seventh sermons on the rosary.

Vieira quickly enters into the world of the black slave by describing the conditions of his daily existence: How did the blacks live in the "sweet inferno" of the sugar plantations? How did their white masters treat them? What was their daily routine, from birth to death?

In posing these concrete questions, the speaker makes a broad analogy that will provide him with an axis by which to orient his sermon, which in turn will support his entire argument: the life of the slave recalls the Passion of Christ.

Vieira's language of identification gains particular strength and projection when the listeners for whom the sermon was written are themselves slaves. This was the case of his fourteenth sermon on the rosary, delivered to a black brotherhood on a Bahian plantation in 1633. Through the intensive use of simile, Vieira causes his audience to feel (or feel again) the labors and the pains of the blacks who are the subjects of his sermon, though they are also sublimated when their suffering is projected onto the human body of Jesus Christ. In this way, they are both the selves to whom he speaks and the Other of whom he speaks.

The transition from subjective immanence to transcendence occurs in a living and suffering present, which takes place here and now though also in light of an exemplary past that the liturgical word brings back to life. Close correspondences guarantee the internal cohesion of what is said:

> You are the imitators of Christ on the plantation, because your sufferings are quite similar to those suffered by the Lord Himself on his cross, and during the entirety of his passion. His cross was made of two beams, and yours on the plantation is made of three. There was no lack of cane there either, for cane entered twice into the story of the Passion, first as the scepter for Christ's ridicule, and second, to collect his vital fluids. Christ's passion occurred over a sleepless night, and a day without rest, just like your nights and your days. Christ naked, and you naked: Christ without food, and you starving: Christ mistreated in every way, and you mistreated in everything.[26]

Vieira is not content to simply describe physical pain but goes further and denounces the social division that is the root of forced labor. At this point in the sermon he names two antagonistic classes, the masters and the slaves, *eles* (they) and *vós* (you): "They command and you serve; they sleep and you keep watch; they rest, and you work; they enjoy the fruits of your labors, and all you take from this is work and more work. There are no tasks as sweet as those you perform but for whose benefit is all of this sweetness? You are like bees, of which said the poet: *Sic vos non vobis mellificatis apes.* The same occurs in your hives. The bees make the honey, true, but not for their own benefit."[27]

Two centuries later Marx would declare: "It is true that labor produces for the rich wonderful things—but for the worker it produces privation. It produces palaces—but for the worker, hovels. It produces beauty—but for the worker, deformity. It replaces labor by machines, but it throws one section of the workers back into barbarous types of labor and it turns the other section into a machine. It produces intelligence—but for the worker, stupidity, cretinism."[28]

In the argument that Vieira constructs, we see two mutually reinforcing discourses: a discourse of sensibility, which views and intensely feels the suffering of the slave, and a discourse of understanding, which denounces the injustice of a society in which men created by the same God the Father and redeemed by the same God the Son are divided into masters and slaves. Having achieved this degree of knowledge, intelligence declares that it has reached the limit of its ability to accept such manifest unreason. In his thirty-seventh sermon on the rosary, Vieira's perplexity indicates the inability of his conscience to understand the reasons for this form of social violence: "Are not these men children of Adam and Eve? Were their souls not saved by the same blood of Christ? Are their bodies not born, and do they not die, just like ours? Do they not breathe the same air? Does the same sky not cover them? Does the same sun not warm them? What star is this, so sad, so hostile, so cruel, that guides their destiny?"[29]

Vieira notes the absurdity of the masters and slaves' disparate destinies, which neither natural laws nor faith in Redemption can explain. Oppression seems even to cloud that which is intelligible: "There are no slaves in Brazil, and in particular, none amongst those whom I see in all their misery, who are not for me the object of profound meditation" and "I compare the present and the future, time and Eternity, what I see and what I believe, and I cannot understand how God, who created these men so much in His image and likeness, just as He created others, could have predestined them for sweet infernos, one in this life, and one in the next."[30] This last passage shines as a ray of modern, enlightened thought, which for a brief moment breaks through the shadows of colonial conformity: "I compare . . . and I cannot understand."

The other sermons on the rosary provide answers, which are contradictory among themselves, to the same doubt. We must take a closer look at these texts.

In Sermon XX, inequality is presented as a consequence of humanity's fall from an initial state, which God created and desired and in which there were neither masters nor slaves. "God made everyone from the same stuff, so that they might live together, and they separated. He made them equal, and they made themselves unequal. He made them brothers and they rejected their common parentage."[31] As the sermon unfolds, we find that it is leavened with libertarian elements that, if we take them in isolation, divorced from the context of the seventeenth century, appear of a piece with the Enlightenment and with Rousseauian thinking: "men, perverting natural equality, distinguished themselves with two names as contrary to one another as those of master and slave." Or consider this: "If between men, the white dominates the black, this is by force, and due neither to reason nor nature."[32]

In Vieira's "philosophy of history," the mission of Christ, as a *novo Adão* (new Adam), was to break the bonds of inequality into which men had become trapped and thus to recover for them their original condition as brothers. Understood in terms of Thomism, natural law accords with the law of reason and recognizes itself, in a sublimated form, in the revealed law. Vieira's writing on this point is categorical: "Jesus Christ came to the world to correct the errors of Adam and his children, and to restore them to their original state of equality, and to return them to their original union, completely undoing the distinctions and differences that they, in their arrogance, had introduced."[33] This theology of universal redemption introduces a corrective and "progressive" meaning to Christ's appearance: "to return men to equality."

But in Sermon XXVII, the same anger caused by the absurdity of slavery is dissipated by another theory of history, one radically opposed to that described just now. Now Vieira appeals to the idea of a compensatory sacrifice. And oppression, which in previous texts had been judged one of mankind's grave sins, is justified here by a providential discourse. The speaker, once anguished by an incomprehensible social division, now searches for supernatural truth to explain "the hidden reasons for such a noteworthy migration (from Africa to Brazil), and its effects."

The explanation that once eluded Vieira ("I compare . . . and I cannot understand") is uncovered here by an elusive *desígnio da Providência* (design of Providence). What was denounced in Sermon XX as the work of human malice is redeemed in the twenty-seventh as the fruit of a divine plan. The blacks' journey to America redeemed their souls, which in Africa would have been lost to paganism or the empire of Islam. This old discourse of salvation, birthed during the crusades against the Arabs and reactivated by the Atlantic and Indian discoveries, reaffirms the neoplatonic distinction between body and soul, the same principle Vieira had so aggressively attacked when it served the political interests of the colonists in Maranhão. Here, however, the dualistic rhetoric returns and has a specific function: only the bodies, and not the souls, brought from Angola are subject to the torments of slavery. The slaves' souls patiently endure the purgatory of the sugar plantations, achieving salvation and eternal life, which Vieira paints in luxuriant terms and with festive colors: "It is God's specific design that for the present you live as slaves and captives so that through your temporal captivity you can achieve freedom, that is, eternal manumission."[34]

Vieira cleverly compares this final happiness to the Roman Saturnalia, in which, for a few days, masters and slaves exchanged clothes and the first served the last, thus inverting the order that governed the rest of the year:

> In the old days among the gods of the pagans there was one called Saturn, who was the god of the slaves, and during the feast dedicated to Saturn, which for this reason was referred to as Saturnalia, one of the rituals of the feast was that the slaves would be seated and their masters would stand, and would serve them. But once the feast came to an end, so would that comedy, and each one would return to how he was before. And in Heaven,

what will the slaves' feasts be like? They will be much better than Saturnalia, because each slave who in this world has served his master as if he were a God Incarnate, will be served by him in Heaven. Who would dare to say or imagine such a thing, if Christ Himself had not said it? *Beati servi illi, quos, cum venerit Dominus, invenerit vigilantes* (Luke 12: 37): "Blessed *are* those servants, whom the lord when he cometh shall find vigilant in their duty."[35]

Note how this final sentence closes. The text from the Vulgate, which Vieira cites, ends with the word *vigilantes*, which may be translated literally as "Blessed *are* those servants, whom the lord when he cometh shall find vigilant," though Vieira adds the words *em fazer a sua obrigação* (in their duty). Thus the words of the Apostle Luke are made to say more than what, in truth, they actually mean to say. In Luke, the servant's "vigilance" is meant to recall the vigilance of the faithful, who in the dark of night await the Savior's return. Expectation makes the soul attentive, it brings it to a state of alert, and it makes it active and not foolish, unlike the mad virgins from the parable. Vieira, however, accentuates labor as a condition *sine qua non*, an idea that he had inserted in an earlier clause by conjugating the verb *servir* (to serve) in the personal infinitive: "*porque todos aqueles escravos que neste mundo servirem a seus senhores como a Deus*" (because each slave who in this world has served his master as if he were a God Incarnate).

Here the paradigm of the Passion is informed by a resolutely ideological current. The cross, which had humanized the Redeemer and given his sacrifice real form in the suffering of enslavement, is interpreted here as the sign of a sacrifice that is valid in and of itself, and propitious in and of itself, in open opposition to the Gospels, which denounce the farce of the judgment, the violence of the sentence, the Pharisees' hypocrisy, the Sadducees' impiety, the stupidity of the masses in calling for the crucifixion of an innocent, and finally the cowardice Pilate showed when he delivered a man whom he had not found guilty of any offense to the fury of the priests and the guards.

The morality of a cross-for-others has down through the centuries served as a reactionary weapon for the legitimation of the theft of human labor for the benefit of a violent order. Giving in to the rhetoric of compensatory immolation, Vieira fails to find in his universalistic discourse those elements that, at the level of praxis, would have worked against the interests of the landowners.

Once again, the colonial condition erected a barrier against the universalization of humanity.

5 Antonil, or the Tears of Trade Goods

> I do not fear Castile; I fear these dogs.
> —Vieira, in a letter to Father Manoel Luís,
>   dated July 21, 1605

In January 1681 a young priest from the Company of Jesus, born in Lucca and who signed his name in Latin as Johannes Antonius Andreonius, embarked from the port of Lisbon en route to Bahia. He was traveling to Brazil at the invitation of the septuagenarian Father Antônio Vieira, whom he had met in Rome when Vieira was a celebrated preacher and favorite of Clement X (who referred to Vieira as "beloved son" and protected him from the Portuguese Inquisition) and who was so dear to Christina of Sweden that she chose him as her confessor.

Once in the colony, Andreoni rapidly rose through the hierarchy of power. He was first named instructor in rhetoric at the Bahian seminary, then director of studies, master of novices, Vieira's personal secretary when Vieira held the post of *visitador geral* (visitor general), rector of the Real Colégio da Bahia (Royal College of Bahia), and finally provincial superior, the highest rank possible within the Societas Jesu in Brazil. Fellow Jesuits quickly discovered in Andreoni a love of calculation, a notable aptitude for describing and classifying all manner of materials, and above all a talent for figures that suited him for the most methodical administrative tasks.

Serafim Leite, who reconstructed Andreoni's career, refers to statistical work undertaken by him while serving as secretary.[1] Using the Livro de Entrada no Noviciado (Book of Entry into the Novitiate), Andreoni drew up profiles of all of the members of the order who were in the province between 1566 and 1688. And thanks to his diligence, we have, in the didactically titled volume *O costumeiro* (The Book of Habits), a catalog of superiors and masters along with a highly detailed account of the customs and practices of the Jesuit colleges. His Annual Letters, written yearly to the superior general in Rome, are models of dry precision and reveal a chronicler's attention to detail.

It was probably this same historian's dedication, married to a due respect for the consecrated leaders of the company, that inspired his greatest work, *Cultura e opulência do Brasil por suas drogas e minas* (Culture and Opulence of Brazil, as Revealed by Its Products and Mines), which he dedicated to those leaders "who would like to see it glorified on the altars of the venerable Father José de Anchieta, priest of the Company of Jesus, missionary, apostle, and new thaumaturge of Brazil."

And clearly it was Andreoni's duty to pay due—and public—homage to Vieira, the order's greatest name during the seventeenth century. This led Andreoni to compose the celebratory, though admittedly brief, pages he dedicated to Vieira's life just after his death in 1697. These would only be translated from the original Latin two hundred years after their composition, when the National Library saved them from obscurity by publishing them in its *Anais*.[2]

Everything appears very correct in João Antônio Andreoni's life and work. However, we must note that the deference Andreoni paid Vieira, that singular man of genius (in whose steps Andreoni had followed for years, from Rome to our Bahia) did not lead him to feel, think, or act in consonance with Vieira's most treasured ideals. On the contrary: though Andreoni was faithful to Vieira in his words and figures, he was unfaithful—nearly a traitor—to his protector's spirit.

Let us take a look at the story.

The conflict between the Jesuits and the colonists in Maranhão and Pará is one of many episodes in a war that lasted a century and a half, and that was fought between two forces struggling for power over the Amerindians, but with unequal material resources. As evidence of this disparity, we may cite the failures of Vieira and his compatriots in the missions in the north—though it was São Paulo de Piratininga, the center of *bandeirante* activity, in which conflicts became routine, from the foundation of the settlement through the repeated missionary-related conflicts and expulsions of the seventeenth century. Serafim Leite and, on the other end of the spectrum, Afonso d'Escragnolle Taunay, an apologist for penetration of the Brazilian interior, offer detailed accounts of the phases of a fundamentally important conflict that would only reach its conclusion with the destruction of the Sete Povos (Seven Missions), the work of the Pombaline Enlightenment.

It is Andreoni's participation that interests us here. The counsel and decisive mediation offered by Andreoni and his Italian confederate Giorgio Benci (author of the *Economia cristã dos senhores no governo dos escravos*, or "Christian Economy of Masters in Their Management of Slaves") would result in the delineation of a new position by certain Jesuits as well as the leadership of the company in Italy. This position might be described as indulgent with regard to the *mamelucos* (mestizos) of São Paulo and worked to "weaken the Jesuits' unbreakable resistance to the enslavement of the natives," in the words of Serafim Leite.

Vieira could not but bitterly resent the maneuverings of Andreoni and Benci, who were supported by the Dutch priest Jacob Rolland, who went as far as to write an *Apologia dos paulistas* (Defense of the Inhabitants of São Paulo). The great fighter complained more than once of the political scheming of the foreign (that is, non-Portuguese) priests, who in all respects differed from the Jesuits in São Paulo, who were zealous guardians of their mission villages and hostile to the rapacious incursions of the *bandeirantes*.

The documents I was able to consult in the Roman Archive of the Company of Jesus lay bare the differences between Vieira, by then an octogenarian, in poor health, and isolated as *visitador* (visitor) in Bahia, and the group secretly led by Andreoni. Whenever he was given the chance, Andreoni would sabotage the projects undertaken by the man who had brought him over from Europe, and who had showered him with praise and secured him a stable institutional position.[3]

In addition to disagreements pertaining to questions of power within the province (as an Italian, Andreoni could not legally occupy leadership positions), there was sharp disagreement between Vieira and Andreoni regarding the freedom of Amerindians.

Vieira, who as a combatant stood in the line of fire during the 1650s and 1660s in Maranhão, had returned from Europe after twenty-five years and had become increasingly animated and forthright in his denunciations of the abuses committed by the colonists and explorers operating in the backlands. In 1687, he proposed to his superiors that he travel as a simple missionary to the villages of the Amazon. One year later, in his "Exposição doméstica" (Domestic Exposition), he urged the fathers of the college to put aside teaching and bureaucratic positions in favor of attending to "the university of souls in the forests and where the natives live." In 1690, seeing that the mission of the backwoods evangelists was in danger, Vieira filled his *Sermões* (Sermons), which were about to be published in Portugal and which were in demand in Spain, France, and Italy, with praise for it.

But his field of action was marked by unseen dangers. It was precisely at the end of the seventeenth century that the inhabitants of São Paulo discovered the gold for which they had long been searching. Luck was on the side of the *bandeirantes* and São Paulo, and luck, wealth, prestige, and influence with the Crown resulted, beginning at midcentury, in royal letters encouraging explorers to found settlements in the interior and tempting them with the promise of privileges and honors if they were successful. Varnhagen relates: "After much effort and unsuccessful attempts the first mines which gave decidedly positive results were found in Itaberaba. This led to the discovery of the others. This first discovery took place in 1694, when Duarte Lopes brought the good news to São Paulo."[4]

The year 1694 was also when the new *Administrações dos Índios* (Governance of the Indians) were written up and signed. The text was approved by Father Alexandre de Gusmão, a provincial, who asked legal advice of Andreoni, who at the time was the priest's secretary and was held in high regard for his study of civil law at Perugia.

Vieira immediately perceived that this amounted to a capitulation by the priests to the interests of the *mamelucos*. In May the College of Bahia met to choose a representative to travel to Lisbon and Rome to discuss the São Paulo agreement with authorities. Vieira would have made known his preference for a specific candidate, but the majority group, led by Andreoni, accused him of attempting to influence the electors, a serious violation of Jesuit bylaws. Vieira was punished both actively and passively, being prohibited from voting and from receiving votes. Undaunted, Vieira protested in a letter to friends, writing of his "escravidão doméstica" (domestic slavery), and he prepared to register a long declaration giving his vote that would be both separate from and openly opposed to the *Administrações*. Vieira then appealed to the judgment of the superior general, Paolo Oliva, who had been Vieira's admirer since their time together in Rome preaching before the pope. But Oliva's solemn correction of the group's decision, which he included in an affectionate and reverent missive to Vieira, would arrive too late to Bahia, three years after Vieira had died in that city.

Vieira's *Voto sobre as dúvidas dos moradores de São Paulo acerca da administração dos índios* (Vote on the Questions of the Inhabitants of São Paulo and the Administration of the Indians) and his letter to Father Manoel Luís, dated July 21, 1695, are testimonies to their author's wisdom. In the letter Vieira complains of "an Italian priest who has never seen an Indian and has only listened to the inhabitants of São Paulo, just like a Flemish priest named Rolando." The Italian priest would have been Andreoni or Giorgio Benci, who was present at the negotiations between Alexandre de Gusmão and the city leaders. And then we have Vieira's very direct declaration: "I do not fear Castile; I fear these dogs."[5]

The *Voto* exposes the continued practice of Amerindian slavery, now described using the specious term "administração" (governance). With royal approval, this "governance" would amount to "approval and public freedom" to capture Amerindians.

Of the pact signed at Piratininga, Vieira states, "all that was good was given to the governors and all that was negative was shouldered by the miserable Indians, who at every turn or with every change are ground under by the wheel of fortune." In making his argument, Vieira looked to the authority of theological moderates on the Amerindian question, namely Joseph de Acosta, who in the *De procuranda indorum salute*, from 1588, had defended evangelization using arguments that recalled Bartolomé de Las Casas (though prudently, Acosta made no mention of him) and Juan de Solorzano Pereyra, who had studied the *encomiendas* and had authored the *De indiarum gubernatione*, in which he tied Acosta's arguments to the violent practices of the first Spanish conquistadors: "My God, what disorder, what ugliness!"[6]

This is not the place to enter into the thicket of the ethical doctrines applied by late Scholastic thinking to the question of colonial rule over the Amerindians. What is important is that we observe a way of thinking coming into existence that rejected the Aristotelian notion that "there are men who are naturally slaves." Francisco de Vitoria (who inspired Grotius and who was one of the precursors of modern international law), Francisco Suárez, and Luís Molina sought to restrict the application of the concept of "just war," which was so often abused to legitimate the conquest of the Amerindians throughout the American continent. It is this juridical tradition that inspired our veteran combatant's *Voto*.

While he was a *visitador*, between 1688 and 1691, Vieira had drawn up a Regimento das Aldeias (Regulations for the Villages) in which he banned the colleges from making use of indigenous labor, even if compensated, in order to prevent abuses that would lead to questions over the correctness of the missionary project. With Vieira dead, Andreoni, who was designated a provincial the following year (1698), petitioned Superior General Tamburini to revoke that restriction, arguing that if landowners could make use of the Amerindians, why could men of the cloth not do the same?

Andreoni, ever the legalist, argued for the generalization of indigenous labor, whether in the form of slavery formally governed by the *Administrações* or semicompulsory salaried labor: "Sed si locantur aliis, quare nos illis utemur pretio *statim* laboris soluto?" That is: "But if the Indians can be rented to others, why can we not use them ourselves, since the price for their labor has *already* been freed of any restrictions?"[7]

In 1704, the superior general overturned the prohibition introduced by Vieira, doing so using the same terms as Andreoni's petition: "Possunt Nostri uti opera Indorum soluto pretio." That is: "We may employ the Indians' labor, without restrictions in price."

While in Vieira we may note concerns owing to his Scholastic education (with the theology implied by the Natural Law of Men limiting the colonizer's powers), in Andreoni moral conscience has been entirely bent to the purposes of colonial mercantilism. Among these mercantilist arguments, we see the argument from the competition among possessors of capital. And while Vieira had fought from his youth for the Crown to extend its hands in friendship to the Jews and to save them from the Holy Office, as an old man Andreoni translated Gian Pietro Pinamonti's anti-Semitic *Sinagoga disingannata* (The Synagogue Revealed) in which he denounces the Hebrews and the Law of Moses, which he termed a "diabolical law." Pinamonti stated, doing little to hide the nature of his prejudice: "If I am to speak sincerely, the Jew is talented in no art except that of making money."[8]

Vieira's messianic hopes, which he placed in the Quinto Império (Fifth Empire) and in the earthly realization of the biblical promise of a kingdom of justice, must have ruffled the feathers of the strictly orthodox Andreoni, all the more so because these prophecies had cost their unlucky author two years' detention in an inquisitorial prison.

Vieira's incomplete final work, the *Clavis Prophetarum*, or *De regno Christi in Terris consummato*, remains unpublished because the manuscripts were lost, though we know that after their author's death, they were entrusted to a locked chest to which Andreoni himself had the key. But we also know that two associates of the Inquisition, who had been advised ahead of time by a clever informant, intercepted this precious cargo at the port of Lisbon, though it was meant to continue to Rome. Andreoni, rector of the college, was the last person to see the original copies of the *Clavis Prophetarum*, which he had read attentively and on which he had commented in a document full of both conventional praise and openly expressed objections. Five days after Vieira's death, Andreoni wrote a letter to Superior General Tirso González, a document summarized in these terms by Francisco Rodrigues:

> Father Andreoni frankly expressed his reservations to the Superior General. He said that Vieira held strange opinions, which would necessarily make the book's approval more difficult. And for this reason he had suggested to Father Vieira that he share his opinions before a universal council. Only there would it be convenient for him to discuss his beliefs so that they could either be approved or rejected. Now, Andreoni insisted that if these opinions were to imperil the work, *it would be best if they were omitted from it*, and that all the rest be published, because all of this was very worthy of publication, and indeed, he had read it with pleasure and admiration.[9]

The mystery remains unsolved: Who prevented Vieira's final prophetic writings from reaching their destination? When did Andreoni's feelings of animosity toward his patron first manifest themselves? We thus must content ourselves with written clues. When I examined letters written by Andreoni, now held in the Roman Archive, I found the following, dated June 26, 1690, and written to Father Fózio, the superior general's inspector (*admonitor*). Below I have included my translation from the Italian of the sections of the letter that refer to Vieira:

> Very Reverend Father in Christ:
> . . . I write as truthfully as if I were to die having celebrated some masses and ministered to the dying. Our Reverend Superior General has a very high opinion of Father Antonio Vieyra, our visitor for the past three years, because he believes that he governs as well as he preaches, though he is very eccentric in his ideas and unfortunate in action. His personality is divided and erratic. He was born in Lisbon, came to Brazil, moved on to Maranhão, returned to Portugal, traveled through Holland, France and Italy, then returned to Portugal, and on to Brazil, and since he is little loved here, it is said that he is writing to the Superior General so that he may return to Portugal. The Portuguese expelled him from Maranhão with much confusion. In Portugal he was one of the principal men responsible for the division of that Province into two, which produced so much regret and division that even today, with the two Provinces reunited, partiality remains. Three years before being named visitor he wanted to make this Province of Brazil a sub-province of Rio de Janeiro, and he discussed this with Our Reverend Father, who very prudently judged the idea very premature. . . . This father has, for reasons of nationality, a great deal of animosity toward Brazilians. I do not deny that Europeans can be better, when they come with a missionary's spirit, as is ordinarily the case when they are from Italy, France, or Germany, but when they come with bad intentions and in search of a place to live, they do little good. . . . The Brazilians know them, react badly to them and cannot bear them.
>
> His way of governing is political, and after getting rid of those who give him good advice, he gathers around him men of little virtue, who over time accommodate themselves to him and who approve everything he does, and they say that they seek his favor. In particular he listens to Father Ignatio Faya, a man notorious for his lack of sincerity, his arrogance, his vengeful spirit, and whose lack of chastity is so commented upon that he left a foul odor in the three principal colleges of the Province, so much so that it got the students talking. And please know, Your Reverence, that in writing to you I say much less than do others, old and young alike, and the Father Visitor himself told me that a representative of the Holy Office had warned him about his manner in the confessional . . . yet even today this man is so ubiquitous that all poor advice given is attributed to him. . . .
>
> The Father Provincial and Father Rector are like the beadle and sub-minister, because they are prejudiced in everything they say, do, and undo. The preacher was a friend of mine, and it seems to me that he does not give

the young men good advice, and there is much discussion on this point, with little deference to his age, and with many judgments and conjectures made. He has shown himself very partial in the administration of justice, forgiving, covering for and defending those of like mind, and behaving less as a judge than as an enemy toward others, to whom he refuses to listen. And I was his adviser . . . but now there is no one who tells him or dares to tell him what should be done. . . . Believe me, my Father, that the young man has in later years fallen to earth. Tobacco, chocolate, meetings with Philosophy students, and what the Father Rector tells me is worst of all: that he could not be freer in his vows of chastity and poverty. . . .

If the Superior General does not find a solution, I have no doubt that Saint Ignatius will do so.

So many poison arrows fired by one who presented himself as a zealous defender of the company! Vieira's voyages, all made on behalf of the missions, some of them dangerous and all standing as evidence of his personal selflessness, are cited as examples of a "divided and erratic personality." Andreoni describes Vieira's expulsion by the colonists in Maranhão, which as we know was caused by the anger of those who did not tolerate the missionary's intransigent defense of the law, as if it were yet another chaotic spectacle: "The Portuguese expelled him from Maranhão with much confusion." His opinions on the administrative organization of the company in Portugal and Brazil enter here merely to sow discord. He does not describe but rather defames the visitor, painting him as an egocentric, unjust man, who schemed along with his adulators, even when corrupt, and who was insolent to the superiors he disdained. It is not difficult to detect a note of resentment on the part of Vieira's old counselor. Within the seminary, Vieira's image is that of an old man so partial and so fallible that the pious, scandalized Andreoni, in the form of a veiled threat, invokes the aid of Saint Ignatius if the superior general fails to put a stop to such abuses.

From the Anti-Vieira to Antonil

Within this Andreoni, wedded to common sense, respectful of all that is firm and established, hostile to utopias and prophecies, conciliatory and diplomatic toward the landowners and enslavers of Amerindians, there hides the man who is literally our first economist: this Antonil is almost entirely present in Antônio, the *Anonymous* man who took pride in being Tuscan and Luccan (from which he took the L in Antonil, which according to Capistrano de Abreu, solves the riddle of authorship), a foreigner and not Portuguese, no longer Baroque, but rational and objective. We unlock the key to the intellectual character of *Cultura e opulência do Brasil* with a term taken from Alice Canabrava, Antonil's most sympathetic reader: objectivity.[10]

Is this objectivity neutral? At bottom it is not, but it is if we consider how forms of social domination appear as "natural." To be objective meant, within a context that had been marked by violence for a century and a half, to accept the fact that the inhabitants of São Paulo utilized Amerindian forced labor in their expeditions to the backlands and that they had sufficient power to continue doing so, as in fact they did. To be objective meant to think, naturally enough, from the point of view of a northeastern slave master or a *bandeirante* from the south. While in Vieira's impassioned sermons this perspective is shown as self-flagellating and contradictory, Antonil adopts it calmly, as a pure reflection of a practice that was part and parcel of the colonial structure.

His book remains bounded by the rationality of a bookkeeper for an agricultural export company. The art of accounting, in Tuscan, is termed *ragionería*. It is nothing more than things and numbers, but it follows them to their ends and their depths, which gives it a general interpretive coherence.

When short-term utility is elevated to the status of absolute criterion for action, the values of "justice" and "truth" are rapidly subsumed by present calculations. This rationale is inherent to mercantile-colonial discourse. This is the thinking that produced the most unemotional and pragmatic account of our colonial riches ever written, *Cultura e opulencia do Brasil por suas drogas, e minas, com varias noticias curiosas do modo de fazer o Assucar; plantar, & beneficiar o Tabaco; e tirar Ouro das Minas; & descubrir as da Prata; e dos grandes emolumentos, que esta Conquista da America Meridional dá ao Reyno de PORTUGAL com estes & outros generos & Contratos Reais. "Obra de André João Antonil"* (Culture and Opulence of Brazil, from Its Drugs, and Mines, with Many Curious Facts as to How to Produce Sugar; Plant, & Nurture Tobacco; and Extract Gold from Mines; & Locate Silver Mines; and the Great Wealth, which the Conquest of Meridional America Has Made Possible to the Kingdom of Portugal in Terms of Goods of These & Other Types & in Terms of Royal Contracts. "Written by André João Antonil").

The author's pseudonym is a near-perfect anagram of João Antônio Andreoni.

Antonil's work was published in 1711 in Lisbon by the Oficina Real Deslandesiana, after receiving the necessary civil and ecclesiastical authorizations. The conditions of its production are rather notorious. The book was confiscated by Dom João V's royal degree, at the request of the Conselho Ultramarino, because of allegations transcribed here:

Here in the Court [i.e., Lisbon] a book was recently published which carried the name and title Culture and Opulence of Brazil, and which, in addition to including many observations concerning the production and resources of the plantations, and the planting of sugarcane and tobacco, on a much different note describes the locations of all of the gold mines which have thus far been discovered, and mentions several other mines not yet discovered or exploited. And since these details and many others of equal importance are included in the book, it is crucial that this information neither be published nor reach the ears of other nations, given the great harm that might thereby befall that state [i.e., Brazil], on which, we might consider, this Kingdom and the entire Monarchy depends to a significant degree.

It was therefore decided that the Overseas Council advise Your Majesty of the great advantageousness of this book being immediately confiscated and thereby prevented from entering into circulation. And further, since the necessary authorizations were granted without the consideration due to a question of such magnitude, a question that concerns the preservation and the interests of the state, and of Your Majesty's Royal Crown, it would be quite proper that these be revoked, since it is safer and more prudent to prevent harm before the effects of this harm make themselves known, than it is to correct a harm which has already come to pass.

The book was confiscated the same year that it was published and was only partially republished in 1800, when Father José Mariano da Conceição Veloso included the part of the manuscript pertaining to the sugar plantations in the volume *Fazendeiro do Brasil* (The Brazilian Landowner). The second, complete edition of the book would be published in Rio de Janeiro in 1837.

A refined expression of the mercantilist ideal, Antonil's work developed to such extremes its method of mapping the mines, for useful and utilitarian ends, that its circulation would have put at risk (if we are to believe the words of the Overseas Council) one of the sacred principles of the old colonizing regime: secrecy.[11] After all, secrets should not be given away to one's most astute enemies, who, subject to the system of international competition, were always on the lookout for good information on one's products and markets. In point of fact, Dom João V ordered all copies of Antonil's book burned.

Antonil's readers are unanimous in recognizing the author's sense of economic reality and his capacity for attentive observation, for perceptive distinctions, for precise description, and for ordered and detailed narration. Everything is presented as if in its proper place, without undue hurry but also without undue delay. *Age quod agis* and *Festina lente* seem to have been the maxims that guided the composition of the book.

The key term, *objectivity* (that is, placing oneself in the service of the object), consistently comes to the commentator's mind. Having dispensed with facile wordplay, the subject of Antonil's text is the object: the cultivation of sugar, the productive and functioning royally chartered mill, the cultivation of tobacco, the gold mines, the abundance of cattle and leather and other goods owing to the conquest.

How do human beings figure in this closed universe in which trade goods are produced and circulate? They appear as convenient instruments for the creation of wealth, marked by need and obligation, which ultimately grant them their identity. Whether master or slave, Antonil's man is in the first instance a body and soul useful to trade goods with which, over the course of his life and through the light of his intelligence and the strength of his arm, he becomes intertwined.

Antonil describes the plantation master as if compiling a list of obligations. This figure is composed entirely of obligations, of worries, of responsibilities.

Como se há de haver o senhor de engenho (How the plantation master should be): thus begins a sequence of titles of recommendations to the landowner regarding such topics as the purchase of *massapê* (fertile, loam-heavy bottom land), the management of water sources and timber (the soul of the ovens!), and how to avoid neighbors who are "scheming, unbalanced, and violent" and who would be future sources of lawsuits and complaints.

Antonil's recommendations range from great to small, even touching on domestic matters that, if mismanaged, will have bitter consequences for the negligent administrator:

> Do not leave papers and written documents in your wife's box or on a tabletop exposed to the dust, the wind, silverfish, and termites, so as to avoid having later to pay for a number of masses dedicated to Saint Anthony to help you find an important paper that has disappeared and which you now need. Because it may well occur that the maid or servant takes two or three sheets from the lady's box in order to embroider what is most pleasing to her, or that your youngest child takes some sheets off of the table, in order to paint faces or make little paper boats, captained by flies or grasshoppers, or that the wind causes these wingless sheets to fly away from the house. (chapter 2)

It stands to reason that here Antonil is addressing landowners without administrative experience, rich men who have not yet achieved a rigorous separation of business and domestic expenses, of the economic public space and the nuances of private life.

And the recommendations do not end here. The plantation master should never appear arrogant or haughty toward his workers, for insolence leads to revolt and a desire to get what one feels is one's due. He should act pleasantly to all, a recommendation that extends to the ladies of the plantation, "who, though they merit greater respect from others, should not be so presumptuous as to assume that they are to be treated like queens, nor that the workers' wives should be their maids and appear among them as smaller stars are to the moon" (chapter 3).

Landowners should be hardworking, prudent in business, and moderate in their habits, as is required by the proper administration of their goods, of which Antonil ranks lands and machines first in importance, followed by livestock, and then male and female slaves.

Throughout the text Antonil evinces the greatest concern for social relations taking place within the closed world of the plantation. Landowners should neither leave to chance their dealings with *lavradores de partido* (producers of sugarcane obliged to provide sugar to the royally chartered mills) nor with slaves. A lack of specifically defined obligations and privileges will lead the strong to arbitrary behavior and the weak to abuse—hence the need for a contractual spirit that, in a certain way, appears more modern and (dare I say) more civilized than the unthinking application of power that takes place in systems guided entirely by favor and servitude.

Antonil formalizes the mutual obligations of master and servant. This rationalization of behavior within the realm of labor serves as a bridge between a rough and archaic mercantilism and the Enlightenment, which was just underway in the Europe of the eighteenth century.

Discoursing, for example, on the *arrendatários* (lessees) and the difficulties that assail the landowner at the always litigious end of a contract, the author advises: "And for this purpose it would be a wise preventative measure to have a formula or lease document drawn up by a very experienced man of letters, and including a declaration concerning how the goods in question should be disposed of, so that the conclusion of the lease will not be the beginning of a period of endless petitions" (book 1, chapter 2).

And concerning plantation officials, who are vital in technical questions, the best contract is one that provides for the prompt and punctual payment of a salary at the end of the harvest, with some sort of bonus ("*algum mimo*," that is, "some kindness") included. The master should conduct himself in this way with the *feitor-mor* (head superintendent), the *feitor de moenda* (mill superintendent), the *feitor de partido* (superintendent of labor), the *mestre-de-açúcar* (sugar master), the *soto-mestre* (underboss), the *purgador de açúcar* (sugar refiner), and the *caixeiro de engenho* (plantation treasurer), whose salaries, calculated in *mil réis*, receive detailed consideration from the author. All things should be subject to regulation and all affairs should be carried out with exactitude. In the particular case of the *soto-banqueiro* (assistant purser), who worked as the underboss's assistant, his condition as a "mulato ou crioulo escravo da casa" (mulatto or black house slave) means that he should properly be paid in coin, but since his job contributes toward the sugar purification process, Antonil recommends that the plantation owner give him, at the end of the harvest, something extra, *algum mimo*, "so that the hope of receiving this small present renews his desire to work" (chapter 4).

* * *

And how did our Jesuit, Vieira's former secretary, feel about the thorny matter of slavery?

At no point in his long discussion of plantation life does Antonil inquire as to the nature, the origin, or the propriety of slavery in and of itself. Enslavement to him is a de facto condition the merits of which are not worth discussing. Certainly this position is part and parcel of his "objectivity." Slavery exists, and slavery is a useful part of the sugar trade. What else needs to be said of it?

Antonil's calculating ratio does not distract itself with queries that might place it on the uncertain ground of metaphysical speculation. If there is a truly relevant question that should be formulated, it is the following: how should the plantation owner behave toward his slaves so that sugar production is both efficient and profitable?

Prompted by this practical question, which is essentially the question of means, Antonil sets himself to reasoning with his customary efficiency and clarity. Chapter 9 of book 1 provides a general answer to his more particular questions.

The opening of this section is possessed of an unmatched power and precision: Slaves are the plantation owner's hands and feet, because without them it is neither possible to produce, preserve, or increase wealth, nor to keep a mill running. The realist will declare that this is evidence of necessity in its most naked form—hence the statement's ironclad logic. "Need, yes, but whose need?" This will be the reply of the reader who seeks to place ideas within their social context and with reference to the historical actors who generated them. The need in question is that of the plantation owners, of the sugar merchants, of the slave traders, of the colonial bureaucracy, of the finances of the Portuguese state, of England, and of other purchasers of tropical products—in fine, it is the need of the colonial system.

But from what social position does the author of *Cultura e opulência do Brasil* speak? From that of the Church as a universal religious institution? From that of the *Corpus Mysticum*? From the standpoint of the evangelical praxis within which Antonil situated himself as a missionary? In truth, Antonil speaks from none of these positions. Rather, his place of enunciation is the colonial system itself, in which even the Jesuits owned sugar plantations. A notable example is the Count of Santo Amaro's famous Engenho de

Sergipe (Sergipe Sugar Plantation), which served as the Anonymous Tuscan's field of observation, as he affirms at the opening of the work: "And one day I determined to see one of the most notable [sugar plantations] of the Recôncavo, bordering the Bay [of All Saints], known as the count's Sergipe Sugar Plantation. And impelled by a laudable curiosity, I attempted, over the course of the eight to ten days I spent there, to take note of everything that made this plantation so celebrated, and nearly the king of all the royally chartered sugar plantations."

The fruit of direct observation, Antonil's text provides useful advice to those future men of commerce who may wish to employ their capital toward the production of sugar: "Let he who undertakes to administer a sugar plantation make use of these practical observations, written so that he may act correctly, which is the goal toward which men of all occupations should aspire and strive to reach."

This is an instruction manual written by Jesuit plantation owners for other plantation owners, who may or may not be fellow Jesuits.

The landowner's economic project constitutes the central, common zone of encounter for this book. It is in his interest that the author evaluates slaves, distinguishing between slaves who are unskilled or skilled, of *arda*, *mina*, or *congo* extraction, of light or dark skin, and who are submissive or rebellious.

The Jesuit Antonil correlates good treatment given by the master to the slave with the maintenance of proper relations between the two on the plantation. He appears as a sort of industrial psychologist of his era when he declares: "What is certain is that, if the master treats his slaves as a father, giving them the necessary food and clothing, and some rest from their labors, he can then act as a master [when punishing them], and they will not protest, but instead will accept their guilt, and will accept their just and deserved punishment, if it is tempered with mercy."

In other words, to act paternally and benevolently toward a slave amounts to useful kindness, an investment that sooner or later will have positive returns for the plantation owner.

Antonil's pragmatism reveals a certain amount of cleverness when, at the conclusion of the chapter, he insinuates that the best guarantee that the labor force will maintain its numbers through natural means is the granting of generous offerings to black women, who will conceive and give birth to children (these are the new generations of slaves, so valuable to the slave masters) in proportion to the amount of food and drink they receive: "If the masters take care to give some table scraps to their young children, the slaves will serve them with good will and will happily give them new male and female servants. On the contrary, some slave women intentionally try to abort, so that the fruit of their loins does not suffer as they themselves have suffered."

* * *

Does this confluence of the assiduous meeting of one's obligations, hard work, correctness in business, observance of religion, and in all things, a spirit of order and economy not recall the Calvinist ethic that Max Weber, in his memorable study, demonstrated to be aligned with the spirit of capitalism? And moreover, consider the notion that earthly prosperity is the guarantee of an eternal reward, because God helps those who help themselves.

In various passages from the work we find signs, sometimes presented together, sometimes separately, of this well-known ideological syndrome. But Antonil was a Jesuit! Any evidence of a connection between the most radical of the Protestant sects and the most orthodox and Roman of the Catholic orders strikes a discordant note within our classifying mind.

But how can we deny what the two have in common? One is the product of the mercantilist ethos, which was the fruit of the Renaissance, which inspired men as distinct from one another as Calvin and Ignatius of Loyala, and which marked Antonil, the latter-day disciple of the Counter-Reformation, with rationalistic "modernity," which he would not merely preserve but would advance a century and a half after the fact. This is the new religion of immanence, which grants excess value to earthly concerns, which celebrates self-evident, solicitous, and prudent reason, and which defends industry and the rigid organization of time. In short, this religion is one of respect for the *vita activa*.

Antonil is a Jesuit, but he has nothing to do with the Baroque splendors of his order as it operated in Rome, Naples, and Lisbon. His was a classical, bourgeois, and Tuscan intellectual background. His homeland, Lucca, was a commune that of old fed Genoa's maritime trade and always counted prosperous bankers among its most illustrious citizens.

When the Object Becomes Subject and the Subject Becomes Object

To observe agents of production is one the objective practices of traditional economics. Living in Bahia, Antonil was so attracted to the feverish activity of the sugar plantations that he spent days on end interviewing an old master "who has enjoyed notable success in this work for fifty years," along with other officials "to whom I inquired in detail as to their specific roles," so as to collect and present all of this information in a well-ordered book.

The manufacture of "white gold"—things, not men—fascinated Antonil: what moved men to produce it day and night, and the machines whose iron laws they obeyed lest they suffer mutilation or death. This is the universe of

Cultura e opulência do Brasil, the same universe into which the young Marx delved in his analysis of the reification of factory labor.

At the heart of the plantation lie the buildings that house the machines: the buildings for the mill, the oven, and the vats, and the building in which the sugar is refined. These are fed by sugarcane that is planted and harvested, and the sugar that is produced and then sold overseas passes through them. Antonil describes, step by step, the transformation of cane into the sweet and clear crystal that all of Europe learned to consume beginning in the first years of colonization. Cane, sugarcane juice, molasses, sugar: these are stages in a story of metamorphosis whose subject is the thing being produced and whose objects are the enslaved bodies, shadows that move through the plantation, illuminated by the fire of the ovens burning day and night.

The slaves are the hands and feet of the masters. This reductive figure robs them of their integrity as actors. They are passive and impersonal verbal constructs that Antonil arranges in describing the planting of cane: the earth is tilled (who tills it?), is burned (who burns it?), and is cleaned (who cleans it?). The cane should not become moist. Stalks of cane should be planted upright and should be cut down entirely and arranged on the ground, one next to the other, head to foot, and lightly covered with earth. So says the traditional grammar for which in all cases the subject is the earth or the cane. And here the formal reasoning of the grammarian coincides with that of the economist of the mercantile era. Antonil's language grants the external object the attributes of a subject. Meanwhile, the real agent (the slave who tills, burns, cleans, wets, lays down, covers, etc.) is omitted through a perverse play of perspectives for which the trade good is omnipresent and all-powerful even before it reaches the market and precisely because it must make it to market whole, white, and unvarnished.

Antonil likewise fails to give us a complete view of men at harvest time, when they are involved in intense labor in the fields. "When the cane is cut, there are as many as twelve to eighteen scythes in the fields." Scythes are used for cutting. The metonym, with the instrument standing in for the worker, communicates what truly matters to the author: the cane to be cut and not the workers who do the cutting. It is then necessary to count the bundles of cane. This operation entails calculation, but how to undertake it given the "ignorance of the dumb slaves, who do not know how to count"? The answer lies in using one's fingers and hands, with each finger representing ten bundles. Since each hand has five fingers, each hand represents fifty bundles. Two hands represent 100 bundles, and seven hands represent 350 bundles, "and each slave must cut in one day three hundred fifty bundles"—that is, seven hands.

Tied in bundles and transported in ox-pulled carts, the cane is brought to the mill building, to be milled "with the machine they so ingeniously invented." There follows the most minute technical description of the milling process: the machine is made to spin around and around in successive cycles, moving wheels whose spokes interlock, the better to grind the cane and extract the juice, the *caldo*, which will be collected and then boiled.

Near the conclusion of these methodically obsessive pages, in which Antonil seems entranced by the gears that never cease their interlocking movements, we are presented with the fleeting image of a "dumb" black woman who, succumbing to exhaustion or intoxication, "is caught between the gears." The distracted slave may escape, if the companion's hand intervenes with time enough to cut off her hand with a large knife—that is, if the miller has not forgotten to hang it within reach in order to prevent the worst.

The reader who is curious about technological information and procedures in preindustrial Brazil will find pleasure in Antonil's incisive observations. Indeed, Antonil was a talented writer, among the best of the Brazilian colonial era. From the mill's gears we move on to the oven room, with its open mouths bordered with iron and topped with chimneys, "which are like two nostrils through which the fire is inhaled and exhaled." We see the wood piled into the oven, which will burn throughout the night, and the various types of cauldrons, *paróis* (tanks), and *tachos* (pots) made in the coppersmith's shop and placed atop the ovens, in which the sugarcane juice boils and is cleansed of surface scum (*escumas*) (the first layer of which, incidentally, is called *cachaça*), and to which ash (*cinza da decoada*) is added to aid the filtration of the juice and to bring it to boil at the ideal temperature, "so that it becomes molasses." The molasses is poured into molds in preparation for the final step—whitening. It is only at this step that the uncrystallized sugar (the "mel," or honey) is separated from the sugar crystals. Clay—or in this case, clay taken from the wetlands of the Recôncavo—is applied to aid in the refining process. Dark, poorly refined sugar in Portuguese is called *mascavo*, that is, brown sugar. Highly refined white sugar was given the name *branco macho* and was the most sought after and the most costly. Antonil extends his account of the process of sugar production to the final stages of drying and packaging, including information on then-current prices for sugar sent to Lisbon and having arrived at its customs office.

With this list of prices given in denominations of *contos de réis*, Antonil appears to prosaically, objectively draw to a close the principal part of his work, tied to the creation of white gold on the count's Sergipe Plantation. However, on the final page of the book's eleventh chapter, Antonil provides the figure of 2535:142$800 (2,535 *contos* and 142,800 *reis*), and, it will surprise the reader to note, describes the following section of his analysis in pathetic terms as "Sugar's suffering, from its birth as cane to its departure from Brazil."

Watermill. Drawing by Franz Post (1612–1680). "Having reached the mill and having been placed between the gears, what force and suffering are used in taking from them what they have to give!" (Antonil, *Cultura e opulência do Brasil* [Culture and Opulence of Brazil]).

This passage could also be titled "The Birth, Passion, and Death of Sugarcane in Brazil and Portugal." In this closing synthesis, sugarcane, which we have accompanied in its transformation from worked natural resource to trade good, recovers its true status as subject—and as suffering subject, whose Calvary repeats the Passion of Christ, the sacrifice par excellence. What has been a fortuitous holocaust now serves to bring about salvation through the European marketplace, which opens to the colonial economy like the heavens.

The phases of the production process for sugar described on previous pages (and these include cutting the cane into pieces, planting, reaping, bundling, transporting, grinding down, extracting liquid, boiling, pulverizing, cooking, purifying with clay, cutting into sections, packaging, and sending into the lofty realms of international emporia) are reiterated in this finale through an analogical comparison with a living thing—that is, active and humanizing—and that suffers indescribable but necessary tortures, for "it is a singular truth for those who contemplate the natural world that those things that are of the greatest usefulness to human beings are not brought to perfection without first experiencing great suffering."[12]

This account of the torments suffered by the sugarcane—which I prefer to transcribe instead of summarize, given the text's elaborate syntax and specific lexicon—evinces a degree of sadism corresponding to the brutal cruelty to which an archaic capitalism submits both man and nature.

Sugar's Suffering, from Its Birth as Cane to Its Departure from Brazil

> It is a singular truth for those who contemplate the natural world that those things that are of the greatest usefulness to human beings are not brought to perfection without first experiencing great suffering. We see this in Europe in the cases of linens, bread, oil and wine, fruits of the Earth that are so necessary, and which are buried, uprooted, stepped on, rung out, and ground down before reaching their perfection. And we see this all the more in the manufacture of sugar, which from the instant it is planted until the moment it reaches the table and passes between teeth before being buried in the stomach, leads a life of such martyrdom that those who invented the tyrant have nothing to compare with it. For if the land, obeying the Creator's command, gave liberally of sugarcane to sweeten men's palates, these men, wishing to multiply their delight and enjoyment, used their wiles to invent one hundred instruments that could be applied to sugarcane to multiply its torments and suffering.
>
> For this reason, they first cut it into pieces and they planted and buried the pieces in the ground. But having come back to life in nearly miraculous fashion, how much suffering is inflicted upon the stalks of cane by those who watched it spring forth from the ground with new breath and vigor! They are chewed upon by a variety of animals, stomped down by beasts, blown over by the wind and finally beheaded and cut with scythes. The stalks of cane leave the field tied together, and oh, how often are they sold before they even leave! They are brought, as prisoners, by cart or by boat and in sight of others who are children of the same land, like condemned men shackled together, and destined for prison or the place of their supplication. They themselves suffer disorientation and cause terror in so many others. Having reached the mill and having been placed between the gears, what force and suffering are used in taking from them all they have to give! With what disdain are their trampled and mutilated bodies thrown into the ocean! With what lack of compassion are their leftovers mercilessly burned!

The liquid in their veins and the stuff in their bones flow out through all of their holes. They are manhandled and strung up, they are boiled in the cauldrons. To increase their suffering, they are sprinkled with ash. Made into something approaching a mush and put into the troughs, they feed the beasts and the pigs, they leave the *paróis* as foam and are held responsible for the intoxication of drunkards. How many times are they run through by hideous strainers! How many times, after having been strained, are they beaten, and how many times are they passed between receptacles which set their flesh afire! How many times are they burned, and how many times are they momentarily relieved from the fire, only to then suffer new torments! The blows and the penetration multiply, and they are left for dead in the molds, taken in tears to the purification building, though they are innocent of any crime, where their unhappy sweetness is cut and wounded. Here their faces are smeared with earth, and to multiply their humiliation, they are washed by slave women in the clay. Their tears run through the channels placed there to receive them, and the tears are so many that they fill deep tanks. Oh what unprecedented cruelty! Their innocent tears are once again brought to a boil, and distilled in stills. And the more they bewail their fate, the more their faces are smeared with earth and then washed by the slave women. They leave this sort of purgatory or prison as pure as they are innocent. And then, placed on a low balcony, they are given over to another set of women, who cut their feet with long knives, and these women, not content to simply cut them, along with other slave women armed with clubs, roll their feet into little balls. From here they pass on to the final theater of torment, which is another balcony, larger and more elevated than the last, on which people fatigued and bored from working the sugar—that is, from breaking it apart, cutting it up with long knives, removing its feet with clubs, dragging it with wheels, trampling it with the feet of the merciless blacks—sit, the cruelty of so many executioners satiated. And so it is weighed with the greatest exactitude, and then made into balls. But the grave torments it has suffered are countless, and there is no one who can truly comprehend and describe them. I thought that having been reduced to this lamentable state, the sugar would be left alone. But here I observe that, buried in a box, it is ground down by a pestle, and beaten across the face with a club. The coffins are finally nailed shut and branded, and thusly enclosed and branded, it is then quite often sold and sold again, held captive, confiscated, and moved. And while it may free itself from the prison that is the port, it cannot free itself from the torments of the sea, nor of exile, nor of taxes and levies, nor of the fear that it might just as easily be sold to Christians as brought to Algiers by Moors. And despite all of this, it is always sweet and never bitter, and will please the palates of its enemies as they banquet, just as it will return the sick to health and make a great profit for the plantation owners and workers who torment it and the traders who buy it and bring it as an exile to the ports, and even more so, for the Royal Treasury in the form of customs duties.

I recall the initial distinction made in this book between colonization as a project oriented toward the satisfaction of present-day material needs (*colo*: I cultivate, I work) and colonization as the transplantation of a past that is shot through with religious images, symbols, and rites (*cultus*, that is, memory of ancestors).

Antonil's mind is centered on the here-and-now of production and on what will become merchandise. His thinking is ultimately concerned with the action of the colonizer as *colo*. But Johannes Antonius Andreonius was also a priest, an Italian Jesuit who imbibed Catholicism's medieval and Baroque-era waters. His imagination retained the memory of the archetypal story of salvation, which secured redemption through the bloody sacrifice of Calvary and the cross. The Christian tradition provides him with his narrative thread and with images of suffering. *Cultus* lends meaning and depth to *colo*. Without *cultus*, *colo* tends toward pettiness and a pedestrian utilitarianism. Colonization is also the reactivation of an arcane identity's signs given figurative meaning through worship.

And even in this marriage of past and present, of religion and economics, Antonil is the anti-Vieira. The secretary who copied Vieira's writing betrays his spirit. Vieira, as a young and inexperienced preacher, spoke on a Bahia sugar plantation in 1633 to the black men who comprised the membership of the Irmandade do Rosário (Lay Brotherhood of the Rosary). Could this have been the count's Sergipe Plantation? In the sermon he described the operations of the mill and of the ovens with words taken from medieval descriptions of Hell. But Antônio Vieira's subject was not sugarcane. Rather, it was the slave.

After proving with an abundance of citations taken from the Old and New Testaments that blacks are children of the same God who created and redeemed all of humanity, Vieira touches on the point that should have an emotional impact on his listeners—the similarity between the slave on the sugar plantation and the crucified Christ:

> There is no work nor any other way of life in the world which is more similar to Christ's suffering on the cross and passion than yours on one of these plantations . . . on the sugar plantation you imitate the crucified Christ. *Imitatoribus Christi crucifixi*, for you suffer in a way that is quite similar to how the Lord suffered on his cross, and throughout his passion. His cross was made of two beams, and yours on the plantation is made of three. There was no lack of cane there either, for cane entered twice into the story of the Passion, first as the scepter for Christ's ridicule, and second, to

collect his vital fluids. Christ's passion occurred over a sleepless night, and a day without rest, just like your nights and your days. Christ naked, and you naked: Christ without food, and you starving: Christ mistreated in every way, and you mistreated in everything. The shackles, the imprisonment, the whips, the wounds, the insulting names—all of this comprises your imitation, which if it were accompanied by patience, would also constitute martyrdom. All that is lacking in making a whole and perfect imitation is the name of the sugar plantation marked on the cross, but Christ has provided this in exact terms. *Torcular* is the name of your plantation, or your cross, and Christ's cross was called, from the very mouth of Christ, *torcular: Torcular calcari solus*.[13] In terms of the type of work done and the sorts of instruments used, it seems that the Lord could find no case that corresponds more closely to your own. The propriety of and motive for this comparison derives from the fact that the juices of all of humanity were extracted, so to speak, by the instrument of the cross and the activity of the entire passion, just as occurs with other toils.[14]

In the next section Vieira compares the sugar plantation to Hell, and more exactly, to the volcanoes of Etna and Vesuvius, an image Antonil would incidentally borrow without any acknowledgment of his source:

> And what is it in the confusion of this world that more closely resembles Hell than your plantations, especially the larger ones? It was for this reason that the succinct, modest definition of the sugar plantation as a *sweet Hell* was so well received. And truly, anyone who sees those great, always roaring ovens in the darkness of night, and the flames being expelled in great jets from their twin mouths, or nostrils, which the fire uses to breathe, and the Ethiopians, or Cyclopes, bathed in sweat and as black as they are strong, feeding the thick and hard stuff into the fire with the forks they use to stoke the fire, and the cauldrons or boiling pools with the liquid bubbling and bubbling again, here vomiting foam, there exhaling clouds of vapor that are more heat than smoke, and causing them to rain down and exhaling them anew, and the noise of the wheels, the chains, of all of the people whose color is like the night itself, working vigorously, and making everything move at the same time without a moment of relief or rest—those who see the chaotic and noisy machine and apparatus of this Babylon cannot doubt, even if they have seen Etna and Vesuvius, that this is like Hell.[15]

Antonil, describing the ovens, calls them "bocas verdadeiras tragadoras de matos, cárcere de fogo e fumo perpétuo e viva imagem dos vulcões, Vesúvios e Etnas [repare-se o mesmo uso do plural],[16] e quase disse, do Purgatório ou do Inferno" (wood-eating fires, prisons of perpetual fire and smoke and the living image of the volcanoes Vesuvius and Etna and I might almost say, of Purgatory or Hell).

There is, however, a significant difference in the relation the two men establish between fire and the slave. Vieira describes strong, robust men, "Ethiopians," Cyclopes bathed in sweat and working vigorously with the strength of their muscles and the skill of their hands: "feeding the thick and hard stuff into the fire with the forks they use to stoke the fire."

Alongside the ovens, Antonil places syphilitic blacks, "slaves afflicted with flesh-eating disease and liquid discharges, forced by their hard existence to purge with violent sweat the bilious humors that fill their bodies." Aside from their sickliness, Antonil describes the perversion of these prisoners, weighed down by heavy chains and forced to labor because of their "extraordinary wickedness, with little or no hope of making amends."

But how much pity he summons when he contemplates the boiling liquid sugar, with the blacks pocking it with ash! How he laments how its foam serves as a form of recreation for the tippling slaves! At the purification stage, "they [i.e., the sugar] are washed by slave women in the clay," and the black women degrade the sugar by hitting it not once but repeatedly. When the sugar, now white, is removed from the molds, "as pure as it is innocent," other cruel-hearted women cut off its feet with knives. On the balconies, ferocious and vengeful slaves, "people fatigued and bored from working the sugar," cut it up. It is chopped, dragged, and trampled by "the feet of the merciless blacks." If trade goods have enemies, these enemies are the workers who take out their frustrations on them.

What interests Antonil are things that are made and sold. In his discourse, the fetishistic element of the mercantile mind comes to the forefront and appears in a nearly pure state.

The eighteenth century, the beginning of which corresponded to Antonil's life, would be rationalistic and would worship utility as the supreme good. It is not a coincidence that among us it begins with *Cultura e opulência do Brasil por suas drogas e minas* and ends with the proslavery works of a bishop opposed to the Jesuit tradition, the wealthy plantation owner José Joaquim da Cunha d'Azeredo Coutinho, who on his plantation, Campos dos Goitacás, would witness the crisis of the sugar plantation that had been ongoing since Antonil's time. From the first to the second, in the span of a century, all but the echoes of Vieira's missionary clamor and his own universalistic ideals, which would inform the notion of the Natural Law of Peoples, were erased.

That dream of salvation and ecumenism, which sought not merely the arms but the souls of the newly discovered people, seems to have been erased for all time in the work of our first economist, who was moved only by the tears of trade goods.

Rome, 1986—São Paulo, 1989

6   A Sacrificial Myth
Alencar's Indianism

It is characteristic of the historical imagination that it creates myths that are often more illustrative of the times in which they were created than they are of the remote universe they were invented to explain.

Accepting this proposition, I will take on the somewhat risky task of revisiting a commonplace of comparative literature scholars, who interpret Brazilian *indianismo* (Indianism) with reference to European Romanticism's exploration of national origins. There, in Europe, we have medieval figures and scenes, whereas here in Brazil we see an indigenous world just as it first appeared to the surprised discoverers. Both here and there we see a movement of return, an effort to meet Michelet's objective of making the past live again, which was the declared goal of Romantic historiography. To what extent is this parallelism defensible?

The approximation of the two visions of the past remains valid within the broad sphere pertaining to the history of worldviews. There was, in point of fact, a nostalgic strain, a loyalty to the ancien régime, which was late in appearing but was by no means less intense than earlier manifestations, within European letters during the post- and antirevolutionary periods. Works by Chateaubriand, Xavier de Maistre, and Sir Walter Scott provide vigorous examples of this worldview at the levels of imagination and style.

In the Brazilian case, one of the principal strains of our Romanticism, which corresponds to the work of José de Alencar, likewise demonstrated its distrust of any sort of social change, and apparently liquidated its feelings of rebellion against the colonial yoke during the political upheaval of national independence. Having moved beyond this historical moment, any sort of measure that threatened to enlarge the quite narrow sphere of liberty conceded by the Constitution of 1824 was seen as subversive.[1] As such, electoral reform and the *questão servil* (literally, "servile question") were blocked, beginning in 1837 with the victory of the Regresso, or "Regression" (the term was coined and enthusiastically adopted by the conservatives), and lasting until the ascent of the liberals in the 1860s. It was precisely the three-decade period that fell between these two moments that saw the rise and peak of Romantic literature in Brazil.

One observes during this period a sort of hardening of the liberal and radical position, which led to Emperor Pedro I's abdication and the tumultuous events of the regency. This phenomenon, which has already been explained in light of the slaveholders' consolidation of power, was not entirely divorced from paradox, as we see in the case of the quite Rousseauian figure of the *bon sauvage*, which became a feature of the most conservative aspects of our collective imagination. A giant by his very nature, the Amerindian entered in extremis into the literary society of the Second Empire.

Let us travel some distance back in time. The process of independence, as it came into being, generated a dialectic of opposition. Even if we accept that society's dominant strata was occupied by the architects and beneficiaries of the *patria del criollo*,[2] we must admit that contradictions were present, both in terms of the material interests repressed by the old monopolies and the delicate weave of symbolic life. This was a time of acute tension between a colony that was emancipating itself and a metropolis that was stiffening itself in order to defend an aging empire. The first quarter of the nineteenth century was a period of rupture throughout Latin America. The distinctions between *nation* and *colony* and *new* and *old* required, in terms of the molding of identities, the articulation of an axis that would divide, on the one side, the pole of Brazil, which was finally raising its head and declaring itself, and on the other, the pole of Portugal, which was hesitant to lose its greatest conquest.

According to this scheme of oppositions, it would have been logical that the Amerindian occupied, within the postcolonial imagination, the role that properly fell to him—that of rebel. He was, in the end, the native par excellence in confrontation with the invader. He was the American, as Amerindians were called in metonymic fashion, in confrontation with the European.

But this is not precisely what occurred in the most significant examples of our Romantic fiction. Alencar's Amerindian enters into intimate communion with the colonizer. Peri is, literally and voluntarily, Ceci's slave, and he venerates her as his *Iara*, or "lady," and is the ever-faithful vassal of Dom Antonio. At the close of the novel, and faced with imminent catastrophe, the nobleman baptizes the Amerindian, giving him a proper name, the concession of which Dom Antonio considered a necessary precondition for this savage to enjoy the honor of saving his daughter from the certain death to which the Aimorés had condemned the inhabitants of the estate:

> "If only you were a Christian, Peri!"
> The Indian was strongly affected by these words.
> "Why?" he asked.
> "Why?" the nobleman replied slowly. "Because if you were a Christian, I would entrust my Cecília's salvation to you, and I am convinced that you would take her to my sister in Rio de Janeiro."
> The savage's face lit up. His chest puffed up with happiness, and his trembling lips could hardly express the storm of words that came from the depths of his soul.
> "Peri wants to be a Christian!" he exclaimed.
> Dom Antônio gave him a tearful look of recognition.
> . . .
> The Indian fell to his knees before the old gentleman, who placed his hands upon Peri's head.
> "Then you are a Christian! I give you my name."
> (*O guarani*, part 4, chapter 10)

Conversion accompanied by a change of name also befalls the Amerindian Poti, from *Iracema*, who is baptized Antônio Felipe Camarão and would become the hero of the local resistance to the Dutch. And Arnaldo, who is Peri's rustic counterpart in *O sertanejo* (The Man of the Backlands), is given the last name of the captain-general during this edifying exchange:

> "And what do you want for yourself, Arnaldo?" insisted Campelo.
> "That you, Captain-General, sir, would let me kiss your hand. That would be enough."
> "You are a man, and from this day forward I would like for you to call yourself Arnaldo Louredo Campelo."
> (*O sertanejo*, part 2, chapter 21)

In these three episodes, it is the colonial master who, through the act of renaming, grants a new religious and personal identity to the Amerindian or man of the backlands.

As for the Aimorés, who appear as the true enemies of the conqueror in *O guarani* (The Guarani Indian), they are described using epithets such as *bárbaros* (barbarous), *horrendos* (horrendous), *satânicos* (satanic), *carniceiros* (bloody), *sinistros* (sinister), *horríveis* (horrible), *sedentos de vingança* (vengeful), *ferozes* (ferocious), and *diabólicos* (diabolical).

Iracema, in the beautiful prose poem that bears her name, falls in love with the colonizer of Ceará, Martim Soares Moreno, for whose love she breaks with her fellow Tabajaras after revealing the secret of how to concoct a hallucinogenic drink made from the Jurema tree.

In the stories of both Peri and Iracema, the Amerindian unconditionally gives him or herself over body and soul to the white man or woman, an act that implies the Amerindian's sacrifice and abandonment of his or her tribal identification. This is a departure without a return. Machado de Assis said the following of Iracema, the virgin of honeyed lips, in an article written shortly after the novel's publication: "She does not resist or ask questions: at the moment she and Martim exchanged glances, she bowed her head to that sweet slavery."[3]

The savage accepts the possibility of suffering and death without hesitation, as if the feeling of devotion displayed toward the white man or woman represented the fulfillment of a destiny, which Alencar presents in heroic or idyllic terms.

I believe that we can detect a sacrificial complex in Alencar's Romantic mythology. Compare the endings of the two colonial and *indianista* novels with the fates of Carolina, the courtesan from *As asas de um anjo* (The Wings of an Angel), who is redeemed and punished in *A expiação* (The Expiation), of Lucíola, from the novel of the same name, and of Joana, from *Mãe* (Mother). These are all works in which the narrative or dramatic plot is resolved through the voluntary immolation of the protagonist, whether an Amerindian man or woman, a female prostitute, or a black mother. Nobility is only achieved for the weak person through the sacrifice of his or her life.

Paradoxically, *O guarani* and *Iracema* are foundational national novels.

In making these observations, I do not wish to call into question Alencar's sincere patriotism, a feeling that, incidentally, does not bear in any way on the aesthetic value of his texts. What we must do is determine how the figure of the beautiful, strong, and free Amerindian was constructed in conjunction with a frank defense of the colonizer. This alignment, which Alencar presents as spontaneous, stands in open violation of the historical truth of the first century of the Portuguese occupation of Brazil (one need only read the chronicles of the majority of the captaincies to learn what took place) and is frankly unbelievable in the case of Peri. Ultimately, Alencar's is a highly ideological interpretation of the colonial process. However, none of this prevents his narrative language from, on more than one occasion, sounding the notes of poetry.

The beauty of Alencar's lyrical prose reverberates within—or in another way, beyond—the representation of the empirical data that the chronicler, inclined toward realism, seeks to convey. And myth, which is woven into this prose, is made both within and beyond the prison of believable narrative.

In terms of "within": myth neither requires proof of verification nor does it make use of the testimonial evidence that sustains historiographical discourse. And in terms of "beyond": the aesthetic value of a mythological text does not respect either the boundaries of the factual or the proper dimensions of the situation it evokes. Myth, like ancient poetry, is first-degree knowledge and is preconceptual, at the same time as it gives expressive form to a desire that wants prior to reflecting.

In the narrative web of *O guarani*, conservative thinking, *indianista* myth, and Romantic metaphor are tightly bound together. In attempting to untie this knot, the critical reader should take care not to confuse the analysis of the author's values, which is a task that falls to historians of ideology, with reflection on the novel's most creative literary features.

Myth is a mediating element, a head with two faces. For the face that looks toward history, myth reflects real contradictions, and in reflecting them converts and resolves them into figures that themselves counterbalance the *concidentia oppositorum*. In this way, Alencarian myth brings together, in the shared image of the hero, the *colonizer*, who is understood as a generous feudal lord, and the *colonized*, who is simultaneously viewed as a faithful feudal subordinate and a noble savage. For the other face, which contemplates literary invention, myth conveys signs produced through an analogical semantics, that is, a figural process, novelistic expression, a poetic image. To the extent that myth achieves this properly aesthetic quality, it resists being integrated into this or that ideology.

These observations attempt, in literary texts in which mythopoetic expressions guide the development of narrative, to differentiate recognition of a text's ideological situation from judgment of its literary value.

But, having made the proper qualifications, which the nature of poetry requires, the interpreter's eye continues to seek out the narrator's point of view. It is here that the culture of a particular context touches on or achieves its state of crystallization, and it is here that values that are peculiar to this or that social class flow or stagnate.

In his representation of colonial society during the sixteenth and seventeenth centuries, Alencar treats the poles of native and invader in an antidialectical fashion that neutralizes the real oppositions that existed between them. In *O guarani*, the mythical return to savage life is permeated by the author's recourse to an imaginary Other. This author's Indianism is not a universe unto itself, existing in parallel to Europe's medieval fantasies, but rather it joins itself to these fantasies. Geometry teaches us that two parallel lines never converge, but here we are not speaking in geometrical terms.

Alencar's understanding of the colonizing process prevents the values he romantically attributes to our Indians—heroism, beauty, naturalness—from shining in and for themselves. Rather, they are arranged as a constellation, pulled by the magnetic force of the conqueror, who is possessed of the power to attract them to him and to incorporate them into himself. I know of no other nation that has formed itself out of the old colonial system in which nativism has, for good and for ill, lost so much of its identity and internal consistency. Augusto Meyer, in a superb study dedicated to Alencar, argued that all of this remits to the concept of Brazilian tenuousness in explaining this and other singular divergences of our culture during the Romantic period.[4]

Suspecting, however, that this ambiguous nativism, because of how it was constructed, could not retain a consistent appearance, I looked for the exception, the rare exception, and finally found it in a short passage, in an ethnographic note concerning the legend of Ubirajara. This was the final work in which Alencar took up the indigenous theme. It consists of a poetic rendering of indigenous life in the time before the discovery. The note suggests a reading of Portuguese colonization as an act of violence. Defending the Tupis from the label of traitors given to them by certain chroniclers, Alencar argues as follows: "It was with colonization that the Portuguese, assaulting them as one would wild animals, and hunting them at the point of a dog's tooth, taught them about betrayal, of which they were heretofore ignorant."

It is true that this cutting judgment, arriving late, does not apply retroactively and cannot alter the Luso-Tupi symbiosis that Alencar had so solidly built up in his colonial novels, in which the native's destiny was understood as one of spontaneous and sublime sacrifice. But Alencar's vehement tone ("assaulting them as one would wild animals, and hunting them at the point of a dog's tooth" recalls the language of missionaries railing against colonists and *bandeirantes*) becomes more comprehensible if we view it in light of the bitter literary polemics in which the author was embroiled during the final, dark years of his life. Portuguese critics and intolerant commentators accused him of creating a false savage, and worse yet, of writing in a language that was full of "Americanisms" and that had strayed from the mother tongue. The irritated and nationalistic qualities of Alencar's rebuttal can be seen in the long preface he wrote for one of his final novels, *Sonhos d'ouro* (Dreams of Gold), which was published in 1872. The text is an interesting document of patriotic Brazilian cultural politics *post festum*.

It is instructive to contrast Alencar's fiction and the Americanist poetry of Gonçalves Dias, who precedes Alencar by a generation.

In the Maranhão poet's *Primeiros cantos* (First Songs), an awareness shines through of the terrible destiny that awaited the Tupi tribes once the European

Dom Antônio de Mariz's home. Set from the opera *Il Guarani* by Carlos Gomes, performed at the Teatro Alla Scala in Milan, 1870.

Ceci's room. Set from the opera *Il Guarani*.

Drawing of Ceci.

Drawing of Peri.

conquest got underway. The poet describes the conflict of civilizations in terms of tragedy. Powerful poems like *O canto do piaga* (Piaga's Song) and *Deprecação* (Supplication) are signs of the massacre that decimated the savages not long after the white men disembarked from their caravels.

The tone of these poems, which lies somewhere between shock and solemnity, recalls the prophecies told by the Aztec priests to their people in the years prior to the Spanish invasion. These are the voices of people destined to succumb, whether through iron or fire, and the means by which they might hope to survive the slaughter are so incomprehensible to the victims that only mysterious, visionary, prophetic words could be used to describe them.

The gods speak though the intervention of the shaman, the entranced "divine *piaga*." Or more precisely, it is a specter who sees the world in reverse who speaks. He sees the darkening sun, the owl hooting during the day, the treetops swaying with no wind, and the moon burning with fire and blood.

> Have you not seen in the sky, a dark cloud
> Blot out the whole face of the sun;
> Have you not heard, during the day,
> The owl's bitter shrieks?
>
> Have you not seen the forest canopy
> Windless, bending and swaying,
> Nor the moon rise, aflame, among clouds
> As if dressed in blood?

In *Visión de los vencidos*, Miguel León-Portilla transcribes prophecies that were first written down in Nahuatl by students of the missionary Bernardino de Sahagún and that were only made available in Spanish during the mid-twentieth century, thanks to the erudition of Ángel María Garibay.[5]

What impresses us in these Mesoamerican songs is their obsession with a fire that engulfs the pyramids and columns and blots out the noonday sun, and the agitation of the lagoon that moves under its own power, "without any breeze" and "windless," an image that recalls the Brazilian poem. In both the words of the Tupi shaman and in the Aztec prophecies monstrous figures emerge from the sea to exterminate a powerless people: "The spirits have escaped from the village / oh, what disgrace! oh, what ruin! oh, Tupã!"

Since it is entirely improbable that there was any direct relationship between the (at that time) ignored Nahuatl manuscripts and our great Romantic poet's American poems, we must then consider the broad affinities of theme and imagery that are opened by an initial comparative reading of the two.

The young Gonçalves Dias retained a relative temporal and geographic proximity to the most exaggerated forms of Latin American nativism. Perhaps the Maranhão poet's familiarity with the struggle between Brazilians and *marinheiros* (sailors), which affected the northern provinces at the time of independence, explains the violent and overawed aura that surrounds these verses, which he wrote as a very young man. In contrast, in Alencar the image of conflict was cast backward toward a remote past through a conscious process of attenuation and sublimation. Gonçalves Dias was born under the sign of the local anti-Portuguese tensions that ran from 1822 through the Balaios revolt. Alencar came of age during the period that ran from the precocious declaration of Pedro II's majority (which his father effectively helped bring about) through the period of conciliation between political parties during the 1850s. The nationalist feelings of both men, though apparently one and the same, deserve a contrastive analysis, since they were the products of distinct political circumstances.

The search for the possible source of our particular Romantic nativism doubtless helps us understand the opposed ways in which the fates of the conquered populations were treated in literature. Respective schemes for how this would be represented were developed in conjunction with the ideological element, which benefitted from an appreciable degree of poetic freedom. The poetic did not suppress the ideological but rather overcame (that is, preserved) it.

I believe that the figures of immanent disaster that we find in the young Gonçalves Dias find their model in the Revelation of John. It is in the closing book of the New Testament that we find images of the blackened daytime sun and the blood-colored moon.[6] This book would provide the basis for the signs attributed to great catastrophes in eschatological discourses articulated throughout the history of Christianity. It stands to reason that this educated Brazilian poet, even speaking through the mouth of a shaman, would draw on biblical imagery in announcing the end of the world. In parallel, the Aztec priests announced their own imminent extermination by narrating events prior to the arrival of the invaders. The affinities in figuration that result from a side-by-side reading of Gonçalves Dias's poems and the Mesoamerican prophecies speak to a shared sense of terror articulated through a broad, transcultural web of apocalyptic signs used to announce a cataclysm that would be both social and cosmic. The end of a people is described as the end of the world.

The poet maintained this tragic vision of the conquest in his final verses. In the last poem he dedicated to the theme of the savage, the unfinished epic *Os Timbiras* (The Timbiras), he returns to the shaman's predictions, though he now laments the fate of America, *América infeliz* (ill-fated America), its nature profaned and its people conquered:

Let he who boasts
Of a hundred-year extermination call it progress;
I, a humble singer of an *extinct* people

> Will weep, my tears filling the enormous graves
> That range from the ocean to the Andes, and from the River Plate
> to the broad and sweet Amazonian sea.

The product of this encounter was a nation

> which has at its base
> The cold bones of its mother nation
> And for cement, the profaned ashes
> Of the dead, ground underfoot by slaves.

The Portuguese colonizer appears as a *velho tutor e avaro* (greedy old teacher), desirous of the beauty of America, its pupil. The signs that describe the convulsion of the elements return, though they are now understood as damage caused by the white invader's firearms:

> The battle raged,
> The fiery sea burned at midnight,
> A thick cloud of smoke
> Blotted out the stars and sky; and the sea and mountains
> Awoke roaring with the thunderous sounds
> Of the never before witnessed clash!
>   (Canto III)

In direct opposition to Dias's *Primeiros cantos* and *Os Timbiras*, the Alencarian historical novel looked back not to the destruction of the Tupi tribes but to the ideal construction of a new nationality, the Brazil that would emerge from the colonial context—hence the attention that must be paid to the means by which the narrator arranged asymmetrical forces in the context of his first novelist synthesis. My hypothesis is that Alencar married the sacrificial myth, which is latent in his vision of the conquered, with his feudal interpretation of our history. Within a context marked by the relationship between master and servant, in which the dominion of the first and the dedication of the second are connatural phenomena, the characters in *O guarani* and the *doce escravidão* (sweet slavery) that Machado de Assis saw in *Iracema* take on a logic of their own.

In the paragraphs that follow I will attempt to test the correctness and the limits of this hypothesis in the context of the novel. In so doing, I will revisit a text that I prepared for an edited volume on the Romantic movement.[7]

A Castle in the Tropics?

The picture of a colonial Brazil created in the image and likeness of a European feudal community appears in a nearly pure state in Alencar's *O guarani*.

But Alencar's intuition as a novelist outran his prejudices as an interpreter of our history, and this almost created gaps in the body of the novel that were so wide that Dom Antônio de Mariz's castle would be reduced to ruins before the narrative reached its conclusion. Let us begin, then, with its construction.

The opening pages of *O guarani* describe the landscape that surrounds the Mariz manor house. This is a haughty landscape whose features are defined by a hierarchical relationship between master and servant. Toward the Paraíba do Sul River, which stretches majestically across its vast bed, flows the Paquequer, "a vassal and tributary that, prideful and domineering against the rocks, humbly bows down at the feet of its ruler . . . a submissive slave, who suffers its master's whip."

The European process of domination will come to define the features of nature, sketching gothic and classical forms onto the forest and channeling the river through green arcades and capitals formed by palm fronds.

How can man be placed within such a grand and pompous setting? Alencar would oscillate between a savage, presocial Romanticism that defined man as a humble accomplice of the elements' majestic dramas and a more coherent and assiduous historical perspective that placed Brazilian nature in the service of the noble conqueror. The nobleman's manor house is solidly grounded in a landscape that protects it on all sides, and if its walls are not built by human hands, this is because they are formed of rock cut with a pike. The eminence of the rock and the surrounding abyss grant Dom Antônio's manor house the security of a medieval castle: "In this way, the home was a true Portuguese nobleman's manor house, without the battlements and the barbican, which had been replaced by a wall of insurmountable rock, which offered a natural, unassailable defense . . . between the trunks of the trees, a high fence of thorn bushes ran, which rendered the small valley impenetrable."

Here the manor house's impenetrable, closed defense is entirely dependent on the union of natural elements with the sphere occupied by the small community, which reproduces in the tropics the model of medieval life. In its transposition, the nucleus of this reproduced European patriarchal complex reappears in sharper and purer form. The imposing, solemn qualities of the castle are reduced in size and spill over into the *casa-grande* (big house), "built in the same simple and rough style as our primitive dwellings of today. In the front there were five windows, low, wide, almost square in shape."

Simplicity, roughness, the square-shaped windows do not give way, on entering the manor house, to a new, rustic way of life. Let us open the heavy jacaranda door and see the inside of the house: "it gave off a certain air of luxury that would seem impossible for that time and in the wilderness, which was what that land was at the time." The walls are simply whitewashed, but the decoration is heraldic, with coats of arms, shields, and helmets depicted in silver above the door, and embroidered into a long, red damask drapery.

A severe, even melancholy taste pervades a style of decoration that would become colonial-Romantic kitsch, which in this case includes high-backed leather chairs in the dining room, and in the alcove, exotic objects, a gypsy guitar, a stuffed gray heron holding in its beak a blue taffeta curtain, and "a collection of curious rocks in pleasing colors and strange shapes." Our first Romantic historical novel constructs its descriptions from heraldic blocks and residue of the tropical forest.

Individuals who take from the feudal holding or the forest their principal defining characteristics move within this environment and the scene painted from it. The principle that defines the characters' interactions is that nature is subordinated to the noble community, such that the original nobility of the former is confirmed by the inherent worth of the latter. Violation of the pact between feudal community and the primitive environment is the only potential source of tension capable of generating conflict in the world of the novel.

Dom Antônio de Mariz, one of the founders of the city of Rio de Janeiro, who had sworn loyalty to the Portuguese crown "before the altar of nature," appears as the agent behind this connection: the conquest of the American land inaugurates a way of life in which the violence of dominion is redeemed by the courage displayed in the initial struggles against the forest, Indians, and pirates. In the case of Dom Antônio, as for Cecília, his favored daughter, the colonial-Romantic synthesis is thorough: both greatly admire Peri and both respect the savages, while Dona Lauriana and their son, Diogo, who represent the high nobility, look disdainfully upon the *bugre* (wild Indian). This attitude will have destabilizing and even fatal consequences in the novel. This internal distinction is the lynchpin of Alencar's simultaneously conservative and nativist ideology: dominion over the land, a right won by the conquering nobility, should recognize in the Indians the natural virtues of pride and nobility that are common to the Portuguese and aborigines alike. In this way, the violation of the second group by the first, which characterized the first contacts between the groups, seems to give way to an honor pact between equals. For this reason, when the young Dom Diogo de Mariz inadvertently kills an Indian woman in the forest, his father severely reprimands him, because killing a woman is "an action unworthy of the name I gave to you."

This offense would not go unpunished: the vengeance of the Aimorés would be one of the causes of the events at the conclusion of *O guarani*. As is well known, honor was the cornerstone of interpersonal relations during the prebourgeois period. It demands all manner of sacrifices, not excluding the sacrifice of one's life, but it also incorporates within it the inevitability of vengeance, as long as vengeance is not taken for any small slight. The aristocratic eye can discern, a priori, which men are capable of naturally living honorable lives and which are villains, of which one may expect ignoble actions. What distinguishes Alencar's Indianism is its inclusion of the savage within the sphere of nobility, in which one sees feelings of absolute devotion (of Peri for Ceci) and also of unrestricted hatred (of the Aimorés for the white residents of Dom Antônio's manor house).

This system, with its expectations of honor, does not simply reproduce the model of coexistence between European noblemen, because these are not relations between equals. He who imposed this model seeks to subject the other, to bring him into his sphere of domination. But because this fact is, generally speaking, implied, what appears most immediately are the relations of the nobleman and savage in terms of their possession of properly feudal virtues: courage and pride, abnegation and loyalty.

These premises are not exhausted in the formation of types. Not being inert, we can see them in action throughout the narrative. It is difficult to count the number of times, from the first to the final chapter, in which Peri's audacity and devotion save the Mariz family from a certain and horrible death. These qualities are also on display in the heroic actions of Dom Antônio and Dom Álvaro de Sá, "who from the former had inherited all of the principles of the old knightly loyalty of the fifteenth century, which the old nobleman preserved as his ancestors' greatest gift."

Peri is, at the same time, just as noble as the most illustrious Portuguese nobles who fought at Aljubarrota with the Mestre de Aviz, the warrior-king, and is the spontaneous servant of Cecília, whom he calls Uiára, that is, lady. Similarly, Iracema, in the novel of the same name, becomes the bride of Martim Soares Moreno, but here the relationship between the sexes is less important than that defined by domination. The Amerindian woman is not the conqueror's lady but rather his servant, and she will die for him.

If the Mariz manor house were in reality what Alencar intended it to be—that is, a castle in the tropics—then the Aimorés' vengeance would be sufficient to provoke within the system the imbalance that would lead to catastrophe. But this predictable element is not the only one present in the plot. As early as the first chapter, the reader is informed that "the rear of the house, which was entirely separated from the rest of the dwelling by a fence, consisted of two large storehouses or servants' quarters, which was where adventurers and protected men lived." And what are these *acostados* (protected men) doing alongside Dom Antônio? It is first stated that they simply receive shelter and protection from him, but it is shortly revealed that they receive this in exchange for granting the nobleman the right to half of the gold they find in their exploratory voyages to the interior. This pact with mercenaries causes a new reality to enter into the novel: profit, money. These are foreign to the feudal value system. This breach, if carefully considered, would have taught

Alencar that the colony could not repeat the Middle Ages and was an open society, one that maintained frequent interactions with the world: "When it came time to sell the goods, which always took place before the departure of the armada for Lisbon, one half of the band of adventurers would go to the city of Rio de Janeiro, calculate their profits, trade for those things that they needed, and settle accounts upon their return. One part of the profits went to the nobleman, as the boss. The other half was evenly distributed between the forty adventurers, who received their share in coin or in goods."

This model of community functions, however, in greater accordance with the Romantic spirit than the social structure to which it is vigorously attached. "This small community of men, governing themselves with their laws, habits, and customs, lived in this way, almost in the middle of the wilderness, unknown and ignored."

In truth, the habits and customs of the mercenary cannot be the same as those of the lord: the shared values that connect the nobleman and Indian do not run between them. By making a pact with a man such as Loredano, Dom Antônio allowed greed, and along with it, lust and betrayal, to enter into his hieratic realm.

Loredano, the son of a fisherman who has left behind the lagoons of Venice, will set traps more fatal than those of the Aimorés. What drives this villain is not wounded honor but *auri sacra fames* and the obscene desire to possess Cecília and make her a *barregã de aventureiro* (adventurer's concubine). A good number of the incidents that define *O guarani* as a serialized novel, full of temporal zigzags, result from this disruptive element, which in the shadows plots the ruin and abjection of the Mariz family. Seen as a whole, however, the mercenaries' actions lead to novelistic action (the threat of evil is given lively, colorful form in a sacrilegious friar) rather than cause a substantial change in the system. The system may be ruined materially, but its most cherished values will endure. Dom Antônio and his family do not flee. They resist heroically, and at the climactic moment, they cause the manor house to explode, hitting the Aimorés in the process. Cecília flees, under the protection of Peri, whom a last-minute baptism has made worthy of saving his lady. The mercenaries are important in creating intrigue, in generating suspense, and as evidence of an adventurous Brazil (neither stable nor feudal) that—with gold, silver, and the legendary mines of Robério Dias—beckoned. But in the overall economy of the work, their principal significance is as the filter that, in the contrast between dark and light, between Cecília's purity and Álvaro de Sá's corruption, between Peri's savage nobility and Dom Antônio de Mariz's innate generosity, reveals.

The final pages describe Cecília and Peri's escape through the forest and down the river. Here the historical limits are annulled, the movements of life in society are undone, and the narration returns to the historical novel's arcane source: legend. We have man and nature, and between the two of them, a more natural humanity—woman. The man must free the woman from death through the mediation of a sheltering nature. It is only at its conclusion, in which life returns to the saving forest, that the novel achieves its ambition to create a closed, natural community. It is as if the chronicler, a reader of Walter Scott, has placed history between parentheses and immersed himself in a timeless landscape. The past, the proper material of the chronicle, quickly loses all of its weight: "She herself could not have explained the emotions she felt. Her innocent and ignorant soul was illuminated by a sudden revelation. New horizons opened to the chaste dreams of her thought. *Returning to the past, she wondered at her life, as eyes are blinded by the light after a deep sleep.* She did not recognize herself in the image of what she once was, a carefree and naïve girl."

In the solitude of the forest, in the canoe that slides across the smooth water of the Paraíba River, the narrative sinuously takes on the form of an idyll. The fundamental relationship between man and woman, in this moment of openness to nature, obscures the issues of race and status that would be constants throughout history:

> Among civilized men, [Peri] was an ignorant Indian, born of a barbarous race repelled by civilization and marked for captivity. While for Cecília and Dom Antônio he was a friend, he was only a slave.
>
> Here, however, all distinctions disappeared. The son of the forests, in returning to his mother's breast, recovered his freedom. He was the king of the wilderness, the lord of the forests, and he ruled by the right of his strength and courage.

For Cecília, the presence of this man, made new and whole and in his natural state, takes on an air of revelation: "Another feeling, still confused, would perhaps mark the completion of the woman's mysterious transformation."

The dialogue between the lady and her slave gives way to confiding and direct conversations between sister and brother, which barely repress other, more ardent feelings. And new situations inspire Peri to tell stories in the form of myths. The first is an amorous allegory, though this is sublimated in the Indian's telling of it:

> "Listen," he said. "The elders of the tribe were told by their parents that a man's soul, when it leaves his body, takes shelter in a flower, and it stays there until a bird from the sky finds it and takes it far away. This is why you see the *guanumbi* moving from flower to flower, kissing one and kissing another, and then flapping its wings and flying away.

"Peri's soul is not in his body. He has left it in this flower. You are not alone."

The savage's fantasy responds to Alencar's declared project of advancing a poetics of romantic love: "What girl does not consult the oracle of a daisy, or see in a black butterfly the fatal Sybil that announces the end of her most beautiful hope? Like humanity in its infancy, the heart during its first years has its own mythology, a mythology more beautiful and poetic than the creations of Greece. Love is its Olympus, populated by goddesses and gods of a celestial and immortal beauty."

The novel's final scene is an epiphany of the great myth of the flood and presents this primitive event in order to again reveal its exemplary function. The cataclysmic rains, the death of all of mankind, the floating palm tree, and the salvation of Tamandaré and his woman are all repeated in the closing episode of *O guarani*.[8] At the hour of supreme danger, the saving power comes from on high: God spoke during the night to Tamandaré, and during the day Tamandaré taught what he had learned at night to the tribe. In the novel, the power comes from within the hero. Peri is inspired by his devotion to Cecília.

From the point of view of the novel's structure, the narration of the new flood plays a decisive role—it allows for a gesture of love and moves the tale into an indeterminate space, just like the myth of rebirth: "The palm tree swept along by the flood was carried away. . . . And it disappeared into the horizon." Alencar's oscillation, which I proposed at the beginning of this chapter between his historical perspective and a savage, presocial Romanticism, is ultimately resolved in favor of the latter. The primitive in its natural state is more remote and purer, and therefore more romantic, than the simple evocation of earlier times.

7 Slavery between Two Liberalisms

It was freedom to destroy freedom.
—W. E. B. Du Bois

Gentlemen, if this were a crime, it would be a crime throughout Brazil; but I sustain that when in a nation all of the political parties hold power, when all of its politicians have been called upon to exercise it, and all conduct themselves in the same way, then it is necessary that this conduct be supported by very strong arguments; it is impossible that it would be a crime, and it would be risky to call it an error.
—Eusébio de Queirós, speech to the Chamber
  of Deputies in 1852

One of Marxist theory's achievements was its discovery that ideologies and symbolic expressions in general are formed within social and cultural practices, which are deeply rooted temporally and spatially.

The thematic nucleus of *The German Ideology*, which Marx and Engels wrote in 1846, describes the intimate relationship that a society's representations maintain with its effective reality. Practices, understood in the broadest sense of the term, are the ferment of ideas to the degree that these seek to rationalize diffuse aspirations in their producers and propagators. Ideology gives rhetorical form (that is, in persuasive registers) to certain particular motives and presents them as general needs. In its discourses, interest and will express themselves or betray themselves in the form of an abstract principle or some overarching rationale.

Twentieth-century historical criticism inherited this skeptical perspective.

Andrade Figueira, a proslavery deputy, made the following statement while combating the proposed Lei do Ventre Livre (Law of the Free Womb) in the Chamber: "Today it is the voice of the general interests, of agriculture and commerce, against the push abolitionist propaganda seeks to give to the emancipation of slavery in Brazil. This is a matter of preserving those living forces that exist in the country and are solely responsible for its wealth. It is a question of *damno vitando*."[1]

In order to understand the connection of liberal ideology with the practice of slavery, we must reflect on the modes of thought that prevailed in the class of Brazilian politicians that came to power during the years of independence and that worked toward the consolidation of the new empire between approximately 1831 and 1860.

What was at work throughout this period, during which Brazil was establishing itself as an autonomous state, was an ideology that was at bottom conservative—and specifically, a system of legal-political norms that sought to defend property rights over land and slaves to the greatest extent possible.

It is not the objective of these paragraphs to once again paint a historical portrait of the agro-export system that characterized Brazilian society during the nineteenth century. Noteworthy works, with a great deal of data and textual support, have already been written on this topic. The reader's familiarity with these texts is assumed, with the diversity of theoretical positions that shape these works serving as a stimulus rather than an impediment.[2]

The objective of this essay is to trace what was, in effect, the ideological profile of the slaveholding regime beginning at the moment in which Brazil was incorporated into the free market.

A False Impasse: Slavery or Liberalism

In the Brazilian case at least, the pairing of slavery and liberalism, which is formally dissonant, was merely a verbal paradox. Together they only constitute a real contradiction if the second term, *liberalism*, is granted real, concrete substance and if it is equivalent to the bourgeois ideology of free labor, which was upheld throughout the Industrial Revolution in Europe.

Now then, this active and developed liberalism simply did not exist as a dominant ideology during the period that began with Brazil's independence and continued into the Second Empire.

This antinomy, so often observed, and the air of nonsense that follows from it (how could a liberalism exist that was dependent upon slavery?) deserve a rigorous analysis aimed at undoing them.

In order to understand the character of the victorious ideology at the center of decision making in postcolonial Brazil, we must examine its internal evolution, which corresponds to the ascent of slaveholding groups. The conservative nucleus, formed from the crises of the regency, defined itself in the voices of its leaders, Bernardo Pereira de Vasconcelos, Araújo Lima, and Honório Hermeto, as the Partido da Ordem (Party of Order) in the critical year of 1837, in the wake of Feijó's resignation.[3] Its history is defined by a flexible but tenacious strategic alliance between the northeastern sugar oligarchies, the oldest in Brazil, and the newest, those of coffee production in the Paraíba Valley, along with export firms, slave traders, the parliamentarians that provided them with cover, and the military, which was called upon various times during the 1830s and 1840s to put down factional movements that sprouted in the provinces. Opposing the impotent radicalism of these local groups from the beginning was so-called moderate liberalism, which held power both during the regency and in the first years of the Second Empire. Internal divisions did not undermine the deeper unity it maintained during moments of action.

The slave trade, more active than ever, brought nearly 700,000 Africans to the sugar mills and plantations between 1830 and 1850. The authorities, despite eventual declarations to the contrary, looked the other way at this form of piracy that allowed for the transport of human beings, a trade that had been formally illegal since Brazil's 1826 agreement with England and the law promulgated on November 7, 1831, during the regency. This law declared free all Africans brought to Brazil from that moment forward. I recall the "Fala do Negreiro" (Slaver's Speech), a character from Martins Pena's comedy, *Os dous ou o inglês maquinista* (The Two, or the English Machinist): "There is such a long coastline here, and there are such tolerant authorities!"

This was in 1842.

This comic playwright's observation accords perfectly with the data provided by Robert Conrad for these same years:

> The judges for the districts to which the slaves arrived received regular payments, which were fixed at 10.8% of the value of each arriving African. The slaves were traded for bags of coffee right on the beach, thus making the economic formula of "o café e o negro" (coffee and slaves) a reality.[4]

Conrad illustrates the collusion of the governments of the regency and the Second Empire beginning in 1837: "During the Vasconcelos government the slave trade entered a phase of renewed expansion that would last for approximately 14 years. It continued through conservative and liberal governments, and was supported and defended by the very authorities tasked with ending the slave trade."[5]

In order to understand the point of view of the other side (i.e., the English government), the best account comes from Gladstone, the prime minister, who in a speech to the House of Commons in 1850 revealed: "We have a treaty with Brazil, which she has broken every day for the last twenty years. We have tried to secure the freedom of the Emancipados; we endeavoured to make the Brazilians declare it a crime to import slaves into Brazil. The treaty has been repeatedly broken."[6]

The Anglo-Brazilian agreement of 1826 provoked nationalistic protests as early as the 1827 parliamentary session of the Chamber of Deputies, in which nothing less than withdrawal from the agreement was proposed. The representative from Goiás, Brigadier Cunha Matos, was applauded by various colleagues when he deplored that Brazilians had been "forced, obliged, made to submit and compelled by the British government to sign an onerous and degrading convention on matters that are internal, domestic, and purely national, and the exclusive domain of the free and sovereign legislature and the august head of the Brazilian nation."[7] Clemente Pereira, whose old Masonic and Enlightenment sympathies were well known and who was one of the pillars of Brazil's independence, also spoke out against Britain's meddling with regard to the slave ships, which he described as "the most direct sort of attack that could be made against the Constitution, against the dignity of the nation, against the honor and the individual rights of the citizens of Brazil."[8] A phrase by José de Alencar stands in for the whole of the rhetoric from this period: "ser liberal significa ser brasileiro" (to be liberal is to be Brazilian).[9]

This line of argumentation managed, in point of fact, to be both nationalistic and aggressively faithful to the principles of free trade. In 1835, Bernardo Pereira de Vasconcelos, a moderate, proposed an amendment to revoke the antislavery law of 1831. His effort received solid support from the deputies of the Provincial Assembly of Minas Gerais.

The patriotic defense of the slave trade was not, however, limited to parliamentarians from Minas Gerais. In the French legislature, where we may reasonably suppose that liberalism was at home under Louis Philippe, the majority of deputies voted to veto an 1841 agreement made by Guizot with England that would have allowed British maritime officials to inspect French ships suspected of transporting slaves.[10]

Enrichissez-vouz! Even during this period, Alexis de Tocqueville was among the skeptics.[11] The defense of national integrity superseded so-called philanthropic arguments, and at the end of the day, the slavers were protected.

Among us, the dominant discourse between 1836 and 1850 was a pragmatic variation on certain positions earlier adopted by the so-called patriots and historical liberals who inherited the fruits of the Seventh of September. And why were these men called historical? Because without a doubt, these were the struggles of the agro-export bourgeoisie, which ended metropolitan privilege in 1808 by opening the ports. These same patriots had guaranteed, for themselves and their class, the freedom to produce and sell goods and to represent themselves politically—hence the functional and topical character of their liberalism. As for the conservatives, called such from 1836 onward, they seconded the moderates, to whose club that had previously belonged, following them into power and toning down their rhetoric. With land, coffee, and slaves under their control, it was enough for them to speak in the dry, prosaic, sometimes hard register of administrative language. This is an efficient style, the *saquarema* style of Eusébio, Itaboraí, Uruguai, and Paraná.[12]

Free trade, which was the first and principal rallying cry of the colonial patriots, was not necessarily—and in effect, was not—synonymous with free labor. Economic liberalism does not produce, *sponte sua*, social and political liberty.

Open commerce with friendly nations, which the end of exclusive trade with Portugal permitted, did not bring about changes in the nature of the labor force: this remained enslaved (not because of inertia but because of the dynamic of the agro-export economy), though the new postcolonial economic order was now honored as "liberal." This is the source of the peculiar pairing at the heart of the economic and political system in Brazil, and beyond, during the first half of the nineteenth century: liberalism plus slavery. The good consciences of the promoters of our laissez-faire were satisfied with the free market.

Given this historical context, it is not surprising that it took twenty-five years for the slave trade to actually be suppressed and for the agreements that expressly prohibited it to be enforced. Total abolition would only be declared in 1888, by which time there was a vigorous flow of European immigrant workers to São Paulo and the southern provinces.

Returning to the quite concrete contextual understanding of the term *liberalism*: as a cultural option of European origin, connected to the struggle of the bourgeoisie in England and France, political liberalism slowly opened itself up to a project of enlarging citizenship. But this was not the case in Brazil, where independence did not amount to an internal conflict between classes. Here the conflict was fundamentally between the colonists and their interests, and Portugal's project for recolonization, an effort that, truth be told, had been reduced to near impotence by the opening of the ports in 1808. Further, our enlightened patriots fulfilled their mission of cutting the umbilical cord in the juridico-political sphere. Under the hegemony of the moderates, and later, the *regressistas*, liberalism in the postcolonial period rooted itself in processes that sought to perpetuate and defend the interests of these same colonists, who were now emancipated. This movement preserved the freedoms obtained during the initial, anti-Portuguese phase of the process, but in no way attempted to extend or distribute these with any generosity among subaltern groups. In this way, our liberalism only accomplished as much as our context allowed.

"Liberalism," says Raymundo Faoro, "did not mean democracy. These terms would later separate, moving along clearly defined paths, and would become, in certain moments, hostile to one another."[13]

The question, at bottom, is this: structurally, what could the name *liberal* denote when used by the landowning class during the period in which the new state was coming into being?

Semantic and historical analysis reveals two meanings for the term, which at times exist in isolation or in variously combined forms:

1) *Liberal*, for our dominant class up until the mid-nineteenth century, could mean *one who preserves the freedoms*, won in 1808, *to produce, sell, and purchase.*
2) *Liberal* could, therefore, mean *one who preserves the freedom*, won in 1822, *to represent oneself politically*, or in other words, to have the right to elect and be elected as a qualified citizen.
3) *Liberal* could, therefore, mean *one who preserves the freedom* (received as a colonial legacy and revived through agricultural expansion) *to bring the enslaved worker to submission through legal coercion.*
4) *Liberal* could, finally, mean *one who is able to acquire new lands in open competition*, thereby adapting the foundational statute of the colony to the capitalistic spirit of the 1850 Lei de Terras (Land Law).

In this way, the class that founded the Empire of Brazil consolidated its prerogatives, both economic (trade, slave-based production, purchase of land) and political (indirect elections and a limited franchise). Both categories gave concrete form to its liberalism, which became, through a process of extension and differentiation between groups, the basis for the prevailing ideology of the 1840s and 1850s.

The historiography on the regency has already provided a detailed account of the transition from the moderate party, in which everyone—Evaristo and Feijó, Vasconcelos and Honório Hermeto—participated, to the *Regresso* (or "Return," a term used from 1836 forward), when the latter pair jettisoned the former pair and substituted themselves, using as a pretext the need to impose an internal order that was being threatened by provincial rebellions. This is the precise meaning of the profession of faith, cited below, by Vasconcelos, a mentor of the reactionary movement that would mark the beginning of the Second Empire:

> I was a liberal. Freedom at that time had recently been won in the country, it was the common aspiration of all, but was not yet in the laws, in practical ideas; power was everything; I was a liberal. Today, however, the condition of society is distinct: democratic principles have gained everything and have made many compromises: society, which was then threatened by power, is now threatened by disorganization and anarchy. Just as was the case, I want now to serve society, I want to save it, and for this reason I am a

regressista. I am not a dissenter. I have not abandoned the cause I defended in its hour of danger, when it was weak. Rather, I put it aside on a day in which its triumph is so secure that its very excesses are what threaten it.[14]

In other words, what this speech is attempting to argue is this: the politics of centralization is the necessary antidote to division in the country which, in turn (and here is its unspoken rationale), would have fatal consequences for the new economic center of gravity in the Paraíba Valley.

Vasconcelos's trajectory and the political success of the Regresso lead one to conclude that the liberals' "moderation" in 1831 would, sooner or later, reveal its true, conservative face. The slave traders were spared, and the few, undeveloped Enlightenment projects to bring about gradual abolition were reduced to silence. It fell to the army to advocate for national unity over and against the centrifugal tendencies of provincial groups. With the defeat of the last of the Farrapos, what was saved was society—which in this case was a state that brought together landowners, their representatives, slave traders, and the bureaucracy. Liberal rhetoric was built around the quintessentially reductive figure, synecdoche, in which the part is named for the implied whole.

Hermes Lima, in his preface to Rui Barbosa's *Queda do Império* (Fall of the Empire), characterizes the Regresso as an element of political strategy employed by groups within the liberal-moderate bloc at the exact moment (1835–1837) at which the expansion of coffee cultivation in the Paraíba Valley required a greater influx of Africans. Slavery, and the slave trade that was at its heart, effectively became the axis around which an economy developed that was based in the opening of the ports and in free trade. In the lapidary words of Du Bois, *it was the freedom to destroy freedom*.

During this period, the coffee growers longed for a strong state, a cohesive and supportive administration, and the preservation of national unity at all costs. This was the rallying cry of the Regresso. Father Feijó, in renouncing his position as regent in the midst of great difficulties, placed the fulfillment of this design in jeopardy by appearing to accept the inevitable secession of some of the more turbulent provinces, such as Pernambuco and Rio Grande do Sul. Along with this apparent abandonment of the fight against the local factions, a fight to which he in earlier days had been so dedicated, the priest from São Paulo appears to have become more interested in honoring the antitrafficking agreements made with England, which were being sabotaged by a legion of conspirators. In contrast, the *saquaremas*, who took Feijó's place in 1837, reasserted *manu militari* the ideal of a unified empire at the same time as they undertook extensive dealings with the slave trade, which breathed life into the agro-export economy.

Everything presented here was imbricated. Centralism presented itself as national and came to depend on the army, which came to the fore during this period. The slave trade was highly useful for the expansion of coffee. Finally, the Party of Order defended all of these interests, which were placed at the center of power in the Court in Rio de Janeiro and would remain firmly entrenched until at the least the end of the 1850s. The Liberal Party, which had been largely deserted, sometimes alternated with the Conservative Party in government and sometimes joined forces with them. But in both cases, official discourse aligned with oligarchic obligations, which were the coin of the realm. Joaquim Nabuco hit the nail on the head in his historical account of this situation: the conservative reaction "presented itself as representing the true liberal tradition of the country."[15] Octávio Tarqüínio de Sousa likewise observed the connections between the moderates and the *regressistas*: "If we think it through carefully, we see that nothing substantial divided them: Vasconcelos's 'return' did not contradict Evaristo's 'moderation.' Rather, the former was simply an evolution, a transformation. In this way, the 'return' consolidated the work of 'moderation.'"[16] The comment's apologetic tone does not negate its perspicuous analysis.

In truth, there was nothing eccentric, anachronistic, or false in the language of those Brazilian politicians who, using the term *liberalism* in a particular historical sense, *pro domo sua*, legitimated slavery for so many years and only began to restrict it under international pressure. What would be anachronistic is if the rural oligarchies had defended a modern and democratic platform in the mid-nineteenth century. But such a project was conceived neither here, nor in Cuba, nor in the English or French Caribbean, all of which were subject to the same plantation regime, nor in the cotton kingdom of the American Old South. In all of these places, politicians who defended orthodox economic liberalism fought to preserve slave labor.

Nor were there truly legal fictions à la Europe that would have whitewashed the plantation, the slave trade, and slavery itself. Granted, plantation masters and other landowners made quite effective use of parliamentary institutions. The legislature served as a tool of the dominant class that, without established legal channels, could not have controlled the administration of such a large country. A paladin of conservative reaction called our parliamentary and monarchical regime a "máquina admirável" (admirable machine).[17]

At the end of the First Empire, the opposition to Dom Pedro I was led by men who were faithful to English parliamentarianism, like Bernardo Pereira de Vasconcelos, who at the same time (1829) scandalized the Reverend Robert Walsh with his proslavery views: "Among Vasconcelos's weaknesses is his defense of the slave trade; and the treaty with England for its total abolition in the short term, and our desire that it be put in place, feature among his reservations with regard to us."[18] Vasconcelos's bitter resentment of the English maritime officials, which recalls the Anglophobia of the southern Confederates, was not unique.

But nothing could dim their admiration for speeches given in the House of Commons. The cabinets and the Councils of State that, year after year, constrained the idea of emancipation (even when encouraged by the emperor, as occurred in his 1867 and 1868 Speeches from the Throne) brought together men for whom so-called liberal principles only inspired vigorous, energetic, and even polemical action in the by-then classic debate between constitutionalists and absolutists. This discussion was neither academic nor byzantine. The struggle, which was of crucial importance for Europe in the post-Napoleonic period, up until the Revolution of 1830, manifested itself here in the efforts by the patriots against the metropolitan yoke, and soon after, against the capricious actions of Pedro I. An English-style liberalism was necessary for the economically dominant class to assume command. This is the reach and the limitation of our oligarchic liberalism.

Analyzing the self-preserving conduct of the liberals during the year in which independence was achieved, Saint-Hilaire commented: "But these were the men who were the king's brains, who complemented him. In no way did they think of the lower classes."[19]

This astute observer might have said, using the argot of the time: "These men were constitutional liberals."

Ardent parliamentarians before the Crown, these were confessed anti-democrats as far as the vast population of slaves and poor was concerned. Neither king nor people, they were "us."

This closed and exclusionary social contract, beneficial to the men who had labored to undo the colonial pact, was described in a solemn document. This was the Constitution of 1824. The charter, though it was granted through Pedro I's authoritarian gesture, satisfied the majority of the signatories who, in fact, held decision-making power in the newly created nation. This was an alliance between the rights of the *beati possidentes* and the privileges of the monarch. The constrained liberalism of the document was not out of tune with the cautiousness of the constitution of Restoration-era France which, in 1814, included within the mechanisms of government the moderating power theorized by Benjamin Constant. The freedoms enjoyed by the *citoyens* (citizen–property owners) exorcised the ghost of an equality viewed as abstract and anarchic, which if achieved would have made the haves and have-nots equal. And why did the half-hearted liberalism of the French charter not fit like a hand in glove for imperial Brazil's quite restricted body of voters? Did the proposals brought to the Constituent Assembly in 1823 perhaps go beyond protection for agriculture, and free and open trade? It left the institution of slave labor intact. José Bonifácio's *Representação* (Report) was not brought up for debate.

The constitution having been promulgated, the myth of its inviolability, the cornerstone of oligarchic discourses until the end of the regime, was quickly developed. Conservative deputies preferred, as late as 1864, to call themselves *constitutionalists* pure and simple. In so doing, they created the space for the liberals to also adopt this vague and appealing label. It was during this period that a liberal-conservative group was created.

The charter became a banner granted sacred meaning through the aura surrounding the heroic years of independence. But behind its heavy gold- and green-colored screen, into whose silken threads branches of coffee plants and tobacco leaves were interwoven, along with the dynastic emblem of the Braganzas (the Portuguese noble family to which Brazil's emperors belonged), the restricted franchise, indirect elections, and the inviolable right to hold slaves as property were all sheltered.

The centralizing tactics employed during the final years of the regency, which the precocious majority of Pedro II would bring to consummation, were yet another guarantee for the landed bourgeoisie. The fact that the majority was pushed forward by a certain number of liberal militants did not prevent the *saquaremas* from quickly harvesting and enjoying its fruits. Beginning in 1843, the chamber was invaded by a "closed reactionary falange."[20]

Turning once again to conditions in Europe: reaction, whether diffuse or institutionalized, represented the dominant ideology between the Congress of Vienna and the Revolution of 1848. Eric Hobsbawm's incisive synthesis effectively describes this situation: "Liberalism and democracy appeared to be adversaries rather than allies; the triple slogan of the French Revolution, liberty, equality, fraternity, to express a contradiction rather than a combination."[21]

There, a utilitarian politics entwined itself structurally to the unnamed exploitation of the new proletariat. Here, our constitutionalism was nourished by the sweat and blood of slaves. Both here and there the reigning powers coined the term "liberal" as a form of easy money.

At any rate, specificity reappears: the agricultural system stalled or slowed the growth of progressive ideals and efforts. At the beginning of the Second Empire, a generation of constitutionalists, sheltered in the shade of coffee from the Paraíba Valley, resisted the English government where the abolition of the slave trade was concerned. Vasconcelos's severe position, which he retained until his death in 1850, is well known. In 1843, the proslavery lobby, which was active in various Brazilian provinces, seemed to Lord Brougham as efficient as it was cynical:

In the first place, we have the expressed declaration of an honorable member of the Brazilian Senate, to the effect that the law that abolished the slave trade is, notoriously, a dead letter, and has fallen into disuse. In the second place, we have a petition or report from the Provincial Assembly of Bahia to the Senate urging that the law be revoked, not because it is onerous, but rather because the clause that states that "slaves brought here after 1831 are free" impedes the sale of slaves and makes it difficult to own slaves who have recently been brought to the country. I have found that another Provincial Assembly, from Minas Gerais, has asked the same thing, citing the same arguments. After insisting on the danger to the country that would come from a shortage of blacks, the report adds: "Above all, the worst of these evils is the immorality which results from our citizens becoming accustomed to violating the law under the nose of the authorities themselves!" I truly believe that in all the history of human shamelessness no passage can be found to rival this—there is no other example of such audacity. We have here a Provincial Legislature, which argues on behalf of pirates and their accomplices, the growers, and in the name of these great criminals calls for the revocation of a law that the people admit to violating on a daily basis, and which they declare themselves exempt from unless it is revoked. They ask for the revocation of this law for the reason that, for as long as the law exists, given that the people are resolved to violate it, they will find themselves in the difficult position of having to commit this immoral act under the noses of the judges who have sworn an oath to execute the laws.[22]

Slave labor was a structural factor of the Brazilian economy, so much so that its internal control became increasingly rigid over time. In 1835, before the *regressistas* came to power, a parliament dominated by liberals and moderates adopted a law that imposed the death penalty on slaves who committed any act of rebellion or who acted against their masters.

This was the national scene. It would be worth undertaking a comparative study on resistance to abolition in the colonies of England, France, and Holland, countries whose bourgeois liberal thought had taken a leading international role. The British government only granted general abolition in its colonies in 1833, with full compensation for slaveholders, which implied the recognition of their rights. The Dutch parliament decreed abolition in Suriname beginning on July 1, 1863, with payment for landowners and "with freed slaves remaining under the special protection of the state."[23] Slaves in French Guiana and the French Antilles would have to wait for their freedom until the Provisional Council's decree of April 27, 1848, which also provided compensation for slave owners. The admirable gesture of the members of the convention, who had given a standing ovation to abolition on the memorable 16 Pluviôse of Year II of the Revolution, February 4, 1794, was shown to have mattered little. In 1802, Napoleon again legalized the institution that would persist for another half century, both there and here.

Laissez-Faire and Slavery

There is a dynamic that is internal to the old economic liberalism that, in taking the citizen–property owner's will toward autonomy to its logical extreme, bridles at any and all legal restrictions on its sphere of action.

The doctrine of laissez-faire dates from the second half of the eighteenth century and the advent of bourgeois hegemony, which dealt a death blow to the corporate orders and the privileges enjoyed by certain social strata. But there was also a colonial and slave-owning application for orthodox principles, an application that in retrospect may appear abusive or cynical but which thoroughly served the interests of the slavers and rural landowners.

A trader on Africa's Atlantic coast, in defending his rights as a "free-born" British citizen, cited the Magna Carta as giving him the inalienable right to trade as he saw fit, along with equal power over all of his property, whether mobile, "semi-mobile," or immobile.[24] This right, claimed by a slave trader in 1772, served as the legal basis for the Brazilian parliamentarians who, in 1884, argued against counselor Dantas's proposal to free slaves over sixty years in age, without compensating their owners. His ministry fell, and Saraiva, who succeeded him, was obliged to maintain the principle of obligatory payment. The individual right to property was as valid in 1884 as it was in 1772.

Celso Furtado perceptively noted that our liberal economists, from the Viscount of Cairu on, were more faithful to Adam Smith than the English or the Yankees. The Americans, under Hamilton's influence, balanced free trade and protectionism as best suited them. Comparing Alexander Hamilton's ideas with those of Cairu, Furtado writes: "Both were disciples of Adam Smith, whose ideas they absorbed during the same period in England. However, Hamilton would transform himself into a champion of industrialization. . . . Cairu superstitiously believed in the invisible hand and repeated: *deixai fazer, deixai passar, deixai vender* (let them act, let them buy, let them sell)."

This observation is especially valid for the period during which the *regressista* hegemony married laissez-faire to slave labor. Vasconcelos, whom we have already witnessed as an open defender of the slave trade (to the point of proposing that the manumission built into the law of 1831 be suspended!), was a bitter opponent of any official measures that would support fledgling Brazilian manufacturing at the expense of the importation of European products. A spokesman for the agrarian way of thinking, victorious in the elections of 1836, Vasconcelos rejected the very idea of a state role in the economy, drawing on classical arguments in so doing:

> What is best for us is that we not try to produce those primary products and trade goods in which foreigners have the advantage over us. On the contrary, we should apply ourselves to producing those goods in which they are our inferiors. It is not necessary that the law indicate which goods are the most lucrative. There should be no government interference. Individual interest is quite active and intelligent. It guides capital toward the most lucrative uses. The contrary views rest on a false opinion, that the government understands what is best for the citizen and the state. The government is always more ignorant than the general mass of the nation, and it has never interfered with an industry that it has not destroyed, or at least damaged. . . . Favor and oppression are one and the same with respect to industry. What is necessary is the most devout respect for the property and liberty of the Brazilian citizen. The professions, commerce, and agriculture ask nothing more of the government than Diogenes asked of Alexander. *Stand out of my light*, they say aloud. We do not need your favor. What we require is liberty and security.[25]

Adam Smith could have not been any more emphatic. *Mutatis mutandis* (*ma non troppo*), this was the language of the UDN (National Democratic Union) and it is the language of the UDR (Rural Democratic Union).

But what, beginning with the agreement of 1826, was the principal obstacle facing this orthodox liberalism that so jealously defended its rights? It was precisely the control the English government exercised over the international slave trade. Vasconcelos reacted indignantly to the preaching of the "philanthropists" and revealed his feelings in the following words, collected by Walsh: "They protest against the injustice of this trade, and cite as examples the immorality of some nations in which [slavery] is practiced. However, what they have not proved is that slavery lowers the morality of any nation. A comparison between Brazil and the nations in which there are no slaves will eliminate any doubt on this point." Shocked, the reverend goes on to state: "He then suggested that the Brazilian government should enter into agreement with England regarding the deferment of the law."[26] Vasconcelos's argument rested upon the differing labor conditions in Brazil and Europe, and it would forcefully appear again in the discourses of the liberals-*regressistas*, and would be taken up once again by José de Alencar in the tumultuous parliamentary sessions that preceded the vote on the Law of the Free Womb.

Here we have sketched out the syndrome of the liberal oligarchy in Brazil (or more specifically, postcolonial Brazil): the country's location within a rigid international division of production, and the defense of monoculture and rejection of any state interference not designed to secure the gains of the exporting class. It was understood that the state's prohibition (in this case, under pressure from England) of the slave trade clearly restricted the freedom of initiative of those who sold and bought slave laborers. The same thought became doctrine among the advocates of slavery in the Old South, which produced a plethora of orthodox economists: Thomas Cooper, author of a Smithian manual that was widely read through the first half of the nineteenth century (*Lectures on the Elements of Political Economy*, 1826); George Tucker, the first degree holder in economics from the University of Virginia; and above all, Jacob Newton Cardozo, an influential editor at the *Southern Review*. All three men questioned the idea that captive labor was unprofitable. These southerners, who were reluctant to judge slavery unprofitable, necessarily held to a unilateral and abstract understanding of the new science of economics, which grew as slowly as it did because "the European economists, in attempting to build systems that would apply equally to all countries, continue, at bottom, to assume that their circumstances are natural and universal. We know that the wealth of nations is generated in very different ways. For example, experience reveals that slavery in the south has produced not only great wealth, but also a greater share of happiness for the slave than occurs in many places in which the relationship between employee and employee is based on wages."[27] The political message that shines through this text is simple: let things be as they are, let us plant our cotton, push back the frontier, buy northern slaves, make money from the slave trade, and so forth.

While our slaveholding regime was compelled to confront England, the laissez-faire southern cotton producers challenged the Union, which was imposing restrictive laws. "By 1854," writes John Hope Franklin in his admirable *From Slavery to Freedom*, "those engaged in the African slave trade had become so bold as to advocate openly for official reopening of the trade." Between 1854 and 1860 there was not a southern business convention that did not consider the proposed reopening of the slave trade. A furious debate erupted on this problem at an 1858 convention in Montgomery. William L. Yancey, the Alabama "fire eater," argued, with a certain logic, that "if it is legal to buy slaves in Virginia and carry them to New Orleans, why is it not right to buy them in Cuba, Brazil, or Africa, and to carry them there?" New Orleans was, in 1858, the most important slave market in the country. Franklin continues: "The following year, at Vicksburg, the convention voted favorably on a resolution recommending that, "all laws, State or Federal, prohibiting the African slave trade, ought to be repealed. Only the states of the upper south, which enjoying the profits reaped from the domestic slave trade, were opposed to reopening the African trade."[28]

The disregard for the antitrafficking law in the United States during the 1850s was as blatant as it was in Brazil during the 1840s. Here and there, the unrestricted freedom of capital required the total subjugation of labor.

It was freedom to destroy freedom: this is the dialectic of liberalism at a moment in which it was expanding at any cost.

In 1844, an erudite Bahian historian wrote an indictment of the disloyalty of England, which, though it pretended to be the friend of the new Brazilian nation, was working against us by preventing Brazilian agriculture from receiving its precious African laborers. I am speaking of Dr. A. J. Mello Moraes and his pamphlet, *A Inglaterra e seos tractados. Memoria, na qual previamente se demonstra que a Inglaterra não tem sido leal até o presente no cumprimento dos seus tractados. Aos srs. deputados geraes da futura sessão legislativa de 1845* (England and Her Treaties: An account demonstrating that England has not been loyal in the observation of her treaties. To the honorable General Deputies of the future legislative session of 1845). Once again, we have this flawless comparison: "An Englishman treats his white servant one hundred times worse than we treat our slaves."[29] Mello Moraes's proposal is simple and drastic: the English cabinet "should either abandon its colonies, for lack of colonial goods to be consumed, or if it wishes to retain them, should allow slavery."[30] Given the close relationship between colonial products and slavery, a historical connection that had been established and cemented over three centuries, this brave defender of our agricultural production exhorts the campaigning general deputies to cut the ties that bound the imperial government to the British: "In order to be happy Brazil does not need treaties with any nation. All that is needed is protection for agriculture, encouragement of manufacturing, free trade, and ports that are open to the entire world. Brazil does not need favors from England."[31] A few lines later, Moraes looks hopefully upon the increase in coffee exports to the United States. The spirit of 1808, which broke with the Portuguese monopoly, now demanded that it be expanded without hindrance.

In the wake of the Latin American countries' postcolonial consolidation, Brazil affirmed the guiding principle of the system—give the greatest possible freedom of action, both legal and illegal, to those who enjoyed rights: the coffee plantation owners, the sugar plantation owners, and those who provided them with their labor force, that is, the slave traders.

The greatest obstacle to the dominant class did not come, then, from our constitutional state, which represented landed interests and was served by them. Rather, the obstacle was imposed by the new international order, the new monopolist, England—hence the defense of the most unbridled laissez-faire and hence the landowners' hostility to the prospect of their nation being controlled by a foreign state.

Since the common ideological factor here was economic liberalism, which during this period was enjoying its golden age, there was only one way around the problem for the proslavery argument: to demonstrate that the guiding principles of the classical doctrine, in being just, should apply fairly to all circumstances, to the peculiar conditions of nations.

The attention and ostensible respect granted the individual, which is affirmed so insistently in the conservative writings of Burke, permeate the Romantic nationalist ideology that runs from Varnhagen to Alencar, from Vasconcelos to Olinda, from Paraná to Itaboraí. This will be the major theme of the argument favoring delay of emancipation: allow time to run its course, for Brazil is not Europe, and differences must be respected.

Ideological filtering and temporization would be the strategies of our intra-oligarchic liberalism during the period in which the national state was being built.

In rationalizing their defense mechanisms, the ideology of the coffee producers from the Paraíba Valley and of the southern U.S. cotton growers, who were contemporaries of one another, did not think to question the absolute right to property or international free trade. The principle of universality served them as much as it served European liberals. There was, however, something added, in accordance with specific ideas and interests. The result of this extension was, and continues to be, the agrarian bourgeoisie's notable swerve to the right whenever a shadow of a threat was seen on the horizon. There exist enough examples of ultraliberal discourse by the political right so that actually citing these is beside the point. Even today, in 1988, a leader of the so-called *centrão* (great center) boasted of being a political reactionary but an economic *anarchist*: down with state interference! All power to private initiative!

In Brazil, for lack of cultural density, the defense of the slave trade and enslaved labor did not take on forms as elaborate as those that can be seen in the case of the American Old South, in which slavery was on innumerable occasions called "the cornerstone of civil liberties."

I follow Gunnar Myrdal's convincing interpretation from *An American Dilemma*: "Politically they [the whites] were all equals, since they were free citizens. Free competition and personal freedom were assured them. The Southern statesmen and writers hammered on this thesis, that slavery, and slavery alone, produced the most perfect equality and the most substantial liberty for free citizens in society."[32]

In a certain way, the ubiquitous presence of blacks placed all white men on the same level, for it united them into a bloc opposing the subordinate race. Slave labor was constituted in the first instance to uphold the social existence of the free white property owner. This is the rationale of Jefferson

Davis, a defender of slavery who was quite popular during the pre–Civil War period. From the perspective of the dominant logic, this was all perfectly reasonable.

The combination of laissez-faire, the landowners' aggressive individualism, a patriarchal culture that was arbitrary and based on favor, antiprotectionist views on industry and the celebration of rural life began coalescing during the 1830s, "under the double influence of the rising profitableness of the slavery and plantation economy and the onslaught from the Northern Abolitionist movement."[33]

A language that was both liberal and proslavery became historically possible. At the same time, the coherence of radical Enlightenment thinking, which had matured during the last quarter of the eighteenth century, was consigned to the shadows.

Beginning in the 1830s in Cuba, another area that typifies the export-oriented plantation, the prosperity of the sugar economy worked to dampen the ideal of freedom and stiffen oligarchic thinking:

> The universal body of ideas was refashioned and adapted to describe or explain the domestic Cuban condition. The Cuban elite showed a cosmopolitanism and a sophistication that were unusual for their time and place—the more surprising in their colonial situation. Forced to defend slavery, they postulated the rights of property and the security of civilization—accepted euphemisms for racial and economic arguments. African slaves were economic assets. Emancipation threatened economic ruin. They reasoned in a convoluted way that slavery was a medium for civilizing Africans. The reasoning and the arguments were neither new nor originally Cuban.[34]

Certain cultural differences aside, what calls out to the historian is the formation of a liberal and proslavery ideology in three regions in which export-oriented agriculture intensified beginning in the 1830s: in coffee-growing Brazil, in the cotton-growing U.S. South, and in the sugar-growing Caribbean, especially Cuba. In all three regions, slave labor underpinned oligarchic reaction. This new growth of the slave economy caught the sharp eye of Tavares Bastos, who saw and criticized everything from his pro-American vantage point.[35]

As for the Andean and Platine social contexts, in which the African presence had been modest or nonexistent, *la patria del criollo* (the country of the Creole), as Guatemalan scholar Severo Martínez Peláez termed it, was erected during this same period and was built upon the same exclusionary ideology.[36]

Franklin Knight's reading of Cuban liberalism draws on concepts like *refashioning* and *adaptation* in describing the processes through which a

European-origin ideology penetrated the mind and heart of the American landowner. Only that which accorded with local practices of domination was filtered through.

It evidently falls to experts in the writing of Smith, Say, and Bentham to provide an answer. Let me elucidate just one point.

Adam Smith wrote *The Wealth of Nations* in the 1770s. His anti-mercantilist struggle is well known. Monopolies, corporations, privileges, legal and cultural obstacles: these were his principal targets. During this period, the slave trade was intense and was primarily in the hands of British maritime commerce. Slavery remained the rule in the United States and in all of the British, Dutch, French, Spanish, and Portuguese colonies. Smith affirmed the superiority of salaried labor, which seemed to him more lucrative and ethical. This was his general principle. However, in addressing the colonies, his discussion takes on a neutral and utilitarian tone. One does not find here an explicit economic critique of slavery. One only finds the observation that "good management" of slaves is always more profitable than poor treatment:

> But the success of the cultivation which is carried on by means of cattle, depend very much upon the good management of those cattle; so the profit and success of that which is carried on by slaves, must depend upon the good management of those slaves, and in the good management of their slaves the French planters, I think it is generally allowed, are superior to the English.[37]

A short while later, he states that in arbitrary as opposed to free societies, "it is much easier for [the magistrate] to give some protection to the slave."[38] Finally: "Gentle usage renders the slave not only more faithful, but more intelligent, and therefore, upon a double account, more useful."[39] The recommendations made by our prudent economic thinkers Antonil and Benci to northeastern sugar planters at the beginning of the eighteenth century would not have differed substantially from this.

A likely hypothesis is that in its early years, caught between empiricism and idealism, the new science of wealth had not yet developed a thorough, unified formulation to explain the problem of the profitability of the slave in the colonies. The value attributed to free labor, which was at the core of political economy, could not entirely obscure the utilitarian vein and the tendency to conveniently relate theory to what was actually occurring in the great plantations of the New World.

On this topic, it is curious how Adam Smith's greatest apostle, Jean-Baptiste Say, confronts the comparison between slave and salaried labor. Say, whose texts were canonical during the nineteenth century in both Brazil and the United States, denounces the degradation of masters and slaves and calls for industrialization and free labor. On the colonies, however, he questions his master Smith and his predecessors Steuart and Turgot on the issue of the cost of slaveholding, and in so doing, illustrates the conflicting positions side by side.

> Steuart, Turgot, and Smith, all agree in thinking, that the labour of the slave is dearer and less productive than that of the freeman. Their arguments amount to this: a man, that neither works nor consumes on his own account, works as little and consumes as much as he can: he has no interest in the exertion of that degree of care and intelligence, which alone can insure success: his life is shortened by excessive labour, and his master must replace it at great expense, besides, the free workman looks after his own support; but that of the slave must be attended to by the master; and, as it is impossible for the master to do it so economically as the free workman, the labour of the slave must cost him dearer.[40]

In the paragraphs that follow Say reproduces, but does not question, the proslavery argument, recalling the slave's scanty consumption ("his food [consists of] the manioc root, to which kind masters now and then add a little dried fish" [87]), his poor dress ("a pair of trowsers and a jacket are the whole wardrobe of the negro" [87]), and his miserable lodgings ("his lodging [is] a bare hut" [87]).

Taken together, these factors point to the great profitability of the colonial plantations: "It is a well-known fact, that the net produce of an estate in St. Domingo cleared off the whole purchase-money in six years; whereas in Europe the net produce seldom exceeds the one twenty-fifth or one thirtieth of the purchase-money, and sometimes falls far short even of that. Smith, himself, elsewhere tells us, that the planters of the English islands admit that the rum and molasses will defray the whole expenses of a sugar plantation, leaving the total produce of sugar as net proceeds: which, as he justly observes, is much the same as if our farmers were to pay their rent and expenses with the straw only, and to make a clear profit of all the grain. Now I ask, how many products are there that exceed the expenses of production in the same degree?"[41]

Having reached this point, after having presented the proslavery argument as valid, or at minimum feasible, Say takes a sharp turn and implies that conditions have changed: "Be that as it may, everything changed. The situation of the Caribbean today is different than it once was." He was writing in 1802, a year in which colonial trade suffered due to competition from European beet sugar. Free labor appeared to have reached a well-deserved primacy, which was a triumph for the new bourgeois orthodoxy. Though his visceral pragmatism compelled him to observe that, in the sugar plantations of Cuba and Jamaica, black slave labor remained in fact the most appropriate form (the European suffered in those conditions, the slave was less ambitious and less needy, and the tropical sun was hot and sugarcane cultivation hard work), his line of thought returned to the Enlightenment thesis that from the last quarter of the eighteenth century had condemned colonial monopolies and the slave trade as barriers against progress and civilization. "Slavery cannot long survive when surrounded by nations of free blacks or even by free black citizens, as exist in the United States. This institution differs from all others and will come to its end through gradual disappearance. In the European colonies, it can survive only with the help of the forces of the metropolis, and as the metropolis becomes more enlightened, it will withdraw its support."[42]

Say's prophecy was long in revealing itself, not only in relation to the colonies (Cuba, the Caribbean islands, Guyana) but also in relation to the now-independent United States and Brazil. And nowhere was the slaveholding regime exterminated without opposition, through the spontaneous action of the masters. Slave desertions and rebellions, the struggle of abolitionist groups, and finally, the action of the state were in all cases decisive. The oligarchies resisted as much as they could.

Say's *Treatise* was published in 1803. In 1807 England outlawed the slave trade. At the same time, however, Bonaparte reestablished slavery after the bloody Haitian revolt. And cotton from the Old South, Cuban sugar, and Brazilian coffee would bring new life to slave labor and would fuel the slave trade to an extent never before seen. The first half of the nineteenth century was a feverish period for slavery, and it is in light of the Afro-American context of the plantation economy that we can understand the *regressista* ideology of liberals from Brazil and from elsewhere.

Oligarchy and Ideological Neutralization

The interests of the rural landowners were represented by a letter, which also served the moderates in the post-abolition period. Old *pais da pátria* (fathers of the country) like Evaristo and Bernardo de Vasconcelos ultimately ran aground in a highly unrepresentative parliamentary system. "No excesses. The line has been drawn, and this line is the Constitution. The liberals' task should be to give practical form to the Constitution that exists on paper." These are the words of one of history's fighters, Evaristo da Veiga, in the issue of the *Aurora Fluminense* for September 9, 1829.[43] "We want the Constitution—not Revolution." The same man, whom histories of the regency tend to place in opposition to *regressismo*, drew a clear line separating his interpretation of liberalism, which he defended, and *democracy*, which he rejected: the principle of popular sovereignty was, in his view:

contrary (1st): to the reality of inequality, established by nature between individual abilities and strengths; (2nd) to the reality of inequality of ability caused by differences in position; (3rd) to worldly experience, in which the timid always follow the brave, the less able obey the more able, and natural inferiority recognizes and obeys natural superiority. The principle of popular sovereignty, that is, the equal right of all individuals to sovereignty, the right of all individuals to compete for sovereignty, is radically false because, under the pretext of maintaining legitimate equality, it violently introduces equality where it does not exist and violates legitimate inequality.[44]

And what would be the party locus of these liberals who, just like Evaristo, viewed inequality as legitimate?

The response is to be found in the changing political biographies of the *moderados* of 1831, the *regressistas* of 1836, the *conservadores* of 1840, and the *conciliadores* and *ligueiros* of the 1850s.

Nabuco de Araújo was first a conservative, then a *conciliador* and *ligueiro*, and finally a neoliberal. Paraná, Torres Homem, and Rio Branco were first liberals and then centrist conservatives. Zacarias, Saraiva, Paranaguá, and Sinimbu were first conservatives, then liberals. Vasconcelos, Paulino de Sousa, and Rodrigues Torres were first moderates and then leading conservatives. All of these men—and their group affiliations matter little here—inherited the very notion of liberty from the generation that preceded them in politics between 1808 and 1831.

Given these circumstances, the political faction they affiliated with corresponded, in each case, with the group that could best defend them. This sardonic phrase rings true: "There is nothing more like a *saquarema* than in *luzia* in power."

Up until midcentury, this discourse—or rather, a collective silence—was complicit in supporting the slave trade. This discourse's liberalism, though partial and selective, was not incongruous. It filtered through those ideas that were compatible with the freedom of the oligarchies and discarded any inconvenient implications, that is, the abstract requirements of European liberalism that did not accord with the particularities of the new nation.

Eusébio de Queirós, whose name is linked to the law that finally banned the slave trade in 1850 after successive confrontations with the British government, provides us with an authoritative example of what I term *ideological filtering*. Speaking to the moral dimension of the slave trade, Eusébio, who was then minister of justice and former chief of police for Rio de Janeiro, proceeds to decriminalize this activity:

> Let us be frank: the slave trade, in Brazil, was tied to interests, or rather to the presumed interest of agriculture. And in a country in which agricul-

ture is so strong, it was natural that public opinion would favor the slave trade. For public opinion enjoys great influence, not only in representative governments but also in absolute monarchies. How can we be surprised that our politicians bowed down to this law of necessity? How can we be surprised that all of us, both friends and enemies of the slave trade, would have bowed down to this necessity?

Gentlemen, if this were a crime, then it would be a general crime in Brazil. But I contend that, when in a nation all political parties have their turn in power and all of its politicians have been called to exercise it, and all of them are of like mind on a question, then it is necessary that their position be supported by very compelling arguments. It is impossible that this would be a crime and one would go too far in calling it an error.[45]

The slave trade had by this time been suspended, but those who had been obliged to prohibit it were still defending it.

The historian finds a more naked expression of opinion when he abandons the official discourse in favor of unadorned testimony, as we find in the words of the owner of an old trading house in Rio de Janeiro. He was bitterly resentful of the expenses that seemed to rain down after the end of the slave trade (had he himself been involved in it?):

Better good blacks from the African coast, brought here for their happiness and ours, than all the morbid philanthropy of the British, who having forgotten about their own home, have let their poor white brother die, have left the slave without a master to care for him, and cry out hypocritically or foolishly when exposed to the ridiculousness of true philanthropy, which is our happy slave's cloak. Better good blacks from the coast of Africa to till our fertile fields than all of the pretty girls on the Rua do Ouvidor, than one *conto* and five hundred *mil réis* for a woman's dress . . . than, finally, dealings so unwise as to exceed the legitimate forces of the country which, having disturbed social relations, and produced dislocations in labor, have resulted more than anything else in scarcity and in the high prices of goods.[46]

José de Alencar, who was one of the champions of the status quo during the debates of 1871, lamented in less brutal terms the evils of financial speculation, of playing the stock market, and of the corrupting luxury that paper money had introduced to the customs of the Court. Further, he identified the slow, heavy rhythm of the old economy (read as: the heyday of the slave trade) with his own values of honor and austerity. This is the substance of his play *O crédito* (Credit), which was staged in 1857 and which can be interpreted as a metaphor for our timid version of capitalism. Taking up the question again in one of his *Cartas de Erasmo* (Letters of Erasmus), addressed to the empire's financial advisor, the Viscount of Itaboraí, Alencar again contended that the new financial credit should be applied to agricultural production—that is, he argued for strengthening ties between the state's monetary authority and the plantation economy. In making this argument, Alencar cited the fact that Brazil was "a new country, in which it can be said that the great landholdings are still in a formative stage." Inflation, which according to Itaboraí's orthodoxy was an evil, was elevated to the level of necessary evil—necessary as long as it benefited landowners. Reproduction and self-defense marshaled in support of public finances: these were the limits of what we might term the dominant postcolonial ideology. According to this thinking, the sin of freely minting money was only judged a mortal sin if committed outside of the legitimate interests of the great landholdings. In these same *Cartas*, Alencar criticized taxes and the *empregocracia* (job-ocracy), and condemned in the same terms as Cairu and Vasconcelos the protection of "factories and goods that are nonexistent and not even dreamt of in this country." A coherent, preindustrial liberalism was made to accommodate our oligarchic routines.

Was this liberalism or conservatism? Ideological neutralization was formulated and carried out through the 1850s. The values that undergirded factional interests were so unified that there was no longer any space for ideological or partisan declarations of faith. Senator Nabujo de Araújo, who was in the process of moving from the Conciliação to the Liga, sought to understand the causes of the doctrinal indifference that allowed the term *liberal* to imply conformism. He identified the cause in what seemed to him the homogeneity of the Brazilian social body: "I concede that in a society in which there are privileged classes, in which distinct and heterogeneous interests exist, in which the principle of feudalism still prevails, I concede that there, as in England, there may be parties that endure for centuries; but where the elements are homogeneous, as in our society, in which there are no privileges, in which the parties merely represent the interests of the moment, which change from day to day, here the parties are fragile."[47]

This speech, delivered on June 13, 1857, should not scandalize us if we understand *nossa sociedade* (our society) as referring not to the Brazilian people in general but only to the circle of men who were economically eligible, and therefore suitable for political activities, as spelled out in the Constitution of 1824. Within this closed space, it was in fact appropriate to question the purpose of ideologically conflicting parties, given that everything was at bottom a lottery for positions, influence, and honors.

The Marquis of Paraná, the head of the *conciliador* cabinet in which Nabuco served, thought in these same terms when, given the "state in which society found itself," he accepted the fusion of the old liberals with the conservatives.

It is also true that this corporatist liberalism at times took on a heated tone when circumstances consigned it to the margins of power. It was in these conditions that a democratic rhetoric based purely in personal or group resentment appeared and managed to deceive its audience for a brief time. A good example of this is found in the pamphlet entitled the *Libelo do povo* (People's Indictment), attributed to Timandro, a pseudonym for Sales Torres Homem. This was a diatribe against the emperor's personal power. In 1849 this pamphlet was considered radical, but its target was not the political oppression effectively committed by the regime. Rather, it targeted the House of Braganza and attacked the royal family and, by extension, Portuguese tyranny. Its author would later enter the ranks of the emperor's defenders and would be rewarded with the title of Viscount of Inhomirim. The son of an African woman in the *Trovas burlescas* (Burlesque Ballads) says the following about these liberals:

> Though an ardent champion of liberty
> Who preaches equality among men,
> He writes fearsome Indictments,
> Composed of venomous, impenetrable lines:
> He abandons the rewards of the mind,
> He bows at the sound of silver,
> He sells his name, glory, position:
> For in Brazil the wise man only wishes to know
> That he may stuff his large belly![48]

In the provinces, with the cycle of revolts having been broken by iron and fire, the political scene likewise degenerated into a low form of partisan adherence, which was symptomatic of its dependence on the Court's edicts. João Francisco Lisboa, a talented journalist, described the political factions in his home province of Maranhão in ironic terms:

> In general . . . they have been favorably disposed to the central government, only declaring war on it when all have lost all hope of obtaining its assistance against enemy parties that have, whether through skill or luck, managed to secure its aid. When the Most Excellent Mr. Bernardo Bonifácio, disturbed by the reciprocal recriminations and by the party chiefs' inevitable declarations of loyalty and support, interrogated them or merely sounded them out, they declared in turn: The motto of the *Cangambás* is "Emperor, Constitution, Order." The *Mossorocas* only support the Constitution along with the Emperor, as our only guarantors of peace and happiness. The *Jaburus* are known for their long-standing and unbreakable adherence to the principles of order and monarchy. Brazil can only prosper under the protective shadow of the Throne. Finally, the *Bucuraus* said: In

theory ours are popular principles, but we are wise enough to know that Brazil cannot yet bear certain institutions. Therefore, we accept without scruples the current state of things, as a consummated fact, as long as we are guaranteed the right to enjoy all the privileges of citizens. We are even willing to offer the most frank and loyal cooperation.[49]

The informational character of the text gives us a detailed, inside view of the oligarchic interests shared by various political clans. But Lisboa's perspective is critical, and in its exposition, dialectical, given that it points toward a greater liberalism that at the time could not have been fully anticipated, but that already existed in latent form, and that sooner or later would erupt onto the scene.

The Formation of the New Liberalism

> The Brazilian agricultural worker must recognize that the age of salaried labor has already arrived, as destiny demanded.
>
> —Quintino Bocayuva, *A crise da lavoura* (The Crisis of Agriculture, 1868)

> Institutions do exist, but by and for 30 percent of the citizenry. I propose a change in political style. One should not say: "consult the nation, the representatives of the nation, the powers of the nation," but rather, "consult the 30 percent, representatives of the 30 percent, the powers of the 30 percent." Public opinion is a baseless metaphor; the only opinion that exists is that of the 30 percent.
>
> —Machado de Assis, "História de quinze dias" ("History of Fifteen Days," *Crônica*, August 15, 1876)

> Either the country or the cities; slavery or civilization; the Agricultural Clubs or the press, the intellectual centers, this country's enlightened thought and morality.
>
> —Joaquim Nabuco, "O terreno da luta" (The Battlefield), *Jornal do Comércio*, July 19, 1884.

If the principal characteristic of the event is its precise location in space and time, the same cannot be said for ideology. Ideology does not emerge unannounced or by chance, from one day to the next. Its raw materials are ideas formed of values, and ideas and values are formed slowly, through comings and goings, as history moves forward, and within the heads and hearts of men. As such, like the tip of the iceberg, it clearly signals the existence of submerged masses whose depth cannot be calculated with the naked eye. Further, certain situations occur that can be precisely dated, and when they occur, they may serve the observer of ideologies as signs of tendencies that are long in the making.

Historiography is unanimous in marking the year 1868 as the dividing line between the first, more stable phase of the Second Empire and its long crisis, which would culminate twenty years later in abolition and the establishment of the republic.

Further, the year 1868 is significant because it is then that we hear the bell (the style of the time, à la Hugo, inspires images of bells ringing and trumpets sounding) that rallied the liberal forces, which were roused by Pedro II's abrupt dissolution of Zacarias de Góis's cabinet, which commanded a majority in Parliament.

This decision, though traumatic, was not illegal, and Pedro II's action fell within the proper exercise of the moderating power. But its effect was to catalyze forces that had previously been dispersed. And the effects of the act brought into being a new situation and represented the tip of the iceberg alluded to earlier. The reactions of politicians, the press, intellectuals, and academic centers throughout the country took the form of a chain of linked meanings and beg the question of the values at play. What liberalism is this, that took to the field in search of a program of broad reforms and that no longer considered itself a mere ventriloquist's dummy for oligarchic dissent?

The crisis of 1868 is the critical moment in the process that, running from 1865 to 1871, culminated in the Law of the Free Womb. Approached from this angle, this crisis marked the passing from the scene of a lifeless, proslavery, agro-mercantile Regresso, in favor of a reformism that was fresh and that believed in the value of free labor. This interpretation of the facts has its value, but one must clearly distinguish the liberal-radical tendency (this expression appears for the first time in 1866, in the newspaper *A Opinião Liberal*) from the hybrid entity that was the Liberal Party up until complete abolition was achieved in 1888.

During the final decades of the empire, progressive tendencies blew through the Liberal and Republican parties but did not coincide perfectly with either party. And there was conservative and even proslavery resistance in both groups.[50]

The history of the *novo liberalismo* (new liberalism), as Joaquim Nabuco described it, can be narrated either over the long term or in terms of certain specific moments.

From the first perspective, which operates at the level of systems, the new ideological current, visible from the 1860s, correlated with the social and economic dynamism the country had enjoyed since the 1850s, thanks to the end of the slave trade. Capital, amounting to nearly 16,000 *contos*, which had been freed by this change, flowed into commerce, manufacturing, transportation networks, and stock market speculation, and accelerated the process of urbanization and the employment of salaried laborers. This situation was further fueled by the continued expansion of export-oriented agriculture, which international demand would sustain through the end of the century. The existence of an internal market and a developing urban pole in the southeast was the necessary condition for the emergence of liberal values that were broader than those professed by intra-oligarchic discourse. "Either the country or the cities; slavery or civilization."[51]

And in terms of infrastructure: in the northeastern region, which had quickly emptied out as a result of the internal slave trade and the sale of black labor to southern plantation owners, contract labor became a fact of life between the 1860s and 1870s. Tavares Bastos, the first ideologue of our capitalistic modernization, noted:

> I shall observe the fact that free men work in the sugar mills and plantations for a salary, in Pernambuco, Rio Grande do Norte, and Paraíba. The same is true of the growing coffee economy of Ceará. Notwithstanding cholera and the export of slaves to the south, production in these provinces has not diminished: Ceará's production has greatly increased. Agriculture there is improving, and the plow and steam-powered motors are being introduced. The plantation owner, in some areas, has almost become a mere refiner of sugar, given that a large part of the sugar produced in the mill comes from cane planted by neighbors or sharecroppers. This represents an economic division of labor.[52]

One of the key ideas of the *Cartas do solitário* (Letters of a Solitary Man), which were written beginning in 1861 for the *Correio Mercantil*, was the need for and superiority of free labor.

A modern liberal mode of thought, which was in all respects opposed to the heavy-handed proslavery thinking of the 1840s, was formulated by politicians and intellectuals from Brazil's principal cities, as well as *bacharéis* (degree-holders, normally in law) from northeastern families who could by then expect little benefit from a slave system in decline.

The new liberalism would be urban in general, and it would be northeastern in particular.[53]

As for the ideological tendencies of the coffee plantation owners, assumed to be more modern in outlook (this was especially true for those of São Paulo's "New West"), these were, for the most part, quite peculiar. For these men, what seem at first glance as antislavery attitudes are in reality pro-immigrant. The fact that these men came to power with the proclamation of the republic placed them in a hegemonic position, which allowed them to resolve the question of rural labor in their own pragmatic and narrow terms. Their plans approximated but could not be confused with the reformist ideas of Tavares Bastos, André Rebouças, Quintino Bocayuva, and Joaquim Nabuco.

Distinguishing between *currents of opinion* and *partisan groups* becomes acutely necessary when we shift from a long-term perspective—that is, what takes place between the 1860s and the end of the empire—to the detailed analysis of actions and group reactions. In the back-and-forth of *petite histoire*, which the reader of the *Anais do Parlamento* (Parliamentary Annals) may accompany, it is not at all rare to see members of the Conservative Party, friends of the Crown, call for the emancipation of children born to slave women (just as the cabinets of the Marquis of São Vicente and the Viscount of Rio Branco proposed) or to uncover reactionary attitudes among members of the Liberal Party, as was the case of Martinho Campos, from Minas Gerais, who more than once declared himself an *escravocrata da gema* (proslavery advocate to the core).

The same occurred on the topic of direct election, a reform defended by radicals during the 1860s: opinions on the question were divided according to regional and group interests, regardless of party affiliation. The old moderate liberals reduced the number of eligible voters to such an extent that, by maintaining the financial and literacy requirements for voting, they reduced the electorate to one-twentieth of the population. This spurred indignant reactions from Silveira Martins, Saldanha Marinho, and the younger José Bonifácio de Andrada, who was the mentor of two men who were making their parliamentary debut, Rui Barbosa and Joaquim Nabuco. Andrada's intervention in the parliamentary session of April 28, 1879, would be anthologized in the compendium of Brazilian democratic thought: "In this country the pyramid of power rests on the summit, as opposed to the base."

Satirizing the official clause that prohibited illiterates from voting, Andrada declared: "This rule by grammarians is an error of political syntax (*supported with laughter*). Who is the subject of the sentence? (*Prolonged laughter*). Is it not the people? Who is the object? Ah, they have discovered a new rule: do not employ the subject (*laughter*)."[54]

But what, in the end, divided the two liberalisms from each other? While the question of direct election was more obvious, the way in which these liberalisms treated the *questão servil* (slavery question) carved out a wider trench: this is the retrospective opinion of Joaquim Nabuco, who theorizes the history of the empire in light of his own abolitionist practice. This fighter's account, in addressing the institutional crisis of 1868, brings Nabuco's father's social misgiving to the forefront: "I translated documents from the *Anti-Slavery Reporter* for my father, who between 1869 and 1871 contributed the most toward the maturation of the idea of emancipation."[55]

André Rebouças.

José de Alencar.

"Once again bringing to Parliament the legitimate deputy for the 1st and 5th districts, the brave Province of Pernambuco teaches a severe lesson to the slavers of the Chamber, represented by their leader." Drawing by Agostini, in *Revista Ilustrada*, June 13, 1885.

Joaquim Nabuco.

This distance is of fundamental importance and would remain so until the abolitionist campaign became irreversible and abolitionism would take on the guise of a true party within the others. "In 1884 the Liberal Party was converted, and in 1888 the Conservative Party followed."[56]

Joaquim Nabuco is fully aware of the contrast between the new thinking and the old *regressista* or *conciliador* discourse. These are two blocs that include all of civil society and manifest themselves in the diffuse form of public opinion. "Public opinion in 1845 thought legitimate and honest the purchase of Africans treacherously brought from Africa, and introduced to Brazil as contraband."[57]

In the article "A reorganização do Partido Liberal" (The Reorganization of the Liberal Party), Nabuco is once again incisive in illustrating liberalism's dialectical relationship with slavery:

> There is a profound difference between the new liberalism and the old, the second of which still exists, with all of its force, but fortunately has reached the limits of its growth, and therefore tends toward decline as opposed to future expansion. The first great difference had to do with abolitionism, which opposed the old partisan political spirit to the truly popular spirit, and replaced the struggle between the *constitutional theses*, which lacked reach and lacked a future, with the struggle against powerful class privileges, which impede the development of the nation. For the first time the Liberal Party moved beyond scholastic discussions, which were only of interest to the governing classes, and entered the terrain of social reforms, which affect the unconscious masses of the people.[58]

This was not, then, a simple liberal renaissance, but rather an oppositional ideology, a self-consciously modern way of thinking about the problems of labor and citizenship, that infiltrated the party. Although the observer of world history might find the defense of wage labor a bit late in coming, this was due to the nature of our capitalism, which in the felicitous worlds of one commentator was a *capitalismo tardio* (capitalism late in coming).[59] The man responsible for this expression, the economist João Manuel Cardoso de Melo, in studying the internal limits to expansion during the old regime, concluded that "the final years of the 1860s mark the crisis of the mercantile and slave-holding coffee economy, and as we shall see, the decisive moment in the crisis of the colonial economy."[60]

The response to the crisis came as much from the urban (and northeastern) abolitionist movements as it did from the pro-immigration policy of the landowners of São Paulo. Their social and moral motivations were distinct but, traveling along different paths, they both contributed to bringing about the end of slavery.

At any rate, the rupture in the political equilibrium that occurred in 1868 could not have led to radical measures for the simple reason that the pro-immigration project had not yet reached maturity, but rather had at this time only been plotted out by certain men of affairs who were sensitive to the lack, whether real or potential, of workers. Practical measures would come ten to fifteen years down the line.

The polemical texts that give expression to the dissatisfaction felt by liberals during 1868 and 1869 did not look to the labor question as their single *punctum dolens*. Rather, this question featured as an item within a program that emphasized electoral reform. The new liberalism, which was urban in origin, sought to give voice to its virtual electors: "At present the most ardent desire of all enlightened Brazilians, as has been the case for all of the opposition parties, is broad electoral freedom. This is the sincere expression of the national opinion as expressed in electoral rallies." So stated José Antônio Saraiva in a public letter to Counselor Nabuco de Araújo, who had asked him his "opinion regarding the reforms that should be included in the liberal program."[61]

This historical moment stimulated the debate on representation. The fall of the Zacarias government and the nomination of a cabinet led by the ultramontane Viscount of Itaboraí had removed the veil and fully revealed the true strength of the moderating power, the impotence of the deputies, and in sum, the precariousness of the entire party system.

Saraiva alleged: "I am also deeply convinced that D. Pedro II enjoys power that is equal to Napoleon III. The French constitution, however, is the base of that monarch's power, whereas the betrayal of the vote is the source of the emperor of Brazil's excessive power."

It is worth focusing particular attention on a symptom of this new way of thinking. The liberals' protest did not end with their call for direct elections that would be free from the interference of the *coronéis*. The idea of salaried labor, as a project for the median term, was also carried in on the waves of this democratic flood. But this was not the first priority of the liberals. They failed to give it a concrete thematic identity, and they failed to respond to the basic question of how to find a substitute, in the here and now, for black labor, which was then sustaining coffee production. At that time, the most radical proposal they would adopt was freedom for Brazilian-born children of slaves with compensation for slave owners. This said, the principle of contract labor was elucidated and would in the future become inextinguishable in more than one context.

From Saraiva's letter:

> All of our difficulties stem from the betrayal of the elections, just as our industrial backwardness stems entirely from our slavery. These are, in my

humble opinion, the two cardinal points on which the whole of the Liberal Party's attention and efforts must converge.

With *free elections*, with the disappearance of the enslaved element, and with the freedom of the press which we already possess, Brazil will find a clear path toward its great and glorious destiny, and in the not-so-distant future, it will stand among the most advanced nations.

However, with the *enslavement* of men and of the vote, despite the freedom of the press we enjoy, we will continue to be, as we are now, looked down upon by the civilized world, which cannot understand how with such natural abundance we have progressed so little.

The semantic polarity is this: our backwardness versus the more advanced nations. The acute awareness of backwardness we see in Tavares Bastos, Nabuco, Rebouças, and Rui Barbosa developed in terms of the opposition between slave and free labor. With their eyes cast toward England and the United States, our progressive politicians issued a severe critique of the regime.

The Manifesto of the Centro Liberal (Liberal Center), published in March 1869, in addition to detailing the abuses that followed in the wake of the conservatives' ascent, expands upon the reforms seen as the necessary median term between reaction and revolution:

> Reform.
> Or revolution.
> Reform to bring about revolution.
> Revolution, the necessary consequence of the nature of things, of the absence of a representative system, of the exclusive, oligarchic rule of one party.
> Do not hesitate in making your choice:
> Reform!
> And the Country will be saved.

The following men signed: José Thomaz Nabuco de Araújo, Bernardo de Souza Franco, Zacarias de Góis e Vasconcelos, Antonio Pinto Chichorro da Gama, Francisco José Furtado, José Pedro Dias de Carvalho, João Lustosa da Cunha Paranaguá, Teófilo Benedicto Ottoni, and Francisco Octaviano de Almeida Rosa.[62]

What was the content of this vital reform? The program was laid out in another text, signed by the same names and first published in the *Diário da Bahia* on May 16, 1869. It consisted of five points, the last of which is literally "Emancipation of the slaves," followed by this proviso: "consisting of freedom for all children of slaves born since the date of the law, and the gradual manumission of all those currently enslaved, in such a manner as shall be deemed most convenient."

One might say that even at the moment at which the abolitionist campaign exploded in Parliament and in the press, in 1879 and 1880, the liberal goals were precisely these: freedom for those born into slavery through compensation and the gradual emancipation of all other slaves.

Further on, the manifesto features a paragraph on tactics that speaks to the fear that the new party might split into opposing wings, which would impede the Centro Liberal from functioning at a time of anticonservative unity:

> The emancipation of the slaves is intimately related to the program's principal object, which is limited to addressing certain abuses. However, it is one of today's great questions, a necessary and urgent requirement of civilization, given the number of states that have abolished slavery, and that Brazil is the only Christian country that maintains it, as in Spain abolition will occur in a matter of days.
>
> It is of course true that the defense of the liberty of thousands of men who live in conditions of oppression and humiliation is a necessary mission, and a great glory, for the Liberal Party.[63]

The progressive elements of this program were the work of the party's more open-minded wing. They reflect the thought of Teófilo Ottoni, who had led an experimental project of German settlement in the Mucuri Valley, as well as Francisco Octaviano, Tavares Bastos, and Nabuco de Araújo. The ideological evolution of Nabuco de Araújo, which his son followed step by step in *Um estadista do Império* (A Statesman of the Empire), leads us to suppose that something profound had occurred as he distanced himself from the politics of the landed interests and began the search for a modern alternative. This new viewpoint, of which Nabuco de Araújo's *discurso de sorites* (Sorites Speech) of July 17, 1868, was paradigmatic, inaugurated, in Joaquim Nabuco's laudatory terms, "the final period of the empire."[64]

This speech lands a masterstroke against the system's narrow-minded formalism, precisely at the moment in which Nabuco de Araújo distinguishes between the legality and legitimacy of institutions. The topic of the polemic was, as has been said, Pedro II's recent nomination of a conservative cabinet without the backing of Parliament. This was a legal act, since it fell to the Crown to choose and dismiss governments, but it was illegitimate, since the liberals held an absolute majority in Parliament.

Having made his point with clarity and distinction, in the name of conscience and justice, Nabuco de Araújo applies it to the institution of slavery: "Slavery, *verbi gratia*, is among us authorized by law, hence it is a legal fact. But no one would say that it is legitimate, because it is condemned by divine law, by civilization, by the entire world."[65]

In substantive terms, what had changed?

The new liberalism now was fully capable of saying that slavery, though formally legal, was illegitimate. Nabuco himself, fourteen years before his speech, had thought and acted differently. In 1854, while he was minister of justice in Paraná's *conciliador* cabinet, he contributed to an infamous official decision that had proscribed—that is, countermanded—the law of November 7, 1831, in which the regency had declared free all those Africans who would arrive in Brazil after that date. Minister Nabuco not only accepted this open violation of the law of 1831 but moreover defended it in terms of the reason of state, advising the president of the province of São Paulo to intervene in the case of Bento, an African slave smuggled into Brazil after the legal end of the slave trade. The slave had fled and, after having been apprehended by the police, was freed by a judge who had managed to determine his date of entry into the country. Nabuco de Araújo, however, defended the rights of the master who sought to recover his slave, citing "the well-being of society's collective interests, the defense of which falls to the government," and concluding: "Rulings should not be made that are against the law, but rulings should be avoided against these interests, rulings that would elicit reactions of alarm and exasperation in landowners."[66]

In 1854, the interests of the landowners were legitimate, whereas the law that protected the freedom of Africans was legal but capable of being infringed. In 1868, however, for Nabuco de Araújo, the freedom of the children of enslaved women became legitimate, whereas now the property rights of the landowner over the children born into slavery were merely legal and thus capable of being reformed.

This inversion of criteria is highly significant: the liberalism of 1868 was not the liberalism of 1854. The concrete content of what was considered legitimate, which lies at the heart of the values that compromise a political ideology, had changed. And the motive force for this transformation had been the civilizing idea of free labor—not the absolute and immediate need for free labor but rather its value. In this same key year of 1868, Quintino Bocayuva (a liberal who favored the republic) published a pamphlet on the crisis of agriculture, in which he advocated in the short term a policy of Chinese immigration financed by the state.[67]

This led to the parliamentary battle of 1871, in which the new liberals successfully fought, and without being unduly constrained by their partisan loyalties. There were members of both imperial-era political parties among the sixty-one voters who favored the Law of the Free Womb, as well as the thirty-five opposed. Coffee from São Paulo voted no. The entrepreneurial thinking of the western landowners, who were on the rise, was not as modern, lucid, and progressive as twentieth-century historiography on São Paulo would suggest. Their thinking was still proslavery.

Reform and Abolition

It is not sufficient to speak of one abolitionism within the broader context of the new liberalism, which set the ideological tone for the end of the empire. The notion of plurality better represents the variety of points of view and specific interests that, in the end, contributed to giving the Lei Áurea (Golden Law) the form it took upon its promulgation, without the compensation for slave owners that was so strongly demanded in the 1880s.

In *Minha Formação*, Joaquim Nabuco identifies five groups that contributed to bringing about this outcome:

1) the *abolitionists* who campaigned for abolition in Parliament, in the press, and in academic contexts;
2) the *militants of the abolitionist cause*, who openly facilitated mass desertions by slaves and instructed them in how to achieve emancipation;
3) the *slave owners*, especially in the northeast and south, who freed their slaves in great numbers in the final years of the abolitionist movement;
4) the *public men* (Nabuco generously terms them *statesmen*) connected to the government who, after the 1867 Fala do Trono (Emperor's Speech), demonstrated their intent to gradually resolve the *questão servil*;
5) The personal actions of the emperor and the princess-regent.

As for the first two groups, these "formed concentric circles and were largely composed of the same elements. The better part of the abolitionist party, the leaders of the movement, belonged to these two groups."[68]

This account can be considered an accurate description of the abolitionist campaign. Nabuco includes himself in the first group, as a deputy for the Liberal Party, defender of legal action, founder of the publication O Abolicionista (1881), and author of a dense, beautiful, and combative text, O Abolicionismo (1883). His testimony merits reflection on the ideological characteristics of the various forms of abolitionism.

We might begin by taking up Nabuco's suggestion and demarcating a broad category that would include the concentric groups of reformists and militants, reserving another category for all the rest. Leaving the exposition of internal differences for another occasion, we are confronted by two types of abolitionist:

I

For the members of the first group, the social and ethical challenge to which Brazilian society was obliged to respond entailed the redemption of a past marked by abjection and the granting of justice to blacks, including freedom in the short term and integration into a modern democracy.

On the horizon, they saw a society built on industry, salaried labor, small and medium landholdings, free primary education, and universal suffrage. Joaquim Nabuco, Rui Barbosa, José do Patrocínio, André Rebouças, Luís Gama, Antônio Bento, and their followers saw abolition as the first step in a program that would entail agricultural reform, *democracia rural* (rural democracy—this is Rebouças's term), and workers' participation in a system based on competition and opportunity.

The cultural roots of this viewpoint are found deep within the discourse of European philanthropists from the first half of the nineteenth century, who were read and quoted by Brazilians during the 1850s and, more directly, in the English and North American economic models that were idealized by the new liberalism.[69]

The progressive arguments in favor of abolition had been articulated in detail in the discourse that came into being following the suppression of the slave trade. The most obvious expressions of this thinking are works by two men who spearheaded a frankly liberal and capitalistic form of social criticism: Tavares Bastos and Perdigão Malheiro.

Both men began writing during the 1860s. The *Cartas do solitário* were published in 1863, the first part of *A escravidão no Brasil* (Slavery in Brazil) in 1866. And if we move a bit farther back in history, we find the name of a pioneering member of our class of Anglophile businessmen, Irineu Evangelista de Sousa.

It is understandable that social differences would exist between the two generations. When Rebouças, Nabuco, and Patrocínio took up the campaign for unconditional abolition, slavery's days were already numbered, and certain farther-sighted politicians from the west of São Paulo had already begun the process of European immigration. But the society in which Tavares and Perdigão operated was still almost entirely dependent on black labor. Compare these figures: 1,175,000 slaves in 1864 versus just 723,419 in 1887.

In 1864, modern, reform-minded liberalism was an ideological value in search of a logical argument but had not yet raised a cry of alarm in response to a problem that required an immediate solution. This explains the gradualism of certain proposals made by the two liberal pioneers. From 1880 forward, the majority was cognizant of the urgency of abolition. The abolitionist campaign sought to build a new society.

It is important to recall that politicians were not alone in the ranks of militants. A vigorous intellectual movement, which sought to approach Enlightenment ideals "scientifically," was active during this period. Sílvio Romero summarized it as "a group interested in new ideas," citing 1868 as its foundational moment.[70] Positivism and evolutionism, Comte and Spencer were their principal points of reference. Their goals were free labor and a more representative political system.

The religious positivists quickly embraced the most radical of the new proposals. In 1884, Miguel Lemos opens the book *O positivismo e a escravidão moderna* (Positivism and Modern Slavery) with a dedication to the black hero of the rebellion of Saint-Domingue:

To the Sainted Memory
    of
the First amongst the Blacks
Toussaint Louverture / (1746–1803),
Dictator of Haiti. Champion and Martyr
    of the freedom
    of his race.

The work is a collection of antislavery texts by August Comte. It features as an appendix the *Apontamentos para a solução do problema servil no Brasil* (Notes toward the Resolution of the Slavery Problem in Brazil), dated Shakespeare 22, 92 (September 30, 1880) and signed by Teixeira Mendes and other orthodox positivists. The text repudiates the "immorality of the criminal colonial inheritance," places the blame for the Paraguayan War on the nation, and argues against the legitimacy of the institution of holding slaves as property. Finally, it contends that once freed, slaves will be transformed into workers with a legally defined number of work hours, weekly rest period, and a reasonable salary. Are these not, in embryonic form, the social policies professed by the Jacobins and, later, by the junior officers who were disciples of the Comtian thinker Benjamin Constant?

In a manifesto dated Dante 21, 95 (August 5, 1883), Miguel Lemos argues for immediate abolition, without compensation for slave owners, and for the use of freed slaves as salaried workers. A good orthodox positivist, he asks the emperor to act as a dictator, without consulting Parliament, "which only serves to guarantee the liberty of intriguing mediocrities," as the august teacher had already observed.

There is a close ideological connection between the new liberals and certain radical republican leaders like Silva Jardim, Luís Gama, and Raul Pompéia. For all of these men, the decisive issue was the question of free labor. For this reason, they kept their distance from the *paulista* group that during the 1870s and early 1880s was still controlled by quite conservative landowners. "Your Phrygian caps are coffee filters"—a declaration Pompéia made openly to the members of the Clube de Lavoura (Agriculture Club) in Campinas—speaks to a rift that would widen into open opposition.

The socially reformist strain within Brazilian positivism has not yet been fully explored. Its bitter struggle against oligarchy influenced young army officers, Jacobins, and junior officers, and the Prestes Column and the Revolution of 1930 were its most complex moments. Elsewhere, Comtian political ideas would create an organizational structure for the modern social preoccupations that would be codified in the *trabalhismo gaúcho* (*Gaúcho* Workers Movement) of Lindolfo Collar, whom the positivist Getúlio Vargas would nominate as first minister for labor in 1931, and who was responsible for almost all of Vargas's social legislation. This legislation, minus its corporatist elements, which were eliminated in the last Constitutional Convention, has survived for more than a half-century and even today serves as the backbone of Brazilian workers' rights.

It is worth noting a difference in terms of how the relationship between civil society and the state was conceived. Orthodox positivism (Miguel Lemos, Teixeira Mendes, and less emphatically, Benjamin Constant) favored a centralized, rational, and tutelary state. Spencerian evolutionism (subscribed to by Sílvio Romero, for example) tended toward classical liberalism and believed in the wisdom of natural selection that, through competitive processes, would reward the most capable. Concretely, the orthodox positivists wanted a strong president, an active mind to head up the state. The evolutionists, in contrast, celebrated bourgeois parliamentarianism for its spontaneous, slow, and gradual reforms. Both groups, however (and this is the sign of their modernity), proposed a political model that would serve as a substitute for the old oligarchic and proslavery empire.

Thus returning our gaze to the crucial years of 1860–1870, we perceive a general tone of disquiet, a desire for renewal that sought to break with the monarchical regime. It was in this climate that the new liberalism coalesced, and it was this dissatisfaction that allowed for a broad ideological filtering of European doctrines.

The American Civil War was another cause of division between the two camps. While Varnhagen, the patron of traditional historiography in Brazil, sympathized with the southern landowners, Tavares Bastos and Perdigão Malheiro saw in the North's struggle and in the figure of Lincoln examples of a new way of thinking that was worthy of imitation. In this, as in other moments in our history of ideas, the relations between the centers of power and the periphery deserve an analysis that does not reduce them to "all or nothing" declarations. By glossing one of John Dewey's theories, on the formation of individual consciousness, we may affirm that cultural and political groups from dependent nations are not only subject to but also choose and work with influences issuing from the system's dominant poles.

Liberal reformism, which would grow from 1868 forward, was the result of an internal struggle whose economic and social elements have already been inventoried: the end of the slave trade, the problem of the lack of available workers, economic growth, urbanization, migration, and so on. At the same time, each of these elements of the system had an international dimension.

The confrontation between our particularities and the course of world history, during this period of ascendant imperialism, alternately points toward variations within a broad process of postcolonial integration (to which the whole of Latin America was subject) and highlights certain discordant racial and cultural features that are interpreted as proper to the new nation in formation. This national element, when recognized as such, can be abstracted—and marshaled—both by conservatives, who adopt it as a sort of traditionalist banner (the *patria del criollo*), or in opposing terms, by reformists, who look upon it as a catalyzing force for dissatisfied groups, as in the radical nationalism of the Jacobins at the end of the nineteenth century or in the critical nationalism of the junior officers during 1922–1930.

Conservative nationalism found organic expression at the height of the proslavery empire. It can be found in the erudite pages of the *Revista do Instituto Histórico e Geográfico*, it permeates the rich bounty of documents found in the Viscount of Porto Seguro's *História Geral do Brasil* (General History of Brazil), and it is the mythical glue of José de Alencar's *indianista* and colonial novels.

At the other extreme, reformist or radical nationalism sought progress, by which was meant the elevation of Brazil to the level of Western civilization. Tavares Bastos preached a national immigration policy and defended the opening of the Amazon River to international traffic, which occurred in 1866, the year in which the first transatlantic cable between Europe and Brazil was also installed. Perdigão Malheiro, who fought alongside Tavares Bastos in the Instituto dos Advogados (Lawyers' Institute), undertook a detailed study of antislavery laws promulgated in the United States, in Europe, and in the English, French, and Dutch West Indian colonies. Brazil would become a great nation when it met international standards. The rhetoric of the younger José Bonifácio, and of his disciples Castro Alves and Rui Barbosa, was similarly oriented, and featured laments and protests against Brazilians' complicity in the massacre of blacks. This is the spirit of "Vozes d'África" (Voices from Africa) and "O navio negreiro" (The Slave Ship). Certain of Dom Pedro II's political views would indicate that, guided by a religious respect for English and French culture, he shifted from the national-conservative pole toward the national-reformist pole.

What is more, we find expressive coincidences that are, quite probably, more than coincidental. One of the arguments made by the proslavery camp was based on the comparison between the life of slaves in Brazil and the hardships suffered by European proletarians chained to a sixteen- to eighteen-hour workday. This was Alencar's thinking. We saw some pages earlier how a businessman from Rio de Janeiro referred to the slaves in the English factories in order to reproach the philanthropists who objected to slavery. It is instructive to accompany the parallel discourse one finds in the debates occurring in France during the reign of Louis Philippe between the opponents and defenders of colonial slavery in the Caribbean. The deputies from Martinique and Guadeloupe described the good treatment given to blacks in their islands and deplored the poor fortune of the workers of the Paris suburbs.

These workers, for their part, closed ranks and sent a collective signed letter to the assembly, disproving the arguments of the colonial representatives. The document is cited in the fine preface written by Aimé Césaire to a new edition of texts by the abolitionist Victor Schoelcher. It is worth transcribing in its entirety:

> Messieurs Deputies: the below-signed workers of the capital have the honor, in function of Article 45 of the Constitution, of soliciting that in this session, you concede to abolishing slavery. This sickness, which is no longer of this century, continues in certain French possessions. It is in order to obey the great principle of human fraternity that we ask that you hear our voice, in favor of our unfortunate brothers, the slaves. We also feel the need to raise our voice in protest, in the name of the working class, against those who uphold slavery, those who dare to argue, and who are knowledgeable of the truth, that the condition of French workers is more deplorable than that of the slaves. In accordance with the *Black Code*, 1685 edition, articles 22 and 25, slave owners must feed and clothe their human chattel, yet official publications of the Ministry of the Navy and Colonies declare that they evade these obligations by giving the slaves Saturdays off. Slaves in French Guiana receive only a *black Friday* once every fifteen days, contrary to the prohibitions enumerated in Article 24 of the Black Code and to the penalties enumerated in Article 26.
>
> Whatever the faults of the present condition of labor in France, the worker is free, and from a certain point of view, freer than those salaried defenders of human property.
>
> The worker belongs to himself. No one has the right to capture him, or sell him, or violently separate him from his wife, from his children, from his comrades. Even if the slaves were fed and clothed by their masters, yet we could not consider them happy. As the Duke of Broglie put it so well, to argue this would be to say that the condition of an animal is preferable

to that of a human being, and that it is better to be a brute than a rational creature. Proud of our sainted and generous gesture, we are certain that our petition will echo throughout the noble motherland, and we have confidence in the justice of the deputies of France.
Paris, January 22, 1844.
Signed: Julien Gallé and 1,505 signatures.[71]

Aimé Césaire comments: "On this day, January 22, 1844, the alliance between the two proletariats, the proletariat of European workers, and the proletariat of colonial slaves, was sealed."

Perdigão Malheiro, in *A escravidão no Brasil*, shows himself to be highly informed regarding the recent French abolitionist campaign. On numerous occasions he mentions the work of Victor Schoelcher (especially the *Histoire de l'esclavage pendant les deux dernieres années*, 1847), A. Cochin (*De l'abolition de l'esclavage*, 1861), and Wallon (*Histoire de l'esclavage dans l'Antiquité et dans les colonies*, 1847), along with official reports edited by parliamentary commissions in the years that preceded the total abolition of slavery in the colonies. Perdigão's work would, in turn, be an obligatory point of reference for Joaquim Nabuco in the abolitionist arguments he made between 1870 and 1880. There is, then, an internal coherence to the project of the Brazilian reformists, who figured out how to incorporate as was appropriate information issuing from the French and English movements that were their immediate predecessors. These close ties with liberal Europe did not alter (but rather reinforced) the doctrinal firmness of the new ideology that was expressing itself in Parliament and in the press.

At the other extreme, the reaction of the elderly Marquis of Olinda to the question formulated in April 1867 by the head of the cabinet, Zacarias de Góis ("Convém abolir diretamente a escravidão?" or "Should slavery be directly abolished?") defines the agro-mercantile ethos that was still clinging to life. Araújo Lima responded: "European publicists and statesmen do not understand the situation of countries with slavery. Their ideas do not apply here."[72]

II

We should now turn our glance to the late but effective participation of those who exercised the greatest influence over the national economy—the landowners of the central-southern region.

In contrast to the positions staked out by Tavares Bastos, Nabuco, Rebouças, Rui Barbosa, Luís Gama, Patrocínio, and Antônio Bento, the social conscience of the coffee growers and their spokesmen in Parliament was slow in forming and remained responsive to their short- and medium-term economic plans. If the objective of the first group was to emancipate the slaves as soon as possible, the goal of the second group was to bring about the transition from slave labor to free labor in good time and without undo cost. While during a certain period (1886–1888) the efforts of the two groups coincided and led to the Golden Law, the rationale for the actions of the first group was never that of the second group.

The abolitionists wanted to free the slaves, whereas the coffee growers wanted substitutes for black labor—hence the difference in rhythm and emphasis between the two groups. The abolitionists worked to accelerate the process, in the interest of alleviating the slaves' suffering, whereas the landowners slowed the state's action on the issue as much as they could, since they were only concerned with the quantum of labor they could manage to squeeze from the remaining slaves before casting them out into the wide world of subsistence labor, that is, of the *lumpen*.

The Partido Republicano Paulista's (São Paulo Republican Party) reservations, which so angered Luís Gama, and its last-minute adherence to abolitionism can only be understood in light of the pragmatic context that produced them. Today, now that the unlimited praise once showered on the landowners of the new west for their lucidity and their modern spirit has come to an end, we can fully retrace the truly pragmatic steps made by the coffee growers, from their open rejection of the Law of the Free Womb (see Rodrigo Silva and Antônio Prado's votes from 1871) to their entry into the already triumphant movement in 1887, by which time the problem of labor had been resolved through mass European immigration underwritten by the imperial and provincial governments.

Studies by Conrad and Gorender, which confirm opinions expressed earlier by Joaquim Nabuco and José Maria dos Santos, lay bare the apprehension of the São Paulo republicans, who in the 1870s were quite reluctant to call for drastic measures.

In opposition to the post-1868 liberals, like André Rebouças, who advocated for a society based on small landholdings, an immediate end to slave labor, and modernization via industry, the republicans among the great landowners focused their efforts on oligarchic decentralization. In line with the Manifesto of 1873, they argued that each province should resolve the problem of finding an adequate substitute for slave labor in its own way and in due course. At this time, the slave trade between provinces was still bringing considerable numbers of blacks from the northeast to São Paulo, Rio de Janeiro, and Minas Gerais. "In 1870, it was stated in the Legislative Assembly of São Paulo that this was the Province that had the least to fear from a shortfall in available labor, since all of the slaves from the North of the Empire were coming here. On that occasion, Paulo Egydio defended the legitimacy of the slave trade, describing it as 'a very legitimate and accepted industry among us.' He came out against the restriction of this freedom through over-taxation: a fee for transfer of title, imperial and municipal taxes, registering of sales."[73]

Abolition, which for the northern and northeastern provinces and for urban professionals could be imposed without harm, was not yet attractive to the landowners of São Paulo, who were only just beginning to develop their immigration projects. Consider this fact: up until 1880 the São Paulo provincial government had spent nothing on the immigration of European laborers. The most convenient ideology for the *bandeirantes* of coffee was the *beautitude physiocratica* (physiocratic beatitude) that was already proving bothersome to the first systematic defenders of national industry. These men, citing French and Yankee examples, fought for a protectionist policy designed to defend emerging industries, but their struggle was in vain. Coffee maintained absolute primacy. The Associação Industrial (Industrial Association) called for the "regenerative protection of the State's Laws, without which [industries] will be cast into the same abyss into which many of their sisters have fallen."[74]

At the moment of its formation, the São Paulo Republican Party was fearful of drowning in the rising flood of the new liberalism, from which it would nonetheless receive a significant degree of assistance during the time in which the embers of the political crisis of 1868 still burned. In order to put things in their proper place, the Comissão do Partido (Party Commission) declared on January 18, 1872:

> Seizing on this opportunity, we ask for your attention and assistance in neutralizing the means by which the forces of obscurantism, aligned with bad faith, have attempted to mischaracterize the friends of democracy, by presenting them as proponents of doctrines that are fatal to the country. Among the arms that they wield, there is one that, if skillfully wielded, may reach its target. We refer to the lie, which has been willfully spread about, that the Republican Party champions and is attempting to put into place violent means to achieve its policies and to bring about the abolition of slavery.... We must not forget that, if Brazilian democracy were to incorporate such ideas into its reforms, then it would alienate the greater part of those who have thus far adhered to it, as well as the sympathies that it hopes to attract in the future. While it is true that the Republican Party cannot remain indifferent to this eminently social question, the resolution of which will affect all interested parties, it is nonetheless necessary to note that it does not, nor will it in future, be responsible for its resolution, for before it leads the government, the question will be addressed by one of the monarchist parties.[75]

From this moment forward, republican propaganda and the abolitionist campaign followed separate paths. The positions were clarified and defined more precisely at the 1873 Republican Congress:

> If the matter is given over to our consideration [so states the Manifesto of April 18], we will approach it as follows:
> 1st) With respect to the principles of federal union, each province will carry out the reform *in accordance with its particular interests*, more or less gradually, as determined by its greater or lesser ease in substituting free for slave labor.
> 2nd) With respect to the rights acquired and in order to reconcile property with the principle of liberty, the reform will be carried out with compensation or redemption.[76]

Luís Gama protested vehemently, but his voice was drowned out by a deafening silence. This would be the neutral line followed by the agricultural republicans, a group principally characterized by Moraes Barros, Campos Salles, Francisco Glycerio, João Tibiriçá, and Prudente de Moraes. Moraes's pragmatism was formulated in tactical terms in his May 1885 parliamentary intervention concerning the Projeto Saraiva (Saraiva Project), which resulted in the Lei dos Sexagenários (Sexagenarians' Law):

> I would say, and I do not believe that the representatives from my province will object, that in the province of São Paulo, especially in the west, which is its richest and most prosperous region, the central question is not that of the freedom of the slaves. The people of São Paulo do not resist, they do not object to this. What does concern them, and with good reason, is the substitution and availability of labor (seconded by Antônio Prado, Rodrigo Silva and Martim Francisco), and provided the government seriously resolves to employ the necessary means to find a substitute for slave labor, provided it facilitates the acquisition of free laborers who will guarantee the availability of labor, and the preservation and development of agriculture, then the people of São Paulo will be satisfied and will not hesitate to free their slaves, even without compensation, for the best, the true form of compensation will be in the ease with which they will be able to find free laborers, to replace their former slaves.[77]

This text, in all of its weighty redundancy, speaks for itself. Full adherence to the abolitionist campaign by the men of western São Paulo was, then, conditional on a satisfactory degree of official support for the acquisition of free laborers. This support would be abundant: between 1887 and 1888, nearly 150,000 immigrants would arrive at our ports. With the proclamation of the republic, to be ruled by coffee, the *grande imigração* (great immigration) could begin.

The problem of salaried labor had been resolved but not that of the former slave, that is, the question of the black. Liberal republicanism had nothing to contribute in terms of this question. This was quickly perceived by those militants of the new liberalism who remained loyal to the monarchy, like Nabuco and Rebouças, whose correspondence is full of accusations against the new, plutocratic regime. Nabuco wrote to Rebouças, who exiled himself to Africa on the day the republic was proclaimed:

> Oh, the sort of people with whom we were involved! I am now convinced that there was not one bit of love for the slave, of disinterest or of abnegation in three quarters of those who declared themselves abolitionists. It was just one more speculation! The proof is that they created this republic and from that point on have only championed the cause of the speculators, of the thieves of finance, and are making the conditions of the poor infinitely worse. It is certain that the blacks are dying and degrading themselves through alcoholism even more so than when they were slaves, whose fate God had put in the hands of others (that is, if God truly consented to slavery). But where are the champions of the new crusade? This time they would be disbelieved to a man. . . . We were involved with financiers, not with puritans, with the lackeys of failed bankers, with mercenaries in the service of loan sharks, etc.; we had it all, except for sincerity and love for the oppressed. The transformation of abolitionism into stock market republicanism is at least as shameful as was the defense of slavery.[78]

But as early as 1884 Nabuco had perceived the opposition between the new liberals' agricultural reformism and the landowners' political agenda: "We are in the kingdom of coffee, and it is coffee that is imposing the greatest obstacles to the rescue of the slaves."[79]

This thinking was shared by Lima Barreto, a mulatto humiliated and insulted by the *República do Kaphet* (Republic of Koffee). But this is another story, the story of the blacks and mestizos after abolition. He who studies it must untie another knot—not that which tied together liberalism and slavery, but rather liberalism and prejudice.

8   Under the Sign of Ham

By the time the Second Empire and reached its midpoint, the aging but still robust conservatism of the oligarchies found itself challenged by a progressive current that was impatient with political stagnation, that defended industry and free labor, believed in Yankee democracy, and in sum, wished to bring Brazil up to the level of the centers of capitalism. The myth of the good savage had little resonance for this intellectual movement, which Joaquim Nabuco termed the *new liberalism*. That myth was the symbol of another time, forged in the period immediately following independence, and it could only survive as an element of schoolboy rhetoric. In the eyes of the new generation, the future was the only thing to be contemplated. The poems of Castro Alves would speak eloquently of the hopes placed in the great and strong century, to cite the words of his idol, Victor Hugo.

But the rank underground recesses of this supposedly modern house, which had opened wide its windows to let in the *sol do porvir* (sun of the future), concealed a dead man, or better yet, a dying man, who disturbed some and caused indignation in others. This man was black slavery.

Alencar had been able to fuse together the Amerindian and the Portuguese in the pages of his novels and in the language of his lyrical poetry. But black and white were arranged as on a chessboard, diametrically opposed to one another. On what images could a critical ideology draw?

The vague perception of a dissonance between the figurations of America and Freedom, which had been signaled as early as Gonçalves Dias's *Os Timbiras*, was taken up fully by Castro Alves and his imitators, who dignified it by giving it thematic substance.

We may perceive an initial sign of this change in the treatment given by the new poetry to descriptions of American nature. In these poets nature loses its status as the savage's idyllic home to become the backdrop for schemes in which it is tarnished. This is a poetry in which the hymn to the tropical landscape serves as a prelude to the execration of a society unworthy of the land in which it lives. This is a strong sign that there had been a change of direction and perspective. "Ao romper d'alva" (At Daybreak), "América" (America), and the powerful description of the forest that opens "A cachoeira de Paulo Afonso" (The Waterfall of Paulo Afonso) are poems written in a contradictory register, for they separate a natural world seen as Edenic from the social inferno into which the greed of the slaveholders had transformed it. It is as if the topos of the American paradise had been preserved with all of the exuberance of sounds and color in which Gonçalves Dias, Alencar, and Varela had painted it intact, but for the sole purpose of impacting the still-Romantic reader with the stridency of its contrasts:

> And the palm trees, tortured, sway back and forth,
> When they hear from the hillsides
>   The cry of affliction.
>   ("At Daybreak")

This was, I believe, the first time in our Romantic-national literature that a feeling for nature and the vision of the nation represented conflicting values. At the end of the poem "América," we encounter a thematic kernel that would be skillfully developed in "O navio negreiro" (The Slave Ship) and "Vozes d'África" (Voices from Africa):

> Oh, my country, rouse yourself
> . . .
> Do not stain the page of your epic
> With the blood of the slave, on the filthy surface!

The Brazilian nation—as a land of slaves—is a blot on a landscape formed of waves of light, green forests, indigo skies. And the *retinir dos ferros do cativo* (clanging of the captive's irons) clashes with the *imensa orquestra* (immense orchestra). It is a *som discorde e vil* (discordant and vile sound).

Beginning with this second wave of liberalism (and with increasing intensity given the critical attitudes of the Escola do Recife, or "Recife School," and of the realists and naturalists), the physiognomy of Brazil would progressively lose its appearance of eternal tropical exuberance, and the lines that cut through an impoverished people, divided in terms of race and class, would be uncovered. One need only look at the gallery of our critical intellectuals. From Tavares Bastos to Joaquim Nabuco, from Raul Pompéia to Euclides da Cunha, from Lúcio de Mendonça to Cruz e Sousa, from Luís Gama to Lima

Barreto, from André Rebouças to Manoel Bomfim, the image of the nation becomes progressively darker, so much so that, put in proper perspective, the apparently triumphant nationalism of the *belle époque* should be considered a residue of official culture rather than a vital line of thought. On the verge of the second Industrial Revolution and imperialist expansion, the former colony looked at itself in the mirror of civilization and, turning its gaze back onto itself, was pained by the contrast it saw.

In 1868, the year "O navio negreiro" and "Vozes d'África" were published, the nation's most depressing malady, its exposed nerve, was slavery. The spokesmen for the oligarchies preferred to treat it as if it were an exclusively private matter, subject to the unassailable right to property. This is how Alencar described it in his comedy *O demônio familiar* (Devil in the Family), in which emancipation is granted by the masters with the dual intent of punishing an intransigent slave boy by expelling him from the patriarchal nest and of freeing the family from a perpetual source of confusion and unpleasantness. In the legislative session of 1871, Counselor José Martiano de Alencar would fight against the proposed Law of the Free Womb using orthodox liberal arguments and would defend the autonomy of the paterfamilias before the imperial state. He argued that if the law were adopted, it would amount to transgressing upon the familial realm to which, having been purchased, the slave belonged. The young girl born to enslaved parents should, according to the senator's appeals to his peers, remain at her mother's side in order to be instructed by her in the shadow of the slave quarters.

In contrast, the new liberals insisted on giving the cause of abolition its legitimate public dimension. Their chosen themes would be work, freedom, and citizenship.

In the midst of the debates over the question of children born into slavery, whose freedom had been proposed in 1866, the liberal cabinet was felled by legal but authoritarian action by Pedro II. Oppositional elements radicalized their discourse, appealing to democratic ideals. They founded clubs and journals, and promoted acts of protest across the country. The law students at the Academia de São Paulo invited the young Castro Alves to publicly recite verses in praise of freedom. By a happy coincidence, he would recite, with enormous success, the most beautiful of his abolitionist poems, "O navio negreiro" and "Vozes d'África," which were written in São Paulo, the first on April 18 and the second on June 11.

These public circumstances gave birth to both texts, and it would be shortsighted to deny the influence of these circumstances in conditioning the oratorical quality of both compositions, which are certainly all the more powerful when recited aloud and punctuated by broad and expressive gestures, and if possible, when read before a sympathetic audience.

The reader seems to touch the current of history as it flows through any of Castro Alves's socially minded poems. Reformist politicians and ideologues quickly recognized in this bard a pioneering proponent of their ideals. The testimonies of Rui Barbosa and Joaquim Nabuco affirm a note of critical praise for Castro Alves that would grow to a crescendo in Euclides da Cunha and Manoel Bomfim. In the twentieth century, militants in the black movements, like Édison Carneiro, and orthodox communists, like Jorge Amado, would cite Alves as a predecessor.

"Vozes d'África" and "O navio negreiro" were understood and beloved as cries of rebellion, which analysis of their reception certainly confirms. However, the use to which successive generations of readers put a poem hardly exhausts its potential meanings. In certain cases a single interpretation, consistently reiterated, consigns to the shadows the truth of other equally valid connotations that might place into dialectical relief the poem's uniform meaning as established by consensus.

The protest and denunciation expressed in both poems are real and reflective of lived experience, and their eloquence is fuel for the purest sort of indignation. But what is the vision spied in these verses of blood, sand, and fire?

If we respond that they describe the slave system, in its here-and-now, then we are being largely unfaithful to their immanent meaning. This sort of interpretation better suits Heinrich Heine's poem "Das Sklavenshiff," which is Brechtian *avant la lettre*, and which Augusto Meyer skillfully translated as "O navio negreiro" (The Slave Ship). It begins as follows:

> O sobrecarga Mynherr van Kock
> Calcula no seu camarote
> As rendas prováveis da carga,
> Lucro e perda em cada lote.
>
> Borracha, pimenta, marfim
> E ouro em pó . . . Resumindo, eu digo:
> Mercadoria não me falta,
> Mas o negro é o melhor artigo.
>
> Seiscentas peças barganhei
> - Que pechincha!—no Senegal,
> A carne é rija, os músculos de aço,
> Boa liga do melhor metal.
>
> Em troca dei só aguardente,
> Contas, latão—um peso morto!
> Eu ganho oitocentos por cento
> Se a metade chegar ao porto.

Se chegarem trezentos negro
Ao porto Rio de Janeiro [sic]
Pagará cem ducados por peça
A casa Gonzales Perreiro. [sic][1]

The supercargo Mynher Van Koek
In his cabin sits adding his figures;
He calculates the cargo's amount,
And the probable gain from his niggers.

My gum and pepper are good: the stock
Is three hundred chests of all sizes;
I've gold dust and ivory too in store,
But the black ware by far the best prize is.

Six hundred niggers I bought dirt-cheap
Where the Senegal river is flowing;
Their flesh is firm, and their sinews tough
As the finest iron going.

I got them by barter, and gave in exchange
Glass beads, steel goods, and some brandy;
I shall make at least eight hundred per cent.
With but half of them living and handy.

If only three hundred niggers are left,
When I get to Rio Janeiro,
I shall have a hundred ducats a head
From the house of Gonzales Perreiro.[2]

Could our poet have been familiar with the French prose version of Heine's poem, which was published in the *Revue des Deux Mondes*, a publication that was widely read by Brazilian intellectuals at the time? Augusto Meyer believes so, though he accentuates the differences in tone and perspective that distinguish the two poems. Heine speaks objectively, dryly, and mockingly of the slave trade, whereas Castro Alves does the same using an oratorical diction designed to invoke pathos.

The broad question this essay seeks to answer concerns the way of thinking about slavery that informed Castro Alves's poetry. His distinction from Heine prompts us to seek out the intimate meaning of his text, without forcing us to concede that his poem was definitively interpreted within the context in which it was written and declaimed—in this case, in the context of the abolitionist campaign.

In other words, I think it legitimate to distinguish, in the interest of analyzing and understanding the poem, between its historical function, its political application, and its internal semantic dynamism.

For this purpose, I will provide a reading of "Vozes d'África," the sister poem of "O navio negreiro," and a text that develops to the furthest possible extent a certain tragic and mythical way of describing the overall phenomenon of slavery.

VOICES FROM AFRICA

God! Oh, God! Where are you that you do not respond?
On what world, on what star to you conceal yourself
     Hidden by the skies?
Two thousand years ago I cried forth,
And in vain my lament has traveled across the infinite . . .
     Where are you, Lord God?

Like Prometheus one day you bound me
Took me from the desert, placed me on the red rocks
     —Like a galley slave for all time!
For a vulture—you gave me the hot sun,
And the land of Suez—was the rope
     You tied around my ankle . . .

The Bedouin's tired horse
Falls face down under the whip's lash
     And dies in the sandpit.
My haunches bleed, the pain flows
When the arm of eternity cracks
the simoom's whip.

My sisters are fair, and fortunate . . .
Asia sleeps in the voluptuous shadows
     Of the sultan's *harems*,
Or on the backs of white elephants
She is wrapped by a jeweled cloak,
     In the lands of Hindustan.

For a tent she has the Himalayan peaks
The love-struck Ganges kisses the beach
     Covered in coral . . .
Mysore's winds inflame the sky;
And she sleeps in the temples of the God Brahman
—Colossal pagodas.

Europe is ever glorious Europe! . . .
A dazzling, capricious woman,
     Queen and courtesan.

An artist—she carves Carrara marble;
A poetess—she performs Ferrara's hymns,
    With glorious dedication! . . .

She wins always the laurel wreath
Now a crown, then a Phrygian cap
    Rests upon her head.
The Universe—sick with love—follows her
Is held captive by the maddening movements
    Of that great harlot.
. . .
Oh but I, Lord! . . . I am desperate, abandoned
Astray among the sands
    Lost I march in vain!
If I cry . . . the hot sand drinks up my lament
Perhaps . . . so that my lament, o merciful God!
    You will not find on the earth.

I have not the shadow of a forest . . .
To shield me, nor does one temple remain
    In this burning land . . .
When I climb the Pyramids of Egypt
In vain I cry to the four winds:
    "Shelter me, oh Lord! . . ."

Like the prophet my forehead is covered in ash,
I hide my head from the sandstorm kicked up
    By the fierce Sirocco . . .
When I walk through the Sahara in my rags . . .
Oh! They say: "There goes Africa, wrapped
    In her white burnous . . ."

They do not see that the desert is my shroud,
That silence runs freely
    Over my breast.
There in the land where only the thistle grows
The colossal stone Sphinx yawns,
    Gazing at the tepid sky.

In Thebes, the storks, from the ruined columns
Crane their necks and contemplate
    The endless horizon . . .
From which appears the wandering caravan
And the lone, breathless camel
    Descended from Ephraim . . .

. . .
Have you not had your fill of pain, oh terrible God!
Do you have an eternal, endless hunger
      For revenge and spite?
And what have I done, Lord? what horrid crime
Have I committed that you would strike me
      With your vengeful sword?! . . .
. . .
It was after the *great flood* . . . A traveler,
Black, somber, pallid, breathless,
      Came down from Ararat . . .
And I said to the wanderer, who was thunderstruck:
"Ham . . . you will be my beloved husband . . .
      I will be your Eloa!"

From that day forward an accursed wind
Has run, blowing through my hair
      Cruel anathema.
The tribes wander along the desert paths,
And the starving *Nomad* cuts across the land
      On his swift horse.

I saw learning abandon Egypt . . .
I saw my people follow—damned Jew–
      The road to perdition.
Then I saw my disgraced tribe
Snatched by the jaws of Europe
      A trained falcon! . . .

Christ! In vain you died atop a mountain . . .
Your blood did not wash from my face
      Its original stain.
Even now, by unkind fate,
My children are animals for all,
      And I—feed for all . . .

Now America grows strong on my blood
—The condor became a buzzard,
      The bird of slavery.
She conspired with the others . . . treacherous sister
Like Joseph and his wicked brothers, long ago
      They sold me.
. . .

Enough, Lord! From your strong arm
Let forgiveness roll down across the stars and space
    For my crimes!
For two thousand years . . . I have cried out . . .
Listen to my appeal, there in the infinite,
    My God! Lord, my God!! . . .

For the sake of greater clarity, let us organize our analysis of the text along three planes that, within the poem, evidently intersect: the plane of subjectivity (of the subject and among subjects), that of time, and that of space.

What are these voices that speak and to whom do they speak? When do they speak? From where do they speak?

The Voices

To allow the Dark Continent to speak for itself, in the first person, was a step forward for a theme that, due to its role in our social drama, tended to be approached in the voice of the other.

Prosopopoeia (from the Greek, *prosopon* = Latin, *persona*), through which the African people are granted the status of an individual being, of a narrating, cursing *I*, is the central figure that sustains all of the poem's stanzas and maintains its coherence of tone from the beginning to the end of the text.

In the course of Western cultural history, this technique became customary in political literature beginning in the post-1789 period, and especially from the post-Napoleonic period, during which peoples and nations came to be seen as living, organic beings, as collective personalities in whose name the Romantic poet should speak. See, for example, "O século" (The Century), by Castro Alves, in which the oppressed nations of Poland and Sweden, Hungary and Mexico, are granted body and soul. Our century, Mazzini said, was the century of nationalities.

The combination of an arcane Africa ("For two thousand years") with Africa-as-subject ("I cried forth") is the poem's first novel element, and the source of its strength, for it grants to the distant past and to enigmatic myths the magnetic power of an immediate presence in which all acts of interlocution take place. Africa is, and has always been, a living being. And through the actualization of its poetic *I*, it is a being that is conscious of its identity and its history.

José Veríssimo, who was far from a Romantic reader, communicates his distance even when celebrating the poem by referring to the process of personalization described above. He praises Castro Alves's "eloquence of the best sort," but he charges this eloquence with an "artistic idealization of the situation of the accursed continent and of the demands that our human idealism attribute to it."[3]

Our critic tends to deconstruct what has been constructed lyrically, that is, to separate Africa's state from the author's voice. Speaking of the "accursed continent," on the one hand, and "our human idealism" on the other, José Veríssimo attempted through analysis to defuse the great impact of the poem's enunciation, which is the very effect of communion between the subject and object, achieved through open chords. From the poem's first to last word, personification is inseparable from subjectification. The cold act of dissection committed by the prosaic reader does not cut to the core of the poem, and the poem's humanization of Africa, a Romantic conquest, resists. People and poet suffer and curse in unison.

As an eminently projective linguistic operation, the intertwining of the *I* and the stigmatized race occurs at the subject's core. The poet who makes his own the cries of a people cursed by the gods and by men is himself a cursed being. In "Ahasverus e o Gênio" (Ahasuerus and the Genius), Castro Alves identified himself with the figure of the damned, the *mísero Judeu* (wretched Jew):

> Have you heard of Ahasuerus? . . . —the condemned,
> the wretched Jew, on whose face
> was stamped that horrible seal!
> An eternal wanderer on an eternal path . . .
> Driven from tent to tent
> Fleeing in vain from the vengeful voice!
> . . .
> The *Genius* is like Ahasuerus . . . alone
> Marching, marching on his way
> Without end.

Fagundes Varela, paraphrasing Byron's *Childe Harold*, likewise saw himself in the figure of the Wandering Jew, who was presented in melancholic tones in Eugène Sue's serialized novel. There is a drastic existential refusal that runs deep in the English poet and flows forth confidently in the Brazilian voice of our Varela:

> It is this perennial, continual disgust,
> ever following in my steps,
> and during the day firing my hot veins,
> that come night holds me fast in its perfumed arms!
>
> These are the seeds of martyrdom and pain
> —Constant companions of the wretched Jew!—

On whose wind-burned face,
A fiery tongue was written in flame!!

Who is there who can be an exile to himself?

This angry, impassioned tone, which to me seems unique to the work of the second generation of Romantics, is partially though not entirely distinct from the tragic poetry of "Vozes." The damnation of a race, century after century, is described in Castro Alves's verses with a certain note of Titanism that recalls Vigny and Lord Byron: "Ham . . . you will be my beloved husband: / I will be your Eloa!"

This said, the similarities do not obscure the poems' differences from one another. If we listen closely to the deeper sound emanating from these outcast voices from Africa and from the poem's *I*, which is also an outcast, we hear supplication or impotent clamoring rather than Promethean defiance. This impression is gained from the silence of the interlocutor. Africa's pleas and those of the poet are one and the same, but they are directed toward a *Deus absconditus*. "God! Oh, God! Where are you that you do not respond? / On what world, on what star to you conceal yourself / Hidden by the skies?"

In this context, the poet's invocation of a "Deus clemente" (merciful God), who in the eighth stanza does not see Africa's tears, which the hot sand drinks up, strikes a sarcastic note.

At the Beginning of Time: The Curse of Ham

The destiny of the African people, which has played itself out over millennia, is the result of a single event, remote in time and irreversible: the curse placed on Ham, his son Canaan, and all of their descendants. The people of Africa will be black and they will be slaves: that is all.

The poem incorporates the mythical account of the origin of slavery as related in the Book of Genesis. Below I transcribe the key biblical passage, in which the legend is formulated in canonical terms:

> And the sons of Noah, that went forth of the ark, were Shem, and Ham, and Japheth: and Ham *is* the father of Canaan. These *are* the three sons of Noah: and of them was the whole earth overspread. And Noah began *to be* a husbandman, and he planted a vineyard: And he drank of the wine, and was drunken; and he was uncovered within his tent. And Ham, the father of Canaan, saw the nakedness of his father, and told his two brethren without. And Shem and Japheth took a garment, and laid *it* upon both their shoulders, and went backward, and covered the nakedness of their father; and their faces *were* backward, and they saw not their father's nakedness.

And Noah awoke from his wine, and knew what his younger son had done unto him. And he said, Cursed *be* Canaan; a servant of servants shall he be unto his brethren. And he said, Blessed *be* the Lord God of Shem; and Canaan shall he his servant. God shall enlarge Japheth, and he shall dwell in the tents of Shem; and Canaan shall be his servant. (Genesis 9:18–27)

The scriptural narrative continues, describing the generations descended from Ham, Shem, and Japheth. The dark-skinned peoples of Ethiopia, southern Arabia, Nubia, Tripoli, and Somalia (that is, the Africans who appear in the Old Testament), along with certain tribes that lived in Palestine before the Israelites conquered the land, were all "Hamites."

Certain commentators have identified two strata in chapter 9 of Genesis. They read the mention of Canaan ("Cursed *be* Canaan") as a late substitution for Ham, a change made to the text after the tribes of Israel had succeeded in subjugating the Canaanites during the time of King David. The land of Canaan, the son of Ham, would become the homeland of the Jewish people. The Canaanites would be excluded from messianic salvation as punishment for their sins (especially lust), while Yahweh would grant the Israelites the right to enslave them.

The Book of Judges states that the Canaanites were forced to pay tribute to the tribes of Israel (Judges 1:28).[4] Joshua reports at the same time: "Yet the children of Manasseh could not drive out *the inhabitants of* those cities; but the Canaanites would dwell in that land. Yet it came to pass, when the children of Israel were waxen strong, that they put the Canaanites to tribute; but did not utterly drive them out" (17:12–13). In short, war was responsible for the sad fate of the Canaanites. The narrator of Genesis, chapter 9, then, created an etiological myth, perhaps grounded in the tradition of Adam's original sin, in order to account for the institution of slavery. The problem remains, and it has fallen to exegetes to search for its solution, all the more so because the Canaanites were, after all, a Semitic people.

On the other hand, it would be worth investigating how the curse of Ham was attributed to all Africans during the time of the Portuguese maritime expansion, which caused the reemergence of the figure of the slave in the Western consciousness beginning in the fifteenth century.[5] Yet this investigation into the archeology of ideas can only be hinted at in an essay on Castro Alves's socially minded poetry.

The fact is that it was in the context of modern culture that the explanation was formulated for slavery as the result of a sin. This sin received exemplary punishment from Noah, the patriarch saved from the great flood in order to perpetuate the human race. References to Ham's fate circulated through the sixteenth, seventeenth, and eighteenth centuries, when Catholic and Protestant theology were confronted by the generalization of forced labor within the colonial economies. The old myth served the new economic thinking, which cited it in order to justify the slave trade, along with the discourse of salvation, which saw slavery as a means to catechize groups that beforehand had been subject to fetishism or Islam. Merchants and religious ideologues saw Ham's sin and his punishment as foundational events that gave rise to a situation that now could not be changed.[6]

Though seemingly paradoxical, it was through the return of the myth of the curse of Ham that Castro Alves in 1868 gave poetic form to his "Vozes d'África." The formal scheme that he adopted for the poem turned its back on the epic traditions of national *prosopopeia*. Now there are no muses to invoke but only an inaccessible God who, if interpolated, conceals himself and remains silent. The Hebrew divinity behaves like the vengeful Zeus of the Greek religion. The victim shares with Prometheus only his unkind fate and not the pride of a semidivine being aware of his worthy gift to mankind. Yahweh metes out punishment like Zeus, but Ham's Africa, unlike Prometheus, bows its head and weeps without meriting even the consolation given to the shackled Titan by the devout Nereids in Aeschylus's tragedy:

> Like Prometheus one day you bound me
> Took me from the desert, placed me on the red rocks
>   —Like a galley slave for all time!
> For a vulture—you gave me the hot sun,
> And the land of Suez—was the rope
> You tied around my ankle . . .

A little less than a month prior to composing "Vozes," Castro Alves had written the poem "Prometeu" (Prometheus), in which the hero remains "still prideful and strong, his eyes on the setting sun, / sublime in his suffering, defeated—but not conquered." These signs of resistance, which allow Prometheus to serve as an allegory for a people, are silenced by the Africans' ignored lamentations. In the Africans' case, what prevails is the absurdity of a punishment that is meted out for an ancient crime—hence the tragic quality of an entire continent, which is placed at the mercy of omnipotent anger:

> Have you not had your fill of pain, oh terrible God!
> Do you have an eternal, endless hunger
>   For revenge and spite?
> And what have I done, Lord? what horrid crime
> Have I committed that you would strike me
>   With your vengeful sword?! . . .

As occurred in the case of Adam and Eve's original sin, all of Ham's descendants are marked by the sinner's fall. In both archetypal situations, sin is identified with knowledge of the forbidden: Adam's nakedness, Noah's nakedness, the father's nakedness, the patriarch's nakedness. Yet there is a difference that, in the end, is decisive. Ham's descendants are given no possibility of remission for their sin. The new Adam, as medieval theology referred to Christ, would reestablish the Creator's original bond with His creation, for the curse of Noah's son could not ever be undone: narrated in a mythic time, it remains outside of history. Within the realm of the archaic, the blind forces of the unconscious reign over man's consciousness of the actions that grant humanity to humankind. Africa ignores the rationale for its punishment: "And what have I done, Lord? what horrid crime / Have I committed that you would strike me / With your vengeful sword?!"

The consequences of anathema are borne out generation upon generation, such that despite time's forward movement, which is observed throughout the poem ("It was after the great flood; from that day forward; I saw learning abandon Egypt; I saw my people follow; then I saw my disgraced tribe"), the original curse loses nothing of its intensity. The open and linear time of history—whether situated in terms of the Christian account of salvation or the secular notion of progress—is incapable of penetrating this other, mythological time, which is self-enclosed, and in which the Son of God has died in vain:

> Christ! In vain you died atop a mountain . . .
> Your blood did not wash from my face
>   Its original stain.
> Even now, by unkind fate,
> My children are animals for all,
>   And I—feed for all . . .

Note the contradiction: the appeal to the redeemer (Christ!) fails, as we see in his useful sacrifice. But the act of identifying destiny by name, as an "unkind fate," is a recognition of a power that centuries of Christianity have not been able to undo "Even now." This confirms the suspicion that it is an archaic perspective that orients the entire poem. The final admission of guilt ("forgiveness . . . for my crimes") partakes of a logic of terror that seeks to find moral meaning in the suffering of millions upon millions of human beings. The silence of the massive stone Sphinx, seated at the entry point of the desert and gazing at the tepid sky, is more eloquent than words. The Sphinx does not ask questions: it is the question.

The poet is confronted by an evil that is absurd and meaningless. His imagination works with mythical, historical, and literary materials that, though they appear diffuse, come together in attacking the millennial scandal of African slavery.

The stanzas in which the other continents are personified are quite conventional, it must be admitted, but they obey the internal logic of the myth of origins in which Ham's brothers are granted privileged positions. The novelty for us, as readers of Brazilian Romanticism, is not to be found in the figuration of glorious Europe or in the image of an Asia immersed in sensual pleasures, but in the charge against America, as the land of liberty that becomes a "treacherous sister, bird of slavery." America and Europe, formed into an oppositional pairing by patriotic *indianismo*, lose their naïve, nationalistic function in light of the new abolitionist consciousness and are replaced by the pairing of Africa and America, in which the former is oppressed and the latter is the oppressor. This also occurs in the final delirious passage of "O navio negreiro."

In "Vozes d'África," the opposition serves to place the idea of the universal rejection of blacks within a mythical and tragic context. In another poem, "Saudação a Palmares" (Salutation for Palmares), written one year prior to Castro Alves's death, the tone is distinct. It is challenging and rebellious, and the image of the *bandido nobre* (noble bandit) signals a revolutionary vision of Afro-Brazilian history. Neither Castro Alves nor the generations of black and mestizo intellectuals that followed the publication of the poem were capable of further developing this vision.

The appearance in "Vozes d'África" of Eloa, a mysterious figure who does not feature in the Bible, must be understood in light of the poem's return to a cyclical time of origins. Eloa is the poetic invention of Alfred de Vigny, who in 1824 published the religiously themed poem "Eloá, ou la soeur des anges" (Eloa, or the Sister of the Angels). Eloa is an angel born from a tear shed by Jesus while he was weeping over the death of Lazarus, whom he would soon bring back to life. A tear of pure compassion then ascended to heaven and was transformed into yet another incarnation of the Eternal Feminine, which since the time of *Faust* has inhabited the fantasies of modern man as a symbol of infinite compassion.

In Vigny's poem, woman's compassion is turned to the most beautiful of the archangels, Lucifer. He calls to Eloa from his kingdom of shadows and bares to her his prideful and noble soul, which "bewails the slave and takes him from his lord."[7] Eloa, attracted to Lucifer, wishes to save him and undertakes a dangerous journey to his home. But instead of redeeming him, it is she who falls under his dominion: "I thought I had saved you." "No, it is I who am dragging you off."

Eloa, though born from one of the Redeemer's tears, is irredeemably lost. Likewise Africa, having wedded herself to the accursed Ham, will find no mercy. In "Vozes d'África," myth and poetry become means to tell the story of black slavery. And as readers came to know and love the poem, from their perspective this account became part of the reality of black slavery, for the image of the real ends up becoming part of reality.

A Fertile Image of the Desert

The phrase "the word *dog* doesn't bite" is one of the postulates of modern logic. The letters that comprise the sign have nothing to do with the object they designate. In the final analysis, this amounts to a renewed affirmation of language's conventional—that is, unnatural—character.

At the opposite extreme, there is a line of aesthetic thinking that runs from Vico to Herder, and from the Romantics to the Symbolists, which postulates language's strongly meaningful character. This is the ancient debate, posed in luminous terms in Plato's *Cratylus*, between a theory of language as conventional and a theory of language as natural.

The reader of "Vozes d'África" will encounter on more than one occasion verses containing an obsessively recounted image, that of the desert. This image accords with the description of the land in which the tragedy of Ham and his descendants takes place. The monotonous repetition of this figure responds to a structural requirement of the poem, which is grounded in a mythical time in which origins are continually invoked. This composition recalls, in its insistence of theme, Ravel's *Bolero*. As a symbol of the endless despair of an entire people, the word *deserto* (desert) and its synonyms and variants are saturated with psychological and moral meaning.

Upon closer examination of Castro Alves's use of this verbal sign, what impresses us is neither its intimate correspondence with its referent nor the degree of expressiveness it attains through its invocation in the tone that dominates the entire poem. Rather, what impresses the analytically minded reader is the range of connotations the poet manages to extract from a symbol that is so closely tied to the idea of sterility. If the word *dog* doesn't bite, then neither is the word *desert* infertile.

In terms of the semantics of the poem, its expansive force is such that it comes to signify something more than the dwelling place of the children of Ham and penetrates into the infinite space of God. The divine heavens are transformed into an empty cosmos in which the cries of the African continent are lost: "God! Oh, God! Where are you that you do not respond?" The heavens too are a desert.

It is only in the second stanza that the word itself appears, here associated, in the form of a curious literary contamination, with the myth of Prometheus. Note the terms of the homology: Ham is to Prometheus as Yahweh is to Zeus. The rocky desert corresponds to the Caucasian boulder to which Prometheus is chained. The hot sun corresponds to the buzzard. The Suez

Cruz e Souza. "You are one of the tribe of Ham, accursed, cast out, damned" ("The Enclosed").

Lima Barreto.

"And I had the sensation that I was in a foreign country" (*Recordações do Escrivão Isaías Caminha*) [Reminiscences of the Notary Isaías Caminha].

isthmus corresponds to the Titan's chains. The grandiloquence of the images perhaps offends our contemporary sensibility, which in general tends more toward intellectualism. "Victor Hugo est le plus grand poète français, hélas!" (Alas, Victor Hugo is the greatest French poet), André Gide complained, and Mário de Andrade said much the same of Castro Alves. But what we must attend to here is the polyvalence of the sign and the desert's function as an instrument of divine punishment.

The third stanza consists of a single simile: the Bedouin's horse falls down dead in the sandpit just as Africa bleeds, having been whipped by the sirocco. The whip is brandished by divinity itself: "when the arm of eternity cracks the simoom's whip." The desert of "Vozes" is the Sahara of the Bible, and the Hebrew vision of the African landscape dominates the spatial representation of the entire poem. The Lord of the Old Testament, zealous of his alliance with the people of Israel and also vengeful toward his enemies, manipulates the strands of this story. The double relationship between Yahweh and Africa, and Ham and the desert, will be reasserted and given new features in the stanzas that follow the description of Asia and Europe.

In the eighth stanza the desert returns as a land of the lost, an idea to which a particularly sadistic connotation is added: the fiery sand drinks the victim's tears, "perhaps . . . so that my lament, o merciful God! / You will not find on the earth."

It has been noted that the verse that opens the following stanza, "I have not the shadow of a forest," reduces an entire continent to the portion of it that is lifeless, as if to ignore the existence of immense forested regions in central and southern Africa, areas from which people were captured and brought as slaves to America. This objection concerns the geography and history of slavery, although it does not negatively affect—but rather helps us better understand—Castro Alves's existential and aesthetic division. In the poetry of "Vozes" what matters is metonymy, the part for the whole, the desert for the continent. The imaginary shrinking of real space allows tragic pathos to prevail and multiply in terms of its figurations: the sandpit recalls the ashes the prophet places on his forehead. It is likewise the shroud of dust, the Bedouin's burnous, the arid soil from which only thistle grows, the land of the wandering tribes, the impermanent home of the starving nomad.

The poetic fantasy presented in the text was, of course, inspired by the Old Testament, but this affirmation must be placed in dialectical relief. For the Israelites the long years spent wandering in the desert, following their flight from Egypt and prior to their arrival in Canaan, represent, as we read in the book of Exodus, a time of trial that was marked by suffering but was also full of hope. This marks the moment of their passage into the Promised Land, the place in which they encounter God, who gives them manna and seals his alliance with his people. Moses and Yahweh speak to each other face to face. In Ham's desert, however, there is no promise of freedom but only agony and the threat of renewed slavery. God is absent or remains silent.

This said, "Vozes d'África" and "O navio negreiro" inspired the first abolitionist campaign seen in the semicolony, populated by masters and slaves, called Brazil.

Exile in the Skin

Afonso Henriques de Lima Barreto is the first great mulatto writer to come of age in Brazil during the postabolition period.

His experience as an intellectual who suffered discrimination because of his race and origin, in the post-1888 context, granted him a perspective that cannot be confused with the abolitionists' limitations in vision. Rather, Lima Barreto's perspective is the obverse of that of the abolitionists. Luís Gama, André Rebouças, and José do Patrocínio, militants from the generation that preceded Lima Barreto's own, believed that they were fighting for the liberation of their race. In truth, however, and with the exception of certain general ideas by Rebouças on a rural democratic future (which also figured in Nabuco's thinking), it can be said that the limitation of the selfless abolitionist campaign was, precisely, what occurred on the day following the promulgation of the Golden Law: the slaves were left to their fate.

In concrete terms, how should we interpret this last statement? With the regime of slave labor no more, its former victims were left with few options:

- remain in their present condition as agricultural dependents;
- join the lumpen proletariat, which had been growing in Brazil with the growth of the white, European-origin proletariat;
- exist on the margins of the subsistence economy.

The first of these options is significant in terms of the occasional favors the impoverished freed slaves received from their patrons. This web of social relations dated from the empire and left deep marks on Brazil's mestizo and black intellectuals. We may cite two notable examples. The childhood and adolescent years of Machado de Assis and Cruz e Sousa, respectively the greatest Brazilian novelist and the greatest Brazilian poet of the nineteenth century, speak to the ups and downs faced by recipients of patronage. And without this patronage, it would have been difficult for them to have overcome the barriers of skin color and class that they faced.

After abolition, what could blacks and mulattos who were dependents, members of the subproletariat, or who otherwise existed on society's margins, expect?

The myth of a people's redemption is not sustainable under these historical conditions. Hopes for collective redemption are only formulated when one is living in, or when one believes oneself to be living in, a period full of promise: this is the messianic hope that there will come a day in which all will be judged, freed, saved. But having lived through this "D-Day," so to speak, one is confronted by the present in all of its contradictions.

Lima Barreto looked his present, which was that of our Old Republic, in the eye, as an observer who knew himself to have been defeated by the societal machine but who would not submit to it.

What I find admirable in his written criticisms of ideology is the equal distance he managed to retain in relation to the two forces that were struggling for power in the recently inaugurated regime. Barreto was just as skeptical of the coffee growers as he was of the soldiers loyal to Floriano Peixoto. This context gave rise to sectarian passions, and intellectuals aligned themselves with one or another party, generally granting their party adherence an overarching nationalistic tone. This was not the case of Lima Barreto: "That republic was complete foolishness. Deep down, what took place on November 15 was the fall of the liberal party and the rise of the conservative party, and especially its most retrograde element, composed of diehard defenders of slavery."

Further on he declares: "The whole of our republican administration has constantly pursued the objective of enriching the old agricultural, conservative nobility through tariffs, support for agriculture, paid immigration, etc."[8]

The clear-eyed view of the interests that impelled the *República do Kaphet* (Republic of Koffee) was also directed with equal intensity toward the military solution, which the Sphinxlike Floriano embodies in *O triste fim do Policarpo Quaresma* (The Sad End of Policarpo Quaresma). Barreto saw an indistinct phalanx of Jacobin cadets surrounding the *marechal*, and behind him, tugging at his pant legs, the dull, stupid, uniformed bureaucracy that expanded during this period.

Barreto's satire of the *bruzundangas* was far-sighted.[9] He was not engaged, as was Olavo Bilac, the poet of an infantile or juvenile patriotism, who alternately critiqued and flirted with the oligarchy, or Raul Pompéia, who was enthralled by his own republican ideals, which only a small number of military men, *sans peur et sans reproche*, could ideally put into practice.

Lima Barreto consciously lived a life in society, and this granted him a weight and density that allowed him to resist dissolution into dominant practices and discourses.

From this vantage point, he also directed his gaze toward cultural criticism. He was not taken in by the false opposition, articulated during the *belle époque*, between cosmopolitanism and nationalism, which were so often reduced to the degraded forms of urbane ultrarefinement and the embrace of folkloric rural ignorance. Lima Barreto, who was labeled xenophobic despite his sympathies for anarcho-syndicalism and the Russian Revolution, rejected and was nauseated by both of these epiphenomena, which are common to cultures of neocolonial extraction.

He knew that Coelho Neto's incursions into the language of the countryside and even the slave quarters were always framed by quotation marks. They were part of that "universe of quotations" that men of letters used to demonstrate to each other their dominion over the Other—that is, the other subjugated and made to parade across the stage of literary style. Lima Barreto saw himself in this Other, and it was for this reason that the peculiarly *sertanejo*-Parnassian mixture of curiosity, folklore, and cultural power saddened him. His was the modesty of someone who saw himself as an object subject to relationships of favor that, to our modern eyes, would seem an objectionable condition.

One likewise finds no evidence of patriotic *mesticismo* in his novels.[10] Among the very few of his characters who were open to universal humanity we find two foreign women: Olga, the daughter of Italians, who until the end and against the tide respected Quaresma's quixotic character, and Margarida, a Russian immigrant and widow of a mulatto immune to the prejudices that assail Clara dos Anjos in the novel that bears her name.[11] In the end, Lima Barreto's nationalism (like his internationalism) was oriented toward the defense of the poor. The relationship between culture and the nation, in the case of Lima Barreto, should be understood from a novel, progressive angle. Let us reread the conclusion of *Quaresma*. The novel's anticlimax is devastating, not only in psychological terms but also as the funeral rite for an ideology that had been ground down to dust through contact with the real.

The major is imprisoned because in a letter he has revealed to the *marechal* the massacre of a group of prisoners who opposed Floriano. Alone in the jail, he is tormented by contradictions:

> And when his patriotism drove him to action, what did he find? Disappointments. Where was our people's sweet nature? Had he not seen them fight like savage beasts? Had he not seen them kill prisoners, so many prisoners?
>
> The country he had longed for was a myth. It was a fantasy he had created in the silence of his study. Neither the physical, nor the moral, nor the intellectual, nor the political country that he had thought existed was real. The country that existed in reality was that of Tenente Antônio, of Dr. Campos, and of the man from Itamarati.
>
> And in truth, even in its pure form, what had the Country become? Had he not been guided for his entire life by an illusion, by an idea that at minimum lacked a solid basis, or the support of a God or Goddess whose empire was evaporating into nothing? Was he not aware that this idea had come into being because of the spread of the Greco-Roman belief that our

dead ancestors continued to exist as shadows and that it was necessary to feed them so that they would not haunt their descendants? He recalled his Fustel de Coulanges. . . . He recalled that this idea meant nothing to the Menenanã, it meant nothing to so many people. . . . It seemed to him that this idea had been opportunely exploited by conquerors who were aware of our psychological tendencies toward subservience. . . . This notion certainly lacked rational consistency and needed to be corrected.

Curiously, this same certainty that historicity was central to the concept of the country would lead a certain line of centralizing thought to defend—throughout the Old Republic—an organic and positive vision of the nation-state. For example, the projects for national salvation proposed by Alberto Torres, Oliveira Viana, and Azevedo Amaral all converged on this point. But what animates Lima Barreto's reflections on nationalism and patriotism is the sense of the relativity, the precariousness, and the malleability contained in these notions, and above all, a fear of an ideology, engendered by fanaticism, that would serve armed tyranny. As such, there is a libertarian impulse in Policarpo's expression of feeling, with its denunciation of the conquistadores and "our psychological tendencies toward subservience."

One finds in Lima Barreto neither *mesticismo* nor statist nationalism, at least as the latter was defined by the antiliberal critics of the Constitution of 1891. In his attack on the society of republican Brazil, Lima Barreto's personal experience and his admiration for revolutionary ideas from Europe allowed him to achieve an independence of vision.

I will now address the other side of the dilemma. If any and all forms of literary exploitation of the poor, of mulattos, of *caboclos*, of *nosso povo* (our people) bothered Lima Barreto, so did its counterpoint, which seems a necessary ill of peripheral bourgeoisies. This is the imitation of styles and signs purchased from the centers of prestige.

This man of culture, poor but two generations removed from slavery, reacted negatively to the patronizing tutelage of the rich, in which he detected a bitter note of disdain, and was disgusted by the servility of the wealthy who licked the boots of those who were even wealthier than they—hence the impatience felt by Lima Barreto whenever he encountered the fetishistic attraction to the foreign that had entranced the Rio of his time. Within the social hierarchy, in which money, status, and race determined position, only those who occupied the lowest rung on the ladder could see, from below, the underbelly of dependence.

He suffered from the desire that his literary words, breaking from the florid language of the period, might achieve absolute transparency. The struggle for authenticity of expression, to be achieved whatever the cost, compelled him, from the standpoint of his individual ethic, to undo the knot tied by the taste and prejudices of his time. We know the degree to which his fiction was forged in the fire of self-analysis. A discourse that is unreservedly and unstintingly confessional takes shape from the opening of the *Recordações do escrivão Isaías Caminha* (Reminiscences of the Notary Isaías Caminha): "Sadness, limitations and differences in mental ability in my family affected me in a curious way: they produced in me a desire for intelligence. My father . . . ."

The narrator's confession transcends the limits of his individual case. It is a testimony of and commentary on typical situations. Let us return to our initial observation. Black and mulatto writers working during the post-1888 period did not enjoy the ideal circumstances that were envisioned for them by the militants of the 1870s and 1880s, who were the children of slaves. The arena had shifted from the slave quarters to the labor market. The young Isaías, barely having left the bosom of his family, is confronted with the hostile environment of the big city: "The woods were so impenetrable, the path I would face so difficult, *that the personality that existed within me changed, or rather, that which I had constructed fell to ruin*. I was like a great modern steamship whose boilers had ruptured, with the steam that powered the ship escaping into the air."

This passage is a metaphor for the mestizo or black intellectual who finds himself both free and confined. Wherever he goes, Isaías finds himself exiled because of his skin color. His personal qualities, those moments in which his intellect and charm shine through, appear as "living, brightly lit mountains" that are drowned in the dark, dull landscape he observes from the window of the train that carries him, as a poor boy, to the capital. They are merely "spots of life on a diseased skin."

The skin, as a mark of identity, a boundary between the gaze of the other and one's intimate space, will reappear in another context. Isaías, from the moment he gets steady work at a Rio de Janeiro newspaper, is afraid to break out of his new shell, since he fears falling back into the anomie of social limbo: "I had crossed a great stretch of sea and had taken shelter on an island and did not have the courage to take to the ocean again and swim to the mainland that I saw on the horizon a few hundred meters away. Crustaceans were enough for me and insect bites had swelled my skin." These are the social forces that cover one's flesh with the scars of daily struggle. In an earlier scene, Isaías, having had his solicitations of employment rejected for no apparent reason, reflects and has the sensation of living in a besieged state: "And I had the sensation that I was in a foreign country."

Working with a more complex range of images and writing in a more vibrant tone, Cruz e Sousa had spoken to the same sense of estrangement in

"Emparedado" (The Enclosed), which was written a few short years before *Recordações*.

The symbolist poet formulated the problem in terms of the situation of the *artista negro* (black artist), to whom the sub-Darwinism of the age denied the possibility of achieving the status of creative intellect. In the febrile language of "Emparedado," the tragedy of the black intellectual is placed in the context of Brazil as a still unformed culture bowing before the "dictatorial science of hypotheses."

The racism of evolutionism, in relegating the black to an inferior position within the spectrum of humanity, rationalized the myth of Ham and gave it worldwide projection between the final years of the nineteenth century and the First World War:

> In a young country, in a land that as yet lacks an absolutely defined ethnic type, in which feeling for Art is uncivilized, local, banal, the effort is surprising and stupendous, the struggle formidable of a temperament fatally marked by blood and who, in addition to suffering from a hostile environment, belongs, descends physiologically from a race to which the dictatorial science of hypotheses absolutely denies the pursuit of Knowledge and principally, artistic knowledge of the written word.
>
> Heavens! A banal question of biological chemistry causes certain rebellious fossils to continue to ruminate on primitive knowledge, to become lost and to perish in the long aquatic chambers of infinite, crushing, irrevocable wisdom!
>
> But what does all this matter? What is the color of my form, of my feeling? What is the color of the killing storm that assails me? What are the colors of my dreams and my cries? What are the colors of my desires and my fever?
>
> "You are one of the tribe of Ham, accursed, cast out, damned!"
> ("The Enclosed," the final prose piece of *Evocações*)

Once again and through crossed paths, the unifying myth of the Brazilian nation is placed in the light of a critical consciousness, and its racial and class fractures are exposed.

In Cruz e Sousa's prose poem and in numerous passages from Lima Barreto's fiction and criticism we can see a sharp intelligence at work, one equipped to confront the dogmas of racial imperialism.[12]

Both men extract a rare counterideological lucidity from their condition as poor and marginalized writers. During this period, a culture of resistance (stimulated, in the case of Lima Barreto, by contact with anarchist and socialist groups) was coming into formation. Its worldview would in no way accord with the official, moderate vision of the young republic.

May 13 is not merely one date among others, a neutral number, a chronological notation. Rather, it is a crucial moment in a process that was advancing in two directions. Without: the black man is an outcast from a cosmetically modern and Europeanized Brazil. Within: the same black man is forced into the nether regions of a sordid, brutish, national capitalism.

The landowner frees himself from his slaves and brings to his lands salaried workers, some of whom are immigrants. The exile of those formerly enslaved was not officially decreed, though they would come to experience this exile in the stigma attached to the color of their skin.

9 The Archeology of the Welfare State

On the Persistence of Long-Held Ideas

In memory of João Cruz Costa

The meaning of positivism for the history of Brazil transcends the limits of the history of a philosophical system.
—Otto Maria Carpeaux, "Notas sobre o destino do positivismo" (Notes on the Fate of Positivism), in *Rumo*, vol. 1, 1943

[A]ll action truly begins with an imagined word
—Guimarães Rosa, *Grande sertão: veredas*

In a chapter from his work on economic backwardness analyzed on a global scale, Alexander Gerschenkron addresses the question of the ideologies that contributed to the processes of national development that occurred after the Industrial Revolution in England. His hypothesis is suggestive. In each case, according to Gerschenkron, there was a peculiar dynamic at play, in terms of values, which accelerated the slow-moving process of social formation. And the theories behind those ideas that stimulated growth varied according to the cultural constellation of each nation that was crossing the boundary line of modernization.[1]

In France in the era of Napoleon III, almost all of the businessmen who achieved long-lasting influence belonged to a well-defined group. They were not Bonapartists but Saint-Simonian "socialists." The French utopian Saint-Simon, for whom Auguste Comte served as a disciple and secretary between 1817 and 1824, envisioned the society of the future as a sort of corporatist nation-state in which leaders of industry would assume important political roles. The term *développement* in the sense of material and social progress appears in Saint-Simon and in the young Comte. In order to establish this, they believed that it would be necessary to install a planned economy that would regulate the development of the nation as a whole. If necessary, the law would intervene, going as far as to abolish inheritance, which comprised one of the greatest obstacles to progress by upholding individual privileges at the expense of social solidarity. Industrialists and their financiers would be the missionaries of a new creed, which Saint-Simon considered to be Christian and which would, through a solid union of industry and government, incorporate and protect "the largest, suffering classes." The financial profits that production would provide for capital could be cleansed of the stain of egoism through the institution of an altruistic society, a term coined to describe a prosperous, distributive form of social organization. The strong would be compensated for their merit, and benevolent aid would be given to the weak. And so the reformist ideal of the welfare state, a vast and organized public apparatus that would both stimulate production and correct market inequalities, was born.

Saint-Simon and Comte would borrow from economic orthodoxy only the recommendation that state revenues and expenses should be kept in balance. But in opposition to the liberalism that predominated at the time, they both believed that moral and political forces should be imposed that could correct "licentiousness" and "industrial empiricism." Capitalism in France began, then, to self-regulate through an alliance of businessmen with a state that provided both guidance and support. It began to follow a path partially distinct from that of English capitalism, whose impasses were being overcome by the systematic pressure of laborers organized into trade unions. Saint-Simonianism, which attracted members of the industrial bourgeoisie who had received a polytechnic education, adopted a reformist strategy that would not have been viable without the direct participation of the state apparatus.

The religious inspiration for this industrialist creed found its expression in Saint-Simon's New Christianity, which Comte, as the creator of another sect, would not follow and from which he would thereby distance himself. A picturesque but meaningful detail: Shortly before his death, Saint-Simon pleaded to Rouget de Lisle, the by-then elderly author of the *Marseillaise*, to write a new hymn, an Industrial Marseillaise. Rouget acquiesced. In his new hymn, the men he had formerly called *enfants de la patrie* were now known as *enfants de l'industrie*, the true noblemen who would secure universal happiness for mankind by "spreading the arts and bringing the world under the peaceful laws of industry." Gerschenkron comments: "There is no evidence that Ricardo inspired anyone to change *God Save the King* to *God Save Industry*."[2]

Gerschenkron moves from the French case to analyze German modernization. Here, the values enlisted to advance the capitalist project were not inspired by the republican tradition of 1789 but, as is well known, were found in nationalistic mysticism. Friedrich List, an influential economist, translated Saint-Simon's entrepreneurial discourse into the language of a centralizing public power whose paladin would be Bismarck. The German path began with official protection of industry. It was in Prussia, which was somewhere between modern and authoritarian, that a term that would cast a long shadow was coined. This was *Wohlfahrstaat*, or "welfare state."

Finally, in the prerevolutionary Russia of the 1890s, Marxism inaugurated a consensus favorable to heavy industrialization, to be brought about by the imperial state, that would achieve concrete form when Bolshevism rose to power and applied its iron fist to the development of the Soviet economy.

The examples of France, Germany, and Russia serve to illustrate the historian's thesis: the technological and economic development of the European nations was not an automatic byproduct of the Industrial Revolution, since it also depended on ideological, and in broad sense, cultural factors. These differentiated ways of thinking confronted archaic, preindustrial circumstances that were peculiar to each social formation. National forms of development were the products of this temporal and spatial play of modernizing and traditional forces.

To what degree did certain positivistic ideals constitute the archeology of Brazilian modernization, which was promoted by a centralizing state? This is the question to which this essay seeks to respond.

Brazil's Positivistic Mold

In their pioneering studies, Cruz Costa and Ivan Lins narrated the vicissitudes of the Positivist Apostolate in Rio de Janeiro and the positions articulated by its two priests, Miguel Lemos and Teixeira Mendes, during the period of transition from the empire to the first years of the republic.[3] Despite at least two decades of intense militancy in favor of Comte, the Brazilian positivists quickly fell out with the French leadership of the movement, which at the time was in the hands of Pierre Laffitte.

This idea of rupture is illustrative and deserves analysis, for it is not just another bizarre episode contributed by positivism to the history of philosophy in our country. Miguel Lemos objected to Laffitte's collaboration with Dr. Ribeiro de Mendonça, a Brazilian coreligionist. Mendonça, who was a landowner in the Paraíba Valley and a slave owner, had violated the master's condemnation of slavery. Miguel Lemos advised Mendonça of this and expelled him from the apostolate. But Laffitte, upon consultation, preferred to take a conciliatory approach, which enraged the orthodox positivists and ultimately caused the separation of the Brazilian contingent from the French leadership in 1883.

Amid this fiery dispute, Miguel Lemos and Teixeira Mendes published a pamphlet that included all of Comte's abolitionist texts, which were prefaced by a dedication to Toussaint Louverture, the hero of the black insurrection in the French Antilles.

Our orthodox positivists consistently complemented their antislavery views with arguments in favor of the republic, adopting for both causes a discourse that was critical of imperial intransigence. Monarchy, according to the master of Montpellier, remained trapped within history's theological and metaphysical stages, which would, through irrevocable laws that were inscribed in the very nature of things, inevitably give way to the positive stage. A society that was industrial and no longer feudal or military, along with free labor and a republican dictatorship, would constitute the new system.

The apostolate, which always kept its distance from political parties, gained a degree of influence during the interregnum of Floriano Peixoto, during which time a group of cadets who were disciples of Benjamin Constant—the so-called Jacobins—managed to intervene in affairs of state. But with the consolidation of São Paulo's role in government with the presidencies of Prudente de Moraes and Campos Salles, and thanks to the hegemony of liberalism in the years that preceded the First World War, positivism as a sect saw its influence reduced—hence the chronology used by its historians, who focus on the year 1900.

The eccentric side of the Positivist Church, with its vestments, its parallel calendar, and its topical interventions—against obligatory vaccination and a national "pedantocracy" that required professional degrees—has generally obscured the important task of investigating a more deeply rooted phenomenon, which Cruz Costa recognized as the persistence of a doctrine that was widespread during the Old Republic and perhaps even during the period in Brazilian politics that followed.

Echoing observations made by Carpeaux, Cruz Costa stated: "Though positivism, like other doctrines, is an imported product, there are elements within it that reveal its perfect adaptability to the conditions of our formation, to the deep realities of our spirit."[4] At any rate, the idea that the golden age of positivism in Brazil came to an end with the republican victory came to be understood as a commonly held truth.

However, recent notable works by Sérgio da Costa Franco and Joseph Love, along with recent university publications from Rio Grande do Sul, have skillfully revisited the question of the mental molding of positivism in that state up to 1930. Our political historiography is beginning to clarify the means through which an imported worldview (has one existed in Brazil that was not so?) fueled an ideology of long duration that first legitimated interventionist actions by government in a local context, and then, after the Revolution of 1930, on a national scale.[5]

This essay seeks to explore the processes of selection, filtering, and adaptation through which a "colonized" intelligentsia carried out an economic and ideological project.

It all began during the period of abolitionism.

The apostolate's 1883 break, in which it rejected Laffitte's global authority, caught my attention during my investigation of the ideological underpinnings of our abolitionism.[6] From the beginning, the differences between the cautious and slow-moving gestures of the São Paulo republicans when faced with the question of slavery and the bold reactions of the propagandists linked either directly or indirectly to positivist circles in Rio de Janeiro and Rio Grande do Sul followed logically from and accorded with the interests and political aspirations of the groups in question.

The republicans who organized the Convention of Itu and formed their party in São Paulo were either coffee growers or *bacharéis* (degree holders, generally in law) involved in the agro-export system. Their objective, which they continually reaffirmed, was to secure the use of slave labor until such time as European immigration could replace it. Taken by surprise by the official decree of abolition, they pleaded for indemnification for the harm done to their business affairs by generalized emancipation. Nabuco openly referred to these men as *cafezistas* (coffee-ists).

The republicans of Rio de Janeiro, whether orthodox positivists (Miguel Lemos, Teixeira Mendes) or sympathizers of positivism (Quintino Bocayuva, Benjamin Constant, Silva Jardim, Lopes Trovão, Raul Pompéia), were liberal professionals who fought for abolition within their respective areas of activity, such as the army, the schools, and the press. These were men of conviction who viewed the evasive actions of the coffee growers with suspicion.

Although for a time the two groups were united in the antimonarchical struggle, they were not cut from the same cloth. Even the positivism of certain spokesmen of the coffee oligarchy was revealed to be heterodox, if not atypical, and was inflected with evolutionist elements. Cruz Costa and Raymundo Faoro perceptively detected in them the influence of a "*paulista* Spencerism." Recent research has confirmed the appropriateness of this designation and has demonstrated the strong influence of Darwin, Haeckel, and Spencer in the discourse of republican medical doctors such as Miranda Azevedo and Pereira Barreto, who intervened in state politics in São Paulo by championing open competition, from which would follow the natural selection of the fittest.[7]

The opposition, which was political as well as theoretical, between Spencerism and Comtism exploded in Sílvio Romero's polemic writing. His pamphlet, *Doutrina contra doutrina* (Doctrine against Doctrine, 1881), directly attacked the positivists from Rio Grande do Sul, whom he judged to be as undesirable as the Jacobins and the socialists. At the same time, Romero lauded the industrious "democracia paulista" (*paulista* democracy) in the name of evolutionist principles. The history of the Old Republic teaches us that this conflict was not experienced merely by Sílvio Romero but, rather, was closely linked to real political groups in Brazil.

On the question of slavery, Sílvio Romero, though an abolitionist, considered the state's promulgation of the Lei Áurea (Golden Law) to have been hasty. Adopting the Darwinian motto that "nature does not make jumps," the critic from Sergipe would have preferred that free rein had been given to the conflict of forces, from which the correct solutions for saving the "national organism" would have naturally emerged.

The contrary position, which was defended by Miguel Lemos, Teixeira Mendes, Júlio de Castilhos, and the orthodox positivists from Rio Grande do Sul, affirmed the superorganic character of society, in which the wisest men would be appointed advisors to the executive and would intervene to guide—and, if necessary, correct—the course of human action. For Comte, colonial slavery was not the fruit of biological evolution but a "monstrous anomaly" to be extirpated from the earth. If would fall to the republican state to do so.

From the beginning, the Rio de Janeiro positivist circle rejected proposals to compensate landowners whose slaves would be emancipated through legal action. To indemnify landowners would mean publically admitting one man's right of property over another. It was the Africans who deserved compensation for the three centuries of forced labor to which they had been submitted by the European colonization of America.[8]

In a text published in *A Gazeta da Tarde* on October 8, 1880, Teixeira Mendes expressed his sincere disinterest in the "possible financial ruin of a handful of slavers," and he defended immediate abolition.

In the *gaúcho* context, Júlio de Castilhos established the *Bases* for the republican candidates who were meeting at the Second Party Congress (1884), in which immediate and prompt abolition without indemnification was advocated. In an article published on July 30 of the same year, Castilhos sought to unmask the slave owners' economic arguments: "Only the blind suppose that our wealth is tied to the strength of slave labor. Labor that is not free has no strength. A country of twelve million inhabitants, whose wealth depends on the exclusive labor of a million and a half accursed slaves, is a nation of the lowest order. Rio Grande do Sul should not wait for a future law, but should anticipate it, just as Ceará and Amazonas did. *Total abolition of slavery within the Brazilian nation!*"⁹

The cohesion of the apostolate and the *gaúcho* republicans invalidates Sérgio Buarque de Holanda's statement regarding the positivists' consistent respect for the right to property.¹⁰ On this topic, Teixeira Mendes confidently declared: "With regard to property, modern civilization cannot maintain the principles that prevailed in the old society. The common good is the supreme law of nations, and all institutions should base themselves on morality and reason."¹¹ He would then outline labor legislation that, "for the time and given local conditions, was truly revolutionary."¹²

During this same period, the cadets of the Escola Militar (Military School) of Rio de Janeiro, who were disciples of Benjamin Constant, wrote a manifesto to the nation, citing "positive reasons" in support of their opposition to slavery's hold on Brazilian life.¹³

The distinguished historian Sérgio Buarque de Holanda was partially correct in stating that the positivists had "a secret horror of our national reality."¹⁴ The truth is that we, looking back, should honor the orthodox positivists' view, which was hardly secret and was repeatedly expressed in public. To swim against the tide and to defend causes that ran contrary to the interests of the dominant class are signs of a salutary nonconformity. However, it frequently happens that proponents of pure historicism are embarrassed to confront this sort of negative dialectic, which to them appears out of place or strange. For the historicist, radicalism carries with it an impertinent—or, in the best of cases, quixotic—air.

The discourse of Benjamin Constant's military disciples would join that of the Jacobins, the so-called *radicais da Primeira República* (radicals of the First Republic), though it is well known that their combined actions would be largely neutralized, beginning in 1894, by the presidents from São Paulo, who were products of the old liberalism. These young officials were quickly excluded from the system of power following the end of the government of Floriano Peixoto.¹⁵ The rapid marginalization of the most nationally visible Comtian militants caused our historiography to conclude that the cycle of positivist involvement in Brazil ended by the first years of the twentieth century. However, one need only recall the ideology that had spread throughout the republican army and the governing classes of Rio Grande do Sul to see that these ways of thinking do not abruptly cease to exist, but rather resist as long as they can serve as useful vehicles for rationalizing interests and agendas. The reformist worldview that was common to the *tenentes* (junior officers) and to the leaders of the Partido Republicano Rio-Grandense (PRR, Republican Party of Rio Grande do Sul) would inform the program of the Aliança Liberal (Liberal Alliance), which was victorious in October 1930. It is not insignificant that the father of Luís Carlos Prestes, Captain Antônio Prestes, was—along with Protásio Vargas, the brother of Getúlio—one of the founders in 1899 of the Centro Positivista de Porto Alegre (Positivist Center of Porto Alegre).

Positivism in the South and the Archeology of the Welfare State

The doctrine of the Partido Republicano Rio-Grandense drew on certain ideas that were directly inspired by Auguste Comte's political views.

This was not, in point of fact, a local idiosyncrasy. The same ideas informed the nation-building projects of the Uruguayan *colorados*, whose leader, President José Batlle, was exposed to Pierre Laffitte's Comtian ideas in the same meetings on Rue Monsieur-le-Prince that Miguel Lemos attended at the beginning of the 1880s. Similar values impelled the "radical" project of Hipólito Yrigoyen, who became president of Argentina in 1916.

A historian eager to make regional distinctions might propose a common *gaúcho-platense* ideology. The response is structural. Despite differences in scale, Rio Grande do Sul, Uruguay, and Argentina constituted similar socio-economic formations. In all three, a cattle-based, export-oriented economy was firmly in place throughout the nineteenth century. But beginning at the end of that century, this economy was forced to face smaller-scale, dynamic alternatives: polyculture oriented toward the internal market, and new industrial and service-based economic activities in urban centers. Hardworking farmers without access to official credit, small- and medium-scale urban industrialists, and a class of salaried workers whose numbers were growing with European migration had needs and aspirations that were often opposed to those of the old landowners and ranchers.

This gave rise, in the three contiguous regions, to pressure groups that demanded state policies that would resist or openly oppose the laissez-faire that had traditionally benefited the oligarchic, export-oriented sector. What sort of ideology could respond to the needs of these new social groups?

Today, when we think of models of interventionist thought, we are confronted by the two principal theories that opposed classical liberalism: Marxism, in its various forms, and post-1929, Keynesian reformism. But if we think back to the nineteenth century, we find Saint-Simon's utopian industrialism and Comte's social positivism at the heart of an ideological current concerned with correcting capitalism through class integration, which would be achieved through a vigilant public management of conflicts. Its deep inspiration was ethical, and in the cases of both Saint-Simon and Comte, it was oriented toward an ideal of distributive order.

Social positivism, which was transferred in a nearly pure state to republican Rio Grande do Sul (or variously combined with Krausist rationalism issuing from the Uruguay of the *colorados*), provided the new economic configuration with models for political action whose internal coherence remains impressive today.

What was it that distinguished the theory and practice of *castilhismo* in Rio Grande do Sul from the main line of bourgeois and progressive thought, as manifested in the Lei Áurea and the proclamation of the new regime? It was its tendency to grant to the government, as the representatives of the popular will, the function of aiding and even controlling the course of economic development.

Its doctrinal bases can be seen in various passages from the *Course on Positive Philosophy* and more specifically, its final volume, which aspired to articulate a theory of *Social Physics*.[16] Here Comte's divergences from what he termed the dogmatism of orthodox political economy are made clear. Orthodoxy's fundamental error was to have removed economic factors from a global vision of society, converting them into "metaphysical" abstractions. One of the liberal principles Comte considered particularly harmful was classical liberalism's tendency to understand processes of production, circulation, and consumption of goods only in terms of individual interest. The elevation of the desire for profit to an absolute principle, present in the egotism of each social participant, tended for Comte to generate a state of anomie or unbridled violence that only a prudent, energetic public administration could successfully avoid: "Political economy has its own way of making anarchy systematic, and the scientific formulas that it has granted to our times will aggravate this danger, and will tend to make it more dogmatic and extensive."[17]

Criticizing Adam Smith and Say's strict disciples, Comte warned: "The most classical among them, especially those writing today, took pains to dogmatically portray their studies' general topic as entirely distinct and independent from the other sciences, and which they always mark as entirely isolated from these."[18]

In other words, Comte deplored one of the typical consequences of the division of intellectual labor in industrial societies: the atomization of areas of scientific inquiry, and specifically, the separation of economics from the science of society, which he himself baptized with the name of sociology. And in terms of political economy, this isolation had particularly negative implications for his ideal of integration.

Our southern Comtians proposed to harmonize the forces that private initiative had set into motion. To that end, they defended the model of a strict, competent presidential regime made significantly representative by virtue of universal suffrage, which would apply regardless of gender, literacy, or religion.

Enlarging the voting public as much as possible would allow a greater degree of power to be delegated to the chosen, who would be selected through open vote, in accordance with the principle of "viver às claras" (living openly). The republican dictatorship, thus legitimated and religiously defended by the Partido Republicano Rio-Grandense, would have as its democratic counterpoint an Assembléia de Representantes (Assembly of Representatives), which would likewise be directly elected and which would be solely responsible for considering, amending, and voting on the budget proposed by the executive.[19]

This model of political organization was transposed onto the Constitution of Rio Grande do Sul, which Júlio de Castilhos drafted in 1891. The *gaúcho* republicans would always speak of their founding charter (incidentally, a model of sober and concise language) with veneration. These were "the sacred principles of the Charter of July 14." And think of how the date chosen for the presentation of the republican constitution resonated!

Among other recommendations by Comte that were incorporated into the constitution we find that of administrative continuity. Castilhos converted this into a constitutional article that permitted a president to be reelected as long as he obtained three-quarters of the vote. This granted the individual who held the executive power the sort of legitimacy conferred by plebiscite.

Translated into laws and decrees, respectfully quoted in presidential and municipal documents during the Old Republic, these principles served, in fact, as the PRR's *instrumentum regni* in its explicit project of "governing above the selfish interests of each class" and, at the same time, "representing all social groups."

Borges stated to the deputies, "In this way a single political bond ties together all of these different cells within the organism of the state, and maintains unity of thought in the midst of the widest possible administrative decentralization," in a speech given on September 20, 1900.

Historians who have investigated the opposition between republicans and liberals differ in their explanations for the origin and meaning of the conflict. Sérgio da Costa Franco and Joseph Love, among others, view the PRR as a mixed group comprised of the urban *petit bourgeoisie*, the Italian settlers of Rio Grande do Sul who formed a small rural middle class, and liberal professionals. These were opposed to the old regionalist elite comprised of cattle barons on the pampas, who were faithful to the Liberal Party and who had been removed from power by the Proclamation of the Republic. This group was also supported by certain old, prosperous communities of German settlers. This is the classical interpretation, which takes us to the nexus between ideology and the locus of relevant political actors. Recently, university-based researchers (Gerardo Muller, Santa Pesavento, and to a certain extent, Dutra Fonseca) have been less inclined to acknowledge the aura of antioligarchical progressivism that the classical interpretation recognizes in the praxis of the PRR, preferring to explain the split as a function of a struggle between segments of the dominant class. This is an interpretation of the facts that joins the rival parties under the common heading of Rio Grande do Sul's bourgeoisie. Here, the emphasis is placed on the process of capitalist accumulation, which certainly figured in the economic designs of both factions. Further, differences of public strategy and of cultural roots are placed into relief.

The crux of the question is to be found in the relations between the state and economic life. Castilhos, Borges, and the intellectuals within the PRR generally held to Comte's account of humanity's passage from the military-feudal phase to the industrial phrase. One may look through the Anais da Assembléia dos Representantes (Annals of the Assembly of Representatives) in order to get a sense for the prevailing character of the proposals issued by the executive.

* * *

In the first place, the PRR consistently defended the land tax, which was increased slowly but surely from its inauguration in 1902 thanks to Borges, who was influenced by Castilhos, and despite the protests of the southern ranchers. Comte had openly expressed his preference for so-called direct taxes.

Not coincidentally, President Batlle in neighboring Uruguay was taking similar measures to tax land as part of a process of energetic, dexterous confrontation with the *ganaderos*.[20] The *colorado* government not only taxed grazing land but also sought to recover for the public those *tierras fiscales* that had been in the hands of landowners who had come by them illegally. The parallel between Batlle's land policy and Castilhos and Borges's interventions in favor of the state's recovery of land is clear and deserves detailed examination.

The argument that a tax on land was the fairest possible tax, which approached the radical proposal that there should be a single, progressive tax, was spelled out as early as Stuart Mill's *Political Economy*, a work that was considered by legislative republicans as an English variation of social positivism. "Land as a good is by its nature held in common by all men," wrote Mill.[21] Liberals who were accustomed to citing phrases from Mill in defending individual interests against the state were taken aback. Each party selected and filtered what it could, and how it could, from writers who were considered prestigious at the time.

The taxation of property, and by analogy, its transmission to inheritors *mortis causa* or *inter vivos* was ethically justified, for it would not be fair to allow "exclusive use, by individuals, of something that was originally common to all, and because the landowner in a certain way rents the land from society as a whole."

Borges de Medeiros invoked this statement, made by Leroy-Beaulieu, in his Message to the Assembly, read on October 15, 1902, and did so in arguing for a proposal that would impose a land tax in the state. This tax had not been levied in imperial Brazil. Castilhos and the contingent of *gaúcho* republicans argued for its creation during the National Constituent Assembly in 1891.

The *Anais da Assembléia* reveal that it was de rigueur for proponents of land and inheritance taxes to cite European sources in making their case. The liberal opposition tended toward a defensive regionalism and described the state as "insatiable" in levying taxes. When the idea of the single tax was introduced, the deputy Gaspar Saldanha could not contain himself, and vehemently protested in the November 23, 1920 legislative session: "I see a subversible [*sic*] socialistic orientation in the single tax on land."

The same legislator, criticizing the PRR's public policies on December 27, 1922, attributed its mistakes "to a certain philosophical doctrine, which in Mexico bore similar fruit to that being produced here. There, the party of *los científicos* upheld the dictatorship of Porfirio Díaz, which ultimately fell. It is this 'scientific' preoccupation, it is this philosophical 'obsession' that have led to the worst ills."

The deputies Lindolfo Collor and Getúlio Vargas, both of *castilhista* extraction, took up the defense of a new tax increase with exact figures in hand. Years later, the speeches made by Vargas while state president of Rio Grande do Sul (1928–1930), though he made them during a period after which time he had reconciled with the ranchers of the Campanha region, preserved traces of his earlier criticism of the *gaúcho* landed establishment, which his praise did little to conceal: "The great expanses of land, where cattle are kept in pasture, and which are managed by a very small number of hired hands, who at times are poorly fed and badly paid, contribute to the poverty of the cities. We must break up the great holdings, and divide them into small parcels and bring the country under intensive cultivation."[22] As can be seen, this is a model inspired by the small landholdings of the immigrant colonies.

* * *

Second, to the same degree that the republicans increased the tax on land (this increase was quite modest, if we trust the comparative calculations made by Lindolfo Collor), they granted exemptions to nascent local manufacturers.

In almost all of the legislative sessions taking place between 1900 and 1930, the majority responded favorably to requests made to the state by small- and medium-scale manufacturers for licenses to build their factories and export their goods.

During these years a fiscal tradition was created that provided incentives for manufacturing. The Comtians zealously defended this effort, arguing that Rio Grande do Sul needed to enter the industrial era. Later, during the 1930s, and with the Generation of 1907's rise to federal power,[23] this argument would be combined with calls for protection of industry and import substitution.

The regionalist liberals of the Campanha looked unfavorably on the granting of so many exemptions to businessmen from Porto Alegre. Gaspar Saldanha alleged that these exemptions were handed out "a granel" (like grain), and he and his fellow regionalist liberals called for comparable support for ranchers. On this fractious point, Borges de Medeiros was on more than one occasion unresponsive to the ranchers' requests, whereas his successor Getúlio Vargas knew how to respond pragmatically, as the situation demanded, to both industrialists and ranchers.

The debate that took place between Gaspar Saldanha and the *borgistas* Lindolfo Collor and Getúlio Vargas is illustrative of the competing positions. The oligarchy's liberal representative objected to the fiscal extortion the state was visiting on the ranchers. These were "disgraceful taxes imposed upon the class of livestock owners, a class that is taxed like no other." In response, Lindolfo, with official figures at his disposal, compared Rio Grande do Sul's fiscal policy to tax increases in São Paulo, proving that in a state guided by the theory of laissez-faire, the taxes paid by coffee growers were proportionally higher than those paid by southern ranchers. Saldanha counterattacked, observing that São Paulo's tax revenues were reinvested to support coffee cultivation. Collor humorously retorted: "In what else could the government of the *bandeirantes* invest?" Getúlio drew for support on his fellow republicans, asking in the name of government efficiency how the state could access the resources necessary to fulfill its administrative obligations other than by levying taxes (December 27, 1922, legislative session).

Getúlio's argument is based on the premise that the government, elected by universal suffrage, should not be confused with this or that sector of the economy. The republicans' efforts were aimed at maintaining an equilibrium that would transcend class conflicts. The state, as the master stated, is the *cérebro da nação* (nation's brain), and due to its central function within the social body, it falls to it to regulate the activities of each organ in such a way that no one part places itself above the others. Vargas's discourse does not contribute to the radicalization of the conflicts between the parts. Rather, he presents himself as a wise architect who only intervenes, through the power of government, when compelled to give to a class that had been lacking (in this case, the industrialists) what had been enjoyed by another (the ranchers). Getúlio's ideological evolution would be guided by the principle that the state should be strong enough to mediate conflicts between sectors of the dominant classes and between the dominant classes and workers.

According to Comte, progress is achieved when a situation of imbalance, or even disorder, gives way to a state in which a proper balance exists between the elements that comprise the whole. In order to reorganize the social whole, "healthy policies, which are the children of morality and reason," should not destroy an organ that has grown disproportionately large, but rather preserve it, by modifying its dimensions and integrating it into a new, higher order. In the case of a nation's political economy, the state should seek to achieve an "organized differentiation" of the productive activities, which is another way of saying that the advancement of production presupposes the establishment of a certain social order: "The intensity of this regulating function, far from diminishing as humanity evolves, should on the contrary become increasingly indispensable, as long as it is competently conceived and exercised, given that its essential principle is inseparable from the principle of development. It is, then, the habitual dominance of the *spirit of the whole* that is the consistent characteristic of government considered from any perspective."[24]

Comte's social physics contains several passages in which he criticizes the principles of classical liberalism, which is always referred to as political economy. For Comte, "the absence of any and all regulatory intervention," when made into a dogma, "evidently equates, in social practice, to this so-called science's solemn surrender before any difficulty marginally more vexing than might be produced by industrial development."[25]

This declaration of principles fit the case of Rio Grande do Sul like a hand in glove. Its economy, which was diversified and oriented toward the internal market, bristled at the hegemony of *paulista* coffee production, for which the federal government sacrificed the interests of states of secondary importance. In 1901—that is, before the successive adjustments in the price of coffee made by the União on behalf of this export product—Borges de Medeiros harshly attacked this particularistic policy, which was pursued at the expense of polyculture and emerging industries: "It is generally accepted that the cultivation of coffee, to the exclusion of other crops, is the principal cause of the country's economic ruin. In fact, the superabundance of this product, which is subject to competition from similar products in the consumer market, has brought about its excessive depreciation in price. Now our principal concern is to actively encourage the development of new crops, which are considered the only possible solution to the so-called economic question."[26]

* * *

Third, in addition to taxing land and granting exemptions to manufacturers, the republicans defended on more than one occasion the socialization of public services, an idea also found in Comte.

Placing themselves on a collision course with foreign-owned businesses, along the lines of Batlle and Yrigoyen's bitter contest with British imperialism, Borges and his coreligionists called in 1919 for the public expropriation of the port of Rio Grande and the Porto Alegre–Uruguaiana railroad. In the same year, the state began administering the coal mines at Gravataí.

These measures might seem tentative, given that we habitually associate state-led economic nationalism in Brazil with the 1930–1950 period, but in point of fact, they are the expression of a doctrine that sought to rein in the abuses of the market through a discipline of "prever para prover" (anticipating in order to provide), which led in turn to intervention.

Borges cited the public good in transferring control of the railroads from the Compagnie Auxiliaire de Chemins de Fer au Brésil to public administration. The speed with which the expropriation was achieved irked the old-line regionalists who viewed the process as authoritarian. Once again it was Getúlio Vargas who rose to speak before the Assembly, in order to defend the action of the republican government: "If a company of firefighters, seeing a house in flames, decided that instead of extinguishing the fire they would first ask the permission of the owner, who happened to be absent, then when the owner returned there would be nothing left to worry about."[27]

There was long-standing dissatisfaction with the Belgian company on the part of the railroad's users. Beginning in 1910, the *castilhista* government petitioned the Assembly to bring various basic services under public administration. Borges's initial argument, as conveyed in his 1913 Message, was unmistakably socialistic. It seems incumbent to me to cite three passages:

> 1) Administration by the municipalities is the death of monopoly, and it is therefore necessary to place under municipal administration all those services for which private initiative cannot provide except through monopoly.
>
> This applies to water, sewage, light, electric power, the tramways, etc. The same principles should regulate the management of public services, at both the national and state levels; September 26 legislative session.

Borges cites as a positive example English municipal administration, which resists "despite the famous school of Manchester, which is the maternal home of laissez-faire and private initiative." Later Borges declares:

> 2) Presiding over the free play of economic forces, it falls to the state to exercise a regulatory function to the degree necessitated by the public good....

From this notion we can derive the principle that advises that everything related to the collective interest should be removed from the realm of particular, privileged ownership: this is the *socialization of public services* [Borges de Medeiros's emphasis], with this generic designation indicating that the administration of these services should fall exclusively to the public power, which suffers from the economic prejudices that continue to prevail within certain social classes.

Finally, the following assertion could not be any more incisive:

3) In terms of the rail lines, if the state is not absolute master of the market, at least it is not its slave.[28]

At a certain juncture of the debate on public control of the port of Rio Grande, the liberal opposition invoked Spencer in condemning the state's interference in economic life. Getúlio wasted no time in responding that, when Spencer wrote one of his final books, *The Man versus the State* (published in 1884), he "was evidently falling into mental decline, in placing the individual in a position of eternal conflict with the state." On the same occasion, in the November 20, 1919, legislative session, Getúlio attempted to convince his adversary that "in young countries like ours, in which initiative is lacking and capital does not yet exist in the proper amount, government intervention in these services is a real necessity."

Reviewing the texts on public matters published by the Positivist Apostolate, the historian Tocary Assis Bastos identified two principles that directly anticipated the antimonopolistic actions by the state:

- That any industrial operation that cannot be carried out through private initiative, in complete freedom, without monopoly or privileges, and the social utility of which has been proved, should be carried out by the Union or by the states, as the circumstances dictate, for the former and the latter both will make opportune use of its privileges, which does not occur with private enterprise.
- That the government should not encourage the organization of companies, which are harmful through the large dividends expected by shareholders and because of the speculation to which directors are prone, in order to avoid association with these fabulous profits. Further, the granting of privileges and monopolies to corporations tends to further harm republican financial policy.[29]

The public expropriations carried out by Borges de Medeiros contrasted with the privatizations taking place at the federal level. Our historian places this opposition into relief in his discussion of Campos Salles's condemnation of the Bahian government's attempt to manage the Estrada de Ferro de São Francisco (São Francisco Railroad). The president registered his opposition in language to which the radical neoliberals of our time would enthusiastically subscribe:

> In my message to Congress, which was solidly grounded in figures provided by the ministry [*of Joaquim Murtinho, a staunch liberal*—Bosi's note], I formally condemned state administration of railroads, and at the same time I frankly defended private administration of the same, which is impelled by self-interest. There is no difference in the nature of administration by the Union and administration by the state. Both are the opposite of private ownership. To lease a rail line to a state would, then, amount to a repudiation of ideas that were so recently articulated. I believe that this would complicate the path taken by my government.[30]

It was common practice throughout the Old Republic to grant the administration of railroads to English companies. In this respect, the Old Republic did not break with the imperialistic interactions that were inherited from the Second Empire. Prominent examples include the Pernambuco Tramway and the Western, in the northeast, the São Paulo Railway and the Rio Claro Railway in São Paulo, and the Rio de Janeiro Tramway and the Leopoldina Railway in the capital.

The opposition between *gaúcho* Comtianism and *paulista* and federal liberalism, in which general principles were applied to measures that circumstances presented to the various political actors, is given tangible form in the case of the railways. João Neves da Fontoura's statement, made while paying tribute to the recently deceased Rui Barbosa, demonstrates the awareness that these agents had of their role and of their contribution to reinforcing the aforementioned opposition: "We, the republicans of Rio Grande do Sul, subscribe to a way of thinking that is structurally distinct from that which guided the life of this celebrated Brazilian."[31]

When did the protectionists first express their anti-imperialist dissention from the proponents of free trade or, rather, when did this dissent burst forth?

Sérgio da Costa Franco refers us to the final sessions of the Congresso Nacional Constituinte (National Constituent Congress) and to those participants who registered a marked dissent. Júlio de Castilhos and this Comtian group opposed a bilateral agreement that exempted from taxes "a large group of industrial and agricultural products from the United States, many of which competed with equivalent national products." The positivist bloc, even when complemented by their sympathizers, represented a minority, and like other minority groups that had broken with the liberals, it was defeated.[32]

The idea that local industries and the internal market should be given priority and protection came to the fore whenever the positivists were confronted with the emerging question of national development. We require a research effort, which Ivan Lins has begun in his fine *História*, that would trace the public lives and economic ideas of progressive leaders like João Pinheiro, Aarão Reis, and Saturnino de Brito in Minas Gerais, Serzedelo Correia and Amaro Cavalcanti—both followers of Benjamin Constant—in Rio de Janeiro, Moniz Freire in Espírito Santo, and Barbosa Lima in Pernambuco. Ivan Lins examines the roles played by engineers, urban planners, and soldiers of positivist background in the principal states of Brazil. What characterizes the lives of all of these men was the joining of knowledge to political intervention. The construction of Belo Horizonte, a city planned by the Comtians Aarão Reis and Saturnino de Brito, is a paradigmatic example of this techno-political culture. Aarão Reis, a professor at the Escola Politécnica (Polytechnic School) in Rio de Janeiro, wrote a *Tratado de economia política, finanças e contabilidade* (Treatise on Political Economy, Finance, and Accounting),[33] in which "verdadeiro socialismo" (true socialism) is described and professed in positivistic terms.

Significantly, the protectionist arguments defeated in Congress would be brought up to date, years later and in another context, by Jorge Street and Roberto Simonsen, mentors to the industrial associations in their struggle to advance the interests of domestic production.

At any rate, the industrialist discourse, with greater or lesser emphasis placed on anti-imperialism, would be officially adopted during Getúlio Vargas's government, which slowly and pragmatically incorporated the suggestions made by the more militant members of our business-owning class. Beginning in the mid-1930s, state command of the economy and bourgeois progressivism demarcated a space of encounter in which both could benefit.[34]

It is worth recalling that the industrializing tendency of the men of 1930 was tempered by an equally Comtian ideal, that of budgetary equilibrium. From Castilhos to Borges de Medeiros and continuing with Vargas himself, austerity in matters of public finance and the motto "Nenhuma despesa sem receita" (No expense without revenue) were taken by the republican administrations as *títulos de honra*, that is, articles of faith. This attitude, which is traceable to a doctrinal imperative, explains an economic cautiousness that otherwise would be considered as simply conforming to classical liberalism. This, however, would amount to an error of perspective. Writing to his old mentor Borges de Medeiros, Osvaldo Aranha wrote, while minister of the treasury for the provisional government: "In general, revolutions are, and have been the world over, profligate, but ours was the first that economized."[35]

We can only understand the apparent paradox in the Brazilian economy during the 1930s, which was simultaneously financially orthodox, industrializing, and centralizing, by studying the positivistic and *castilhista* orientation of the Generation of 1907.

The more advanced among the industrialists never formed themselves into a single party and only intervened through their respective class-based organizations, which allowed the executive to call on businessmen to act as advisors on questions of official economic policy. This pretechnocratic scheme was inaugurated in 1931, with the creation of the Ministério de Trabalho, Indústria e Comércio (Ministry of Labor, Industry, and Commerce), which was entrusted to Lindolfo Collor, a convinced, methodical *castilhista*. Generally speaking, the government's deliberations were preceded by meetings of mixed commissions of men of industry and high-level government functionaries. Getúlio defended this aspect of his administration, which he placed within a modern, international frame of reference in which the executive made decisions with the aid of a committee of experts: "The age is one of specialized assemblies, of technical councils integrated into the administration."[36]

To recapitulate: the republican praxis of Rio Grande do Sul, which was broadened by the group that rose to power with the Revolução de Outubro (October Revolution), interfered with the bourgeoisie's accumulation of wealth through fiscal measures by taxing or granting exemptions, and more directly, by bringing transportation networks under state control, in accordance with the principle of socialization of public services. The manner in which this policy addressed, before and after 1930, the so-called *questão social* (social question)—that is, the working class—proves that the policy was not contingent but rather was animated by the *esprit géométrique*.

* * *

The formula applied by Comte to the relations between capital and labor— that is, the incorporation of the proletariat into modern society—became a cliché. And it is here that we arrive at the PRR's fourth fundamental adaptation of positivism.

Much of what is said concerning the corporatist bases for the labor legislation of the Estado Novo (New State) can be clarified by studying the protective measures included in the program of the Positivist Apostolate, as defined in Júlio de Castilhos's and Borges de Medeiros's public interventions.

Castilhos, in drafting the Constitution of 1891, took the first step toward formalizing the sort of incorporation envisioned by Comte. Article 74 of that legal document reads: "All distinctions between salaried public employees and laborers are abolished, and the privileges that have been enjoyed by the former are extended to the latter."

As a member of the National Constituent Assembly, Castilhos failed to win approval for his proposal, which shocked the liberals, that salaries be equalized. But as the undisputed leader of Rio Grande do Sul's republicans, his support was sufficient for the article to become law in the state.

After the death of Castilhos, the social policy pursued by Borges de Medeiros, as the five-time reelected state president of Rio Grande do Sul, was guided by two complementary principles:

- The first, which in the context of oligarchic Brazil we could term progressive, called for the executive to support and grant his authority to certain demands made by urban workers, such as a reduction in the workday, better living conditions, and less miserable salaries;
- The second, which was frankly centralizing, granted the state the function of mediating, or in extreme cases arbitrating, conflicts between workers and bosses.

The history of strikes in Rio Grande do Sul has been largely told. We know that Borges, on more than one occasion, sought to meet the workers' demands while repressing protests that he felt were violent. In this way he played the role of privileged arbiter of labor issues, a function that would be institutionalized when Vargas and Collor created the Ministry of Labor.[37]

The role of the state government in the strike of 1917, for example, illustrates a tendency that would later be termed paternalistic. Borges appeared at that time as the protector of Porto Alegre's labor unions for effectively supporting their demands and for having regulated the prices for certain necessary staples. The PRR government's attitude differed, in this regard, from the systematically violent approach to workers' strikes taken by the oligarchies of other states.

If we analyze the structure of the Consolidação das Leis do Trabalho (Labor Code), or CLT—which is quite familiar to us, which was promulgated in 1943 and which with few changes continues to define the legal relationship between capital and labor in Brazil—we are confronted by the continued presence of this double register, both progressive and authoritarian, which appears as an unresolved contradiction.

The aspects of the law that address the rights of workers, as workers, fall within the reformist and humanitarian mode of thought initiated by Saint-Simon and which was later integrated into the social morality of positivism. They presuppose that labor should be recognized, that its poverty should be granted dignity, and that it should be protected from selfish interests defended by industrialist empiricism. These are all expressions taken from Auguste Comte.

The labor protections enshrined in the law had been developed, throughout the nineteenth century, by the English trade unions and European labor unions. They corresponded, at times in integral form, to the basic programs of the socialist parties that were gradually being organized in Argentina and Uruguay, where social legislation was adopted early on (and more episodically, in our case), thanks to the leadership of workers who arrived with the great migrations of the 1890s.

Among these protections we find: the reduction in the workday, that is, the long-sought-after eight hours, which was only achieved in the twentieth century; the regulation of nighttime labor and its prohibition for women and children; holidays; maternity leave with compensation; security and health protections in factories; and later on, minimum wage.

With regard to the minimum wage, which had been proposed by the apostolate in its publications: those historians who describe the minimum wage as copied from Italian fascism are incorrect. To the contrary, the *Carta del Lavoro* reads: "La determinazione del salario è sotratta a qualsiasi norma generale e affidata all'accordo delle parti nei contratti colettivi (Declaration XII).[38]

The right to participate in nonviolent strikes is a demand that is common to moderate socialism and the program of the religious positivists. It bears mentioning Teixeira Mendes's articles, which he wrote in support of the striking workers of the Companhia Paulista de Estradas de Ferro (São Paulo Railroad Company) in 1906.[39]

The manner in which a cohesive program of social legislation came to exist depended on the local and national styles of modernization referred to by Gerschenkron, when he insisted on the relevance of cultural and ideological factors for the development of capitalist formations. In England, the *primum mobile* was the pressure exerted by organized labor, along with the House of Commons; in France, it was Saint-Simonianism that filtered into the industrialists identified with Napoleon III's protectionist policies; in Germany, it was Bismarck's "Prussian" approach in the 1880s.

Among us, the positivists left their mark on practically everything that was systematic among the rights of workers as defined by the state, or concerning the state's intervention in their defense. Recall, for example: the famous circulars sent by the apostolate to Dom Pedro II and to the republican presidents; the sections of Rio Grande do Sul's constitution that concerned workers, which were the work of Castilhos; Borges de Medeiros's handling of the strike of 1917 and his success in convincing bosses to accept the striking workers' demands; and above all, Lindolfo Collor's codification of workers' rights, a project undertaken at the request of Vargas that endorsed the views of old socialist militants like Evaristo de Morais, Joaquim Pimenta, and Agripino Nazareth, the Ministry of Labor's foremost "leftist" advisors.[40]

The transition from the slaveholding regime to salaried labor was the initial catalyst for our Comtians' precocious concern with labor issues. The following items are included in the program of the Partido Republicano Histórico (Historical Republican Party), written by Júlio de Castilhos: an eight-hour workday for government and industrial workers; worker holidays; protections for minors, women, and the elderly; the right to strike; "arbitration court for the resolution of conflicts between employers and workers"; and pensions.[41] In sum, this is the program of social legislation of a welfare state that does not want to leave the working conditions of salaried workers, newly freed from slavery, to be determined by capital.

In the abolitionist article "Organizemos a vitória" (Let Us Organize for Victory), Castilhos said:

> To free the slaves—is to remove them from the centuries-old exploitation to which this oppressed race has fallen victim. This race, with its sweat and its blood, established the initial bases for the Brazilian nationality. We must admit that the problem is complex. And in bringing the great mass of freed slaves into the Brazilian communion, we must give them certain guarantees, so that the freedom granted them by law is not denied by systematic oppression by the practical heads of industry.... It falls to the legislator, then, to define the new situation of the freed slaves who confront the heads of agriculture, who, with no prejudice toward them, cannot be permitted to threaten the freedom of the newly freed.[42]

There is in this text a lucid recognition that, if abandoned to the whims of the market, the relations between salaried workers (*o proletariado liberto*, or "the freed proletarians") and the business owners and directors (*os chefes práticos da indústria*; *os chefes agrícolas*, or "the practical heads of industry"; "the heads of agriculture") would run the risk of *opressão sistematizada* (systematic oppression). And the legislator is also granted the responsibility of defining the conditions in which free labor will operate, that is, *a nova situação dos libertos* (the new situation of the freed slaves). This describes the most basic function of the welfare state.

In 1887 Castilhos was writing under the direct influence of Comte and the orthodox positivists of the apostolate.[43] His followers, united in the Bloco Castilhista Acadêmico (Castilhista Academic Bloc), would be the future architects of the centralizing state inaugurated in 1930.

Progressivism and authoritarianism: the latter, perpetuated through the high degree of centralization in the Partido Republicano Rio-Grandense,

Auguste Comte. "In all normal states of society, each citizen is truly a public functionary" (*Discours sur l'ensemble du positivisme* [*General View of Positivism*]; see note 44).

Júlio de Castilhos. "All distinctions between salaried public employees and laborers are abolished, and the privileges that have been enjoyed by the former are extended to the latter" (*Constitution of the State of Rio Grande do Sul*, Article 74; July 14, 1891).

CENTRO POZITIVISTA BRAZILEIRO

REPUBLICA OCIDENTAL

ÓRDEM E PROGRESSO.   VIVER PARA OUTREM.

O POZITIVISMO

E

A ESCRAVIDÃO MODÉRNA

Trechos estraídos das óbras de
Augusto Comte, seguidos de documentos pozitivistas
relativos á questão da escravatura no Brazil
e precedidos de uma Introdução

POR

MIGUEL LEMOS

Prezidente Perpétuo da Sociedade Pozitivista do
Rio de Janeiro

RIO DE JANEIRO
NA SÉDE DA SOCIEDADE POZITIVISTA
7 Travéssa do Ouvidor 7
96 — 1884

A' SANTA MEMÓRIA

DO

PRIMEIRO DOS PRETOS

TOUSSAINT-LOUVERTURE

(1746 — 1803)

Ditador do Haiti. Promotor e Martir da liberdade
de sua raça

Á PROVÍNCIA DO CEARÁ

Ao torrão brazileiro que primeiro purificou-se do crime
ocidental

(25 DE MARÇO DE 1884)

O. D. C.

O Centro Pozitivista Brazileiro.

would inform the CLT, which would be inaugurated during the era of the Estado Novo.

The law, which affirmed the rights of the worker as a worker, ignored his rights as a citizen.

Title V of the Labor Code absorbed (the organic metaphor is significant) workers' unions and employers' organizations into the ministry's orbit. In the 1930s the growth of these associations was encouraged, which is understandable given the cooperativism pursued by Borges and Vargas as state presidents of Rio Grande do Sul. But at the same time, these groups were solidly coopted by the state apparatus. The public power was compelled to recognize the unions, to legalize them, and to provide them with funds through the application of a compulsory union tax. The government, through its technical organs, would negotiate with class-based groups in moments of crisis. This would prove a defining feature of Brazilian labor relations until at least 1964. The CLT was a two-way street, connecting the ministerial bureaucracy and the unions. For Comte, "[i]n all normal states of society, each citizen is truly a public functionary."[44]

There is a parallel question, which as yet has not been clarified by scholars of our social history. This concerns the tenacious survival of the centralizing model after the fall of the Estado Novo. The Constituent Assembly of 1946, whose ostensible motto was to "re-democratize the country," did not alter the syndical structure inherited from the Estado Novo, nor did workers' organizations, led at the time by the orthodox left, work to nullify the corporatist aspects of labor legislation. Is this another case of institutional survival over the long term?

* * *

Finally, no study on the role of social positivism in Latin America can ignore the high degree of support within positivist discourse for free, secular primary education. Here, it should be acknowledged, Comtians and Spencerians were wholly in agreement, for they shared an unbreakable faith in science's capacity to spur progress and in education as the primary means by which it could do so.

Despite these shared values, the orthodox positivists defended certain ideas of their own, which were taken directly from canonical texts.

A reconstruction of Comte's educational thinking would fall outside the scope of this essay. Indeed, the French scholar Paul Arbousse-Bastide offers an exemplary, detailed analysis of Comte's *Discours sur l'ensemble du positivisme* (*General View of Positivism*).[45] In this text Comte drew a connection between universal basic education and the formation of the *bon prolétaire*, a term invented by Arbousse-Bastide as an analogy with the *bon sauvage*. At a certain moment in the *Discours,* Comte states: "Each proletarian constitutes, in more than one way, a spontaneous philosopher, just as every philosopher represents, in a variety of ways, a systematic proletarian."

Free primary education is thus viewed within the broader context of popular education, or as Comte preferred, "proletarian" education. This was, for Comte, the only level of education that should be provided for by government, with the responsibility for university education falling to the various social groups. Let the state take responsibility for the people's fundamental education and abstain from contributing to the proliferation of counterfeit doctors, those degree-holders who swell the ranks of the *pedantocracy.*

As is well known, the educational reforms undertaken in Mexico and Uruguay at the end of the nineteenth century were the work of positivists. By examining documents related to these projects, which are now accessible thanks to Leopoldo Zea's panoramic *Pensamiento positivista latinoamericano,* we can appreciate the degree to which Comte, Littré, and Laffitte's ideas shaped the public policies and educational thinking of these national governments.[46]

In Brazil, the statistics show that no state government dedicated more attention to primary schools or to technical and professional education than did Rio Grande do Sul during the presidencies of Castilhos and Borges. On the other hand, the same republican government faithfully dispensed with the need for those who wished to exercise one of the liberal professions to hold a degree, which slowed the creation of state institutions of higher education.

By analyzing the executive's messages to the Assembléia dos Representantes (Representative Assembly), as well as the statements made by that body, we find evidence of the interest with which the goal of secular and free fundamental education was addressed. In the budgets that were proposed and faithfully approved, funding for education and rail lines was generally provided for first, and in amounts far greater than was dedicated to other areas of expense. And in justifying this amount of funding, phrases from the master of Montpellier were inevitably cited.

What can be said about the quality of this education? Any judgment of quality would lack the necessary comparative data, which today are difficult to come by. As a sign of the government's interest in ensuring that its teachers were well instructed, we may cite Borges de Medeiros's decision in 1913 to send a delegation of primary school teachers to Montevideo, "on an educational mission," in order to get direct access to the "methods and work" of public education in Uruguay, which at the time was considered the best in Latin America. "Further, a group of the best students from our Normal School will travel to Montevideo to study in its corresponding institution."[47]

The argument continually invoked in Borges's speeches and adopted to justify the need to allocate greater resources to elementary education was that the government, in so doing, would obey "a postulate that has become a constitutional item." In truth, there was no law in the Old Republic that determined how educational spending should figure in a government budget, and in this sense, the *castilhistas* in the south were ahead of the curve. It was only with the Constitution of 1934 that a certain percentage of the government budget would be reserved for primary education.

As for the relationship between education and productivity, this was cited as if by law in all proposals made to found technical schools during this period. It should be noted that this argument at its core did not change significantly as the twentieth century progressed. If certain terms and antiquated stylistic elements are removed, the following text makes for a fine example of the developmentalist discourse of our present day:

> We are experiencing a period of true economic evolution. Industries must abandon archaic methods and adopt those deemed by science to be the most efficient. They must substitute their old, deficient, and nearly useless tools for machines that multiply the force of creative action. They must produce a great deal and produce better so, that through the quality and economy of their projects, they might conquer consumer markets. In order to achieve this goal, capital that has already been accumulated should come to the aid of production so that, through labor, new capital can be generated, and should be lightly taxed, so that the liquid wealth produced by the land is not absorbed.[48]

The leaden syntax of the period, rather than suggest the inelegance of a bureaucratic report, invokes a series of linkages between causes and effects, means and ends. Industrial development plus technical education plus public credit equals conquest of consumer markets. This government program, which firmly tied together education and economics, placed the wheel of the republican ship in the hands of modern entrepreneurs and wise planners. Symptomatically, this policy coincided with the administrative practice of João Pinheiro, the state president of Minas Gerais and a sympathizer of the Positivist Apostolate, whom the *gaúcho* legislators cited as a champion of professional education for the poor.

João Pinheiro, the son of an Italian metalsmith, Giuseppe Pignataro (hence his last name *à brasileira*), pursued a policy in Minas that was an alternative to export-oriented large-scale agriculture. Instead, he promoted polyculture, the division of land among agricultural colonists and industry. He subscribed to *Proteccionismo* (Protectionism), a term that was always written with a capital P. His 1907 message to the Congresso Mineiro (Congress of Minas

Gerais) served as a point of reference for Rio Grande do Sul's Assembly in evaluating Borges de Medeiros's educational proposal. João Pinheiro gave the name *economism* to his program of modernizing reforms.[49]

At any rate, from the beginning, Castilhos and Borges de Medeiros's projects were marked by an interest in technical and professional education. In 1913 a "taxa profissional" (professional tax) was created to provide funds for a program of instruction designed to produce specialized workers. In 1896 a group of Benjamin Constant's followers and former professors from the Escola Militar de Porto Alegre (Porto Alegre Military School) founded in that city the Escola de Engenharia (School of Engineering). An autonomous institution, though one supported by the government, the school was responsible for training the state's technical workers in the areas of engineering, agronomy, zootechnics, veterinary medicine, meteorology, industrial chemistry, and domestic and rural arts, professions, and education. It offered courses at the superior, intermediate, and eventually lower levels. Among its objectives was to graduate *rural workers*, along with teachers and master teachers, who would be guaranteed employment in local businesses. In 1934, with the creation of the Universidade de Porto Alegre (University of Porto Alegre), which was later renamed the Universidade Federal do Rio Grande do Sul (Federal University of Rio Grande do Sul), the School of Engineering was integrated into the system of public education despite the opposition of its founder, João Simplício Alves de Carvalho, who was an orthodox Comtian. Between 1914 and 1934 the school published a bimonthly magazine, *Egatéa*, which was unquestionably the most important scientific publication of the Old Republic. The magazine publicized Brazil's advances in scientific, agricultural, and industrial modernization. It addressed topics as varied as the recently formulated Montessori method, new refrigeration technology, Hertz's work in physics on electromagnetic waves, and useful information for viticulture and shoeing horses.

In their best moments, republican Rio Grande do Sul's positivist intellectuals and politicians managed to lay down the tracks for the civilizing process.

Ideological Persistence over the Long Term

The nineteenth century in Brazil gave us three reasonably consistent ideologies. All three were imported, as was to be expected in a peripheral nation, but each was rooted in the day-to-day intellectual life of our political classes, as their long-term persistence implies.

The first comprised the *conservatism* of the Second Empire's oligarchies, based in the sugar plantations of the northeast and Rio de Janeiro, and beginning in the 1840s, in the coffee plantations of the Paraíba Valley.

The second was the *new liberalism* ("new" in opposition to the prior liberalism, which likewise termed itself "liberal"), which from the 1860s through the 1880s fought for abolition and electoral reform. It was not always republican. At times, and in the case of its best men (Nabuco, Rebouças, and the young Rui Barbosa) it defended parliamentary monarchy. With the proclamation of the new regime, this official liberalism pursued purely formal solutions, principally because its base of support was still found in the rural oligarchy. This was true of the *paulista-mineiro* hegemony of 1892 to 1930. In any case, it had the merit of preserving the ideal (if not the practice) of the representative system.

Finally, the third, positivist mode of thought manifested itself in two strains that ultimately converged: *Jacobin radicalism*, which ran from the cadets who supported Floriano Peixoto to the *tenentes* of the 1920s, and the *gaúcho republicanism* of Castilhos and Borges de Medeiros, which has been the subject of this article.

The old conservatism of the *saquaremas* did not entirely die out. Rather, it was absorbed, like sugar into coffee, into the routine of the state republican parties of the Old Republic. In order to understand it, we must analyze the phenomenon of *coronelismo* in each province.[50]

This third ideology did not come to power until the 1930s, when the tactical coalition of southern republicans and *tenentes* dislodged an oligarchic liberalism in decline from the center of decision-making power.

Positivism's degree of persistence in the minds of our men of state is proved by its capacity to receive and adapt to itself powerful modern tendencies like leftist social reformism and rightist authoritarianism. When Getúlio Vargas asked Lindolfo Collor to put together an advisory commission for the new Ministry of Labor, Industry, and Commerce, the *castilhista* leader from Rio Grande do Sul did not hesitate to bring together socialist militants, progressive industrialists, and landowners identified with centralizing nationalism. Evaristo de Morais sat at the side of Jorge Street and Oliveira Viana, and together, under the banner of a statist ideology that presented itself "acima das classes" (above classes), created our Social Law, which is at once progressive and authoritarian, modern and conservative—in a word, positivist.

The Comtian mold, which is less rigid and dogmatic than it appears at first glance to the student of philosophy, revealed itself at a number of junctures to be flexible and pragmatic, and only hardened in moments of crisis—that is, when rebellious groups from civil society (communists and integralists, in the 1930s) attempted to bring down the very order that those in power considered indispensible for the consolidation of their modernizing project. But in moments of calm, it efficiently engaged in paternalistic co-optation, and it tightened the relationship between unions and the state's executive and legal apparatuses in a way that deeply marked our labor model. This model would, ultimately, define capitalism's mode of operation in Brazil, especially in the largest urban centers.

Doubts of Yesterday and Today

I am fully aware that I am writing this final section at an important moment in world history, and therefore also in Latin American and Brazilian history, in which the ideal of a reformist state engaged in economic planning finds itself vulnerable and assailed from all sides. The attacks launched from the right and the center are not nearly as surprising as those coming from the left, which finds itself dispirited by recent events in Eastern Europe.

The republicans who brought about the Revolution of 1930 were perhaps firmer than the social democrats of today in their belief that the state should direct economic life—though the republicans were not absolutely sure either. Osvaldo Aranha declared to the members of the 1934 Constituent Assembly: "I do not know, honorable deputies, and no one can know, if the state's tendency toward totalitarianism, which characterizes our age, marks the end of a civilization, or marks the beginning of a period of rectifications and improvements for the miserable contingent of the tormented, impoverished peoples of today."

Later on, however, he notes the social necessities that can and should only be satisfied by the state, in accordance with Comte's motto, anticipate in order to provide:

> The Public Power presides over the intimate relationship between the functions of the state and social necessities, and the whole of national life, and indeed, is its raison d'être. This power cannot be exercised if the resolution of collective problems is left to private initiative. The state increasingly participates in, cooperates with, and intervenes in private activities, so that society can reap the material benefit generated by human action. . . . These activities are directed, controlled, [and] dominated by the sovereign, selfish, and exclusivist arbiters that are the firms and enterprises that, in a variety of ways, govern and monopolize the world of business.[51]

In his swearing in of the Assembly, Getúlio Vargas brought the institutional aspects of this question to the forefront: "The state, whatever one's theoretical view of it, is in reality nothing more than the coordinating and disciplining agent of collective interests, that is, society organized as a power, so as to direct and ensure its progress. For this reason, any constitutional structure implies the structure of the functions of the state."

Allow me to pose an apparently casual question: to whom would this National Constituent Assembly delegate the powers of president? The man chosen was Getúlio, with 175 votes. In second place, with 59 votes, the deputies and class representatives did not choose a member of the opposition to *gaúcho* republicanism but rather voted for none other than Borges de Medeiros. *Castilhismo*, rejected in 1891, became in 1934 the cornerstone of the national political system.

* * *

Given that the first experiment in state-led centralization was announced and partially achieved by the Constitution of Rio Grande do Sul in 1891, we may declare that the model contained therein, which prevailed between 1930 and 1964, and which survived from 1964 to our present day, has already achieved an honorable one hundred years of age. If we were to say to the ghost of Auguste Comte that the dead should be buried and forgotten, he would probably respond that, to the contrary, "the dead govern the living." And he would advise us that it remains a prudent course of action to "continue improving by conserving." This piece of advice, directed toward "the miserable contingent of the peoples of today" to which the wise man of affairs of 1930 referred, today means the democratization of the state and the elevation to the highest possible degree of the citizenry's consciousness. This is the republican ideal. The anarchic alternative would certainly not have figured in the master's philosophy.

10 Brazilian Culture and Brazilian Cultures

From the Singular to the Plural

We are accustomed to speaking of Brazilian culture in the singular, as if there were a preexisting unity that incorporated all of the Brazilian people's material and spiritual manifestations. But it is clear that such unity and uniformity does not exist in any modern society, much less in a society determined by class. We could perhaps speak of Bororo culture or Nhambiquara culture in referring to the material and symbolic lives of these groups during the time prior to the invasion of their land and their subsequent acculturation by whites. But in later periods, as internal divisions appear within groups, culture tends to fracture, to generate tensions, and to lose its primitive appearance that, at least in our case, appeared homogeneous.

The tradition of cultural anthropology in Brazil used race to divide the country into distinct cultures: indigenous culture, black culture, white culture, mestizo culture. Arthur Ramos's *Introdução à antropologia brasileira* (Introduction to Brazilian Anthropology), an excellent study completed in 1943 that remains useful for its information and method, is divided into systematically organized chapters dedicated to non-European cultures (indigenous cultures, black cultures—always using the plural) and European cultures (Portuguese, Italian, German, and so on), and concludes by examining racial and cultural contacts.

The criteria we utilize can and should change. We might shift from race to nation, and from nation to social class (the culture of the wealthy, the culture of the poor, bourgeois culture, working-class culture), but in any case, recognition of plurality is essential.

The sort of understanding I propose here departs from an initial analytical point of origin and, hopefully, aims toward a final dialectical horizon.

If we understand the term *culture* as referring to the inheritance of values and objects that are shared by a relatively cohesive human group, then we can speak of an erudite Brazilian culture, centered in the educational system (and principally in the universities), and a *popular culture* that is basically oral and that corresponds to the material and symbolic mores of the rustic man, whether from the *sertão* or the interior, and of the poor man who lives on the urban periphery and who has not yet been entirely assimilated into the modern city's symbolic structures.

We might add to the aforementioned two well-defined currents (in brief, Academia and Folklore), two other strains that urban, capitalist society has reinforced. First, there is the individualized creative culture of writers, composers, visual artists, playwrights, filmmakers—that is, intellectuals operating outside the universities and who, whether grouped together or not, would appear from the outside to constitute a system of high culture that exists independently of the particular ideological motivations of this or that writer, or this or that artist. And second, there is mass culture, which, because it overlaps with systems of production and the market for consumer goods, was termed the *culture industry* and the *culture of consumption* by the members of the Frankfurt School.

Thus we have, analytically speaking: university culture, creative culture, the culture industry outside the universities, and popular culture. From the point of view of the capitalist, techno-bureaucratic system, the university and mass media may be placed within institutions, whereas creative and popular culture should be placed outside of institutions.

Clearly, this spatial distinction between "within" and "outside" should be relativized, as it defines *institution* rigidly, as an organization of the dominant classes. In truth, if we consider the question in greater depth, a typically "popular" cultural phenomenon like the *procissão do Senhor Morto* (Procession of the Dead Lord) during Holy Week is also an institution, just as *candomblé* and indigenous rites are also institutions. Or speaking in terms of creative culture produced by individuals, theatrical pieces are public institutions, whether their authors approve or not. Though if we utilize this sociological criterion, then everything necessarily becomes a socially codified institution, and in antihistorical fashion we erase our initial distinction between cultural systems organized to function as institutions (schools and television networks, for example) and manifestations that are more closely tied to individual or group life, such as poems, *rodas de samba* (samba circles), *mutirões* (volunteer neighborhood building crews), and so on.

The State of University Culture

In terms of the scheme outlined in the previous section, university culture appears as a privileged entity, that is, an entity protected and supported by particular groups that invest in it, as well as by the state, which in Brazil provides a good part of the support for public education. University culture, as a primary goal of young people from the middle and upper classes, has a capacity for self-perpetuation that today can only be compared to that of the large media enterprises. Some would consider university culture one of the state's basic supports, given that the university continually produces graduates who have been trained for positions in an ever-growing bureaucracy.

For this reason we must analyze university culture more closely, in order to determine how certain tendencies that are constructive of worldviews, which run through all of Brazilian culture, operate within it.

Our initial observation concerns the rapid and perhaps irreversible decline of the traditional humanistic disciplines (Greek, Latin, philology, French), which today are consigned to curricula in *Letras* (Letters). As a result of this disappearance, a type of classical humanistic education—which forty years ago enjoyed a prominent position in secondary instruction and which provided the educational basis for members of the clergy and legal system (two sectors that at the time occupied preeminent positions)—has vanished. The intimate relationship between classical erudition and social status disappeared from contemporary society, and the university, with the Church following closely behind, abandoned the teaching of these subjects.

Education in Greek, Latin, classical and vernacular philology, French, Roman law, and related subjects was no longer crucial to the formation of secondary school teachers, priests, or jurists. These subjects became specializations and have since then been taught without the aura that once surrounded them, and as a result, have been stripped of the power that was once invested in them.

One notable consequence of this emptying out was a tendency, which was especially pronounced during the 1960s, to analyze linguistic, literary, legal, and even religious culture from a structural and achronic perspective. That is, the notion that letters, laws, and rites move through diverse periods and styles was displaced by an ahistorical approach restricted to the analysis of texts to which supposedly universal formal categories could be applied. If one loses the sense of context that is necessary to understand a text, one loses the possibility of concrete historical interpretation. Literary studies, at least during the high point of this tendency, were placed at the mercy of a violent synchronization of forms and meanings that were presented as if all readers shared an aesthetic consciousness or even a common ideological orientation. The results were ambiguous. In adhering to this method, one might detect what is not historically present in the text, and one might miss what is present within it. These both constitute grave academic shortcomings. In compensation, this approach, in seeking to extract from the literary past a code or message that would be intelligible to our way of thinking, unexpectedly recovered texts that had long been buried under the weight of an uncreative erudition. Literary culture has depended, during the past few years, on the discovery or rereading of classic texts that are approached from this structural-synchronic perspective, which is based only on the immanent analysis of the text.

This antihistoricism is significant for a specific reason: it signaled the senescence of an earlier vision of the world (humanistic traditionalism), though it shares with the old rhetoric a key feature that has not yet been explored. This is the act of removing the text from the contingency of time, whether this time is past or present. The old rhetoric also approached the text in absolute terms and made it immune to and exempt from social conditions. Achronic structuralism, *mutatis mutandis*, does the same by refusing to study the text as the expression of a given social moment and instead inserting it, without any form of mediation, into the system of ideas and values that is proper to the analyst's present. These poles, seemingly at opposite ends of the spectrum, in fact touch: the classifying, Aristotelian spirit of the old rhetoric tends to reconcile itself to the rigor of structuralist analysis, just as during the nineteenth century philology and positivism joined forces.

Having elucidated the similarities, let us return to the essential difference. Traditionally, classical vernacular and legal studies occupied a position that, beyond formalistic, was also normative. The mapping of literary forms implied their strict use as correct moral and aesthetic criteria. The normative criterion was so entrenched that, at least within institutions, it survived Romanticism, which in the Western world was the antiformalistic movement par excellence. But this value was cast into serious doubt with the configuration of a new structuralist rhetoric that, with the normative option foreclosed, was merely analytical or descriptive.

The state of literary and legal culture since the 1960s is as follows: techniques of formal or immanent analysis have been adopted, but the assumption of normativity has been abandoned to the extent that particular historical formations are no longer granted a privileged status. (If any sort of privilege is granted, it is granted to forms of expression that are absolutely contemporary. The tendency to synchronize texts results in their placement within the subjective frame of reference of the interpreter, who is immersed in his own temporal reality).

During the 1970s (many would specify 1968 as the crucial year), the mere inventorying of linguistic structures came to be considered insufficient. Structuralism no longer satisfied the dynamics of reality, which after all, also impact university education. University culture began to energetically survey its work for meanings and values, and it was precisely in this search that formalistic tendencies began to change, splitting between an inward-looking movement of extreme and epigonic rigidity and a movement of overcoming oriented toward the negation of negation. Within this second tendency, formal analysis was connected to the meaning of expression and communication, with this meaning being interpreted in alternately psychoanalytical and historical-social terms. At this historical moment, literary and linguistic studies, which in 1960 had reflected the prevailing technical worldview, shifted to support a culture of resistance, which in the Brazilian context corresponded to the political opening of the mid-1970s.

Let us recapitulate the process, strictly within the context of the Brazilian university. The old classical and philological studies were replaced by a formalism that was, generally speaking, non-normative, or opposed to grammatical and lexical normativization. The decline in the prestige of classical and vernacular erudition was accompanied by a positive assessment, or even a defense, of any and all contemporary forms and tastes. There was a period during which, *tout court*, intellectuals celebrated any manifestation of so-called mass culture simply because it was contemporary. Finally, the practitioners of the structural method embarked on a search for values. Some found structural analysis sufficient in and of itself, and fetishized the word, the aesthetic of formal materiality, or the immanent value of the legal proceeding. Others found meaning in the text's relationship to intersubjective experience, as revealed and produced by the text.

Analysis of the cultural terrain reveals the simultaneous presence of these extreme positions, a phenomenon I referred to previously in the text "Um testemunho do presente" (Witness to the Present): "The paroxysm of the attacks accompanies the paroxysm of epigonic manifestations."[1]

At any rate, in humanities and law programs, the most narrowly focused analytical techniques and the broadest possible ideological critique exist side by side, or rather, side against side.

Awareness of the ideological risks of this or that method is particularly acute in the broader field of the social sciences. Here, purely technical and purely historicist approaches have especially grave interpretive consequences. During the 1970s, evidence of an alliance between neutral technique and ideological oppression caused researchers to develop a profound distrust of the positivistic and functionalist prescriptions that had been methodically applied from the founding of the social sciences in Brazil, beginning in the

1930s. The imbrication of sociology and dialectical thought is, now more than ever, a problem of cultural politics experienced by all those social scientists who hope to utilize their knowledge as an effective instrument of change.

But the techno-bureaucracy would not be what it is today if it did not counterattack by quite directly and substantially responding to cultural criticism's lingering doubts. The following are five of its most effective measures:

- First, it implanted at all levels of instruction a body of sociopolitical doctrine full of neocapitalist ideas. Courses of study entitled *Organização Social e Política do Brasil* (Social and Political Organization of Brazil) and *Estudos de Problemas Brasileiros* (Study of Brazilian Problems), both of which are taught at the primary level, present a nation-state calmly experiencing technological advances and social progress in which there is space for all, as long as one works and assiduously meets the obligations implied by one's job. The ideology of *Brasil Grande* (Great Brazil) and the *Milagre Brasileiro* (Brazilian Miracle) has until recently permeated education (and in primary school has tended to persist, given the structural inertia of primary education), though it was administered in the largest doses during the Estado Novo (New State).
- Second, and in line with the spirit of the aforementioned measures, the central educational administrative organs replaced the study of general history, cultural geography, Brazilian history, and Brazilian geography—constant features of traditional midlevel educational curricula—with the hybrid discipline of social studies, which in addition to suffering from methodological deficiencies due to its vast, undifferentiated content, brought about competition in the labor market between degree-holders in a variety of subjects, including social sciences, history, geography, education, and finally, the self-same social studies as taught at the undergraduate level. As might be expected, this had negative consequences for all of the aforementioned areas of study by removing them from their specific place within secondary education.
- Third, the study of philosophy abruptly disappeared from secondary education. This form of theoretical and critical reflection par excellence, which questions the meaning of the natural sciences, of the social sciences, of the development of culture and its ideological implications, was jettisoned from education at a crucial moment in adolescents' development. For analogous reasons, it has all but disappeared from advanced courses of study. Many programs of philosophy exclude, in pure and simple terms, the study of philosophy from their undergraduate courses of study. Here, the coup d'état un-

dertaken by techno-bureaucratic power has had a greater and more public impact than in any other area of higher education in Brazil.

- Fourth, the economic dominance of the United States of America has been directly reflected in the gradual exclusion of French from the curriculum, even as an optional language in mid- and even higher level courses of study. An absolute majority of programs of letters have eliminated the study of French. This is yet another reversal, in this case suffered by one of the most fully articulated instruments available to the social sciences in the modern world. The results have been extremely negative for programs in philosophy, letters, and social sciences, as it has been impossible to fill the hole created by the lack of French instruction with translations, which are insufficient in number and are generally of unsatisfactory quality. In today's world, a literary or humanistic culture without French is the equivalent of a classical culture without Latin.

  What remains as far the teaching of modern languages, English included, has generally been oriented toward the goal of acquiring basic conversational skills, along the lines of the Yázigi language schools or the programmatic study of languages, which are built on behaviorist notions. These techniques have an advantage over the old methods of teaching language through translation, in that they create certain automatic audio-linguistic responses in the student, though they bar the student for too long a time from accessing the literature and culture produced within the language of study. The instrument becomes an end in itself. This is the very definition of technocracy. The emphasis placed on the student's command of a (few) phonetic and syntactic structures, though valid, tends to eclipse the goal of attaining a command of educated language, a goal that while arduous, cannot be postponed to the extent that a student might complete his basic courses in a given language without having the opportunity to read the important authors who have written in that language. This has, however, occurred in a systematic fashion.

- Fifth, the unified vestibular university entrance examination—which gives the test-taker alternatives but does not emphasize writing, a change that was partially inaugurated in 1977—has had the effect of orienting precollege education, and specifically, precollege test preparation courses, toward information. This is to the evident detriment of the stated goal of secondary education in Brazil, which is formative and axiological.

The five official measures mentioned above affect the internal curricular dynamics of university- and secondary-level teaching in the humanities. Clearly, however, the bureaucratic mind-set that brought about these changes did not restrict itself to removing or suppressing elements of courses of study. Indeed, it acted in powerful fashion at the macro-structural level of the university system by facilitating, if not frankly supporting, the increase in the number of private institutions of higher learning in Brazil, the majority of which are exclusively motivated by profit. Oriented toward instruction in humanistic and social sciences disciplines such as education, history, literature, social studies, and communications, which are considered of low operating cost, these private institutions have contributed to a perceptible impoverishing of teaching in our country, at both the informational and critical levels. In general, instruction in the social sciences and the humanities in these private institutions is limited to the repetition of formulas from instructional manuals, which makes the ideological repression practiced by their administrative organs particularly heavy-handed and threatening.

If we reconsider relevant dimensions of the situation in which literary, philosophical, and social studies currently find themselves, we will perceive a field of tension, which has now been placed in relief, between a way of reading culture that is closely aligned with the pragmatic needs of neocapitalism in its most savage form and a way of reading this same culture whose objective is to demystify the ideologies that undergird culture. Again: alienation coexists with a language of protest against the illusions of developmentalism and its authoritarian masks. And once more: it is ideology that separates these strands.

Similar tensions can be seen in the overall cultural development of Brazilian society. They can be detected outside of the realm of literary and humanistic education *in sensu strictu*. The affirmation and denunciation of the technical mind-set are also visible along the disciplinary borders between the social and biological sciences (in psychology, medicine, and public health), and between the social and exact sciences (in economics, administration, demography, engineering, architecture, and urbanism). Conflict has erupted in these areas, which have grown as capitalism has evolved, between technocrats and those scholars who seek to place their area of study in the service of social democracy.

After a good many years of developmentalist policies, years in which the sciences were encouraged by the state and by private enterprise to contribute to the rational planning of society, its most gifted practitioners now find themselves confronted with a system guided by forces that are not oriented toward the democratization of cultural goods. Multinational enterprises involved in engineering, urbanism, administration, and the pharmaceutical industry are exclusively guided by profit, while the strong state, in turn, is guided exclusively by the accumulation of power and security. It matters little that the ideological expressions of all concerned make use of a moribund developmentalist rhetoric.

These pages will not concern themselves with specifying the ways in which, in all of these areas, tensions between technocrats and critics are resolved. The objective here is distinct and necessarily broader: to observe, within the practice of university culture, the contradiction between specular tendencies and critical tendencies. I term the first group of tendencies *specular* because in mirroring the interests of dominant groups, they bring to bear the force of facts.

This is not an academic contradiction that manifests itself exclusively in classrooms or in graduate seminars. University courses of study flow into the liberal and technical professions and into print culture—in short, the various realms of civil society and the bureaucratic apparatus. In making the leap from a medical education to the medical-mercantile practice of private clinics, one generally observes a process of rapid adaptation to the real, which in this case is represented by Brazil's class society. Functional information and techniques quickly become routine. The transition from the university to professional practice follows established formulas, prescriptions written beforehand by those who profit—in this case, the pharmaceutical industry and providers of medical equipment. This world of prescriptions is the direct result of specular culture. What was, perhaps, something to be problematized, investigated, and critiqued during one's higher education becomes, once one has fallen into a professional rut, a formula, a functional design, a mechanical calculation that can be made and handed over to the consumer. We must be aware of this brutal simplification, which today's consumer society inflicts upon academic culture.

The world of prescriptions is the form through which the dominant culture operates in all of the professional paths opened by a university education. The situation is particularly depressing when one considers how university culture impacts secondary education, generally at the informational level. What is transmitted to schoolchildren (and here we reach the heart of the educational dynamic), what is presented in terms of primary education, is almost always the final, reduced, reified manifestation of a by-now outmoded trend in higher education. Worse yet, the routine of secondary education is marked by the inertia of structures that are much more deeply entrenched than those in the universities.

The transformation of innovative ways of thinking into schematic, abstract, and self-satisfied language is one of the most frustrating problems entailed in the diffusion of culture in a consumerist society. Thinkers like Adorno and Umberto Eco have expounded upon the theme of the "institutionalization of the vanguards"—that is, critique that becomes a product, a trend, and that is diluted through verbal abuse and is ultimately incorporated into the clean consciences of well-meaning thinkers. This critique thereby loses sight of its objective of changing the status quo. The neutralization of all possibilities for dissent by a broad and flexible modernizing process seems an almost physiological reflex of neocapitalist societies that at times, and seemingly at random, reprimand certain expressions and attitudes that they consider inconvenient, that is, most capable of awakening or sharpening one's awareness of contradictions.

The system appears to give a certain leeway to that which does not imperil its economic self-preservation. The liberalization of customs and language occurring today falls within this category. But the absence of a coherent philosophical system of values (aside from self-preservation) grants a certain instability, and even an incoherence, to the censorship standards applied to politics, journalism, literature, cinema, theater, and so on. Developmentalism-oriented neocapitalism, even in its politically authoritarian phase, has no morality, no set of values other than that of appearances. And the ideology of modernization will occasionally change its appearance in order to sell itself more effectively—hence the inconsistencies in the norms that regulate verbal expression, which is our cultural form par excellence, and hence the practice of incorporating the jargon of criticism into official discourse. An illustrative example of this facility for rhetorical assimilation is found in the half-sociological, half-dialectical language that permeates the most recent Plano Setorial de Cultura (Sectional Plan for Culture, 1975–1979), which continues to govern us and which was prepared by the Secretaria do Ministério de Educação e Cultura (Secretariat of the Ministry of Education and Culture):

> All education that is active and rationally implemented maintains a dialectical relationship, of agreement and assimilation, of criticism and overcoming, with the society it serves. In this way, education can also act as the motor of the social process, and the educational project should be conceived in light of the goal of achieving a society better able to mold the human person. This point accords with the Faure Report in its affirmation that there exists a close, simultaneous, and differentiated correlation between socio-economic transformations and educational structures and mechanisms, and that education contributes functionally to the forward movement of history. Further, education, by instilling knowledge of the context in which it occurs, may help society become more aware of its problems, and if it focuses its efforts on the molding of complete men, may contribute significantly to the transformation and humanization of society.

This is a perfectly hybrid text. We have a personalist discourse, a functionalist sociological discourse, and a dialectical veneer in which education and society, superstructure and infrastructure, are negated or mutually reinforced.

This example was offered merely to accentuate the main argument presented in these pages, which affirms the existence of disparate specular and critical currents as well as their coexistence and the centripetal character of the cultural system. At certain moments, the cultural system incorporates the language of the opposition into its discourse, though naturally, it makes sure that these ideas are diluted within a vague progressive and developmentalist agenda inherited from the 1945–1964 period, during which, however, this agenda was joined to a more democratic politics.

Culture Outside of the University

At this point, we should observe that there exist cultural currents outside of the university. As such, we must retain the anthropological definition of the term *culture*, referring here to the ways of being, living, thinking, and feeling proper to a certain social formation. But at the same time, we must abandon a more restrictive definition that associates culture exclusively with verbal expression and, preferably, with verbal expression issuing from university-level teaching and research institutions.

In point of fact, literary culture occurs now more than ever within the university or around it. Open the magazines and cultural supplements published by the best newspapers: their culture sections are filled with articles, interviews, reviews, and reports written by intellectuals or about intellectuals from the country's best universities (Rio de Janeiro, São Paulo, Campinas, Brasília, PUC-Rio, PUC-São Paulo, etc.). Cities no longer support the type of cultural and literary life that existed in tangible form up until the 1940s, a period in which the university was just coming into formation and had not yet professionally absorbed the intellectuals. Today, it seems that the social division of labor has also brought specialization to the life of the spirit, which is now channeled through institutions of higher learning.

Given that this culture, regardless of its wide diffusion, is still the privilege of the minority, we must ask if Brazilian culture is not articulated and expressed in places, in moments, and in ways distinct from those of academic life.

Now then, what characterizes culture outside of the university is precisely its diffuse character and its intimate relation with the psychological and social life of the people. This is exactly the opposite of academic practice, which is focused and specialized, and which addresses second- or third-hand materials that have already been addressed in the thematic literature. In the university, culture becomes prematurely formal and professional. This culture, whether technical or even critical, is quickly reduced to the articulation of formulas on which it will depend until new formulas arrive to replace the earlier ones. This is a context that produces branded, thematically specific discourse. Culture within the university equates to speaking programmatically "about something."

In the world outside of the university, symbols and cultural goods are not the objects of detailed analysis or systematic interpretation. They are sporadically experienced and thought but not analyzed in the abstract.

The Culture Industry

Outside of the university, symbolic goods are primarily consumed through the mass media.

This entails a process of diffusion that is proper to today's consumer society. The man in the street turns on his battery-powered radio and listens to Brazilian popular music or, more frequently, North American popular (or mass) music. The maid turns on her little radio and listens to the soap opera or the police drama or the women's program. The housewife turns on the television and watches the prime-time soap operas. The man of the house turns on the television and watches the soccer match with his sons. The children turn on the television and watch action movies. Almost everyone listens to the evening news. Music and images arrive from the outside and are consumed en masse. On a smaller scale, newspapers and magazines report on crimes or construction projects or the horrors of the drought or the frost in Paraná. On an even smaller scale, couples go to the movies. They watch police dramas, science fiction films, light comedies, and slapsticks. Adolescent boys read comic books. Adolescent girls read *fotonovelas*. All of this is mass-produced according to certain successful formulas. There are women's magazines for working- and middle-class women that sell 500,000 copies weekly and reach over one million readers. This is mass culture, or more precisely, *culture for the masses*. Certain radio and TV programs have similar, if not larger, audiences.

In general, the psychological processes involved in these programs are those oriented toward immediate appeal—to sentimentality, aggressiveness, eroticism, fear, fetishization, curiosity. There is a dose of realism and conservatism that, simultaneously, stimulates the desire to see, disturbs the primary emotions, and placates them with a happy ending. Everything that is placed in a state of crisis during the program or in the image-heavy text is ultimately restored to order. Umberto Eco is correct in using the term *consoling structures* to describe the underlying meaning of the interpolative processes that hold the attention of millions of consumers of culture.

In diachronic terms, it does not seem to me that this type of consumption of symbolic goods has changed significantly from the 1960s through the 1970s. Censorship and massification continue. The formulas for success and the large audiences continue. Intensive and insidious advertising, which employs all available resources to increase the sales of its products, continues. Perhaps a more detailed analysis would find, here or there, isolated changes, though nothing substantial.

What marks an important, observable change is the intellectual's critical position with regard to the culture industry. The favorable attitude toward the culture industry, with was common and in certain cases enthusiastic during the 1960s, the golden age of academic work on mass communication, became critical beginning in the 1970s. The number of dissertations and theses produced by academic departments, which sought to denounce the conformist ideology that underlay the most popular TV programs and certain heroes from the best-selling comics, multiplied. Under the aegis of Adorno, there occurred a radical denunciation of the culture industry, a denunciation that extended to all media and that has become a quite common counterideological strategy. It even committed the sacrilege of critiquing the soccer-centric ideology advanced by official propaganda. This critical position, adopted by a culture of resistance, has not, as can be easily perceived, changed the fact that, objectively speaking, the culture industry and its respective market remain intact.

Umberto Eco termed the negative understanding of mass culture, formalized by the scholars of the Frankfurt School, like Horkheimer, Adorno, and from a distinct perspective, Herbert Marcuse, *apocalyptic*. This occurred in the context of his division of intellectuals into the apocalyptic and integrated categories. In responding to these radical critiques, certain voices recall the socializing character of mass media, which theoretically gives the same amount of information to all, and from time to time, provides the spectator with the tools to make nonalienated judgments regarding the system to which he is subject. Further, the defenders of mass media insist that certain programs, when guided by artistically or intellectually sophisticated persons, can have a pedagogical character. In truth, and considering the historical record, we must suspend our judgment regarding a process of communication that is far from having exhausted all of its remaining resources. In the contemporary Brazilian case, the political censorship and aesthetic and ideological massification that one sees at work in popular programs do not inspire confidence in the more alert and demanding viewers.

This said, a politics that seeks to educate a large number of Brazilians must necessarily make use of mass communication. This does not mean that these forms, in terms of their materiality and quantity, will transform the thinking of their users, in the positive sense of humanization and socialization. Rather, they will transform their thinking in terms of the guiding philosophy of the political-social project that makes use of these forms. So far, this has amounted to a modernizing neocapitalism that has been marked by more or less accentuated phases of conformity and innovation. One should not hope that mass culture, and especially the culture industry as its capitalistic expression, will provide what it does not want to provide: lessons in social freedom and support for the construction of a world unchained from money and status.

Popular Culture

Academic culture and mass culture are institutionalized formations generated by the state and by corporations for the purpose of transmitting knowledge or occupying the leisure time of a significant portion of the Brazilian population. Modern, complex organizations oversee the production and circulation of symbolic goods. Their growth and their basic intellectual orientation have developed in line with the country's economic growth.

But if we strictly adhere to the anthropological definition of culture, which is by far the most productive definition of the term, we will quickly perceive that a nearly limitless number of symbolic phenomena that give expression to Brazilian life have their point of origin in the popular imagination. This popular imagination takes on a diversity of forms, from indigenous rites to *candomblé*, from *samba de roda* to the Feast of the Divine Holy Spirit, and from the Pentecostal Assemblies to *umbanda* houses of worship, as well as rustic and cultivated expressions of Catholic piety.

Within this complex range of cultural expressions, the institution (in the classically sociological sense of the term) exists. These are group manifestations, and they adhere to certain canons, but they do not have access to the network of economic power, nor do they have the expansive ideological influence enjoyed by the university or by communications enterprises. These are micro-institutions, dispersed throughout the space of the nation, which maintain a significant distance from official culture. They serve the expressive needs of more enclosed groups, though the members of these groups are also exposed to academic culture and to the mass media.

The tendency of conventional, evolutionistic sociological studies is to label as *residual* all manifestations typically termed *folkloric*. With this point of view firmly established, everything that exists beyond the pale of writing, along with, in general, the habits of rural persons and of those on the urban periphery, is seen as a remnant of indigenous, black, *caboclo*, slave, and even archaic Portuguese cultures—cultures that were invariably produced in conditions of subordination.

It is extremely important that we rethink the generative process for this culture, which existed and continues to exist beyond the pale of writing. A certain Westernizing intellectual tendency, which at its core is colonialist, stigmatizes popular culture as a fossil of earlier states of primitivism, backwardness, slowness, and underdevelopment. According to this perspective, what is inevitable (and what ultimately corresponds to its most cherished ideal) is the wholesale disappearance of these residual elements, and the integration of all those linked to them into the two most powerful institutional forms: culture for the masses and academic culture. This is a linear, evolutionistic vision that, drawing on the authority of official science, argues the case of the winners.

At the other extreme, a Romantic-nationalist, Romantic-regionalist, or Romantic-populist current (the details change according to the context) sees the values transmitted by folklore as eternally valid, ignores or denies folklore's ties to mass and erudite culture, and identifies group expressions with a mythical spirit of the people, or in a more ideological fashion, with the nation. What, from the opposing point of view, an abstract universalism would erase, in this case is lost in excessive particularism.

The problem becomes significantly more complicated in the present day, given that we must now consider the imbrication between popular and mass culture (or popularesque culture, according to Mário de Andrade), or between popular culture and the culture of artistic creation. In the final analysis, what is called for is a theory of acculturation that would exorcise the ghosts of elitism and populism, both of which are aggressively ideological and the source of deep-rooted prejudices.

A theory of Brazilian culture, if it exists one day, will draw on the daily physical, symbolic, and imaginative lives of people who live in Brazil. There it will find content and values. In the case of popular culture, there is no separation between a purely material sphere of existence and a spiritual or symbolic sphere. Popular culture entails ways of living: food, clothing, male-female relations, shelter, sanitation, medicine, kinship relations, and the division of tasks throughout the workday, along with beliefs, songs, dances, games, hunting, fishing, smoking, drinking, proverbs, greetings, verbal taboos, euphemisms, ways of seeing, ways of feeling, ways of walking, ways of visiting and receiving visitors, pilgrimages, vows, feasts of patron saints, ways of raising chickens and pigs, ways of planting beans, corn, and manioc, knowledge of time, ways of laughing and crying, of attacking and consoling, and so on.

This enumeration is intentionally chaotic in its movement from the material to the symbolic and back again from the symbolic to the material, given that the intent is to express quite clearly the indivisibility, in the daily life of rustic man, of body and soul, or of organic and moral necessities.

The educated observer will have difficulty perceiving this indivisibility, because he does not experience it in his own life. He will attempt to divide popular experience into parts or topics, converting it into a list of separate items, of which some are material and others are not.

However, the life of the body, of the group, of manual labor, and of religious beliefs overlap with one another in the daily experience of the impoverished in such a way that one can almost speak of animistic materialism as the underlying philosophy for all radically popular culture. This phrase, which I have used once before to describe the perspective of Guimarães Rosa, merits clarification. The impoverished man experiences materialism through his daily obligations that require him to make use of material, to labor over the land or with mechanical tools, which are his only means of survival. This grants him a realism, a practicality, a lively sense of the limitations and possibilities of his actions, which together comprise a deeply rooted empirical knowledge that is his principal defense in a hostile economy. It falls to the impoverished man and the impoverished woman to face the strongest sort of resistance from nature and from life. But this world of need is not entirely disenchanted, to cite the term Max Weber used to describe the universe of bourgeois rationality. Even the most destitute believe that they maintain a tacit relationship with a higher power (God, Providence), a relationship that in terms of religious syncretism produces a number of spiritual manifestations that are invested with energy and intention, such as saints, celestial spirits, evil spirits, and the dead. This pantheon also assimilates the idols elevated by mass communication and, eventually, the most admired persons within society.

In this way, a solid empiricism or realism in the world of work and in the sphere of basic economics is joined with a potentially magical universe, alternately good and evil in orientation, built on chance events, bad and good luck, favor, the evil eye, and right and wrong feet. All of this is given concrete form in objects that rationalistic criticism tends to view as superstitious, such as likenesses, photos, *figas*, ribbons, amulets, medals, holy objects, stones, herbs, and animals. Together these comprise the symbolic system of Brazilian animism in its most impoverished contexts, though these appear in other contexts as well.

Animistic materialism (grounded, as semantic analysis of the term demonstrates, in the overcoming of the opposition between body and soul) was passed down from century to century within a predominantly rural context. For this reason, it is highly cognizant of the cycles of nature, clearly marking the seasons, the arrival and departure of periods of drought and rain, the high and low ocean tides, the phases of the moon, the parts of the day, women's biological cycles, and the ages of man. Further, it gives each of these a weight, a quality, and a meaning, the knowledge of which is an integral part of popular wisdom from all corners of the globe.

Animistic materialism has a cyclical vision of nature and history, a vision that to rationalistic culture appears static but that has an inner dynamism and is fully aware of changes, of dangers, of the incessant movement that alternately quickens and slows the movement of the cycle.

In general, this view of the world easily accepts a belief in reincarnation, which can be proved by the very large number of spiritist Catholics throughout Brazil. According to cyclical materialism, nothing dies—not even the dead. All can return and live among us. There is neither sin nor definitive punishment, and everything that once was can be once more, as the forces that guide our destiny will it. The heart of every man of the people holds within it both a fundamental resignation and an ever-renewed hope.

Materialism, animism, and a cyclical vision of existence (or reversibility) are constant features of our popular culture. It is implicit in the term *popular* that this culture is, above all, *of the group or supra-individual*, which guarantees its perpetuation despite the loss of individual elements.

As for the expansive potential of each of these currents of Brazilian culture: erudite culture grows principally in the upper classes and in the more protected segments of the middle class, and it grows in line with the educational system. Mass culture, or the culture industry, cuts vertically through all layers of society and grows most significantly within the middle classes. Popular culture traditionally belongs to the poorer classes, though this does not prevent its appropriation by mass culture and by erudite culture, which in their flexibility and rootlessness may take on popularesque or populist airs.

Relations between Brazilian Cultures

Given the impossibility in this sort of essay of specifically developing the aforementioned theme—which, incidentally, is a very broad topic within cultural anthropology—I will limit myself to indicating combinations adopted by the previously discussed currents.

Erudite Culture and Mass Culture

Though they are apparently opposed in terms of the points of view that gave birth to them, erudite culture and mass culture may nonetheless intersect at more than one point. University-level professionals, and especially technicians and technocrats, are fascinated by the products of the culture industry that make use of a true plethora of mechanical and electronic elements and that reproduce and distribute objects that can only be developed after careful research in universities. There is, then, an evident contiguity between academic research and the electronic, optical, acoustic, mechanical, pharmaceutical, surgical, and other consumer products generated by technology that intersect with mass culture through advertising.

But it is not only in the technical arena that university education and intensive consumption converge. This convergence also takes place in the world of literature and the arts. In Brazil, for example, certain writers and avant-garde composers have sought to take advantage of advances in electronics and computing, and have given chance and chance combinations a dominant aesthetic weight. This intimate relationship with technical means prompted certain experimentalist ideologues to condemn any and all art forms that did not make use of the most modern programming and communications technology. Within this field, television enjoyed a special prestige. According to Marshall McLuhan's key theory, television revolutionized the perception of all men, shattering the barriers between the social classes and instituting the "Global Village," which, using electronics, reorganized humanity and wiped clean the regional and cultural differences that for millennia characterized the various peoples of the planet. This is an evocative case of incorporation of mass media into a project whose origin was educated and elite.

In fields more closely tied to the applied sciences, such as engineering and economics, mass culture is an important source of information and values for a large number of people who, throughout intellectual history, have done without the corpus of humanistic culture. In this way mass culture, despite its name, has transformed itself into the middlebrow culture of technicians.

Such an interrelation can be inverted. Mass culture—that is, the industry that generates symbolic objects in serial form—draws on and grabs hold of erudite culture, transforming not a few of its representations into style and consumption. This is the phenomenon of kitsch, which has been studied by Abraham Moles and which consists of the distribution to upper- and middle-class consumers of words, tastes, melodies—in sum, cultural goods—initially produced by so-called higher culture.

In turn, the university, making due adaptations or concessions to middlebrow taste, is called upon to offer up images, words, and ideas to be bundled and sold to the mass market, or to the middle or upper classes through newspapers and magazines. We are presently witnessing massive solicitation of the universities on the part of communications enterprises looking for material. The culture industry has popularized (especially among its most refined costumers) as well as diluted and exploited critical and creative academic work. Certain academic figures, whose activities were previously restricted to academic life and whose work reached a very small public, have quickly been transformed into figures of cultural consumption, narrowing the divide that for some time separated higher education from the average reader of these publications. The university did not, however, develop these means of publicity. Rather, they came to the university, they solicited it, and to a certain extent they incorporated it into a modernizing project already in progress.

Mass Culture and Popular Culture

The expansive economic power of the communications media seems to have destroyed manifestations of popular culture issuing from a variety of contexts, reducing them to folklore destined for tourists. Such is the degree of penetration of certain radio and TV programs among the poor, such is the appearance of modernization that attaches itself to the life of the common people throughout Brazil, that at first glance it does not appear that any space has been retained for traditional-popular ways of being, thinking, speaking—in sum, living. Were this in fact true, we might understand it as a necessary effect of neocapitalist penetration of countries whose origins are found in colonialism.

Mass culture enters into the home of the *caboclo*, or the worker living in the urban periphery, and occupies the leisure time in which he might otherwise develop some creative form of self-expression. This is its first objective. On another level, mass culture makes use of various aspects of popular life and exploits them as popularesque reportage and tourism. This vampirism is dual in nature and is on the rise. It destroys from within the temporality proper to popular culture and exhibits what remains of this temporality for the benefit of the television viewer, through handcrafts, festivals, and rites. Here we have a more complete picture of the relationship between the industrial and commercial apparatuses that exploit and the popular culture that is exploited. One cannot escape from the fundamental struggle: capital seeks out raw materials and labor in order to manipulate, produce, and sell. *Macumba* on television and samba schools that allow tourists to participate in Carnaval for a price are typical examples of this.

However, the dialectic is a more profound truth that is dreamt of in our philosophy. The exploitation, the abusive use by mass culture of popular manifestations, has not yet succeeded in entirely stopping the slow but sure, powerful, and dynamic progress of archaic-popular life, which reproduces itself on the micro level within family and community networks, and with the support of kinship networks, of neighbors, and of religious groups.

The people assimilate, in their own ways, certain television images and certain songs and words from the radio, translating these signs into their own system of signification. There is a filter that allows them to reject undesirable material and pragmatically adapt themselves to information that can be assimilated. Further, advertising cannot sell to those who have no money. It ends up doing what it is least inclined to do: it gives out images, distributes words, and popularizes rhythms, all of which are freely incorporated or re-incorporated by a generous popular imagination.

Though the fan of the Corinthians soccer club may acquire, through loans and through much effort, the newest digital television, complete with remote control, he will still light a candle in honor of Our Lady of Aparecida or for one or many figures associated with *macumba* in order to guarantee victory for his team.

What does it matter that in the dance clubs of the urban periphery the patrons dance to the latest rock song released by the Yankee music industry, if the young people dance and flirt in accordance with an almost ritual relationship reproduced down through the centuries by the moral education of the *sertão*?

These peculiar reactions to receptors determine, up to a certain point, the content and forms transmitted by the media that attempt to satisfy the people's tastes, and which in so doing become popularesque or pseudo-traditionalistic (given that they cannot be authentically traditional), as occurs with certain more or less sentimental, more or less modernizing, and more or less moralizing radio programs and *fotonovelas*. The typical in a popular sense, with all of its tendencies toward caricature, is a mode through which the culture industry depicts the people as an Other. This Other is a people that is simultaneously exploited and untouched.

Relations between mass culture and popular culture are, then, quite delicate. From the point of view of capitalist dynamism, mass culture invariably tends to scatter and supplant popular culture. This phenomenon does occur, both on the moral and aesthetic planes, but as with the detribalization of indigenous groups, it is more the product of a violent technical and economic campaign undertaken by the capitalist system than it is a case of gradual exposure by the primitive or the rustic to forms of mass culture.

Erudite Culture and Popular Culture

The culture industry's use of folklore is similar to expropriation. Just as industry takes the labor power of the dispossessed person and pays him a pittance, mass culture steals as much as it can from the popular sensibility and imagination, and repays it with a minimal amount of leisure, which is shot through with the images and slogans of advertising.

And yet, or perhaps for this very reason, because we are a society made up of consumers of objects, of news, and of signs, the culture industry is the thing that penetrates us most deeply, invading, inhabiting, and modeling us. The cultured consumer is a jaded voyeur, a pervert.

And what about erudite culture?

Erudite culture either ignores, purely and simply, the people's symbolic manifestations, and remains for the most part distant from them, or it leans in, sympathetically and inquisitively, perhaps even enchanted by things that appear strong, spontaneous, whole, energetic, vital—in sum, distant from and opposed to the coldness, dryness, and inhibition that are peculiar to intellectualism and to academic routine. Erudite culture hopes to feel goosebumps when faced with the savage.

This contact can yield a variety of fruits, ranging from the blindest and most demagogic populism, which represents the resounding guilty conscience at the heart of all class societies, to the most beautiful works of art, formed from popular motifs, such as the music of Villa-Lobos, the narratives of Guimarães Rosa, the paintings of Portinari, and the Afrocentric poetry of Jorge de Lima.

To get to the crux of the problem, there is only one valid and productive relationship to be had between the educated artist and popular life: a relationship of love. Unless he becomes deeply rooted in the popular, unless he feels sincere and sustained empathy for it, the writer or the university-educated man, who speaks a reductive dominant language, will become entangled in prejudice, or will irrationally mythologize everything that seems popular to him, or will perhaps project the full weight of his misgivings and inhibitions onto the culture of the other, or might even interpret the ways of living of the primitive man, the rustic man, or the man of the urban periphery in a fatally ethnocentric or colonizing way.

The errors of the ethnocentric gaze and the sympathetic but distorted interpretations made by a nationalist (and ultimately, populist) anthropology amount to a look at the inside from the outside, to a projection, to an unfamiliarity that is poorly disguised as familiarity. This unfamiliarity, and the judgments to which it gives rise, have well-known ancestors in the chroniclers and catechists of the first centuries of colonization. Is there anyone who has not read, in either Gabriel Soares de Sousa, or in Gândavo, or in a Jesuit writer, that because the Tupi language lacked the letters *F*, *R*, and *L*, the Tupi could have neither *Fé* (faith), nor *Rei* (king), nor *Lei* (law)? The errors and prejudices of colonial philology are deeply rooted. Another observer, writing in the eighteenth century and concerned with Afro-Brazilian religious habits, looked for the root of Africans' wickedness in the etymology of the word *calundu*, which he, oddly enough, believed was derived from the Latin *calo duo*, that is, "two have fallen silent." He then inferred that when two have fallen silent, some evil thought much certainly be circulating through their minds and that certain individuals who fall silent are possessed by Satan, that is, the mute demon. Even Gregório de Matos, for all of his familiarity with Afro-Bahian life, attributed *candomblé* ceremonies to the devil, to *padre-mestre Satanás* (father-master Satan), and included them in a list of sins against the First Commandment.

With independence, erudite culture changed in tone, shifting toward nativistic exaltation of the Alencarian type, and drawing on Tupi images and myths to defend a nationalistic and conservative ideology. At any rate, interest in the savage—and beginning in the second half of the nineteenth century, in the black and the *sertanejo*—continued, and embarked on a search for a methodology, which it would borrow from the emerging disciplines of sociology and ethnology. In this way, Brazilian high culture assimilated, to the extent that was possible, certain evolutionistic notions taken from Darwin and Haeckel, and strictly divided our population into primitive, archaic, and modern segments. Fundamental works written from this perspective include *O Selvagem* (The Savage, 1877) by General Couto de Magalhães, *L'animisme fétichiste des negres de Bahia* (The Fetishistic Animism of the Blacks of Bahia, 1900) by Nina Rodrigues, and *Os sertões* (Rebellion in the Backlands, 1902) by Euclides da Cunha. These works deal, respectively, with the Brazilian Amerindian, the black, and the *sertanejo*.

How were an interest in popular culture and scientific prejudices and colonialism expressed in the classic books and the ethnographic literature produced at the end of the nineteenth century? The answer can be found in the substantive essays written at the turn of that century by Sílvio Romero and João Ribeiro, authorities on our folklore and oral literature. The Amerindian, the black, the mestizo, the mulatto, and the *caboclo* were seen as deserving of sympathy, though they were considered rougher, less educated, more instinctive—in sum, more primitive—than, or even inferior to, whites. Their prelogical or illogical character (this prejudice was gradually undone during the twentieth century) was emphasized, and a series of negative or degenerative changes was postulated as peculiar to miscegenation. Attention to pathology and delinquency defines the tone of the work of Nina Rodrigues, who was a medical doctor. In Euclides da Cunha, who was Rodrigues's disciple, this tone is counterbalanced by a frank admission of the personal valor and physical and expressive energy of the *sertanejos*, whom he observed in Canudos. This perspective, which mixes interest, condescension, and attribution of mental inferiority, recalls, *mutatis mutandis*, the attitude of certain sixteenth-century chroniclers. One constant, which strikes me as curious and prone to a number of variations, is the attribution to the primitive man of more pronounced natural characteristics—of power, desire, and intuition—than could allegedly be found in civilized, white populations. Erudite culture is fascinated by what it perceives as the unconscious energy of savage peoples and illiterate populations, an energy that is lost in the civilizing process. Rousseau, who for Lévi-Strauss was the "founder of the social sciences," is a constant presence here.

Modernist writers like Mário de Andrade, Oswald de Andrade, Raul Bopp, and Cassiano Ricardo addressed the specific theme of cultural mixture. I will limit myself to noting two strands of thinking: Mário de Andrade's aesthetic and critical nationalism and Oswald de Andrade's *antropofagismo* (cannibalism). Mário was inclined toward a fusion of supranational technical skill with a search for a semiprimitive, miscegenated, fluid, and romantic Brazilian psychology. Oswald preached the violent and indiscriminate ingestion of international content and form through a Brazilian cannibalistic process that would devour everything and incorporate it into its unconscious organism, which was somewhere between anarchic and matriarchal. These two theses, though quite distinct in their formulation, both postulate an assimilation of European codes by a presumed Brazilian national character (or noncharacter), characterized by a combination of a prelogical mentality (this expression is taken from Lévy-Bruhl) and civilized forms superimposed by historical forces such as colonization and catechization.

The ways in which these hypotheses (in which anthropology drew on debatable ideas of national psychology) contributed to modernist literary works should be analyzed within the context of Brazilian literary interpretation and history for the period. For the purposes of this discussion, it should be noted that modernism, especially among the modernists who were *paulistas* or were based in São Paulo, addressed the relationship between erudite and popular culture from a decidedly mythopoeic perspective. The authors of *Macunaíma* and the *Manifesto antropofágico* (Cannibalist Manifesto) understood popular culture, in the first place, as the expression of a Tupi sensibility, as articulated in legends, myths, and rites recorded by the chroniclers, the Jesuits, and certain contemporary anthropologists. At a later moment, Mário de Andrade, an indefatigable researcher, would additionally dedicate himself as a semiprofessional folklorist to the study of the black and mestizo worlds. However, this was no longer the heroic moment in which modernism's fundamentally primitivistic definitions were formulated. It would fall to the regionalist novelists, and in particular the northeasterners and *gaúchos* responsible for the best examples of our literary neorealism, to explore impoverished modern Brazil. Radical primitivism issued from São Paulo, an industrial, capitalistic region and ground zero for cultural modernization, as if the choice presented in Oswald de Andrade's famous pun "Tupi or not Tupi, that is the question" were genuine. But this was merely an aesthetic choice faced by the modernism of the 1920s. Pure primitivism or the future: that was the question faced by that modernism. There likely exists a structural relationship between ultramodernizing historical moments and irrationalist (or to use the preferred term of today, countercultural) aesthetics. The call to fuse technique with irrationalism was symptomatic of the late 1960s, a period in which Brazil experienced the first wave of consumption of technology and mass media. It is not coincidental that this was the high point of Tropicalism, which proposed a return to modernism's cannibalistic thinking, though the Tupi Amerindians were replaced by the masses, whose ways of feeling and speaking were found in narratives and theatrical pieces focused on the theme of violence. Erudite culture seeks to renew itself through the appropriation, somewhere between brutal and sophisticated, of what it perceives as popular spontaneity and vitality. The most common risk in this process is that one repeats, perhaps without the richness of modernism's aesthetic fantasy, the ideological and psychological phenomenon—from which the modernists, incidentally, did not escape—of projection: projection of the intellectual's neuroses, imbalances, prejudices, repressions, and recoveries onto popular material interpreted as an escape valve for petit bourgeois subjectivity. But isn't this risk a deep tendency of all cultures engendered by class societies? If this is this case, analysis of the crucial relationship between erudite and popular culture should begin with a self-diagnosis of erudite culture. The best observations I have yet encountered concerning the intellectual's obligations to his class are found in Antonio Gramsci's *Prison Notebooks*. These must be reinterpreted so that their degree of applicability to Brazilian cultural life can be understood.

More easily understood, because of its abstract and unilateral character, is the confrontation of a certain sort of self-focused erudite culture with folkloric manifestations. The erudite gaze denies these folkloric manifestations their status as culture and accentuates their simple, poor, elementary, crude, and vulgar content and their monotonous, repetitive, and unoriginal form. This is a lamentable case of ignorance, pure and simple, and in most cases, points to the inability of pseudo-culture to distinguish between folklore (with which it is, in reality, unfamiliar) and folkloric counterfeits exhibited by the mass media.

Purely academic intellectuals and technical professionals are, for the most part, satisfied with their efforts to pursue an international lifestyle and are content with the economic and social benefits their status gives them. For this reason, they can move through life without ever knowing about, caring about, or entering into real contact with popular culture. Further, they are impeded from accessing popular culture by barriers of race and color. When they do encounter popular culture, they most often see it transposed onto the television or as tourists during their periods of leisure. In both cases, they receive an image of popular culture-as-spectacle, a view that only accentuates the elite's disdain or sadness at the backwardness of the Brazilian people.

The crux of the problem is always this: there is only one valid and productive relationship to be had between the erudite man and popular life—a relationship of love. Populism, if we call into question its easy sympathy for the object known as the people, always makes use of popular culture. This is a necessarily passing and superficial use, given that the intellectual (even the countercultural intellectual) lacks the conditions or effective intention of sharing in what Jacques Loew termed a "community of destiny" with the poor. Populism in journalism, fiction, theater, and so on makes verbal or iconic use of fragments taken from popular daily life, just as political populism episodically (or rather, regularly) makes use of the electoral aspirations or illusions of the mass.

Elitism functions in a distinct way. Grounded in the experience of enjoyment, elitists take voluptuous pleasure in the cultural goods that have been determined to be the best by well-meaning academics from the world over. They buy the best and seek whenever possible to prove the excellence of their selections: this is a culture of citations, which seeks to elevate the smallest kernel of an idea through the irresistible endorsement of "so-and-so said," and if possible, elaborates on that happy, carefully remembered moment when, in casual, friendly conversation, "so-and-so said to me . . ."

The intellectual, the educated consumer, in his frequently unconscious cult of authority (at bottom, elitism considers itself liberal), inserts a structure of domination at such a deep level that he cannot perceive it. In his alienation, he excludes the concrete existence of the dominated from his mental universe. He is aware of the dominated but only through citations. He sits on a chair skillfully built using techniques he will never observe. He receives the tributes, the fees levied on a largely illiterate people with whom he will never find the time to converse. But this will not worry him much. He will resolutely carry on in his career and in his most deeply held convictions, which are the most widely popularized and up-to-date talking points of the dominant pseudo-rational ideology. Though describing this type of culture is a thankless task, we must not, because of idealism, ignore the fact that it has methodically lodged itself in the heads of thousands of professionals who have graduated from our public and private universities, and who often are the same persons who plan and administer our material life and the powerful symbolic system known as propaganda or advertising. Its most visible objective is to enjoy consumption of the sophisticated type, to use an adjective that these privileged consumers would never use. It is not necessary to repeat that the people only enter into this universe as picturesque or malicious objects to be consumed, to be enjoyed in passing as a cheap pleasure in which the Brazilian upper bourgeoisie cannot help but indulge. For example, the ideology, which lies somewhere between epicureanism and morbidity, of the high-priced "better" pornographic magazines that often are the only aesthetic component of Brazilian executives' leisure hours has not yet been studied in detail. In these magazines, money, status, luxury, and the human body are intertwined to such a degree that it is difficult not to make the intellectual leap to high-class prostitution. The fundamental pattern of domination again rears its head, this time with greater exhibitionism and self-confidence.

But does popular culture receive something from erudite or institutional culture? Historically, we cannot forget that Brazil's poorer classes (Amerindians, *caboclos*, enslaved and later freed blacks, mestizos living on the urban periphery, and the lumpen proletariat in general) were colonized by Portuguese rustic, and eventually urban, culture as well as by the Jesuits' ritualized Catholicism. And now, having been thoroughly miscegenated and living within a capitalistic class society, they are being recolonized by the state, by primary schools, by the army, by the culture industry, and by all those acculturating agents that spread out from the center toward the periphery. This expansive culture is the dominant one. It is literary culture distributed and diluted by official and private actors, by schools, and by factories. To what degree will these cultural agents' images, ideas, and values penetrate into and condition the people's system of values? Will they have the same influence, for example, as Catholicism, with its rites and precepts, enjoyed during colonial times?

There are well-known examples of forms of medieval aristocratic culture that passed into the popular culture of the *sertão*: the peers of France were projected onto northeastern Brazilian tales of horsemanship and served as a paradigm for the believers who participated in the Condestado rebellion. In the largest urban centers, Carnaval, which is European in origin, provides a space and time for black and mulatto music to be performed. *Nagô*-origin *candomblé*, which is fundamentally syncretic, fuses Christian saints with African supernatural entities. The North American Negro spirituals provide an illustrative example: blacks drew on the holy book of their oppressors in order to express their hope that their race and people might be freed. Herskovits, a great anthropologist, insisted on the phenomenon of reinterpretation, through which the dominant culture is absorbed and decoded by the dominated culture, so that nothing remains of the superior culture except, perhaps, the desire of the dominated to learn the skills and powers of their oppressors. The ways in which the illiterate refashion cultured content are permanently open topics of analysis for researchers of popular culture. See, for example, the evolution of the *modinha* in Brazil, which moved from bourgeois balls to serenades performed in poor neighborhoods. See also the complex and surprising phenomenon that is *literatura de cordel*: the singer, who is literate and has been inserted into the realm of education and mass culture, addresses a public that is often illiterate or semiliterate in order to explore rural themes and values that no longer exist in a pure state but rather exist in permanent contact with urban life. In a certain way, he also reinterprets in magical or religious terms events that have occurred outside of a strictly *sertanejo* context. These events run the gamut from man walking on the moon to the singer Roberto Carlos's descent into Hell. For those interested, I would recommend Mário de Andrade's quite beautiful studies on Brazilian dramatic dances and cultural mixture in Aleijadinho's art. Roger Bastide's work (see the bibliographical references at the end of this chapter) provides another source of information and interpretation.

From Union to Creation

In analytical terms, this chapter identifies three quite distinct cultural contexts and then observes how they come together: erudite culture (concentrated in the universities), the culture industry, and popular culture. There is a fourth possibility, which because of its genesis is much less uniform: individualized creative culture. Relative to the other three, this final option experiences more intensely and more dramatically the relationship between individual and society, with its effects of uprooting and disenchantment, which are proper to the systems of class and consumption that define relations in our country.

The fate of Brazilian cultures appears to be predetermined, given the class system presided over by a state that alternates between economic liberalism and political authoritarianism. A technocratic university culture and the cultural industry are supported and reproduce themselves. The various forms of popular culture are ignored when they are not actively exploited. Manifestations of individual creativity are, to a certain extent, absorbed. Forms that are openly critical are repressed, regardless of their context.

Institutionalized censorship is the visible sign that most greatly preoccupies intellectuals. We should add to this negation, which is full of violence and arbitrariness, an organizing and imposing affirmation that represents the support given by the state for the purpose of producing, purely and simply, and with greater or lesser efficacy, the sort of professional required by the market. This short-term pragmatism, which is quick to sacrifice the human and social sciences, as well as more purely academic projects, is useful to the imperialist system when coupled with an autocratic state. Nothing is more disruptive to this alliance than a flourishing and self-sufficient national technical culture or an organized critical culture. Both challenge the ascent of imported technology and of political rhetoric destined for internal use.

If we view the problem through this lens, we must call into question the belief that Brazilian culture can democratize itself as a function of the

Photo by Maureen Bisilliat.
"Living things hurt,
 they have teeth, edges, are heavy.
 Living things are heavy
 like a dog, a man,
 like that river."
João Cabral de Melo Neto,
"O cão sem plumas" (The Featherless Dog)

Photo by Maureen Bisilliat. Masterpieces like *Macunaíma* by Mário de Andrade, *Vidas secas* (Barren Lives) by Graciliano Ramos, *Grande sertão: veredas* by Guimarães Rosa, and *Morte e vida severina* (The Death and Life of Severino) by João Cabral de Melo Neto could never have been produced without their authors' prolonged and difficult effort to break through the ideological and psychological barriers that separated them from the people's daily life and imagination.

simple expansion of educational institutions. The most we could claim is that such an expansion would more widely distribute a certain form of institution that, barring innovation in even the most elementary areas, simply transmits the world of citations referred to earlier to a large number of children and adolescents. In a thoroughly democratic society, primary school (which joins the old *primário* and *ginásio* levels) and secondary school should provide a continually renewed means of accessing nature, an in-depth introduction to man and society, and a continual opportunity to develop one's own language as subjective expression and intersubjective communication. In short, it should awaken in the student an awareness of the most humane and beautiful visual, musical, and poetic works produced in Brazil and abroad. This ideal, which is the living consciousness of humanity's achievements, cannot be pawned or traded for lifeless programs or scraps of scientific or historical information. The ideal should guide the unified schooling that the democratic state has the written obligation to provide to all children and adolescents in Brazil. The neocapitalist state, though it will only become democratic with great difficulty, has at least the obligation to be liberal.

All of these obligations, in entering the problematic territory of what "should be," end up constituting a political discourse, a discourse of ends and a discourse of values. It cannot be otherwise. A theory of Brazilian culture must either be a mirror of the system, a duplication of its inequalities and its basic irrationality, or be a discourse that exists in a relationship of tension with this same system, after having moved through its structure with an eye toward transforming it.

At the heart of this *should be*, this politics of proposals, we find the cultural process with its interconnected currents of erudite culture, individualized creative culture, the culture industry, cultural commerce in symbolic goods, and the cultures of popular expression. If the Brazilian educational project were truly democratic, if it sincerely wished to delve into the richness of civil society, it would give priority to that which in erudite culture (generated both within and outside of the universities) represented an attentive study of the life and expression of the people, and to that which constituted a reflection on the possibilities (or acts of imposture) provided by the culture industry and by cultural commerce. I would like to emphasize both actions: the first, a deep receptivity and understanding of popular manifestations and aspirations; the second, control and critique—or in positive terms, guidance—of the messages transmitted by the media to the mass of the population.

The principal aim of the educational project, as Paulo Freire admirably reveals in his theory and practice, should not be to provide the illiterate man with letters themselves (with dead or lethal letters), but rather with awareness of self, of the Other, and of nature. This consciousness is the true test of the human sciences, of the natural sciences, of the arts, and of letters. Without this, the man of letters falls prey to the world of citations and manipulation.

At the basic level, culture should represent a continuation and reflection of daily life. It is in man's experience with the land, with tools, with machines, with his fellow laborers, and with his family that he gains knowledge of the real and of the drama of life within society. The scholarly disciplines render this awareness formal, at times prematurely.

Erudition and the most modern technology cannot by themselves remove man from barbarism and oppression. They merely grant him one more "means of life," that is, a means of defense and attack within a competitive society.

Thus far, and with the exception of occasional achievements in the other direction, Brazil's modernizing state has worked in lock step with the growth of capitalism. At times it has taken a step forward, as when it acted to create a university system, and at times it has taken a step back, as when it fails to provide industries and the labor market with the ideal number of technicians and professionals demanded by the division of labor. When the latter occurs, the techno-bureaucratic state removes itself and cedes the role of educating and producing professionals to private entities, and moves in the blink of an eye from democratic planning to liberal capitalism.

A philosophy of Brazilian education should not be developed in the abstract, disconnected from the practice of Brazilian culture and from a critique of contemporary culture. It is, then, important that we describe and interpret those differentiated subcontexts (erudite, mass, popular, and individualized creative culture) and observe how they mutually penetrate one another within concrete historical forms that are determined by economic context, class relations, internal group dynamism, and yes, by the individual sensibility of those who create and receive culture. It is only at this stage in our analysis and historical interpretation that we can respond to the basic question: education, yes, but to what cultural end? I assume that the analysis provided thus far allows us to respond to another question posed earlier: within what culture are we educating and being educated?

Given the democratic and socialist project within which this analysis takes place, the answers to these questions must necessarily be pluralistic and as broad as possible. We must educate in order to work alongside the people, to rethink cultural tradition, to create new values of solidarity, and now more than ever, to put into practice the ideas of the greatest teacher of education in Brazil, Paulo Freire: we must educate for freedom.

"Individualized" Cultural Creation

Relatively speaking, it is easier to trace the present-day lines of force (or of projection) that guide institutionalized cultural contexts, such as the university, the church, and mass media, than it is to map the present and even the future of the creative culture of writers and artists.

Literature, music, painting, and theater both exist and do not exist within social institutions, to the extent that they exist within distinct and often conflicting temporalities, such as the bodily time of sensibility and imagination and the social time of the division of labor.

The creation of a poem, of a novel, of a painting, or of a drama is frequently the result of very strong tensions that are internal to the individual creator. Among these tensions we find, as an exemplary model, a (successfully or unsuccessfully resolved) balancing between creative forces anxious to find expression and a historically grounded formal tradition that conditions modes of communication. Personal expression and public communication are needs that come to regulate the creator's language and place his work at the intersection of the body and of social convention.

Within this struggle, the work gains in richness, density, and permanence as its creator participates in the dialectic experienced by his culture, which like cultural creation is torn between high, internationalizing, and popular instances. Masterpieces like *Macunaíma* by Mário de Andrade, *Vidas secas* (Barren Lives) by Graciliano Ramos, *Grande sertão: veredas* by Guimarães Rosa, and *Morte e vida severina* by João Cabral de Melo Neto could never have been produced without their authors' prolonged and difficult effort to break through the ideological and psychological barriers that separated them from the people's daily lives and imaginations.

The contradictions of our social formations are accentuated in José Lins do Rego's memorialistic, regionalist novels and in Érico Veríssimo's *gaúcho* epic. The middle class and the poverty of the urban periphery find their voice in the early Dyonélio Machado and in Dalton Trevisan's and João Antônio's short stories. Bourgeois violence, strategically combined with their opposite and symmetrical corollary, the rich *bas-fond*, is expressed in Rubem Fonseca's narratives. Contrary to what some have mistakenly supposed, regionalism is not so dead as to have precluded its rebirth in Bernardo Élis's novels and short stories, which tell an epic of Goiás, or its adaptation to the odd scenarios of J. J. Veiga's sober writing. Bridges have been built, or are being built, in the music of Adoniran Barbosa, Chico Buarque, Gilberto Gil, Caetano Veloso, Milton Nascimento, Geraldo Vandré, Clementina de Jesus, Edu Lobo, and Sérgio Ricardo, among so many others. Despite differences in aesthetic orientation, the theater of Guarnieri, Boal, Oduvaldo Vianna Filho, Plínio Marco, and Ariano Suassuna has made mediation possible between an educated public and popular themes, if not popular language. Within the performing arts (which are distinct from literature, which is consumed individually) it is even more difficult to speak of the separation of mass culture from popular culture. Physical presence, voice, gesture, and the search for interpolative, provocative, and encompassing communication give rise to a new form of art that aspires, deep down, toward the overcoming of long-lasting barriers erected by social divisions.

Within this universe and speaking generally, in terms of creative work, it is essential to adopt an attitude of respect and of hope. It does not fall to the state, nor the university, nor the church, nor the press, nor to any institution to assume responsibility for literature and the arts. The natural environment of these forms is one characterized by freedom to investigate and to encounter themes and perspectives. Art has its own ways of fulfilling the highest purposes of human socialization, among which are self-consciousness, communion with the Other, communion with nature, and the search for transcendence in the heart of immanence.

Supporting Bibliographical References

The following is neither a thematic bibliography, which would be quite extensive, nor even a list of works consulted. What follows is merely a list of those supporting works that I drew on directly in writing this essay and were indispensable references.

Amaral, Amadeu. *Tradições populares*. 2nd ed. São Paulo: Hucitec, 1976. The first edition was published in 1948 and collects published and unpublished articles from the 1920s.

Andrade, Mário de. "O Aleijadinho." In *Aspectos das artes no Brasil*. São Paulo: Martins, 1928.

———. *Danças dramáticas do Brasil*. 3 vols. São Paulo: Martins, 1959. Posthumous volume edited by Oneyda Alvarenga, written between 1928 and 1934.

Bastide, Roger. *Estudos afro-brasileiros*. São Paulo: Perspectiva, 1975. A collection of essays written between 1944 and 1953.

Bosi, Éclea. *Cultura de massa e cultura popular*. Leituras de operárias. Petrópolis: Vozes, 1972.

———. "Problemas ligados à cultura das classes pobres." In *A cultura do povo*. Edited by Edênio Valle et al. São Paulo: Cortez e Moraes, 1979.

Couto de Magalhães, General J. V. *O selvagem*. Belo Horizonte: Itaiaia, 1975. The first edition is from 1875.

Cunha, Euclides da. *Os sertões*. São Paulo: Cultrix, 1972. The first edition is from 1902.

Eco, Umberto. *Apocalittici e integrati*. Milan: Bompiani, 1965.

Freire, Paulo. *Educação como prática da liberdade*. Rio de Janeiro: Paz e Terra, 1967.
Gramsci, Antonio. *Obras escolhidas*. Lisbon: Estampa, 1974.
McLuhan, M. *Os meios de comunicação como extensões do homem*. São Paulo: Cultrix, 1969.
Ramos, Arthur. *Introdução à antropologia brasileira*. 3rd ed. Rio de Janeiro: Casa do Estudante do Brasil, 1962. The first edition is from 1943.
Romero, Sílvio. *Folclore brasileiro*. 3 vols. Rio de Janeiro: J. Olympio, 1954.
Weil, Simone. *A condição operária e outros estudos sobre a opressão*. Rio de Janeiro: Paz e Terra, 1979.
Xidieh, Oswaldo Elias. *Narrativas pias populares*. São Paulo: USP, Instituto de Estudos Brasileiros, 1967.

This text was originally written in 1979 and 1980. I [Bosi] have made some changes in language, but the ideas presented remain the same. The original version of the essay was published in *Filosofia da Educação Brasileira*, a volume edited by the fondly remembered educator Durmeval Trigueiro Mendes (Rio de Janeiro: Civilização Brasileira, 1981).

Postscript to "Brazilian Culture and Brazilian Cultures" (1992)

The hour is very late, and the choice between good and evil knocks at our door.
—Norbert Wiener

The essay "Brazilian Culture and Brazilian Cultures" was written in 1979 and 1980. With twelve years having passed since its composition, I prefer to leave it basically untouched, rather than make changes that would be like patches on old clothes. In this way, at the very least, the character of the historical moment in which the essay was written will remain intact.

But the situation described in those pages has changed in part, and it behooves us to rethink the ways in which these changes have been significant.

While firmly maintaining the basic orientation of the text, which centered on the plural quality of culture, I believe that today we can go a bit further in terms of the differential analysis of the cultural contexts that were examined in the original essay.

If one looks principally at literary culture, both within and outside of the universities, as well as at broader sectors of the mass media, one perceives a certain appearance of disintegration, which today's labels attribute to a postmodernity that has marked capitalist societies since the mid-1970s.

Disintegration is the word that is used, but in what sense is it utilized? To begin, let us play a memory game. Recall the systematic approaches and the strong and interconnected concepts that guided the analysis of symbolic processes until the 1960s. Sociology, functionalism, Marxism, structuralism, and semiology competed for the attention of intellectuals, both within and outside of the university. Social scientists drew on models that oriented their particular observations toward unity, continuity, the centering of perspectives—in sum, toward a coherent theory of meaning.

What happened to these schemes that aim toward unity and the closing off of meaning?

They came, or are coming, under suspicion of excessive abstraction or even of authoritarianism. An illustrative example: Roland Barthes, perhaps nostalgic for anarcho-surrealism or having soured on his long love affair with the structural method, said in a lecture that language, as a system, is "fascist." And in the wake of this provocative condemnation (which had the flavor of May 1968), institutions that other philosophies had already critiqued—such as science, the university, schools in general, as well as businesses, the church, and the state—would be tarred with the same brush. But ultimately, what Barthes and shortly thereafter his followers throughout the world were confronting was the idea of system, with all of its implications of unity, completeness, and connection.

These days, the cultural observer's gaze is drawn toward the multiple, the ambivalent, the sparse, the aleatory, the centrifugal. Is this a matter of a new sensibility, a new ethos?

Let us, then, continue our description. At the end of the millennium, anthropology within and beyond Brazil is drawn to minorities, to difference, and to the atypical, and its greatest pleasure would be to challenge the ancient Aristotelian certainty that a science of the individual does not exist, for *individuum est ineffabile*. In this context, Foucault's alluring ideas are effective and ubiquitous both in academic circles and in their journalistic by-products. Academic sociology (*où sont les neiges d'antan?*), grounded in classes and functions, models and types that once tied everything together, now lacks an area of analysis specific to itself. What remained of its patrimony is now being filtered, ad hoc, through social history, which was sociology's poor cousin until the 1960s but which today is growing and widening its reach, though at the cost of a certain *émiettement* of documental and oral research, as was advised by a bewildered editorial published in the *Annales* journal.

The goal of a history of sensibilities prompted a decided shift toward the study of phenomena in which the institutional sphere finds itself marked by subjective impulses. This unstable ground was explored until very recently by social psychology. The history of dreams, fantasies, compulsions, sexual perversions, fetishisms, witchcraft and its repression, from the dawn of modern times until the present, is being written. In doing so, it challenges, to the extent that it can, the barrier that once divided and now brings together the historical chronicle and prose fiction.

The leveling of the walls that once separated the various humane sciences spurred an ambition to forge a new type of writing that would be comprised, in apparently paradoxical fashion, of quick microanalyses and a luxuriant conceptual fluidity. This recalls, *mutatis mutandis* (because there are no repetitions in the strict sense of the term), the sounding of a series of notes, each one emitted at random, which was typical of nineteenth-century literary impressionism.

But so much has changed at the instrumental level, that is, in terms of the *means* that knowledge has at its disposal. The most salient aspect of cultural reproduction today is the expansion of information technology, which now defines not only communications but also a limitless number of industries and services. In the First World, there is now discussion of a postindustrial era as a descriptive term for a new period in which systems are defined by computing and automation. Cybernetics, computer science, and robotics appear in varying degrees in any context that claims to be postmodern.

The apparently positive effects of these new technologies for learning and for academic research are widely commented upon. Reports are searched for, obtained, assessed, arranged, indexed, combined, multiplied, and retransmitted—in a word, processed—with extraordinary speed, which facilitates the capture and organization of data in all areas of knowledge.

Is the era of mechanical reproduction, announced in Walter Benjamin's celebrated essay, reaching its peak? All indications are that electronic means will continue to develop toward the most extreme forms of artificial intelligence such that the active and cortical functions of inventing and organizing knowledge will eventually be attributed to "machines" (though I hesitate to use this antiquated word). As far as I can see of the present moment, computers, which the French call *ordinateurs*, are effective reactive agents, receiving and executing programs that human intelligence gives them. However, science fiction has already reached further than this.

If it is true that, as per "postmodern reason," a large quantity of information obtained within a brief period of time will eventually transmute itself into a superior intellectual process, then there truly is hope that the expert users of ultramodern technology will produce works of learning and art that are ever more beautiful, profound, and complex, not only in their preparation and material presentation but in their cognitive and expressive value as well.

> Sarà vera gloria?
> I posteri diranno.
> —Alessandro Manzoni

> And this was glory? After-men
> Judge the dark problem.
> —Translated by W. E. Gladstone

For the time being, and for well-regarded educational and research institutions as well as for the more sophisticated agents of the culture industry, the advancements made by computer science consist of greater speed in storing and transmitting signs. Hence order, precision, detail, and speed are identified as signs of modernization, which coincide with our so-called postmodern age. These effects produce the impression that the cultural level of the country is rising, at least in those cultural contexts that are internationalized.

It would be more accurate to state that the pace (that is, *timing*) of culture has been accelerating since the 1970s and has come into sync with North American, Western European, and Japanese time. As for the substantive problem of quality, which itself remits to the crucial question of values, we know that things are a bit more complex.

What spurs the search for knowledge is the will toward value. I understand this expression as entailing the desires that lead individuals and groups to seek out and communicate knowledge. Only that which has worth is worth the effort. Information itself and for itself alone cannot produce a new theory of the real that is worth studying. It is only the sense of value that guides the effort to understand men and things, selects themes, drinks from the fount of primary sources, awakens dormant memories, stokes the embers buried under the ashes of lived experience, sharpens one's perception of formal connections, and almost compels the mind toward certain conclusions. And, so that the resulting science does not regress to being a simple mask for the interests that motivate it, an additional metavalue is necessary. This is the will to truth, which maintains the subject's honesty before its object.

Within this sort of reflection, the question of the quality of recent literary culture does not so much concern the visible efficacy of the electronic media in use as it does the identification of the values and guiding ideas desired by the consumers of these new technologies. What, on the axiological level, is the equivalent of the mosaic of bit upon bit of information that has been so rapidly compiled and reproduced? My response is merely tentative: The empirical dispersion of signs and themes corresponds to the will toward, and discourse of, decentering.

So-called high culture and its channels of diffusion are presently experiencing an unprecedented dispersal of icons, indices, and symbols, which gives the impression of a cyclone or whirlwind, previously projected by the futurist avant-garde during the second Industrial Revolution—hence the first equation that I will propose:

*post*modern = *plus*-modern

At times, and without being fully aware of it, we fall back on singularly monotonous ideas in attempting to interpret this battery of imagistic and aural stimuli.

The dispersing effect is a result of the plethora of objects of pleasure and interest that the market offers to the educated man and to the consumer of symbolic goods who is hungry for novelty. The mass of bits of information available on an elevated number of topics leads to a mushrooming in the number of subareas of specialization. Looking through an academic journal, or the catalog of a large American or French publishing house, or the academic and events calendars of a modern university causes vertigo and cognitive depression.

The production of information presents itself as a remedy for the sensation of chaos that the flurry of messages provokes in even the most gluttonous of readers. At the same time, the use of the computer functions as an invitation to expand, *ad infinitum* and *ad libitum*, programs, data, memories, and files. Babel requires alertness and an ability to constantly reorder, which in turn leads the inhabitants of this Babel to add ever larger new levels to their electro-computerized tower. The sky is the limit. The multiple and the unified try to pull ahead of one another in a race that has no apparent finish line.

The consumer's space and time become saturated with increasing amounts of informational pollution. The process's pathological quality is the result of an inability to give intelligible form to the excesses of content that have proliferated like stray cells within the weave of contemporary mental life. The receiver, whose internal defenses are not always sufficiently strong, can literally become intoxicated with signs that are images, words, opinions, judgments, or stimuli.

This is the congested marketplace of a civilization that produces in order to produce or, more exactly, produces so as to preserve its means of advertising and selling images and symbols. The technical or liberal professional who finds himself immersed in this mutable context, in which the distance between information and intellectual disciplines becomes ever larger, barricades himself within his area of specialization, which often comes at the price of a cultural and political impoverishment that can border on idiocy.

A production engineer, who incidentally was celebrated by his peers, once told me with the forthright audacity that is proper to idiots that psychoanalysis was the nineteenth century's last superstition. This opinion was substantiated by a specialist in the sexual behavior of caged rats, who observed that Freud wrote stories for nervous babysitters. In another corner of the room (this was an academic party), a wise professor of semiotics made use of her sememes to inveigh against the exact sciences, which in her opinion were nothing more than skillful binary constructs. More than one journalist who had recently completed graduate school decreed the death of Hegel and Marx, attributing the *causa mortis* of both to automation. They made use of citations from a Japanese author reputed to be clever and who had declared the end of history, the death of ideologies, and the beginning of a post-utopian age.[1]

These examples have the air of caricature, but it is through extreme examples that the style of an age apparently lacking in style most clearly reveals itself.

The discourse regarding this fragmentary knowledge and the fractures that cut through the terrain of high culture prompted me to begin thinking about a situation of spiritual decentering that can also be described as a refusal of totality. This attitude tends, through repeated unconscious repetition, toward ideological monotony.

This is a new, strange form of mental simplification that has nothing to do with the forms of semantic cohesion that preceded it and therefore is deserving of close analysis.

Up until the 1960s, the theoretical unity of the humane sciences was grounded in the belief that social and symbolic phenomena were organized around structures. Marxism provided us with a systemic explanation that, beginning with the relations of production, delineated a process of class conflict. This was a totalizing vision of the world, which was tangible and which fused evolutionistic anthropology with the critique of classical political economy and cleared the path for a transformative praxis guided by historical materialism. For its part, structuralism, which came to prominence in the 1970s, placed diachronic accidents in parentheses, did not hide its disdain for subjective inclinations, and not only preserved but ossified the image of a system composed of elements in the mode of the phonemes and morphemes of structural linguistics. An element's worth was determined by its position within the syntax of the object, whether this object was an Australian totem or a sibylline poem by Mallarmé.

In both cases, what appears is the idea of a unified, internally articulated whole that is only accessible through scientific rigor. This denies the possibility of aleatory or impressionistic readings.

Today, on the contrary, it is the desire for discontinuity and decenteredness, along with its corollary figures, that lends an air of familial resemblance to cultural expressions. Attraction to the unformed and atypical, to the stray and occasional, to the changeable and volatile, gives rise to a scattered taste that presents itself as no longer modern, and therefore, for lack of a better term or lack of conceptual imagination, as postmodern.

The arbitrary, self-satisfied caprice, the pun crafted from phonetic coincidence, bad taste, the mixing of registers as an end in itself, and the abandonment of all epistemic ties occupy the place held previously by all-encompassing doctrines and positive or dialectical certainties. There are academic theses published today that are collections of allusions and citations. The best suffer from a sort of tourist's erudition and lack logical connections, while the worst are comparable to the "Samba do Crioulo Doido" (The Crazy Black Man's Samba) in their illogical connections and profusion of confused references.[2] A number of contemporary novels celebrate themselves as pastiches and stylistic collages. Articles published in important publications and news presented on television present as objective truth the mathematical sum of two opinions that, in reality, merely mention distinct aspects of a particular situation. The principle that one must have access to distinct points of view becomes degraded when the same weight is given to the accounts of the criminal and the victim, or to the words of the guilty and aggrieved parties. The naked self-interest of the participants is accepted as valid testimony to be delivered, without any mediation, to an unarmed mass of readers and viewers. The ability to judge truth is cheapened when it is confused with the cherry-picking of details, the importance of which is exaggerated and which are removed from their context of signification. The rush to inform at any cost leads journalists to prematurely abandon the search, which demands both effort and patience, for an explanatory criterion worthy of the assembly of facts and words being presented. In order to not "lose time," time for reflection, which would connect the part to the whole and which is so important to the scientific spirit, is abandoned. Who will judge the truth of the simulacrum?

There seems to be a certain recurring ethos in contemporary culture that informs cognitive, aesthetic, ethical, and political habits. As for political habits, which are a thankless object of analysis, I offer this affirmation: whoever followed on TV the electoral machinations of the 1989 presidential campaign, which were immediately followed by marketing for the candidates' economic plans and counterplans, has already clearly seen what in the context of the political circus "Brazilian postmodernity" is becoming. If these viewers are inclined toward skepticism, they will conclude that *plus ça change plus c'est la même chose*, a phrase that challenges the consistency of all labels.

"Em política, o que parece é" (In politics, what appears to be, is), said the now-deceased Portuguese dictator Antônio de Oliveira Salazar, whom no one would accuse of being postmodern *avant la lettre*. The natural tendency would be to judge these words, made by a man so famously conservative, as those of a Machiavellian, a Jesuit, a man of the Baroque. But disturbingly, a certain commonality can be found between his view and the contemporary scene. The great theater of the world represented by the courts of Vienna, Madrid, and Versailles is nothing more than a crude trompe l'oeil when compared to the ultramodern triumph of the simulacrum. Today, what appears to be is, or at minimum, must be. The recent Gulf War was projected into homes the world over as a fantastical spectacle similar to a video game. The glare of the missiles exploding in the Baghdad sky prevented billions of viewers from seeing the physical horror of bloodletting, which is the naked truth of war. The planet became a screen the size of which was previously unheard of (note the use of the term *setting* by both politicians and economists), onto which the ancient art of appearances was projected by the fearsome tools of mass communication.

If this is the case, then why insist that the term *postmodern* be applied to the contemporary industry of appearance? In the end, isn't this nothing more than the warping of certain tendencies that are proper to capitalism and the modern state, as described and deplored by the philosophers associated with critical theory? Haven't Benjamin, Bloch, Horkheimer, and Adorno, with a mixture of acuity and melancholy, already placed into relief alienation, disposability, cynical individualism, political apathy, the prevalence of the immediate, consumerism, cold brutality in the treatment of erotic relations, and a resounding indifference to the question of truth—themes given luminous treatment in *Minima Moralia* and the *Dialectic of Enlightenment*? In recent years, with greater technical resources available, these behaviors have multiplied on a scale unimaginable in the 1930s and 1940s.

For this reason, they termed these behaviors *apocalyptic*. After them came those thinkers who were integrated into the system, with Marshall McLuhan leading the way. Over time the polemic cooled, as neoliberalism placed the First World during the 1970s and 1980s into a state of anesthesia.

However, the equilibrium of this *plus*-modern appears precarious. As part of a broad and profound movement of self-defense, those intellectuals who have not yet given up on the possibility of understanding the whole are acting dialectically and are not concerned with appearing out of step with the majority, whose means are disconnected from their ends. And here we can formulate a second, negative equation:

*post*modern = *anti*modern

The global green movement, which came into being precisely during the 1970s, is becoming radicalized in the face of the effects of blind and dirty industrialism. Three Mile Island and Chernobyl were highly visible catastrophes, but they were no worse than the proliferation of atomic waste, acid rain, the greenhouse effect, the poisoning of the water, the threat of pesticides, and the inferno of the megalopolis.

A "modernity" that preys on the environment is provoking protests the world over, though the possibility that it might be replaced by clean industry is remote. The world's nonrenewable resources are continually diminished, and in this respect, awareness of the problem on the part of poor populations lends a dramatic tone to a debate that the Global North can no longer ignore. Here we find one of the dialectic of colonization's far-reaching consequences.

There is something both disturbing and promising to be found in the fires of the ecological conflicts—specifically, the desire to establish an honest understanding between society and nature. The purely predatory tradition of evolutionistic reason, which preaches *Homo faber*'s dominion over all living beings, has been cast into doubt. Environmentalists see farther than those interested in productivity, and they are asking capital and the technocracy to stop and think. They move in the direction of what Simone Weil asked of twentieth-century culture: that a new pact be established between man and the universe that surrounds and constitutes him. The austere anticonsumerist stance taken by critics of the obscene waste that continues to be produced by the upper classes and which threatens everyone's well-being is entirely understandable. The agents of superproductivity have not yet absorbed the polemic provoked by the Club of Rome's report.[3]

A new science for which *ethics* is a key word, along with a new technology and new public policies, are coming into being, stimulated by a consciousness that in some cases is "too little too late."

In this way, that which the *plus*-modern, in its indifference to the totality, destroys, the *anti*modernist attempts to recover. That which the advance of instrumental ratio continues to divide (separating body from soul, economics from ethics, means from ends), a new way of thinking centered on an awareness of the living world attempts to reunite, within the flux of experience.

Given that, as Habermas argues, the project of modernity remains incomplete and therefore open and receptive to differences, it will be a pleasant task to look back upon the Renaissance and Enlightenment to recover a "modern" tradition of balance between man and nature, individual and society. One thinks of Leonardo, Montaigne, Vico, Montesquieu, Rousseau, Goethe, Schiller, and Humboldt, among others.

A civilization that in the midst of fratricidal conflicts and during capitalism's violent birth managed to uphold the ideal of the Rights of Man and Citizen, and which through artistic invention brought into harmony a passion for freedom and the inherent rules of form in Beethoven's symphonies and Blake's poetry, and which thought through human destiny with the depth and beauty of *Faust*, of *War and Peace*, and of *The Brothers Karamazov*—this is a past that is not only found behind us but within us as well. The man of today can remember this whenever his identity and dignity are placed under threat. In this way, contemporary culture is free to choose its matrices and its guiding stars. The choice imposes itself. This is the "choice to choose," so to speak, which Søren Kierkegaard in *Aut Aut* defines as the first step of ethical existence, outside of which the subject's time flows away into the gutter of labile curiosity and inconstancy.

One must choose. *Vivre n'est plus qu'un stratagème*, said Louis Aragon in one of his poems from *Le crève-coeur*. What should interest us in terms of the tradition of modernity is that which points us toward an intelligent approximation between things and signs, which makes the planet habitable, and which makes relations between men happy (or at least dignified).

A postmodernity that accepts the delirium of consumption and disposability, of immediacy and competition, lacks the mental and moral strength to confront scarcity of resources, disparities in income, and inequalities in power and status. When one refuses to acknowledge the natural and human whole, which constitutes us and invites us to exist in the world, one may gain an air of epistemological modesty (were that this were the case). However, in the long term, those who adhere to this as a program of thought and action will gradually lose all standards of value and will find themselves the accomplices of the forces of disintegration and death. The common people say that a fish out of water rots beginning with its head.

After freeing ourselves from the reductionism of vulgar Marxism and linear evolutionism, a salutary course of action would probably be to carry forward certain patient phenomenological analyses. This possibility does not imply that the intellect should submerge itself in the Lethe of forgetfulness of the past, for we have again discovered that Mnemosyne is the mother of the muses and that the future must be disentangled from the interpretations of the world that we inherit from those who thought and acted before us. I have the sense that many people would like to adhere to the letter of Nietzsche's radical call for us to free ourselves from the nightmare of history. They do not lack reasons for wanting to do so. However, here again we are forced to choose. What past should we throw overboard as dead weight? And what past should we preserve as ballast so that our ship can survive the storms?

There is a type of postmodernism that carries the modernism of the recent and more distant past forward to a hyperbolic degree. But there is also a postmodernism that rejects the traumatic efforts of an instrumental reason that an angry German philosopher called (on the bicentenary of Kant's *Critique*) cynical reason.

The two equations that we have proposed form a system that it both contradictory and simultaneous:

Postmodern = *plus*-modern
Postmodern = antimodern

Postmodern = *Plus*-Modern

Even a nonspecialist in the physical and mathematical sciences knows that the evolution of computing and robotics was only made possible by research and discoveries in statistics and electronics, which began during the second half of the nineteenth century. Large states like the British Empire, czarist Russia, and the United States needed a technology capable of dealing with large numbers for censuses and later for military purposes. The first computers were developed during the Second World War. During these same years, Norbert Wiener was preparing his masterpiece, *Cybernetics*. However, discoveries in information theory and the large-scale use of hardware and software did not occur until the 1970s. It is for this reason that an industry that is, in fact, *ultra*modern has been described as *post*modern.

In the version of Wiener's *The Human Use of Human Beings* (1950) that was destined for the general public, we read: "It is the thesis of this book that society can only be understood through a study of the messages and the communication facilities which belong to it; and that in the future development of these messages and communication facilities, messages between man and machines, between machines and man, and between machine and machine, are destined to play an ever-increasing part." The accuracy of this prediction is proved at every moment of our daily life in 1992.

Cutting-edge technologies are the result of vast efforts by scientists and technicians who, over the past four centuries (beginning at least with Galileo), have not stopped exploring the properties and applications of matter and energy, terms that we still use today, through force of habit, despite all of the theoretical impasses thrown up by contemporary science.

What has appeared over the last few decades that is new, in terms of cultural emphasis? The answer can be found in processes of communication and language, the primacy of which has impacted social scientists, artists, and writers, who for the most part lived until the middle part of this century with their backs turned against technological innovation. Achievements in computing and cybernetics have built a bridge, with traffic running in both directions, between the physical and mathematical sciences, and in particular, between electronics and studies centered on signs in linguistics and semiotics. Those art forms that are oriented toward the general public—that is, music, cinema, and naturally television (the communications vehicle par excellence of today's world)—interact with information technology, which provides them, formally, with a way to appear ultramodern. I have intentionally used the adverb *formally*. The extreme rationalization presently employed by electronic means of communication recalls the first calculating machines used in the West, which were developed under the sign of Cartesian mathematics.

Pascal and Leibniz created them, and both men did so in the context of a classical rationalism that feared passion and imagination as the madwomen in the attic. The rationalizing of computers and synthesizing technologies is the child of a science that is numerical, ordinal, calculating—in sum, formalizing. The paradox, which ultimately represents the truth of the contemporary world, lies in the fact that these ultramodern means of mass communication transmit the most irrational messages, in which all of the passions (and especially the most unruly and offensive passions) and all of the deliria of the imagination are manifested with an often demonic violence. The dialectic of classical rationalism follows the dialectic of Enlightenment like a shadow: the madwoman agonizes when all the cells are of equal shape. Technological abstraction, immediacy of will. The machine's passivity encourages and allows for the most grotesque willfulness. I do what I like because the machine is efficient, it does not think, and it obeys my commands.

When reason is automated, it can only reiterate the rules that have already been established. And so the will, which dominates it, is transformed into mere inclination and, in looking toward instrumental discourse, cannot find any arguments to clarify or restrain its capricious actions. This abstract freedom believes itself omnipotent, and as Hegel feared, is capable of the most heinous crimes, and the reasons it cites for committing these acts seem the rationalizations of a criminal.

Pascal was touched by grace and changed course: after his geometric and mechanical discoveries he began looking for a humanity that, in being human, was *ni ange ni bête*, neither pure spirit nor pure matter, and he wisely warned that he who would act the angel acts the beast. The brain, as a solitary calculator, is the source of a frightening order: rational and obtuse, docile and dangerous like automata. Pascal stated further, with the simplicity proper to free spirits: "Great thoughts come from the heart."[4]

Postmodern = Antimodern

"The hour is very late, and the choice between good and evil knocks at the door." Thus Norbert Wiener concludes his pioneering book on automation.

The true scientist, like Wiener, asks us to choose. It was not by chance that, during the 1970s, a culture of resistance that I have referred to in a prior chapter on the various cultures of Brazil took hold among the intelligentsia. This resistance continues despite having confronted both ups and downs. The environment, human rights, democracy as a substantive value, disarmament, the universal minimum wage: it can be said that the struggle to protect the fundamental relations between man and nature, and between man and man, began as an internal reaction within contemporary industrial societies, as an emission of antibodies to counteract the pathology of modernization.

Is this antimodernism a case of a good negativity struggling against the bad positivity produced by those who control economic and political power? The culture of resistance sees itself as a nonreactionary reaction. It fights so that during the third millennium, *Homo sapiens* does not have to pay in disease, pollution, disintegration, and death for blind and unequal growth between peoples and within national contexts.

The twentieth-century "modernity" that would lose its way along the paths leading to the Nazi concentration camps, the destruction of Hiroshima by the atomic bomb, the dictatorships of the East, the Vietnam War, and the Gulf War was the result of a combination of will to power and the use of new technologies indifferent to the values of humanization and socialization. All that remains is for us to unmask the animal unconscious that is hidden behind a façade of rationalization.

A higher form of reason, which can only operate through a certain degree of integration and only acts for the purpose of upholding universal values, might be capable of carrying forward the ideal of truth championed by men like Leonardo, Galileo, Newton, and Einstein. For the great physicist Ampère, the word *cybernetics* referred to an art that, as per its Greek root (*kybernétes*: pilot), should "secure for all citizens the opportunity to fully enjoy the benefits of this world."[5]

The culture of resistance, because it conceives of parts as an expression of a whole, looks toward the same goal as Ampère.

Brazil 92

Is there anyone who has not heard it said, with an air of ridicule, that the Brazilian elites believe themselves to be engulfed by postmodernity without ever having experienced modernity? In this way, the bourgeoisies of the periphery continue to suffer from an incurable provincialism at the very moment at which they affect to have entered into lockstep with the centers of the First World.

But doesn't this statement perhaps betray a subtle, nonreflective prejudice in its propensity to see Brazilian thinking as substantially behind the times and to judge conjunctures in national life in terms of the distance that necessarily separates us from the advanced countries?

Isn't a petrified concept of the colony responsible for this obsession with our inability to keep pace, which at times impairs our capacity to examine the situation in detail? Metropolis and colony: must there always necessarily be two parallel temporal lines—one long and which has already traveled a great distance in the direction of development, and for that reason deserves the seal of modernity, and another shorter line, whose slow rhythm will always impede it from traveling the same distance as the first?

Before attempting to respond to these difficult but crucial questions, it might be enlightening to read what Sergio Solmi, who wrote the preface to the Italian edition of *Minima Moralia*, said of his own "national case," recalling that Italy, like Brazil, also experienced industrialization later than England and France:

> The world that Adorno describes for us is modern American society, and the term of comparison available to him is that of Nazi or pre-Nazi Germany. The context in which he lived when he was writing *Minima Moralia* was that of a German immigrant in the United States. It is necessary to understand these circumstances in order to make a thorough evaluation of his book. In more than one regard, our country presents a panorama that is very different from that seen by Adorno when he wrote his pages. On the other hand, it would be an error to underestimate all that an advanced monopolistic society like the USA has in common with a *sui generis* bourgeois society like ours. Despite all of the differences at the structural level, there exists something like a spirit of the age. And this is even truer today, now that the technical apparatus and instruments for the diffusion of mass culture constitute a cultural *koiné* that often anticipates economic development. The exportation of the American "way of life" finds particularly favorable terrain precisely where the economic conditions that produced it do not exist—and perhaps will never exist. The future of the backward countries is not at all promising. They run the risk of finding themselves assimilated without having moved one step forward, and of suffering all of the disadvantages of the present added onto those of the past. Despite all appearances, the world described in these pages is also our own. Let the following stand as a warning to impatient critics: *de re vestra agitur*.[6]

The following suggestive idea, which was previously formulated by Trotsky, should be kept in mind in order to understand the Third World: techno-economic backwardness within the capitalist race does not in itself prevent the emergence of progressive, reformist, or utopian ideological groups (rather, it tends to stimulate them), nor does it block the rise of artistic and cultural avant-gardes *in sensu lato*.

Sergio Solmi speaks of a spirit of the age, an idea dear to culturalists and Hegelians. He speaks of diffusion, a term that works to correct linear evolutionism and—and this strikes me as very insightful—gives appropriate emphasis to the anticipation of cultural currents and products of the imagination in relation to the slow rhythm of infrastructure.

Theoretically, what is at stake in the confrontation between center and periphery is the true reach of economic determinism. To the degree that we grant language and culture freedom and do not reduce them to epiphenomena of systems of production, we correct the simplistic theses that divide advanced cultures from backward cultures according to the indices of industrialization and urbanization for the countries in question.

At any rate, the risky game of "all or nothing" does a disservice to the complexity of the theme and impedes the understanding of particular situations.

The reflections presented in previous chapters of this book—on Vieira's advanced thinking as compared to that of the nobility and the Portuguese clergy, on the "new liberalism" of the Second Empire, and on the social positivism of the Old Republic—suggest that the diffusion of ideas is not impeded by a cultural system that has become progressively more globalized, beginning with the discoveries and the European expansion of the sixteenth and seventeenth centuries.

Thought is or can be universally available. But the question formulated at the beginning of this section remains the same: is there a specific difference in the way these ideas are manifested when they develop in a colonial context?

Analysis of specific situations is necessary in order that our answer not be overly hasty. In poor and dependent countries, ideas transplanted from modern centers sometimes fall into the empty hole of irrelevance or are watered down in the rhetoric of epigones and academics. But sometimes, and to the surprise of skeptics, they bear significant, lasting fruits.

What is responsible for these divergent fates? In the first case, what we have are what John Dewey perceptively defined as inert ideas, which are in reality nothing more than foam bubbles, dust from errant asteroids that shine and fall dark, erratic objects lacking their own light and without sufficient energy to rally individuals around a coherent course of action. To paraphrase Guimarães Rosa, these are *nonadas*. They might last a bit longer within provincial circles, in which possession of an exoteric or pseudo-original jargon grants an aura of prestige to members of certain educated groups, but they remain what they are—empty words, *vana verba*.

Brazilian literature has developed a biting tradition of satire against this verbal dance that is ignorant of our context. Though the targets and details vary, one can find criticism of our compulsion toward imitation in texts by Machado de Assis, Raul Pompéia, Araripe Jr., Manoel Bomfim, Lima Barreto, Mário de Andrade, and Oswald de Andrade. This criticism was given razor-sharp form in the disdain Graciliano Ramos directed toward the false and *safada* (shifty) language of the old Republic of Letters. This is a topic in need of treatment by a good historian of ideas in Brazil.

By the simple fact that it continues to exist and has remained vital for more than a century, this critical tradition (which should not be confused with vulgar nationalism and which was already present in the first movements toward democracy and abolition) reveals the capacity of ex-colonial cultures to remain vigilant in the face of the mere repetitions of ideas that have been generated in dominant centers. Those who choose between opposed doctrines (parliamentary monarchy or republican dictatorship, *belle époque* conformism or anarcho-syndicalism) are not passive recipients, gorillas condemned to imitate the actions of more evolved animals. Just as real as the "transoceanism" of Brazilian intellectuals, identified by Capistrano de Abreu, is the thinking that recognizes it as such and seeks out means to place it in dialectical relief.

Of the diverging options listed above, it is the second that interests us. In some cases ideas and currents of opinion born beyond the borders of the dependent nation may graft themselves onto contexts lacking in conceptual models. To the degree that these ideas are adapted to the movement that seeks them out and selects them, the worldwide expansion of culture takes on new, unique forms.

Ideas imported from abroad may cease to be inert, depending on the use to which they are put. With their content filtered by new recipients, they may energize—in certain cases over the long term—the institutions that were inspired by them. For instance, this occurred with the ideas of *rule* and *system*, which during the nineteenth century migrated from Napoleonic law and administrative codes to almost all European states and arrived intact in Latin America. This occurred with positivism in education in Mexico and Uruguay, and was so active at the beginning of the twentieth century that it left its mark on two or three generations. And this happened at the dawn of modernity, with the ideas of free access to the Bible that were developed in Luther's Germany and Calvin's Geneva, and which made a quick and lasting impression on the Christians of Scandinavia, Holland, Scotland, and in the American colonies, in which they established deep institutional roots. These were ideas that were not confined to the space in which they were initially developed.

Just as local altitude corrects general latitude in terms of climate, so does a correct understanding of the processes of diffusion and ideological filtering call into question the notion of linear evolution, according to which backward economies can only produce ideas that are behind the times.

All this said, we may ask, how are Brazilian intellectuals reacting to the ultra/anti-modernist dialectic, which seems to constitute postmodernity on an international level?

Brazil today is a sufficiently diverse country so that there is space both for those who refuse to pay an unfair "price of progress" and for avid consumers of habits, fashions, and signs that are imported at any cost. Among us—and, I believe, in all parts of the world—those who are apocalyptic in thinking and those who are integrated into the system coexist.

Movements that rejected the model of development that was imposed *manu militari* by the coup of 1964 and that fought, and continue to fight, for the respect of human rights and in defense of a balance between nature and civilization, tend to counteract certain illusions held by bourgeois ideology or by Marxist doctrine that correlate the growth of industry with democracy, and state control with social justice.

The culture of resistance is democratic (and borders on the notion of "civil disobedience") because it was born under the sign of dictatorship. It is ecological because it sees the damage done by a savage industry to country and city alike. It is distributive because it came into being in a country with one of the least equal distributions of wealth in the world. When molded by religious doctrines (in particular, liberation theology, which was formulated during the 1970s in Latin America), it is open to progressive movements that fight at its side and against the same enemies. When it is secular, it respects the values that call believers to fight for equality and liberty. In both cases, it is the product of a political choice and a refusal to deny that meaning can be found amidst the apparent chaos of contemporary history.

With a perspective opposed to that of *plus*-modern dissipation, the culture of resistance sees a society of thoroughly humanized men as a goal worth reaching, and this teleological imprint teaches it to approach technological means precisely for what they are: instruments, useful objects, products of practical intelligence, and not ends in themselves. It does not need to be said that, surrounded by the play of disposable messages that typifies neocapitalism's intellectual index of values, this intellectual position may at any moment be judged passé. But nature, and men's bodies and minds, have a very long history, and perhaps an equally long future, in whose defense the work of memory is indispensable. For this reason, the recovery of memories that feed one's sense of time and desire to survive is also a part of the culture of resistance.

It was the creator of the science of automation, Norbert Wiener, who best clarified the relationship between past and present: "Like a tradition of scholarship, a grove of sequoias may exist for thousands of years, and the present crop of wood represents the investment of sun and rain many centuries ago."

From Dependency Theory to Internal Reform

The question of the condition of men in Brazil in recent years leads to a series of complications. The temptation toward pessimism is difficult to exorcize. The global context of the 1980s, viewed in raw numbers, is threatening and depressing. Along with the other countries of Latin America and the majority of the nations of the Third World (now referred to as the [Global] South, in opposition to the wealth of the [Global] North), Brazil entered into an economic recession that was plainly visible. Poverty increased significantly, affecting at least two-fifths of the population. Stagnation in industry led to unemployment and underemployment. Rural poverty, especially dramatic in the northeastern interior, led to the migration of 15 million Brazilians during the past decade. There was an overall decline in quality of life, as determined by measures such as malnutrition, infant mortality, lack of basic sanitation, the very precarious state of medical care and hospitals, the poor quality of basic education in public schools, lack of housing, and the chronic problems faced by public transportation.[7]

Dependency theory, the holistic theory given to us by the social sciences during the early 1970s, entered a state of crisis and was questioned or abandoned by its creators. Dependency theory was a Latin American variation on anti-imperialist doctrine in that it closely correlated our underdevelopment with the [Global] North's development. Its anticolonial emphasis was replaced by a distinct, if not opposed, priority: to look within each impoverished nation and "clean house." This was a program that, whether it openly aligned itself with social democracy or avoided this label for any number of ideological reasons, ended up entering into the thinking of the vast majority of Brazilian intellectuals, whether liberals or ex-leftists.

However, in descriptive terms, the situation of Latin America as analyzed by dependency theory did not change between the 1970s and the present decade. If anything, the situation worsened. What changed was its interpretation and, by extension, the sorts of projects proposed for resolving the crisis. Internal reform, which is championed by the liberal press and by many regretful socialists, presents itself and sees itself as an ideology that is more pragmatic, more efficient, more agile, more feasible, and (and why not just come out and say it?) more modern than the socialism that was defended until quite recently. Social democracy, which cannot be reduced to the party label that explicitly endorses it, is the expression, formerly timid and now vocal, of the confusion of a political culture that is no longer anticapitalistic because it accepts all of the changes imposed by modernity, but that has not yet been entirely incorporated into the system for the simple reason that Brazilian society is marked by all manner of inequalities. So then what should Brazil adopt? How should it adopt it? Should it adopt an ideal or a model exclusive to Western Europe or Japan? Should it adopt a short-term course of action?

The answers to these questions constitute an invitation to establish tactical agendas, an appeal for immediate reform. Without forcing the comparison—which incidentally, would not be unfavorable to either party—I would venture to say that Brazilian social democracy, which is weighed down by an unprecedented national crisis, seems to have adopted the Comtian motto of *conservar melhorando* (continuing to improve by conserving). Positivism revered the republican principles of 1789 but was horrified at the prospect of bloody revolution and any type of anarchy, though it was neither unmoving nor retrograde in its thinking. Comte and his disciples believed in the decisive power of the intellect and in the organizing role played by scientists, and in particular by "social engineers," and they preached a progressive and harmonious incorporation of the proletariat into industrial society, which in this way would leave behind humanity's feudal and military stages. Comte called on more than one occasion for the state to intervene moderately and on a supplementary basis, though also energetically, but he respected the principle of balanced budgets as dogma, and he shared with classical economics a fear of inflation. He was a convinced reformist, though his tactics were gradual, for he believed in the coming of a positive era as one believes in the coming of divine revelation.

Brazil's integration into the First World system (some are openly calling for closer economic relations with the United States) would come about through the relentless application of competition in labor, which would increase levels of production, and through austerity, which would increase domestic savings at the same time as some degree of monetary stability would be achieved. These professional and civic virtues would wipe from our memory General de Gaulle's phrase: "Brazil is not a serious country."

Dynamic, competitive, and one would assume, honest businessmen; conscientious, assiduous, and proficient workers; punctual, helpful public servants invested in the success of their departments and institutions: this is the Abraham's bosom aspired to by reformists who are tired of selfish and unpatriotic industrialists, unqualified and inadequately compensated workers, and above all, slow, negligent, and irresponsible functionaries, a category that includes medical doctors, teachers and professors, and public sector workers. Once again, what is called for is seriousness and efficiency—that is, morality and professionalism in public life—which would cure our problems of poverty, stagnation, inflation, and corruption—in a word, our backwardness. Brazil must regulate conflicts, work to be deserving of foreign credit, imitate the Japanese or German examples, or as some more modestly propose, study how the Asian tigers work, or lowering expectations even further, refer to the "Chilean experiment" and the "Mexican solution."

This way of thinking, which has the best of intentions and a declared aversion to the old left's excessive verbosity, is oriented toward a project that does not see postmodernity, even on the distant horizon, but rather Brazil's entrance into modernity *tout court*, which is assumed to be blocked not by external dependence but above all by the persistence of certain behaviors on the part of Brazilians—that is, by Brazilian politicians, Brazilian businessmen, Brazilian workers, and the Brazilian public sector.

Is this (once again) a case of a "national culture" that is resistant to the appeals of the spirit of capitalism, as Max Weber unforgettably described it?

A sense of aggravated guilt and a consequent desire for relief through work have caused the previous generation's revolutionary élan to be replaced by the furrowed brow, the harsh word, and the finger raised in disapproval of the chronic torpor of Brazilian public life.

The image of an interconnected global system—described in such detail in work published by Celso Furtado and Fernando Henrique Cardoso before 1970—has been shifted or suspended, and what has now come to the fore is an internal psycho-social web, a set of bad behaviors against which it is necessary to apply a barrage of Skinnerian shocks that, if the reaction is positive, can be complemented by rewards.[8]

Production under competition seems to be the objective of the new reformism, which has no patience for utopian visions and wants to see, and as soon as possible, the effects of a politics of results.

But why is it that so reasonable and sensible a project should encounter so many difficulties in being implemented in a country that is, after all, capitalistic?

The concrete situation has become somewhat convoluted, but not for reasons of national psychology, which appears as the culpable party in only the worst of academic subliteratures. The complication is due to other factors.

In the first place, the regimes of production and control that are necessary to carry out the efficient model of modernity the social democrats propose do not coincide, but rather conflict, with the supposedly post(*plus*)-modern values adhered to by the upper rungs, and by extension, the middle rungs of society. These favor an ethos of dissipation, informality, rupture, caprice, guiltlessness, and if we venture to use an accusatory term, irresponsibility. In this way, the same modern culture that would like to throw its faith in the working class's revolutionary virtues into the trash bin of history must ask the youth of all classes to believe in and resolutely hope for redemption through work, which is seen through the lens of bourgeois convention as the only means available for obtaining individual happiness.

Just as invasive as Marxism, reformism proposes to shift the hope for a material transformation of society to the realm of personal motives. In order to be convincing, it must utilize the rhetoric of liberalism, which it is already using assiduously. But social democracy is also, or believes itself to be, the standard bearer of a globalizing vision of society according to which increased production should, in the decisive moment of distribution, also result in greater equity. The achievement of this ideal of harmony between individualism and justice (would it to inappropriate to recall Saint-Simon and Comte?) demands constant regulation and vigilance against social inequalities, and requires individuals to adhere to supra-individual motivations. It calls, in short, for an order to achieve progress.

Now then, the *plus*-modern man revels in the material and symbolic evidence of progress, but he does not defer to order unless the reward is immediate and significant, which in Brazil is rarely the case. The young person born after 1970 is satisfied with the inherent rule provided by the computer, and he looks to the computer to find pleasure in games and combinatory freedom rather than the coercive order found in labor. The upper and middle classes, in their post(*plus*)-modernity, want more leisure, more consumption, more disposable labels, more gadgets, more electronic kits, more video games, and more shows that dazzle with sounds and images, as opposed to new and strict civic and professional obligations oriented toward a reduction of national poverty, which would be difficult to achieve.

Reformist pedagogy is currently taking on neoconservative airs, which are complementary to the intellectual and moral anomie that has been the coin of the realm since the 1970s. There is little or no theoretical novelty in the social democratic "modernity" that is visible today; we all remember what "rationalization" means according to the Weberian lexicon. There is, however, a great deal of political novelty in the Brazilian case. Perhaps for the first time, the majority of Brazilian politicians, regardless of their ideological background, have come to adhere to certain features of classical international modernization.

In order to get an up-close look at the sorts of contrasts that this rhetoric of productivity must confront, one need only open one of the large-circulation newspapers of São Paulo or Rio. They are a conspicuous part of a press that aspires to be modern and that most certainly influences the minds and hearts of thousands of educated and semieducated readers. What do we find in these newspapers? On the second and third pages we find editorials that circumspectly praise managed labor, economic austerity, honest government, rigorous schools, responsible politics, and an end to inflation, waste, corruption, and the threat of coups. The social democratic superego speaks through these texts. Later on in the newspaper one finds sections devoted to "culture," leisure, daily life, travel, money, and style. These are loaded with bait encouraging unhinged consumption, the use and abuse of the disposable, as well as asocial speculation, transgression, anomie, perversion, and barbarism. They are instruments in an immense orchestra that, apparently, cannot get in tune. "Let's play!" is their inherent law. Are these the readers who are meant to adhere religiously to the grand pact of austerity, economy, and productivity? Aren't these the same readers whose desires to buy and sell, to consume and do everything, are stimulated by the newspapers, readers for whom the newspapers provide a spectacle of universal venality and then wash their hands of this vortex of nonsense?

The orchestra cannot stop playing. There is no synthesis, only agglutination. The international market, which is modernization's ultimate object of desire, requires a legion of men and women who will hand over their arms, hands, and eyes to continually fashion and refashion the parts of a "whole" that can be sold and, therefore, can be altered and replaced. This shameless play on consumers' instincts using the most sophisticated advertising and commercial techniques is, without a doubt, *plus*-modern, but it does not negate the existence of the mute force, concealed in the background, which operates just in time and with appropriate self-control. But for the Brazil that is poor, what does this collective effort toward modernization mean? So far it has meant the poor's more efficient insertion into a vast inequality-producing machine. Surely, it must be said, this cannot be the intention of the social democrats, "all honourable men," who in their speeches combine competitiveness and equity.[9]

But properly speaking, the greatest obstacle to reformism does not derive from the opposition between the modern "morality" of work and the ultramodern "amorality" of consumption. After all, this combination, though unstable, has held together in rich and highly industrialized countries like Germany and Japan, in which the majority of the population behaves as if persuaded that it is worth the difficult struggle to enjoy the fruits of an abundant and diverse marketplace. In many Japanese firms, the purgatory of hard work is accepted as necessary in order to enter the paradise of consumption.

It is on the other side, on the side of those *de abajo* (from below) (to use the Latin American expression), where the mysticism of production and of high quality in industry fails to interest all but a very small cross-section of qualified workers. The stagnation of salaries, which is plaguing all peripheral economies, is too strong a dose of reality and hits too close to home for the laboring masses for a language of productivity to convince them to quickly accept the need to contribute to neocapitalism's projects. The modernity of some has little or nothing to say to the majority, who live in squalor.

In recent times, the official strategy has been to bet on educational reform as the only hope for raising the greater part of the Brazilian people above the low levels of development in which they presently live. But I repeat, the poor lack strong, immediate motivation to make the jump into the darkness in the hope of reaching the light of redemption. Nor do the objective cultural conditions appear to exist for there to be a full-scale brainwashing of the Asian type, which might jolt the absolute majority of Brazilians out of their present state of indifference.

If, however, a movement in this direction were to take place, we would witness the search for some sort of unity and coherence at the level of values and a corresponding discourse of social integration, though this discourse would likely not be nationalistic in the style of the 1930s or 1950s but would be productivity-centered, neoliberal, and competition-oriented. However, for now, and if the observations presented at the opening of this essay are correct, things are moving in the opposite direction, both within literary culture and among the various agents of the culture industry. One need only open a large-circulation newspaper or magazine to appreciate the degree of mental and moral dispersion, decomposition, inconsistence, and anomie presently afflicting Brazil.

The language of modernization, which one hears everywhere, is quite vague and rhetorical, for it lacks specific social content and its message consists of proposals for technical improvement that are understood as steps toward, well, postmodernity. On the other hand, we have the precariousness of our overarching theories, seen in light of the deterioration of the Latin American economy, which in many cases has been coupled with a perplexed reaction toward the crisis in Eastern Europe. This has added more fuel to the fire of skeptical reason. Efforts toward synthesis, long-term intellectual discipline, and the search for global objectives—in short, the will to change present conditions—have all lost steam.

All political crises are in fact cultural crises and directly involve representations and collective values. This explains the significant opportunity we have at present to more profoundly appreciate the ethical significance of forms of resistance implied in the critical equation: postmodern = antimodern. These forms of resistance understand how to undo the perverse mechanisms of what Vico termed the *barbarism of reflection*, an expression that registered as paradoxical during the period in which it was formulated, which was dominated by Cartesian thinking. The barbarism of reflection: the cruel moment in history in which instrumental reason, divorced from the meaning of the natural and human whole, comes to serve the forces of oppression and destruction.

Environmental science and practice, militancy in the area of human rights—which include the right to live in an international community, the belief in democracy as a substantive value, and a guaranteed universal minimum wage—are part of the system of ideas and values that proposes itself, here in Brazil as well, as an agenda aimed at ensuring survival with dignity.

If at heart our thinking turns decisively toward this program, then the tactical plans for economic growth as developed by planners and executives should be properly reclassified as instruments—that is, necessary means for the material achievement of ends that transcend them in importance.

The mediocrity and emptiness of the social liberalism preached by official circles and the private entities attached to them are caused by the lack of a sustained reflection on social liberalism's core values and priorities. The impression one takes from the pragmatic arguments made in defense of efficacy and competitiveness as necessary conditions for renewed growth is that, in the minds of those who make these arguments, the means take the place of values and ends. Now then, these qualities, which are inherent to classical capitalism, lost their appeal and their perceived reliability precisely when they were viewed as values and ends of the process of humanization. These qualities have already amply demonstrated, in Germany and Japan during the years of the fascist Axis, for example, that in being instrumental, they can be made to serve any ideological formation, including those that are the least compatible with the practice of citizenship. Further, all of us who have lived through the 1970s and 1980s in Latin America know that there exists no intimate relationship between productivity and democracy. When growth is made an end in itself, other values are either discarded or subordinated to it.

The intellectual disintegration and the ethical and political anomie of the past few years have deeply impacted university culture and the industry and commerce surrounding symbolic goods. As I observed in a previous chapter, the university and the communications media drew closer together during the 1970s, and even more so during the 1980s. At times, the two could hardly be told apart, with classes and seminars imitating the "informal" style of television programs, which in turn glossed or utilized academic discourses in their own way.

Sameness attempts to counterbalance dispersion and manages to do so for a time, but it cannot manage (nor does it even attempt) to impede the tendencies toward dissipation and decentering that attack cultural life from within.

* * *

As poles of modernization, the university and the media have tended to grow and have received a certain level of attention from the state and from civil society. This attention has evidently not been bestowed on everyday popular symbolic life.

The relations between this *tertius* and other cultural formations were the object of analysis of the previous essay. In reviewing this discussion, it did not seem to me that anything substantial should be added. The condition of rootedness, lacking which popular life cannot survive, remains precarious and has even deteriorated, given the "lost decade" experienced by Brazil and all of Latin America. But what managed to survive demonstrates that the core elements of popular culture (flexibility, reversibility, animistic materialism, gregariousness) remain.

As for the use to which academic researchers and mass media in search of material put the symbolic life of the people, this speaks in the first instance to the ideological fluctuations occurring within the dominant culture. This culture aspires to bestow meaning on its objects. It is precisely the dominant culture that offers interpretations—sometimes reductive, sometimes open—of popular life. Elitist rejection of, rationalistic critique of, or romantic adhesion to popular culture do not concern the meanings internalized and experienced by the people. Rather, rejection, critique, or adhesion are revealing only of ideological shifts within the ranks of the educated. As viewpoints, they directly correlate with the class divisions that mark our society.

It is less difficult to evaluate the ways in which the university or the press views the ethos of poverty than it is to uncover the internal changes that potentially affect the representations, symbols, and feelings that together make up the daily life of the people. We have made little progress within this area of understanding.

Within the terrain of the popular imagination, what one perceives is the coupling of an archaic and providential religiosity with certain behaviors and even secular forms of expression that are proper to modern rationality. In this way, for instance, the numbers of devotees of charismatic and Pentecostal sects, which along with *umbanda* and *candomblé* continue to grow, often couple magical thinking and the experience of trance with economic behaviors aligned with the competitive individualism that conditions us all.

To get to the heart of the question would require one to determine, in terms of the real intentionality of these religious practices, what is defensive (of the person, family, group, race) and what resists the threats posed by an insecure day-to-day life, and in terms of the free experience of the sacred, what there is of consolation and what there is of faith.

Orthodox sociological and psychoanalytic analyses err in their drastic oversimplifications, which are presented as demystifying but which fail to capture the ways of being and appearing inherent in symbolic processes. They attempt to locate what is "behind" these behaviors but end up touching on what, phenomenologically speaking, is not there.

At the other extreme, a hermeneutics that is grounded in existentialism seeks to delve into the interior of phenomena—which is certainly laudable—but runs the risk of abstracting these phenomena from the web of conditions, means, and ends that makes them intelligible on a social level.

This disjunction in observation (from the outside or from the inside), which only a reimagined and liberated anthropology can overcome, has been responsible for unilateral approaches to popular culture. In Brazil, religious manifestations as well as the symbolic language of the poor—whether plastic or musical, ludic or dramatic, resigned or rebellious—suffer from these mutually exclusionary readings.

There are those who view the poor as ever more closely tied to the process of consumption and who consequently believe that archaic-popular culture is experiencing a kind of final agony. And there are those who perceive in archaic-popular culture a symbolic web that is flexible, lively, and resistant to the commodification of human relations that is brought about by the universalization of commerce.

In these pages I have merely provided one more perplexed formulation concerning the question of popular culture. This question's degree of relevance, in the context of the crisis of conventional modernity, is not insignificant.

A Retrospective Glance

If there is a common thread that runs through the essays that comprise this book, it is an idea that can be formulated synthetically, as follows:

Colonization is a process that is at once material and symbolic. The economic practices of its agents are linked to their means of survival, to their memory, to their ways of representing themselves and others, and ultimately, to their desires and hopes.

To put it another way: there is no colonial condition without a weaving together of labors, of cults, of ideologies, and of cultures.

The relations between these fundamental dimensions of all civilizing processes (which Marxism summarized at the levels of infrastructure and superstructure) are modified, throughout time, by positive determinants of adjustment, reproduction, and continuity. Situations arise, however, in which it is the asymmetries and, in extreme cases, the ruptures that appear before the historian and anthropologist of colonial life.

Within this process of cultivation of old seeds and new transplants, grafting is not always successful. At times the present seeks or needs to free itself from the weight of the past. At other times—and this perhaps occurs more frequently—the force of tradition demands the *ritornello* of signs and values without which the system would collapse.

Those who propose to discover geometric or unchanging laws governing the interactions between metropolis and colony—or, from a vertical point of view, between the economic and the symbolic—risk losing themselves in mental formulas. A dialectic of potentialities, which are sometimes achieved and sometimes frustrated, can more accurately tell us how things have occurred.

In the conquest of the New World by the Old, violent and barbaric practices, like the reinvention of slave labor, were accompanied by what are generally considered progressive changes, such as the transition from feudalism to the slow, difficult, but irreversible ascent of the bourgeoisie, which occurred in the centuries following the discovery.

As a mercantile machine and a system, colonization cleared the path for the surge of global capitalism in which the future country would take its place as a dependent nation. But as a condition, daily life in the colonies reproduced, *intra muros*, old ways of thinking, feeling, and speaking. The transformation of this existential ballast into ideology would later be responsible for conservative currents such as Luso-Tropicalism, *bandeirismo*, and certain tenacious regional and class syndromes. One must distinguish what is alive from what is dead in each of these tendencies, and carefully separate what hearkens back to the memory of deeply rooted experiences, which art expresses, and what has been reified or transformed into clannish self-deception or a source of prejudice.

To return to the principal effects of colonization in the sphere of symbolic creation: we are faced alternately with reflections of erudite innovations, whether Iberian or Italian, and which can be seen in Mannerist, *arcádica*, and neoclassical art, and with frontier expressions, in whose creation the semieducated artisan only partially conformed to the aesthetic standards of the Catholic Church, which was a powerful unifying institution.

In the first case, the historian's gaze contemplates phenomena marked by motifs and themes that were imported, which circulated, and that were common to intellectuals in the dominant strata of society. In the second, however, one notes singular combinations of rustic and learned styles, which together give form to expressions of a living and whole popular devotion. Examples of this frontier art include the figures representing the Stations of the Cross at Congonhas do Campo, as well as the nineteenth-century *paulistinhas*, and the *romances de cordel*, which are written even today.

* * *

Viewed in retrospect, these currents of thought and action, which gave rise to a historical scene that Machiavelli described as *verità effettuale*, ended up resolving themselves into clearly opposing positions. If times of peace allow for openness to a variety of options, during times of war choice imposes itself, and multiplicity is reduced to an imperious *either this or that*.

Let us return to history.

I. What were the Jesuits trying to achieve?

They were attempting to transplant to the New World a universalistic culture—*Ide e pregai a boa nova a todos os povos* (Go ye into all the world, and preach the gospel to every creature)[1]—grounded in medieval Christianity and fueled by Iberian redemptive fervor. The Company [of Jesus]'s project, which had been outlined in Loyola's *Constitutions*, runs through the missionary writings of Nóbrega, Anchieta, Simão de Vasconcelos, Vieira, Montoya, and the founders of the Paraguayan missions. Over the medium and long term, their plans were revealed to be incompatible with the expansion of the "Portuguese of São Paulo" and with the Spanish and Portuguese states' strategic interests in the southern half of the continent. Thus, these two colonial complexes—the Company [of Jesus] on one side and the *bandeiras* and the army on the other—would come into conflict, and the result would be the destruction of the seven missions followed a short time later by the expulsion of the Jesuits.

The conflict between a militant religious order and a predatory economic force, which was sublimated as the inherent logic of conquest in the prose of the writers of lineages and of Enlightenment *epos* (see the *Nobiliarquia paulistana*, the *Uraguai*, and *Vila Rica*) can be viewed as the first key moment in the dialectic of mercantile colonization. Material and moral dominion over indigenous labor gave brute reality to an antimony of political views and wills.

II. Another battle, also concerning the role of slave labor, would take place between the 1860s and 1880s:

The country had achieved its legal independence and was subject, as with other societies living under colonialism, to the gravitational pull of British imperialism. The core question was whether to inaugurate a system of free labor and to fully accede to the mechanisms of capitalism.

During this period, the harsh and pragmatic language of slavery described itself using the sacred designation of "liberal." In this context, this adjective was not entirely inappropriate or paradoxical in that liberalism affirmed the principles of free trade and the state's noninterference in production. Both had received the approval of Adam Smith and, here in Brazil, had been embraced by a precocious and convinced Smithian, the Viscount of Cairu, a man who opened ports and doors. This liberalism, which was modern in its opposition to the old monopolism but which remained conservative in its agrarian and proslavery inclinations, would come into conflict with the new liberalism of Tavares Bastos, Joaquim Nabuco, Rui Barbosa, and André Rebouças, who as proponents of free labor were also abolitionists.

Two ideologies: one close to the clannish sugar and Paraíba Valley–based coffee economies, which parliamentary theatrics presented as representative of the general will; the other, open to broad international horizons. One tied to the immediate present and so apparently more sensible and closer to its roots, the other clairvoyant and far-sighted, and for this reason denigrated by the proponents of the first as out of step with and inappropriate for Brazil's national reality.

III. With abolition and the declaration of the republic, it would seem that those who had bet on the future were victorious. The relentless critique that realists, evolutionists, and positivists had launched against the stale routine of the empire had a visible impact not only at the rhetorical and discursive levels but in terms of institutions as well.

Once again, however, the historian is confronted by a division of the waters.

In the main branch of the river, class interests create a federative, pseudo-national structure, ensuring that the state will support the coffee economy to which everything else will be subordinated. In this republic, which was born Old, the model of *saquarema* hegemony from the Second Empire will return, with the difference being that by this time, rural *coronelismo* will be even more entrenched.

The Darwinian liberalism of the largest state associations, the PRP and the PRM—that is, the Partido Republicano Paulista (São Paulo Republican Party) and the Partido Republicano Mineiro (Minas Gerais Republican Party)—joined regionalist passions, to the point of suffocation, with the cosmopolitanism of their *enfants gâtés*, and therefore *terribles*, which made for an interesting mixture that remained visible in the oscillations and ambiguities of the modernists of 1922.[2]

In secondary branches of the river, political and cultural groups that were, existentially speaking, distant from the privileged main branch gravitated toward other ways of thinking. Though their ideas were as European as those of their opponents, these ideas allowed them to conceive of the nation-state as a system that had yet to be built, an integrated and "organic" formation, and a country that depended upon more than the destiny of one class. The social positivism that united the *gaúcho* republicans of the Generation of 1907 with the *tenentes* was a courageous alternative that made the movement of 1930 possible. Once more, a totalizing way of viewing Brazilian society would be opposed to the mental habits of a defensive oligarchy that was increasingly incapable of leading the nation politically or economically.

The *castilhistas* of the south, with the support of the *tenentes* (a sort of neo-Jacobin group that revered the memory of Benjamin Constant and Floriano Peixoto), came to national power and tactically absorbed certain ideological traces from doctrines that—from the right and from the left—rejected the dogma of laissez-faire that had been weakened by the crisis of 1929. During this period a Brazilian welfare state was created, which for good or for ill remains with us today.

The foreign provenance of all of these ideas, including radical forms of nationalism, led me to question the interest of discussions concerning their origin. It seemed that by tracing the evolution of these ideas in the West beginning in the Middle Ages—ideas that gained in strength and speed with the formation of a world system in the sixteenth century—we might free ourselves from a preoccupation with examining the locus of this or that theory. What is important is to examine social history as a means to accompany the paths through which ideology has spread and to analyze specific contexts in which certain sets of values were incorporated, at the same time as these contexts filtered out certain conflicting messages.

The Portugal of the sailors and traders, the Spain of the inquisitors, the Rome of the Jesuits, the England of Smith and Spencer, the France of the *Encyclopedia* and Comte, the Germany of Bismarck, the Russia of Lenin, the Italy of fascism: these have become nearly mythical topoi from which ideologies have spread, both to other European nations and to America. The colonial situation merely reinforces a feeling of distance or of ethnic difference, particularly in the thinking of the elites. But as the common structures of urban, industrial capitalism began manifesting themselves, grafting became necessary. A logic of roles became apparent, along with that logic's sharp edges and violent features. Here, as everywhere, the march of modernization could no longer conceal its pseudo-rational aspects.

The dialectic of colonization described in these pages is less a seesawing between nationalism and cosmopolitanism (which one also observes in European cultures) than it is a struggle between localistic ways of thinking, which reflect calculations made concerning the here-and-now, and projects that imagine the transformation of society using discourses developed elsewhere but supplemented with universal arguments.

* * *

This summary would not be faithful to the spirit of my book if it failed to comment on one of its recurrent methodological features: the recognition of mythical ties that bind a variety of cultural expressions, not only those that are conservative but those that have a progressive function as well.

Signification sustains itself through metaphors and allegories developed by prior generations. Those who deal with symbolic networks, which are what poems, sermons, and novels in effect are, end up discovering within the weave of sentences images derived from social memory ("o que lembro, tenho," that is, "what I remember, I have," Guimarães Rosa said), as well as echoes of old, periodically intoned expressive movements, melodies of love and hate, of hope and anguish. Ghosts come to life in ideas, as Vico taught, and what yesterday was desire is today reason.

In the history of colonization I hear a dialogue, often muffled, between what the mind writes and passion's impulses, and I see the osmosis that takes place between the poet or prophet's imagination and the figures of tradition. Recall the myths of Titans and their opposite in the contradictory voices heard in *Os Lusíadas*, the medieval sins and suffering of Baroque Bahia as described in Gregório de Matos, the cross borne by the black plantation slaves in Vieira, the Calvary of the cane fields in Antonil, the indigenous apocalypse in Gonçalves Dias, the voluntary immolation of the Guarani in Alencar, the call of Prometheus and the sign of Ham in Castro Alves, and the shadows of the imprisoned being and the exiled soul in Cruz e Sousa and Lima Barreto.

Situations that are experienced or imagined within the broad circle of individual or group existence give to writing, which reveals them, its primary source of potency, a body of intuitions and feelings that nothing can replace. But the original lived experience absolutely requires the mediation of a universalizing form, without which it would not have crossed over the border into the terrain of literary expression. That which lives cannot speak without defining a point of view.

The coming together of force and signifying form, of event and word, gives birth to the symbolic process, which lives and is transmitted in the history of cult and culture.

Metaphors, which appear within the magnetic zone of translation, and allegories, which tend to crystallize meaning, are protoconcepts, near-concepts, "fantastic universals" (Vico), which men drew on and will always draw on when prompted by their limited ability to communicate. In these moments, which are vital for the signifying process, it would be prematurely abstract to reduce these figures to logical universals, to pure concepts. It is at these moments that mythical images from earlier times are made actual in the memory of a culture attempting to be true to the continually renewed density of the human condition.

In the case of Brazil as a colonial formation, these symbolic transfers, which cut across time and space, occur in the context of social experiences that are particular to our history. At the same time, as ways of producing meaning and values, they are constants of the process of acculturation, from at least oriental and Mediterranean antiquity forward.

* * *

In sum, as we examine the course of contemporary thinking, a weave of technically new signs makes its imperious presence felt: these are the mass media. Beginning in the mid-twentieth century, the souls of all social classes, the world over, would be colonized.

Today, to colonize means to utilize certain power matrices of images, opinions, and stereotypes to transform on a mass scale.

Despite the thousand and one academic studies that have been published and all of the plaudits and curses that for the past half-century have been heaped upon the culture industry, and in particular, upon television, the work of intellectuals continues to determine what takes place in the hearts and minds of a very large public, over which, in a certain way, erudite and popular culture retain influence.

This book's final chapter, which addressed the plural character of cultures, and its postscript were the products of my lingering questions concerning these issues, questions that the passage of time has only made more difficult to answer.

That the dialectic of civilization has sporadically produced thoughts, words, and acts identified with a culture of resistance that has yet to be defeated by the forces of disintegration—this is a small flame of hope that flickers at the end of this journey.

Epilogue (2001)

As a historian of Brazilian literature, I have always been interested in texts by poets, prose writers, and essayists that work to find meaning in the web of material and symbolic processes that comprise the history of our people. With so many years gone by, as well as so many interpretations (some evolutionist and Eurocentric, others Romantic and nationalist, others psychological and concerned with capturing the essence of our "national character," and still others economic and guided by so-called orthodox Marxism), what appears to have remained, and what continues to generate new research, is the enduring theory of Brazilian multiplicity and miscegenation.

Our cultural process, which begins with the constitution of a language, Brazilian Portuguese, and moves toward a coexistence, alternately difficult and peaceful, of customs, beliefs, values, and poetic and ludic expressions, has been multiple and mestizo.

The previous pages do not aspire to be a new history of a culture that, despite its five centuries of existence, is still in a process of formation that is not yet complete and that is becoming increasingly dense, both objectively, thanks to accumulated interactions of its component parts, and subjectively, through the lived experiences of its participants. There is a great amount of research to be completed in the field, the archive, and the library. These projects await scholars and devotees who can collect a larger amount of data than we currently have so that, at least, we can trace the outline of a synthesis.

The objective of this book is more modest: to identify and interpret certain moments in our cultural production, whether these moments are ideological or counterideological. Beginning with the colonial period, this production reveals contradictory aspects of our social life, and thus, our cultural history. Contradiction implies the multiplicity and simultaneity of divergent tendencies.

The contrasts engendered within and outside of texts are captured in the works of Anchieta, Gregório de Matos, Vieira, Alencar, Joaquim Nabuco, Castro Alves, Cruz e Sousa, Euclides da Cunha, Lima Barreto, and other intellectuals engaged in the project of understanding or critiquing the society in which they lived.

The following are some prominent episodes from this long process:

The Jesuit project survived with the support of the Catholic Portuguese monarchy until the moment in which the internal dynamism of the colonizing expansion of the *bandeirantes* brought the Jesuits and *bandeirantes* into conflict, ultimately leading to the end of the Jesuit project *manu militari*. The attitudes of the missionaries, alternately characterized by skillful compromise and open resistance, reveal the varied facets of a point of tension in which the vast Jesuit project looked to Scholastic theology for weapons that would help the Jesuits alternately compose arguments justifying their position and issue impotent expressions of protest. We should observe, within this project, that the dualism between compromise with the colonists and defense of the Amerindians was interiorized by the Jesuits and took on a dramatic tone in the writings of Antônio Vieira. And how tense and agonized his writing seems when compared with the cold and reliably colonial and mercantile style of Antonil, who was a fellow Jesuit. Though Antonil was Vieira's secretary, he can be viewed in certain respects as the anti-Vieira.

Moving forward to the postindependence period: José de Alencar founded the national novel, defended the validity of a Brazilian literary language, and argued with Portuguese critics. He was, in short, the patriarch of Romantic *indianismo*. This said, his most heroic and poetic Amerindian characters, who are symbols of a new Brazilian-ness, Peri and Iracema, voluntarily serve the white, "noble" colonizer as a form of "*doce escravidão*" (sweet slavery), as Machado de Assis perceptively termed it. This is an ideological knot that entangled rebellion and veneration, pride and sacrifice, which has yet to be thoroughly untied.

A generation later, Castro Alves would in 1868 sound the first trumpet blast of the abolitionist movement with *Vozes d'África* (Voices from Africa). Abolitionism had not yet invaded the public square, nor had it reached the press or Parliament. This would occur in 1871 and then in the 1880s. But the Africa of his poem is more of a tragic than epic figure. The black man who weeps for Africa is not the longed-for rebellious Titan who will call upon his blood brothers to fight against the injustice of slavery but is a descendent of Ham, the victim of a ridiculous curse that cannot be lifted. But is the tragic discourse not the most intense expression of a negative dialectic that places a language of despair against the arbitrary actions of gods and men? We now know that the feeling and awareness of the tragic has a progressive face in that it shows us the reverse side of a superficial and illusory optimism.

The end of the nineteenth century saw abolition and the proclamation of the republic. Was this modernity at last? Would the luster of the European *belle époque* shine throughout the federal capital? A cultural history understood as a collection of *faits divers* would claim as much. The contrast between the voice of liberation and the racial Darwinism that marked this golden age of European imperialism would be dramatically experienced by the great black poet Cruz e Sousa, the *Emparedado* (Enclosed), and by the mulatto novelist Lima Barreto, a humiliated and offended intellectual and a reader of the Russians and the anarchists who refused to participate in Rio de Janeiro's early twentieth-century literary circles. Deterministic science or individual freedom, racist anthropology or the equality of peoples: these followed opposite paths. This disjunction could be felt and resented more strongly in the mestizo, impoverished ex-colonies than in the metropolises that were fascinated by the new century's inventions. Cruz e Sousa, Euclides da Cunha, and Lima Barreto show us the physiognomy of a Brazil that is precisely the opposite of the pleasant image of the years during the Old Republic in which "o Rio civilizou-se" (Rio became civilized).

Ideological Struggles and Their Place in Society: Liberalisms and Positivism

When the corpus of contradictory discourses is comprised of political sources, this method pays in kind. It seemed to me that, in speaking of dialectic in a Brazilian cultural context, one should not omit the black-and-white study of the two forms of liberalism that entered into confrontation with one another beginning in the 1860s over the heated question of black slavery.

Examination of the arguments made by the political actors of the Second Empire during the 1871 debate over the liberation of slaves' children led me to distinguish between an old intraoligarchical, and therefore exclusionary liberalism, and a "novo liberalismo" (the term "new liberalism" was coined by Joaquim Nabuco, one of its proponents), which was oriented toward the promotion of free labor and ideas of democratic representation.

Analysis of the *Anais do Parlamento* (Parliamentary Annals) for this period confirms the extent to which the old liberalism accommodated and functioned in lockstep with an agro-mercantile, slave-holding Brazil. This was the proper place for an intraoligarchical liberalism. In parallel, I propose that we examine the ideology, which is simultaneously classically liberal and proslavery, of the dominant political classes in Cuba and the U.S. Old South during the mid-nineteenth century, in order to understand the degree to which these liberal forces accommodated the interests of those who held power over the plantation economy, and to explain why the new urban, pro–free labor liberalism had to rise up against the solid ideological bloc (to use Gramsci's synthetic expression) represented by the old liberals and the agro-mercantile, plantation economy. These were two liberalisms opposed to one another, each anchored in its place in society.

Moving a bit further forward in time: I was greatly impressed with the coherence of a regional political practice located in Rio Grande do Sul and based in Auguste Comte's doctrine. In the context of a republic guided by orthodox liberalism and based economically in the exportation of coffee, the state of Rio Grande do Sul, over a period of forty years, pursued its own form of politics that was distinguished by the intervention of the executive power, the promotion of small-scale urban industry and rural family smallholdings, the development of the domestic market, and state takeover of public services. These measures provoked the ire of the great cattlemen and beef exporters, who were leaders of the Liberal Party.

The opposition between positivism and oligarchical liberalism was not limited to this period in the history of Rio Grande do Sul. When in 1930 the southern republican leaders came to national power on the coattails of a political movement led by Getúlio Vargas, these same ideals of industrialization and central control were given a broader space to express themselves. This was the beginning of the Brazilian welfare state, which continued in one form or another until the beginning of the 1990s and which is now staggering from the blows dealt by the neoliberalism that has inserted itself into the dominant political group.

As we see once again, ideologies take root in the soil of the interests and aspirations of the groups that defend them. An ideology's origin (whether from beyond or within national boundaries) matters little, though its function and capacity to consolidate institutions matter a great deal. For this reason, ideas like diffusion, filtering, grafting, and ideological remodeling seem to me more pertinent and productive than the antiquated debate regarding the foreign or national place or provenance of ideas.

Five Working Hypotheses

In examining the dynamics of Brazilian culture from the colonial period forward, I came to formulate some working hypotheses, which I will summarize below:

1. Colonization, Cult, and Culture

Colonization is a process in which at least three planes overlap:

a) the plane characterized by the conquest of the land and the exploitation of the labor force (I chose the Latin verb *colo*, in the present indicative, meaning "to occupy, cultivate, dominate," to designate this economic and political dimension);

b) the plane corresponding to the memory of the colonizers and colonized. This is responsible for a great part of their symbolic and affective expressions (I used the past participle *cultus* to designate this religious, and *in sensu lato*, traditional dimension);

c) the plane corresponding to the generally secular projects that envision the construction of a modern future and a national identity. Here I linked the word *cultura*, taken from the future participle, to an intellectual and technical dimension that took on an autonomous identity beginning with the Enlightenment.

The verb *colo*, the participle forms of which give us *culto* and *cultura*, is at the root of both the noun *colônia* (colony) and the verb *colonizar* (to colonize).

There are periods in which the relations between these three dimensions are characterized by accommodation and harmonization, and in which they form the historical blocs of which Gramsci spoke when referring to the solidity of the French national bourgeoisie, which emerged victorious during the nineteenth century. During these periods the economy, political power, and the dominant ideology are firmly intertwined. However, instances of conflict and dissonance do occur. Indeed, in *Os Lusíadas*, the quintessential epic of maritime adventure and conquest, Camões paradoxically inserted the speech of the Velho do Restelo (Old Man of Restelo), in which the voice of tradition (*cultus*) inveighs against the maritime exploratory project and the modern values of the Portuguese Renaissance.

Examples can be cited in which political power (*colo*) and traditional religion (*cultus*) unite against freedom of culture. These are cases in which the forces of reaction identify with the past in order to impede the democratic diffusion of Enlightenment ideas. These are the so-called periods of restoration in which fundamentalisms rule. At the other extreme, there are cases in which religion is influenced by and unites with secular culture against the abusive power of money and status. Beginning in the 1960s, the Brazilian and Latin American secular left strategically allied themselves with progressive religious forces in order to unmask the most notorious figures in international finance and their local puppets. Finally, there is the alliance of *colo* and *cultura* against *cultus*, in which those who fetishize bourgeois modernity create a world of things and values that marginalizes all forms of tradition, lowering them to the condition of unused merchandise.

This broad, combinatory hypothesis runs through the entire book and presupposes the revision of the dogmatic view according to which superstructures are always a reflection of the infrastructure. This dogma, despite or perhaps because of its unsophisticated reductionism, has survived the sharp critiques of German historicism, culturalism, Crocian idealism, Weberian sociology, psychoanalysis, phenomenology, existentialism, hermeneutics, and the critical theory of the Frankfurt School.

2. A Culture beyond the Pale of Writing

During the three centuries of Portuguese colonization and throughout the long period of our national history that followed independence, popular culture was characterized by its production and reproduction beyond the pale of writing. Its oral character, combined with its gregariousness and animistic materialism, persist and resist despite the presence of an all-encompassing mass culture—though at times popular culture enters into close contact with mass culture. A surprising effect of contact between literary culture and oral and traditional language has been the creation of masterpieces like Guimarães Rosa's *Grande sertão: veredas*.

3. Frontier Culture

Between traditional oral culture and the practices of literary culture we find an interstitial zone I call frontier culture. This consists of examples of contact that are marked by the dualism of the process by which they are constituted. For example, rustic sculptures of religious images (the "paulistinhas" found in the interior of São Paulo state) were based on learned or semilearned models taken from medieval and Baroque religious art, though effectively they are examples of an art whose formal characteristics and devotional function remain popular in character. Similar observations can be made when we analyze images taken from the Sete Povos (Seven Missions) of the Jesuits, which have only recently been collected and evaluated. Or in another context, we may consider how authors of *literatura de cordel* adapt situations taken from mass culture to the images and rhythms of oral tradition. Frontier culture ignores the compartmentalization of space and time. Its generosity is ecumenical, though this does not negate its rootedness in the region.

4. Two Contrary Meanings of Postmodernity

Moving to more recent times, since the 1970s, Brazil has experienced the global phenomenon of postmodernity. The hypothesis I presented in this book's final chapter observed the contradictory duality of the term. Postmodern might consist of nothing more than the development of global capitalism taken to the extreme. In this case, postmodern is simply ultramodern, or *plus*-modern. But postmodern can also entail a movement of critique of and reaction to the negative effects of capitalistic modernization. These effects have become more profound in the context of a Third World passing through a period of crisis. For instance, the destruction of nature gave rise to environmentalism, a deeply antimodernistic movement supported by ecological science. Further, the coupling of savage capitalism with technological blindness summoned ethical antibodies that today call for the preservation of communities and the urgent participation of minorities (and in Brazil, the majority as well) in the direction of public affairs. Quality of life, community, and citizenship are values that in the vocabulary of the left today occupy the place once held by the Leninist expression "dictatorship of the proletariat."

In parallel, various manifestations of the so-called counterculture of the 1970s launched a critique of technology-focused modernization. In sum, those who speak of the postmodern today should specify whether they mean ultramodernity or antimodernity. The question of the hour, which is difficult to resolve, is in knowing what "modernity" itself means.

5. A Culture of Resistance

Finally, we come to a theme that is partially related to certain nonconformist notions taken from critical theory. This is the culture of resistance, an idea that has preoccupied me since I wrote the essay "Poesia-Resistência" (Poetry-Resistance).[1]

The sense that there is a tension present in great works of literature, between writing and dominant ideologies, is at the heart of my hypothesized culture of resistance. In bringing the objects of their attention into singular focus, poets and narrators remove them from a mental routine that typifies or reifies everything. The aesthetic result is a particular, strange form that represents the reverse side of established convention. The understanding of resistance sometimes coincides with the idea of estrangement, as elaborated by the Russian formalist poets, but its strong dialectical and moral elements place it in closer relation to Benjamin's and Adorno's propositions, which describe the subject's negativity when confronted by the positivity of the capitalist system and an alienating bourgeois mentality.

It is likely that this same idea of resistance will recall for my French readers a revolutionary tradition that, during the twentieth century, included surrealists and reached its highest expression during the Second World War. And while the concept of resistance transcends the limits of this tradition, I should recognize, in conclusion, that the figures of Antigone, Prometheus, and Sisyphus, which Simone Weil and Camus loved so much, endure for this Brazilian reader as indelible symbols of that which is most dignified in human nature.

This epilogue is, barring a few changes, consistent with my preface to the French translation of my book, published as *Culture brésilienne. Une dialectique de la colonisation*, trans. Jean Briant (Paris: L'Harmattan, 2000).

Notes

1. Colony, Cult, and Culture

1. Augusto Magne tells us that "*[c]olo* is derived from *Kwelo*, which means to move around something, to circulate. The meaning of the root is clearly illustrated by the second part of Greek compound masculine nouns like *bou-kólos* (cowherd), *ai-pólos* (goatherd), *amphi-pólos* (servant, he who moves around a cow, a goat, or the master of the house, and takes care of them). The idea of 'taking into one's care,' which is apparent in these terms, explains some of the applications of *colo* in Latin. Its agrarian connotations are explained, on the other hand, by the rural character of its ruling class during Rome's earliest days. While in Greek *Kwel-* carries the meanings of 'to move' and 'to habitually find oneself in,' the Latin *col-* carries the specific meaning of 'to inhabit' or 'to cultivate.' Compare how the aforementioned compound words convey the idea of 'occupying oneself with.' The ideas of habitation and cultivation are present from the earliest times because of the connection drawn between these ideas by the rural population" (*Dicionário etimológico da língua latina*, vol. 4 [Rio de Janeiro: MEC, 1962]).

2. In the *Lexicon totius latinitatis*, Aegidio Forcellini distinguishes, with lapidary definitions, between colony and municipality: "A *colony* differs from a *municipality*: municipals in truth are citizens of a municipality, who live by their own laws and their own right; colonists are citizens of a city who are brought to another, and who live by the laws of the city from which they originated." And he specifies one meaning of colony: "A colony is the part of a city (state) or society that has been displaced to another land in order to cultivate and inhabit it; 'colony' also refers to the place itself" (Aegidio Forcellini, *Lexicon totius latinitatis*, 4th ed. [Padua: Typis Seninarii, 1940], 692–93).

3. See Vitorino Magalhães Godinho, *Economia dos descobrimentos henriquinos* (Lisbon, 1962).

4. Gordon Childe, *Man Makes Himself* (London: Watts, 1965), 101–2. On the ancientness of funerary rites, see Henri Gastaut's succinct but well-founded "Alguns comentários a respeito do culto do crânio," in *A unidade do homem. Invariantes biológicas e universais culturais*, ed. Centro Royaumont para uma Ciência do Homem, vol. 3 (São Paulo: Cultrix/Edusp, 1978), 254–56.

5. See Werner Jaeger, *Paideia: The Ideals of Greek Culture*, trans. Gilbert Highet (New York: Oxford University Press, 1939–1944), the first German edition is from 1936; Henri-Irénée Marrou, *A History of Education in Antiquity*, trans. George Lamb (New York: Sheed and Ward, 1956).

6. Jacob Burckhardt, *Force and Freedom: Reflections on Universal History*, ed. James Hastings Nichols (New York: Pantheon Books, 1943), 140.

7. Antonio Gramsci, *Il materialismo storico* (Roma: Ed. Riuniti, 1975).

8. Here I refer to the entire tradition of progressive critique, of Max Scheler, Mannheim, Benjamin, Adorno, Sartre, and Merleau-Ponty, which beginning in the 1920s called into question the certainties of the bourgeois thought of the Enlightenment, along with its positivist or evolutionist derivations.

9. Karl Marx, *Capital: A Critique of Political Economy*, vol. 1, trans. Samuel Moore and Edward Aveling (Chicago: Charles H. Kerr, 1906), 823.

10. Marx, *Capital*, vol. 3, 320.

11. Manuel Galich, in *Nuestros primeros padres* (Havana: Casa de las Américas, 1979), 390, quotes this account from Rex González y Pérez, *Argentina indígena, vísperas de la conquista*.

12. On Montaigne's knowledge of Las Casas, see Juan Durán Luzio, "Bartolomé de las Casas y M. de Montaigne: escritura y lectura del Nuevo Mundo," *Revista Chilena de Literatura* (Universidad de Chile, Santiago), no. 37 (April 1991). The theme of the *leyenda negra* has been ably taken up by Gustavo Gutiérrez in *Dios o el oro en las Indias. Siglo XVI* (Lima: Instituto Bartolomé de las Casas Rimac, 1989).

13. Quoted in Aimé Césaire, *Discours sur le colonialisme* (Paris: Présence Africaine, 1955), 20.

14. Karl Marx, *Pre-Capitalist Economic Formations*, trans. Jack Cohen (New York: International Publishers, 1980), 119.

15. Translator's note: In Portuguese, *fazenda* refers to an agricultural property, a mid- to large-sized farm. It is distinct from the terms *sítio*, which is used to describe a small farm, and *engenho*, which describes a sugar plantation.

16. Marx, *Capital*, vol. 1, 340.

17. Raymundo Faoro offers an excellent analysis of the linked themes of centralization and authoritarian tradition in Brazil in *Os donos do poder: Formação do patronato politico brasileiro* (Porto Alegre: Globo, 1958).

18. Translator's note: *Literatura de cordel* is a form of popular Brazilian literature, especially prevalent in the rural northeast, that tells folkloric and popular narratives, often in verse form. It is published in small booklets, some of which feature lithographs on the cover.

19. Caio Prado Jr., *Formação do Brasil contemporâneo* (São Paulo, 1942); Nelson Werneck Sodré, *Formação da sociedade brasileira* (Rio de Janeiro: José Olympio, 1944); Celso Furtado, *Formação econômica do Brasil* (Rio de Janeiro: Fundo de Cultura, 1959); Fernando Novais, *Portugal e Brasil na crise do antigo sistema colonial* (São Paulo: Hucitec, 1979); Jacob Gorender, *O escravismo colonial* (São Paulo: Ática, 1977); Maria Sylvia Carvalho Franco, "Organização social do trabalho no período colonial," *Discurso* (São Paulo, USP—Depto. de Filosofia, Hucitec), no. 8 (1978).

20. Translator's note: *Bandeirantes* were colonial-era adventurers and explorers who generally departed from São Paulo and journeyed through the interior in search of precious stones and metals as well as indigenous slaves. They are considered heroic symbols of Brazilian, and especially São Paulo, culture. They are also credited with early exploration of the Brazilian interior, which allowed Brazil to expand its borders to the west, beyond the line demarcated by the Treaty of Tordesillas in 1494.

21. Translator's note: *Paulista* is a term used to refer to an inhabitant of the state of São Paulo; *paulistano* is a more specific term referring to someone from the city of São Paulo.

22. In Sérgio Buarque de Holanda, *Raizes do Brasil*, 3rd ed. (Rio de Janeiro: José Olympio, 1956), 188. The author's broader thesis rests on the assumption that "the Portuguese, in their ability to adapt themselves to all environments, many of which ran counter to their own racial and cultural characteristics, revealed a greater colonizing capacity than the other [European] peoples, perhaps more closely tied to the peculiar conditions of the Old World."

23. Karl Marx, *Critique of Hegel's Philosophy of Right* (Cambridge: Cambridge University Press, 1970), 131.

24. T. S. Eliot, *Notes toward the Definition of Culture* (New York: Harcourt, Brace, 1949), 64.

25. Alphonse Dupront, *L'acculturazione. Per un nuovo rapporto tra ricerca storica e scienze umane*, 3rd ed. (Turin: Einaudi, 1971), 89.

26. José de Anchieta, *Cartas, informações, fragmentos históricos e sermões (1554-94)* (Rio de Janeiro: Academia Brasileira de Letras, 1933), 334.

27. Anchieta, *Cartas, informações*, 334.

28. Anchieta, *Cartas, informações*, 334.

29. Anchieta, *Cartas, informações*, 375.

30. See Eduardo Hoornaert, "Rio de Janeiro, uma igreja perseguida," *Revista Eclesiástica Brasileira*, Petrópolis, Vozes (1971); Américo Jacobina Lacombe, "A Igreja no Brasil colonial," *História geral da civilização brasileira*, ed. S. B. de Holanda, book 1, vol. 2 (Difel, 1977). On the situation in Bahia, see Thales de Azevedo's exemplary study *Igreja e Estado em tensão e crise* (São Paulo: Ática, 1978).

31. Vico wrote the following: "In children memory is most vigorous, and imagination is therefore excessively vivid, for imagination is nothing but extended

or compounded memory." Giambattista Vico, *The New Science*, trans. Thomas Goddard Bergin and Max Harold Fisch (Ithaca, NY: Cornell University Press, 1984), 75. This translation follows the 1744 edition of Vico's text (book 1, section 2, paragraph L).

32. "History shows that all peoples who are superior in civilization are moved by an instinctive force, and sometimes in spite of themselves, to found colonies" (*Larousse du XXe Siècle*, ed. Paul Augé [Paris: Librairie Larousse, 1928], s.v. "colonisation.)"

33. English translations from *Os Lusíadas* are taken from the following edition: Luis Vaz de Camões, *The Lusiads*, trans. Landeg White (Oxford: Oxford University Press, 1997).

34. Why did the poet choose an anonymous old man, someone of whom we know nothing other than his advanced age and his "venerable appearance," as the poem's spokesman of discontent? The weight of the Old Man's experience was certainly a strong factor in this choice, as was, moreover, the uniqueness of this very experience. The little we know of Portuguese demographics during this period leads us to believe that the average life expectancy could not have been more than forty years. Vasco da Gama was not yet thirty when D. Manuel appointed him to lead his fleet to India, and Pedro Álvares Cabral was only thirty-two when he reached the Brazilian coast. The youth of those who crewed the Portuguese ships can easily be guessed. In this context, old age conveys a kind of uncommon wisdom, as well as prudence and a groundedness that stand in contrast to the daring of the youthful sailors.

35. In *A literatura portuguesa e a expansão ultramarina*, Hernâni Cidade writes of what he expressively calls the "shadows in the painting," assembling various literary and historical episodes that communicate sadness, anguish, and even open indignation at the dark side of Portugal's overseas enterprise. Among the "chords in the great elegy" are passages from Garcia de Resende's *Cancioneiro geral*, João de Barros's *Décadas*, Diogo do Couto's *Soldado prático*, and later the tormented *História trágico-marítima*, whose twelve shipwreck narratives provide effective testimony of the disasters suffered by the Portuguese in the Atlantic and Indian Oceans. Camões was well aware of the sinister side of the expansionist adventure: the lies, raids, killings (some of which involved attempted cannibalism by starved Portuguese shipwreck victims), rapes, escapes, and suicides provided him with ample material for an anti-epic of colonization.

36. See the following exemplary studies: Maria Isaura Pereira de Queiroz's *O messianismo no Brasil e no mundo* (São Paulo: Dominus, 1965); Maurício Vinhas de Queiroz's *Messianismo e conflito social*, 3rd ed. (São Paulo: Ática, 1977); and Duglas Teixeira Monteiro's *Os errantes do novo século* (São Paulo: Duas Cidades, 1976). Behind all of this is Euclides da Cunha's *Os sertões* (1902).

37. See O. E. Xidieh, *Narrativas pias populares* (1967) and *Semana santa cabocla* (1972), both published by the Institute for Brazilian Studies, University of

São Paulo. "Popular culture," states Xidieh, "is a historical phenomenon, but whose date of origin can only be sociologically or anthropologically established through identification of situations in which old and new sociocultural models enter into conflict. By the time history 'speaks,' it has already occurred. . . . Yet what I want to underscore is that popular culture, while it is no longer primitive culture, nonetheless perpetuates, through inheritance or discovery, innumerable of its traces and patterns: *tradition, analogy, consideration of the natural world's laws, a magical approach to life, a sense of repetition*. But its dynamic can also be expressed through a popular saying, 'God makes things better hour by hour' (*De hora em hora Deus melhora*), which demonstrates its capacity for renovation and re-elaboration," in O. E. Xidieh, "Cultura popular," *Feira nacional da cultura popular* (São Paulo: Sesc, 1976), 14.

38. In Sílvio Romero, *Folclore brasileiro. Cantos populares do Brasil*, 3rd ed. (Belo Horizonte: Itaiaia, 1985), 294. See also João Ribeiro's commentary in *O folclore*, 27.

39. Translator's note: *Leixa-pren* is a poetic term associated with medieval Galaico-Portuguese poetry, and specifically, *cantigas de amigo*; it consists of the use of the second verse of a pair of stanzas as the first verse in the following pair of stanzas.

40. See Eduardo Etzel, *Imagens religiosas de São Paulo* (São Paulo: Melhoramentos, 1971).

41. Luís Saia, *Escultura popular brasileira* (São Paulo: Gaveta, 1944).

42. Etzel, *Imagens religiosas de São Paulo*.

43. Nina Rodrigues, "Ilusões da catequese," *Revista do Brasil* (1896); *Os africanos no Brasil*, 5th ed. (São Paulo: Nacional, 1977), written in 1916.

44. Mário de Andrade wrote the very first essay dealing with Aleijadinho's artistic and social significance. His "O Aleijadinho" (1928), later included in *Aspectos das artes plásticas no Brasil*, deals particularly with the artist's sculptural expressiveness and his condition as a mulatto.

45. Morales de los Rios, cited by Afonso Taunay, *A missão artística de 1816* (Rio de Janeiro: MEC, 1956), 51.

46. Published in 1872 in *O seminarista*. For criticism on this point, see Lourival Gomes Machado's article "Muito longe da perfeição," in *Barroco mineiro* (São Paulo: Perspectiva, 1978).

47. According to Pierre Verger, the term *candomblé* only came into use in Brazil in the first years of the nineteenth century or, more precisely, in 1826: "Before this time, the most common term used to describe the body of African-origin religious practices seems to have been *Calundu*, an Angolan word. Another term used was *batuque*, though this was used to describe both religious rituals and secular forms of entertainment" (*Notícias da Bahia—1850* [Salvador: Corrupio], 227).

48. Nuno Marques Pereira (Bahia, 1862–Lisbon, 1731), *Compêndio narrativo*

do Peregrino da América. Em que se tratam vários discursos espirituais, e morais, com muitas advertências e documentos contra os abusos que se acham introduzidos pela malícia diabólica no Estado do Brasil, 6th ed., vol. 1 (Rio de Janeiro: Academia Brasileira de Letras, 1939), 123.

2. Anchieta, or the Crossed Arrows of the Sacred

1. Translator's note: *Língua geral* is the standardized form of the language of the Tupi-Guarani, one of Brazil's largest indigenous groups; it was used as a vehicle for communication between Europeans and Amerindians during the colonial period, especially by Jesuits.

2. Joseph de Anchieta, S.J., *Poesias. Manuscrito do século XVI, em português, castelhano, latim e tupi*, transcription, translation, and notes by Maria de Lourdes de Paula Martins (São Paulo: Comissão do IV Centenário, 1954), 556.

3. See Hélène Clastres's reconstruction of Tupi-Guarani beliefs in *Terra sem mal* (São Paulo: Brasiliense, 1978). Anthropologists have thus far not come to an agreement regarding the degree to which the Judeo-Christian God is equivalent to Tupã. H. Clastres subscribes partially to the God = Tupã equation. Her analysis centers on the Guaranis' beliefs regarding the Apocalypse (leading her to emphasize Tupã as a destructive figure). In contrast, Alfred Métraux, Egon Schaden, and Léon Cadogan view this equation as arbitrary and a product of the Jesuit imagination. According to Curt Nimuendaju, who lived in intimate contact with the Ñandava-Guarani during the first years of the twentieth century, the correspondence between Tupã and the Christian God of creation is the product of the "missionaries' fantasy" and is not borne out in the narratives he himself collected. His volume, *As lendas da criação do mundo como fundamentos da religião dos apapocuva-guarari* (São Paulo: Hucitec/Edusp, 1987), is a key reference; the original German volume was published in Berlin in 1914.

4. Letter to General Diogo Lainez, of São Vicente, 16 April 1593, in *Cartas, informações, fragmentos históricos e sermões* (Belo Horizonte: Itaiaia, 1988), 199–200.

5. Anchieta, *Cartas, informações*, 339.

6. Anchieta, *Poesias. Manuscrito do século XVI*, 684–86.

7. Anchieta, *Poesias. Manuscrito do século XVI*, 684–86.

8. *Tarracón* or *tarrascón*. "Augmentative of *tarasca* (Fr. *Tarasque*; mod. Prov. *tarasco*): ghost; fantastic creature; monstrous serpent, with an enormous, biting mouth, that in certain regions would appear depicted in the procession of Corpus Christi. In Portuguese, the word comes into use in the 16th century" (Edith Pimentel Pinto, *O auto da ingratidão* [São Paulo: Conselho Estadual de Artes e Ciências Humanas, 1978], 258).

9. English translation of Dante: Dante Alighieri, *The Divine Comedy*, trans. Allen Mandelbaum (New York: Alfred A. Knopf, 1995).

10. Walter Benjamin, *A origem do drama barroco* (São Paulo: Brasiliense, 1984). The German original dates from 1925.

11. George Lukács, "Símbolo y alegoria," chapter in *Estética 1*, vol. 4 (Barcelona: Grijalbo, 1967), 405. Translator's note: I do not know which Lukács work Bosi is quoting from, but a rough translation of Bosi's quotation is: The old allegory, determined by a religious transcendence, had as its mission to humiliate the earthly reality, comparing it to the ultramundane or celestial, until its full nullity.

12. Translator's note: This is Brenda Machovsky's English translation of number 749 of Goethe's *Maximen und Reflexionen*.

13. See Helmut Hatzfeld: "Saint John of the Cross effectively considered lyrical expression a stylized cry and writes in the introduction to his *Llama de amor viva* (Living Flame of Love) that poems should occasionally make use of exclamations such as *oh!* and *ah!* in order to give adequate expression to the ineffable. In the same way, Valéry declared: 'Poetry is an attempt to represent . . . by articulate language, those things or that thing, by way of tears, cries, caresses, kisses, etc.'" (*Estudios literarios sobre mística española* [Madrid: Gredos, 1968], 329).

3. From Our Former State to the Mercantile Machine

1. Francisco Rodrigues Lobo's fine sonnet, "Formoso Tejo meu" (My Beautiful Tagus), comes immediately to mind, for the similar stylistic game it plays:

Fermoso Tejo meu, quão diferente
Te vejo e vi, me vês agora e viste:
Turvo te vejo a ti, tu a mim triste.
Claro te vi eu já, tu a mim contente.

A ti foi-te trocando a grossa enchente
A quem teu largo campo não resiste:
A mim trocou-me a vista em que consiste
O meu viver contente ou descontente.

Já que somos no mal participantes,
Sejamo-lo no bem. Oh! quem me dera
Que fôramos em tudo semelhantes!

Mas lá virá a fresca primavera:
Tu tornarás a ser quem eras de antes,
Eu não sei se serei quem de antes era.

My beautiful Tagus, how changed
I now see and saw you, and you see and saw me:
I see your waters murky, you see me sad.
I saw your waters clear, you saw me happy.

You have been changed by the great flood
Which your vast plain could not resist:
It changed for me my view
Of whether my life was happy or sad.

As we have participated together in bad things,
Let us do so in good. Oh! God willing
That we would be alike in all respects!

But the cool Spring will come:
You will again be what you once were,
I know not if the same will be true of me.

Although the two poems share lexical and grammatical forms, an analogy of function cannot be said to exist between them. In Rodrigues Lobo's sonnet, the lyrical word invokes and evokes the Tejo, Portugal's national river, and conveys a sense of union with it: "Oh! God willing / That we would be alike in all respects!"). In Gregório, however, censure and punishment violently divide the man from his city. Once again, a Mannerist poet from the seventeenth century draws on an illustrious precedent to lend greater nobility to his diction by enriching it with classical references. However, in placing one's ear against the conch shell of the poem, the echo one hears takes on a distinct meaning.

2. See Roberto Simonsen, *História econômica do Brasil (1500–1820)*, 3rd ed. (São Paulo: Nacional, 1957); Magalhães Godinho, "Portugal, as frotas do açúcar e as frotas de ouro," *Revista de História*, no. 15 (1953): 69–88; Frédéric Mauro, *Nova história e Novo Mundo* (São Paulo: Perspectiva, 1969).

3. Mauro, *Nova história e Novo Mundo*, 112.

4. Apud Celso Furtado, *Formação econômica do Brasil* (Rio de Janeiro: Fundo de Cultura, 1959), 46.

5. Bahia laments its invaders

"I remember that there was a time
(this was when I was young)
when the seed that they gave me,
was good, and from good stock.
And so my lands
produced fine fruit,
of which there are still
some faint signs.
But after you arrived
weighed down like a goldsmith
with jealous seeds,
some with wicked vices;
I declined along with you,
and I have suffered such a change,
that what once gave roses
now only gives thorns."

6. See "Vida do excelente poeta lírico, o doutor Gregório de Matos e Guerra,"

transcribed in the seventh volume of Gregório de Mato's *Obras completas*, ed. James Amado (Salvador: Ed. Janaína), 1689–721.

7. See Antonio Gramsci, *Gli intellettuali e l'organizzazione della cultura* (Rome: Ed. Riuniti, 1977), 3–23.

8. Amador Arrais, *Diálogos* (Lisbon: Sá da Costa, 1944), 167. Pages earlier, Arrais exclaimed: "Fortunate is the land, whose king is noble!" (132).

9. Translator's note: The English expression "sore point" probably best conveys the meaning of the Latin phrase *punctum dolens* in this context.

10. Abdias do Nascimento takes another look at the problem of the meaning of miscegenation in "Nota breve sobre a mulher negra," *O quilombismo* (Petrópolis: Vozes, 1980), 229–44.

11. M. Bakhtin, *La cultura popular en la Edad Media y en el Renacimiento. El contexto de François Rabelais*, Spanish translation (Barcelona: Barral Ed., 1974); the Russian edition is from 1965.

12. Armando Plebe, *La nascita del comico* (Bari: Ed. Laterza, 1956).

13. On this broad topic, see João Adolfo Hansen's complex and wide-ranging analysis in *A sátira e o engenho, Gregório de Matos e a Bahia do século XVII* (São Paulo: Companhia das Letras, 1989).

14. Gracián, *El Comulgatorio—Meditación XLIV* [1655], (Barcelona: Ed. Labor, 1947), 163.

4. Vieira, or the Cross of Inequality

1. See Artur Cézar Ferreira Reis's study, "O comércio colonial e as companhias privilegiadas," in *História geral da civilização brasileira*, 2 vols., ed. Sérgio Buarque de Holanda, vol. 1, *A época colonial* (São Paulo: Difel, 1977), 311–51.

2. Antônio Vieira, *Sermões*, vol. 3, book 8 (Porto: Lello), 55. All quotations from Vieira are from this edition.

3. Vieira, *Sermões*, vol. 1, 1:42.

4. Vieira, *Sermões*, vol. 1, 1:56–57.

5. Vieira, *Sermões*, vol. 1, 1:57–58.

6. Vieira, *Sermões*, vol. 1, 1:58.

7. Vieira, *Sermões*, vol. 1, 1:212.

8. Vieira, *Sermões*, vol. 1, 1:208.

9. In *A Contribution to the Critique of Political Economy*. Engels's text was first published in the *Deutsch Französische Jahrbücher*, in Paris in 1844. The Portuguese translation I utilized is by Maria Filomena Viegas, revised by José Paulo Netto and published in the journal *Temas de Ciências Humanas* (São Paulo, Huitec), no. 5 (1979). These quotes are taken from the following edition: K. Marx and F. Engels, *Karl Marx/Friedrich Engels Collected Works*, 50 vols. (London: Lawrence and Wishart, 1975–).

10. Vieira, *Sermões*, vol. 3, 1:155.

11. Vieira, *Sermões*, vol. 3, 1:157.

12. Vieira, *Sermões*, vol. 3, 1:158.

13. Vieira, *Sermões*, vol. 4, 1:372.

14. Vieira, *Sermões*, vol. 2, 4:203–4.

15. The presence of an anti-Baroque—or more precisely, antirhetorical—vein in Vieira's work, which is in the final analysis Baroque, demands a study that would assess the weight of mercantilist thinking in the discourse of the great preacher. The perplexity one notes in Antônio José Saraiva's essay on the *Sermão da Sexagésima* seems to me a signal that Vieira's modern readers have become perplexed in the face of his contradictions. See Antônio José Saraiva, *O discurso engenhoso* (São Paulo, Perspectiva, 1980), 113–24.

16. Vieira, *Sermões*, 210–11.

17. Vieira, *Sermões*, vol. 1, 2:44.

18. Pope Paul III, "Sublimus Dei," *Papal Encyclicals Online*, May 29, 1537, available at http://www.papalencyclicals.net/Paul03/p3subli.htm.

19. Vieira, *Sermões*, vol. 1, 2:42–43.

20. On this topic, see José Oscar Beozzo's study, *Leis e regimentos das missões* (São Paulo: Loyola, 1983). For related documents, including various letters written by Vieira, Serafim Leite's *História da Companhia de Jesus no Brasil* (Lisbon: Rio de Janeiro, 1983) is indispensable, especially volumes 3 and 4.

21. Vieira, *Sermões*, vol. 1, 2:32.

22. See the *Defesa perante a Tribunal do Santo Ofício*, with an introduction and notes by Hernani Cidade (Salvador: Publicações da Universidade da Bahia, 1957), two volumes.

23. Vieira, *Sermões*, vol. 1, 3:16.

24. Vieira, *Sermões*, vol. 1, 3:20.

25. "According to the *Informação que por ordem do Conselho Ultramarino deu sobre as coisas do Maranhão ao mesmo conselho* (Report on Things Pertaining to Maranhão Given by the Order of the Overseas Council to the Same Council), Vieira reported that the Amerindian population of Maranhão decreased by two million between 1615 and 1652! In 1650, the Portuguese population of Maranhão was no larger than eight hundred persons. In truth, these numbers are comparable to those given by Bartolomé de las Casas regarding the slaughter of Amerindians during the Spanish conquest of the Caribbean" (Eduardo Hoornaert et al., *História da Igreja no Brasil. Primeira época* [Petrópolis: Vozes, 1977], 88).

26. Vieira, *Sermões*, vol. 4, 11:315.

27. Vieira, *Sermões*, vol. 4, 11:315.

28. Karl Marx, *Economic and Philosophical Manuscripts of 1844*, trans. Martin Mulligan (Moscow: Progress Publishers, 1959).

29. Vieira, *Sermões*, vol. 4, 12:330.

30. Vieira, *Sermões*, vol. 4, 12:331.

31. Vieira, *Sermões*, vol. 4, 12:81.

32. Vieira, *Sermões*, vol. 4, 12:91.
33. Vieira, *Sermões*, vol. 4, 12:82.
34. Vieira, *Sermões*, vol. 4, 20:357.
35. Vieira, *Sermões*, vol. 4, 20:358.

5. Antonil, or the Tears of Trade Goods

1. Serafim Leite, *História da Companhia de Jesus no Brasil*, vol. 8 (Lisbon: INL, 1949).

2. This is the *Compendium vitae pereximii patris Antonii Vieyrae*, a copy of which is found in the Archive of the Company in Rome (Lusitania 58[2]: 520–27). In the *Anais da Biblioteca Nacional do Rio de Janeiro*, XIX (1897), it was published under the title "Carta do p. reytor do Collegio da Bahia em que dá conta ao p. geral da morte do p. Antonio Vieyra e refere as principais acçoens de sua vida. Bahia, 20 de julho do ano de 1697" (Letter from the Rector of the College of Bahia in Which He Informs the Superior General of the Death of Father Antônio Vieira and Discusses the Principal Events of His Life. Bahia, July 20, 1697).

3. See a letter written by Vieira to the Bishop of Pernambuco, in *Cartas*, edited by the University of Coimbra, vol. 3, 554.

4. In *História geral do Brasil*, 9th ed., vol. 2, book 4 (São Paulo: Melhoramentos, 1978), 98.

5. *Cartas*, ed. Lúcio de Azevedo, vol. 3 (University of Coimbra, 1928), 670.

6. Acosta, apud Lewin Hanke, *Aristóteles e os índios americanos* (São Paulo: Martins, s.d.), 116.

7. Apud Leite, *História da Companhia de Jesus no Brasil*, 7:111. The adverb *statim* may be translated as "already," but it can also be translated as "always" or "normally," as the Latinist Flávio Vespasiano DiGiorgi explained to me. He considers this alternate meaning in line with Andreoni's desired outcome. [Translator's note: My translation is somewhat speculative. My assumption is that Andreoni is arguing that if priests can rent out "their Indians" and be paid, then they should be able to use them as laborers themselves and profit from them directly.]

8. In *La Sinagoga disingannata, ovvero via facile a mostrare a qualunque ebreo la falsità della sua setta e la verità della legge Cristiana* (Bologna: Longhi, 1694). Andreoni's translation was published by the Officina da Musica in Lisbon in 1720.

9. In Francisco Rodrigues, "O p. Antônio Vieira. Contradições e aplausos. À luz de documentação inédita," *Revista de História* 11 (Lisbon, 1922): 114. The *Index manuscriptorum p. Antonii Vieyrae, quae post mortem in eius cubiculo inventa sunt. Bahiae, 22 Juli 1697*, which is a list of the documents found in Vieira's cell, and which Andreoni placed in a chest and sent to the Italian headquarters of the company, is found in the Roman Archive.

10. See Alice Canabrava's substantial introduction to the eighth edition of *Cultura e opulência do Brasil* (São Paulo: Nacional, 1967).

11. José Paulo Paes perceptively observed this in "A alma do negócio," *Mistério em casa* (São Paulo: Comissão de Literatura, 1961).

12. From Antonil, *Cultura e opulência do Brasil*: "Having reached the mill and having been placed between the gears, what force and suffering are used in taking from them what they have to give" (168–69).

13. Isaiah 63:3. The King James Bible renders this phrase as follows: "I have trodden the winepress alone." Isaiah refers to the container in which the grapes were crushed by the feet of the vineyard workers. Ruy Gama notes that such presses "were used on more primitive sugar plantations before the invention of the mill powered by three vertical arms" (Ruy Gama, *Engenho e tecnologia* [São Paulo: Duas Cidades, 1983], 97).

14. Antônio Vieira, *Sermões*, vol. 4 (Oporto: Lello & Irmão, 1959), 2:305–6.

15. Vieira, *Sermões*, 312. I have retained the punctuation from this edition.

16. "Note the use of the plural." This is Bosi's ellipsis—Trans.

6. A Sacrificial Myth: Alencar's Indianism

1. The reader will find a good deal of reactionary thought from Brazil, which remained dominant until the 1860s, in the *Anais do Parlamento*, printed in Rio de Janeiro by the Tipografia Villeneuve. See also the following chapter, "Slavery between Two Liberalisms."

2. This phrase is taken from a classic work of Latin American historiography, *La patria del criollo*, by Severo Martínez Peláez, who applied this idea to Guatemala's national formation (Costa Rica: Editorial Centroamericana, 1973).

3. Machado de Assis, "*Iracema*, por José de Alencar," *Diário do Rio de Janeiro*, January 23, 1866.

4. Augusto Meyer, "Alencar e a tenuidade brasileira," in José de Alencar, *Ficção completa e outros escritos*, vol. 2 (Rio de Janeiro: Aguilar, 1964), 11–24.

5. Brazilian version published in Porto Alegre by L&PM, 1985.

6. See Revelation, chapter 6. See Curt Nimuendaju's *As lendas da criação e destruição do mundo como fundamentos da religião dos apapocuva-guarari* (São Paulo: Hucitec/Edusp, 1987) on the language of the Tupi-Guarani apocalypse. There is no evidence to suggest that Gonçalves Dias could have been aware of the legends that Nimuendaju collected and translated at the beginning of the twentieth century. At any rate, the figures included in the Guarani narratives, which center on erosion and especially on floods, do not match the cataclysmic signs evoked in the "Canto do piaga."

7. Around 1972, at the request of Anatol Rosenfeld, I [Bosi] wrote an essay entitled "Imagens do Romantismo no Brasil" (Images of Romanticism in Brazil). This topic, in somewhat expanded form, is addressed in the section of this chapter entitled "Um Castelo no Trópico?" (A Castle in the Tropics?).

8. Translator's note: The indigenous legend of Tamandaré relates the story of a great flood in which Tupã (God) tells Tamandaré that he will flood the Earth.

Tamandaré and his wife flee to the top of a mountain to wait out the storm, from which they later descend.

7. Slavery between Two Liberalisms

1. A. Figueira, *Anais do Parlamento* (Rio de Janeiro: Tip. Villeneuve, 1871), appendix, 26.

2. *Casa-grande & senzala* and *Sobrados e mocambos*, by Gilberto Freyre; *Formação do Brasil contemporâneo*, by Caio Prado Jr.; *História do café no Brasil*, by Affonso de Taunay; *Capitalism and Slavery*, by Eric Williams; *Formação econômica do Brasil*, by Celso Furtado; *Vassouras, a Brazilian Coffee County, 1850–1900*, by Stanley Stein; *Capitalismo e escravidão no Brasil meridional*, by Fernando Henrique Cardoso; *As metamorfoses do escravo*, by Octávio Ianni; *Da senzala à colônia*, by Emília Viotti da Costa; *Homens livres na ordem escravocrata*, by Maria Sylvia Carvalho Franco; *A formação do povo no complexo cafeeiro*, by Paula Beiguelman; *The Destruction of Brazilian Slavery, 1850–1888*, by Robert Conrad; and *O escravismo colonial*, by Jacob Gorender. These titles provide us with an analysis of the process through which the owners of the sugar and coffee plantations regulated the economic life of the new nation and imposed, beginning with the breaking of the colonial pact, their hegemony in close connection with international commerce and the slave trade. The political activity of this class found able interpreters in Tavares Bastos (*A província, Cartas do solitário*), Joaquim Nabuco (*Um estadista do Império*), José Maria dos Santos (*A política geral do Brasil*), Victor Nunes Leal (*Coronelismo, enxada e voto*), Raymundo Faoro (*Os donos do poder*), José Honório Rodrigues (*Conciliação e reforma no Brasil*), and Sérgio Buarque de Holanda (*Do Império à República*).

3. Translator's note: Father Diogo Antônio Feijó (1784–1843) was a moderate liberal politician who served as regent prior to Emperor Dom Pedro II's majority.

4. R. Conrad, *Os tumbeiros* (São Paulo: Brasiliense, 1985), 103–4.

5. Conrad, *Os tumbeiros*, 118. See also the following analysis from Stanley Stein: "The increased importation of slaves during the 1840s benefitted plantation owners and public finances alike. In 1848, taxes collected on the sale of slaves accounted for nearly 60% of the tax revenue collected in the town of Vassouras, in the Province of Rio de Janeiro." (Stanley Stein, *Grandeza e decadência do café no vale do Paraíba* [São Paulo: Brasiliense, 1961], 161). [Translator's note: All quotations from Conrad are my translations of Bosi's quotations from Conrad's original work.]

6. O. Duque-Estrada, *A abolição (esboço histórico)* (Rio de Janeiro: Leite Ribeiro & Maurílio, 1918), 28. [Translator's note: The quote is taken from Gladstone's March 19, 1850, speech to the House of Commons.]

7. L. Bethell, *A abolição do tráfico escravo no Brasil* (São Paulo: Edusp, 1976), 73–74.

8. Bethell, *A abolição do tráfico escravo no Brasil*, 74.

9. José de Alencar, *Cartas a Erasmo*, VI.

10. W. Cohen, *Français et Africains. Les Noirs dans le regard des Blancs (1530–1880)* (Paris: Gallimard, 1981), 42–49, 271–78.

11. Tocqueville's overriding preoccupation seems to have been guaranteeing that freed slaves would quickly become workers. This would explain his proposal (which Aimé Césaire considers "cynical") to prohibit freed slaves from owning land, so as to speed their entry into the proletariat:

> If the freed blacks, neither being allowed to remain vagabonds nor acquire a small plot of land, were obliged to make their living by selling their services, it is quite realistic to suppose that the greater part of them would remain on the plantations. . . . Pay closer attention to this matter and you will see that *the temporary ban on possessing land* is not only, of all exceptional means to which one might have recourse, the most effective, but is also the least oppressive. By temporarily banning the blacks from owning land, what do we do? We place them artificially in the position in which the European worker naturally [sic] finds himself. There is surely no tyranny in this, and the man upon whom this restriction is imposed, in leaving captivity, does not seem to have the right to complain. [Translator's note: This is my English translation of Bosi's Portuguese version of Tocqueville's original work.]

See Victor Schoelcher, *Esclavage et colonisation*, with a preface by Aimé Césaire (Paris: PUF, 1948), 9.

12. Translator's note: *Saquarema* was the informal name given to the Conservative Party during the Second Empire. The Conservatives and Liberals (known informally as *Luzias*) dominated the imperial government until the 1870s, which witnessed the emergence of antislavery and republican elements in Brazilian politics.

13. R. Faoro, "Existe um pensamento politico brasileiro?," *Estudos Avançados* (São Paulo), no. 1 (October/December 1987): 44.

14. Apud Joaquim Nabuco, *Um estadista do Império*, 2nd ed. (Rio de Janeiro: Nova Aguilar, 1975).

15. Apud Nabuco, *Um estadista do Império*.

16. O. Tarqüínio de Sousa, *Evaristo da Veiga* (Belo Horizonte: Itatiaia, 1988), 153.

17. P. Silva, "O Brasil no Reinado do sr. Pedro II," in *Escritos políticos e discursos parlamentares* (Rio de Janeiro: Garnier, 1862), 28 (written in French and published in the *Revue des Deux Mondes*, April 15, 1858).

18. O. Tarqüínio de Souza, *Bernardo Pereira de Vasconcelos* (Belo Horizonte: Itatiaia, 1988), 77.

19. Saint-Hilaire, *A segunda viagem do Rio de Janeiro a Minas Gerais e a São Paulo*, trans., rev., and pref. by Vivaldi Moreira (Belo Horizonte: Itaiaia, 1974), 94.

20. Nabuco, *Um estadista do Império*, 77.

21. Eric Hobsbawm, *The Age of Revolution 1789–1848*, 1st ed. (Cleveland: World Publishing, 1962), 240.

22. J. Nabuco, *O abolicionismo*, 4th ed. (Petrópolis: Vozes, 1977), 117–18.

23. P. Malheiro, *A escravidão no Brasil*, 2nd ed., vol. 2 (Petrópolis: Vozes, 1976), 301.

24. *A Treatise upon Trade from Great-Britain to Africa; Humbly Recommended to the Attention of Government by an African Merchant* (London: R. Baldwin, no. 47, Pater-Noster Row, 1772).

25. Glowingly cited by Sílvio Romero in his *História da literatura brasileira*, 5th ed., vol. 5 (Rio de Janeiro: J. Olympio, 1953), 1727–29. The reference to Diogenes' request that Alexander stand out of his light appeared earlier in Bentham's writings against the protection of national industry.

26. R. Walsh, *Notícias do Brasil* (Belo Horizonte: Itatiaia, 1985), 109.

27. J. Dorfman, *The Economic Mind in American Civilization* (New York: Augustes M. Kelley, 1966). See especially the chapter "The Southern Tradition of Laissez-Faire." The entanglement in the South of liberalism with a proslavery ideology caught the attention of a contemporary essayist, John Cairnes, who was read by Marx and Engels and who wrote *The Slave Power* in 1863.

28. J. H. Franklin, *From Slavery to Freedom*, 5th ed. (New York: Alfred Knopf, 1963), 182.

29. A. J. Mello Moraes, *A Inglaterra e seos tractados . . .* (Salvador da Bahia: Tip. Correio Mercantil de F. Vianna e Comp., 1844), 26.

30. Mello Moraes, *A Inglaterra e seos tractados,* 33.

31. Mello Moraes, *A Inglaterra e seos tractados,* 41.

32. G. Myrdal, *An American Dilemma: The Negro Problem in a Modern Democracy* (New York: Harper & Brothers, 1944), 442.

33. Myrdal, *An American Dilemma*, 441.

34. F. W. Knight, "Slavery, Race and Social Structure in Cuba during the 19th Century," in R. B. Toplin, ed., *Slavery and Race Relations in Latin America* (Westport, CT: Greenwood Press, 1974), 221–22. The fusion of liberalism, anti-Spanish nativism, and the defense of slavery was also observed by Eugenio D. Genovese in *O mundo dos senhores de escravos* (Rio de Janeiro: Paz e Terra, 1979), 75–80.

35. T. Bastos, *Cartas do solitário*, 4th ed. (São Paulo: Nacional, 1945), letter 11.

36. S. Martínez Peláez, *La patria del criollo* (Costa Rica: Editorial Universitaria Centroamericana, 1973).

37. A. Smith, *The Wealth of Nations.*

38. Smith, *The Wealth of Nations.*

39. Smith, *The Wealth of Nations.*

40. Jean-Baptiste Say, *A Treatise on Political Economy*, trans. C. R. Prinsep and Clement C. Biddle (Philadelphia: Claxton, Remsen, and Heffelfinger, 1880), 86.

41. Say, *A Treatise on Political Economy*, 87.

42. Say, *A Treatise on Political Economy.*

43. Tarqüínio de Sousa, *Evaristo da Veiga*, 61.

44. In *O Independente*, March 14, 1832, apud Augustin Wernet, *Sociedades políticas* (1831–1832) (São Paulo: Cultrix, 1978), 67.

45. Apud Nabuco, *O abolicionismo*.

46. Apud Nabuco, *Um estadista*, 217–18.

47. Apud Nabuco, *Um estadista*, 319.

48. L. Gama (Getulino), *Primeiras trovas burlescas*, 3rd ed. (São Paulo: Tip. Bentley Júnior & Comp., 1904).

49. "Parties and Elections in Maranhão," *Jornal do Timon*.

50. J. M. V. Santos, *A política geral do Brasil* (São Paulo: J. Magalhães, 1930), 133–54.

51. Joaquim Nabuco, "O terreno da luta," *Jornal do Comércio* (July 19, 1884).

52. Bastos, *Cartas do solitário*, 268.

53. "On plantations in northeastern Pernambuco, for example, where slave labor had predominated at the time of independence, by the 1870s free labor had become more important" (Peter L. Eisenberg, "A abolição da escravatura: o processo nas fazendas de açúcar em Pernambuco," in *Estudos Econômicos* [São Paulo] 2, no. 6 [December 1972]: 181).

54. Apud S. B. de Holanda, *Do Império à República*, 4th ed. (São Paulo: Difel, 1985), 204.

55. J. Nabuco, *Minha formação* (Rio de Janeiro: J. Olympio, 1957), 34.

56. Nabuco, *Minha formação*, 201.

57. Nabuco, *Minha formação*, 59.

58. In *O País*, December 9, 1886; transcribed by Paula Beiguelman, *Joaquim Nabuco. Política* (São Paulo: Ática), 136–37.

59. J. M. Cardoso de Melo, *O capitalismo tardio* (São Paulo: Brasiliense, 1982).

60. Cardoso de Melo, *O capitalismo tardio*, 72.

61. *O Centro Liberal* (Brasília: Ed. Senado Federal, 1979), 44.

62. *O Centro Liberal*, 1000.

63. *O Centro Liberal*, 102.

64. Nabuco, *Um estadista*, 662.

65. Nabuco, *Um estadista*.

66. This is taken from a confidential letter written by Minister Nabuco to Saraiva when the latter was president of the province of São Paulo. The date is September 22, 1854 (Nabuco, *Um estadista*, 207).

67. Q. Bocayuva, *A crise da lavoura* (Rio de Janeiro: Tip. Perseverança, 1868).

68. Nabuco, *Minha formação*, 196.

69. Richard Graham, *A Grã-Bretanha e o início da modernização do Brasil* (São Paulo: Brasiliense, 1973). The richest sources for details on the agricultural reform projects are André Rebouças's articles, written beginning in 1874 for the *Jornal do Comércio* and later compiled in the defining text of the new liberalism, *A*

agricultura nacional. Estudos econômicos. Propaganda abolicionista e democrática (Rio de Janeiro: Lamoureux, 1883).

70. Sílvio Romero, "Explicações indispensáveis (Prefácio)," in T. Barreto, *Vários escritos*, Editorial do Estado de Sergipe (1926), xxiii–xxiv. Euclides da Cunha speaks of an *Era Nova* (New Era) in his characterization of the post-1868 period (*À margem da história*).

71. V. Schoelcher, *Esclavage et colonisation*, preface by Aimé Césaire (Paris: PUF, 1948), 11. The English translation included in the footnote is my translation from Bosi's Portuguese translation.

72. Nabuco, *Um estadista*, 613.

73. Machado de Assis ironized—and auto-ironized as a narrator—the mode of thought by which the ruling class, at the end of the imperial regime, upheld modern liberal norms *in abstracto*, at the same time as they rationalized the use of slave labor, this class's principal economic and political support. In this context, and seen from the outside inward, this boastful classical liberalism is nonsensical, though it nonetheless had implications for the daily lives of the national bourgeoisie. This is, in sum, the hypothesis Roberto Schwarz proposed and successfully defended in his study of Machado de Assis, *Ao vencedor as batatas* (São Paulo: Duas Cidades, 1977).

74. *Atas* of the Legislative Assembly of São Paulo for 1870, apud Emília Viotti Costa, *Da senzala à colônia*, (São Paulo: Difel, 1966), 132.

75. "O trabalho nacional e seus adversários," *Biblioteca da Associação Industrial* (Rio de Janeiro, 1881), 13, apud Edgard Carone, *O pensamento industrial no Brasil (1880–1945)* (São Paulo: Difel, 1977), 151.

76. J. M. Santos, *Os republicanos paulistas e a abolição* (São Paulo: Martins, 1942), 118–19, 150.

77. Santos, *Os republicanos paulistas e a abolição*, 225.

78. Letter to Rebouças, Rio de Janeiro, January 1, 1893, transcribed in Joaquim Nabuco, *Cartas a amigos*, São Paulo, Ipê, vol. 1, p. 219.

79. *Jornal do Comércio*, September 11, 1884.

8. Under the Sign of Ham

1. Heine's original is part of the cycle *Gedichte, 1853–54*. The parentheses with [sic] were inserted by the Brazilian translator. Augusto Meyer comments, in comparing Heine's text first to Béranger's "Les nègres et les marionettes," and then with Castro Alves's poem: "Heine approaches the subject with a realistic objectivity not seen in the others. For him the question of slavery was part and parcel of the question of class relations and the economic structure of capitalism. In a text from 1842, collected in the *Französische Zustade*, the poet, criticizing the innocuous liberalism of certain circles of German nobles, represented by Count Moltke, stated: 'Count Moltke certainly considers slavery the great scandal of our

age, and a flagrant monstrosity." But in the opinion of Myn Heer van der Null, a Rotterdam slave trader, the slave trade is a natural and justified activity, and on the contrary, what to him appears monstrous are the privileges of the aristocracy, titles and inherited privileges, the absurd prejudice that favors nobility of blood" (A. Meyer, "Os três navios negreiros," *Correio da Manhã*, August 19, 1967). I thank Marcus Vinicius Mazzari for providing me with Augusto Meyer's translation and article.

2. Translator's note: Translation is from the following edition: Heinrich Heine, *The Poems of Heine*, trans. Edgar Alfred Bowring (London: George Bell and Sons, 1981), pp. 508–9.

3. Translator's note: From an article published in the *Jornal do Comércio*, August 14, 1899, trans. R. Newcomb.

4. Translator's note: Bosi's original says Judges 1:29 and Joshua (17:10); the organization of the King James version seems at odds with Bosi's Portuguese version.

5. There is an allusion to Ham's curse in Zurara's chronicle, which narrates the first instances in which the Portuguese captured slaves along the African coast. Scholastic theology, which was codified in the centuries prior to the Iberian discoveries (c. 1100–1400) did not need to develop a discourse to justify slavery. Saint Thomas Aquinas linked slavery to war, and war to the degeneration suffered by mankind due to original sin: "in statu innocentiae non fuisset tale dominium hominis ad hominem" (S. T., 1, 9.96, 4c). Aquinas speaks generically of "dominion of one man over another." Concretely, what the theology of his time was familiar with was feudal servitude, which in several respects was distinct from the black, colonial, and mercantile slavery of the modern age.

6. Numerous examples of this interpretation of slavery can be found in David B. Davis, *The Problem of Slavery in Western Culture* (Ithaca, NY: Cornell University Press, 1966). The conservative theology of the Catholic and Protestant missions made use, during the nineteenth century, of the curse of Ham to justify colonialist attitudes in Africa. See Albert Perbal, "La race nègre et la malédiction de Cham," *Revue de l'Université d'Ottawa* 4 (1940): 156–77.

7. Translator's note: This and the following Vigny quote in English are from Alan D. Corré's translation, available here: http://minds.wisconsin.edu/bitstream/handle/1793/61400/eloaweb.html?sequence=1.

8. In *Careta*, Rio de Janeiro, January 24, 1920. Transcribed in *Coisas do reino do Jambon* (São Paulo: Brasiliense, 1956), 110.

9. Translator's note: *Bruzundanga*: the fictional inhabits of Bruzundanga, a country invented by the writer Lima Barreto to satirize Brazil of the First Republic; Barreto's book *Os Bruzundangas* was posthumously published in 1922.

10. Translator's note: Here, *mesticismo* refers to the celebration of ethnic and cultural miscegnation. In Portuguese a multiracial person can be referred to as a *mestiço*, and miscegnation is termed *miscigenação*.

11. See D. Brookshaw's observations in *Raça e cor na literatura brasileira* (Porto Alegre: Mercado Aberto, 1983), 169.

12. For analysis of this theme in the work of Lima Barreto, see Zenir Campos Reis's essay, "Vidas em tempos escuros," in *Nossa América*, São Paulo, Memorial da América Latina, no. 3 (July/August 1990): 32–38.

9. The Archeology of the Welfare State

1. A. Gerschenkron, *Economic Backwardness in Historical Perspective* (Cambridge, MA: Belknap Press, 1966), 22.

2. Gerschenkron, *Economic Backwardness*, 24. Translator's note: This is my translation back to English from Bosi's translation to Portuguese of the original English.

3. J. Cruz Costa, *Contribuição à história das idéias no Brasil* (Rio de Janeiro: J. Olympio, 1956); I. Lins, *História do positivismo no Brasil* (São Paulo: Nacional, 1964).

4. Cruz Costa, *Contribuição à história das idéias no Brasil*, 285. In Carpeaux's view, the authoritarian elements within our political history most fully assimilated the positivists' message.

5. Sérgio da Costa Franco, *Júlio de Castilhos e sua época*, 2nd ed. (Porto Alegre: Editora da Universidade, 1988), the first edition was published in 1967; Joseph Love, *O regionalismo gaúcho* (São Paulo: Perspectiva, 1975). The following university publications are worth consulting: Sandra Jatahy Pesavento, *A burguesia gaúcha. Dominação do capital e disciplina do trabalho* (Porto Alegre: Mercado Aberto, 1988); Guilhermino César et al., *RS: economia e política*, ed. J. Dacanal and S. Gonzaga (Porto Alegre: Mercado Aberto, 1979); Décio Freitas et al., *RS: cultura e ideologia* (Porto Alegre: Mercado Aberto, 1980), see particularly Nelson Boeira's essay, "O Rio Grande de Augusto Comte"); Hélgio Trindade, "La 'Dictature Républicaine' au Rio Grande do Sul: positivisme et pratique au Brésil," *Cahiers du Brasil Contemporain* (Paris: Maison des Sciences de l'Homme) (no. 12, December 1990); Hélgio Trindade, *Poder Legislativo e autoritarismo no RGS* (Porto Alegre: Sulina, 1980); Céli Regina Pinto, *Positivismo. Um projeto politico alternativo (RS: 1889–1930)* (Porto Alegre: LP&M, 1986); Pedro Cézar Dutra Fonseca, *Vargas: o capitalismo em construção* (São Paulo: Brasiliense, 1989). Published before this bevy of works from Rio Grande do Sul, we find Tocary Assis Bastos's article, "O positivismo e a realidade brasileira," in which the author directly ties the interventionist actions of the 1930s and 1940s to Getúlio Vargas's positivist values and those of his closest advisors (*Revista Brasileira de Estudos Políticos*, Belo Horizonte, 1956).

6. See chapter 7, "Slavery between Two Liberalisms."

7. See Terezinha Collichio, *Miranda Azevedo e o darwinismo no Brasil* (São Paulo: Edusp, 1988). See also an incisive note by Miguel Lemos, who in his

capacity as president-for-life of the Positivist Society censured certain opinions expressed by Pereira Bastos regarding the benefits for Africans of slavery. M. Lemos countered the articles published by the medical doctor from São Paulo in 1880 in the *Província de São Paulo* with Comte's categorical doctrine on slavery in *O Positivismo e a escravidão moderna* (Rio de Janeiro, Sociedade Positivista, 1884), 6.

8. Miguel Lemos, *O positivismo e a escravidão moderna* (Rio de Janeiro: Boletim do Centro Positivista Brasileiro, 1884). Comte proposed that the French Antilles be given to freed blacks from all of the Americas for resettlement. See also *A incorporação do proletariado escravo: protesto da Sociedade Positivista do Rio de Janeiro contra o recente projeto do governo*, in which Miguel Lemos exclaims indignantly: "No! A thousand times no! They have the right neither to indemnification nor to the air that we breathe" (Recife: Typographia Mercantil, 1883), 3.

9. In *Idéias políticas de Júlio de Castilhos*, ed. Paulo Carneiro (Senado Federal, 1982), 163–64.

10. S. B. de Holanda, "Da maçonaria ao positivismo," *O Brasil monárquico*, vol. 2 (São Paulo: Diffel, 1977), 290.

11. In *A incorporação do proletariado na sociedade moderna*, 2nd ed. (Rio de Janeiro: Templo da Humanidade, 1908), 10.

12. Cruz Costa, *Contribuição à história das idéias no Brasil*, 247.

13. In *A cruzada* (Rio de Janeiro, July 1883).

14. S. B. de Holanda, *Raízes do Brasil* (Rio de Janeiro: J. Olympio, 1936), 120.

15. For an explanation of the tensions between the Jacobins and the government of Prudente de Moraes, see Suely Robles de Queiroz's study, *Os radicais da República* (São Paulo: Brasiliense, 1986).

16. The *Cours de philosophie positive* was published between 1830 and 1842. Statements can be found affirming that it was read in Brazil beginning in the 1850s.

17. *Cours de philosophie positive*, vol. 4 (Paris: J. Baillière et Fils, 1877), 200. Translated by R. Newcomb.

18. *Cours de philosophie positive*, vol. 4, 191, translated by R. Newcomb.

19. It is worth accompanying João Neves da Fontoura's precise argument in defense of the Comtian concept of republican dictatorship. In a speech given before the legislature of Rio Grande do Sul on October 11, 1927, João Neves offered a reverent defense of the apostolate, of Benjamin Constant, and of Castilhos. The text proves the doctrinal continuity among the *gaúchos* between the earlier orthodox group and the men of 1930.

20. V. Milton Vanger, *El país modelo. José Batlle y Ordóñez, 1907–1915* (Montevideo: Arca, 1983).

21. Translator's note: This is my translation of Bosi's Portuguese-language quotation, which reads: "A terra é um bem por natureza comum a todos os homens." I have been unable to find the English original of this quote, but assume that it is

found in Mill's *Principles of Political Economy*. The closest quotation I could find from *Principles* is the following from book 2, chapter 4: "If individual property ... were excluded, the plan which must be adopted would be to hold the land and all the instruments of production as the joint property of the community." John Locke notes in more lapidary fashion: "[T]he earth and all inferior creatures be common to all men."

22. Getúlio Vargas, "Discurso de abertura do III Congresso Rural," *Correio do Povo* (Porto Alegre), May 25, 1929.

23. The phrase "Generation of 1907" was coined by Joseph Love, who includes in the group second-generation republican politicians who were admirers of Júlio de Castilhos (who, after his death in 1903, became a figure of myth) and who were supported by Borges de Medeiros. The seven principal names are: Getúlio Vargas, Flores da Cunha, Osvaldo Aranha, João Neves da Fontoura, Lindolfo Collor, Maurício Cardoso, and Firmino Paim Filho. The majority of these were members of the Bloco Acadêmico Castilhista in 1907, the year in which they entered public life. All of them served as state or federal deputies for the PRR, and all would participate actively in the Revolution of 1930 and hold key positions in the provisional government that followed.

24. *Cours de philosophie positive*, vol. 4, 189.

25. *Cours de philosophie positive*, vol. 4, 202.

26. Borges de Medeiros's Message to the Assembly, read on September 24, 1901.

27. Text of the *Parecer da Comissão* (Opinion of the Commission), read on November 23, 1920.

28. This is a variation on Henry George's phrase from his *Social Problems*: "Either government must manage the railroads, or the railroads must manage the government." This sentence was transcribed in the December 1914 issue of the magazine *Egatéa*, a publication of the Escola de Engenharia (School of Engineering) of Porto Alegre, which at the time granted technical assistance to projects aimed at bringing public services under state control.

29. In *A política positiva e a liberdade bancária*, principles 14 and 15, publication no. 81 of the Apostolado Positivista no Brasil, apud Tocary Assis Bastos, "O positivismo e a realidade brasileira," 141–42.

30. Campos Salles, *Da propaganda à presidência* (São Paulo: 1908), 301, apud Tocary Assis Bastos, "O positivismo e a realidade brasileira," 149.

31. *Anais*, November 30, 1923 legislative session.

32. Costa Franco, *Júlio de Castilhos e sua época*, 93–95.

33. Rio de Janeiro, Imprensa Nacional, 1918.

34. See Nícia Vilela Luz, *A luta pela industrialização no Brasil* (São Paulo: Difel, 1961); Edgard Carone, *O pensamento industrial no Brasil, 1888–1945* (São Paulo: Difel, 1977). An important detail: in 1934, Getúlio created the Conselho Federal de Comércio Exterior (Federal Council on Foreign Trade), which would coordinate the project of import substitution carried out a few years later.

35. Letter written from Rio de Janeiro, dated May 1932, apud John Wirth, *A política do desenvolvimento na era de Vargas* (Rio de Janeiro: FGV, 1974), xxi.

36. Speech given on May 4, 1931, transcribed in *A nova política do Brasil*, vol. 1 (Rio de Janeiro: J. Olympio, 1938), 11. In his writings, Jorge Street, a pioneer among protectionist businessmen, clarifies the relationship between the provisional government and the industrialists of São Paulo. See *Idéias sociais de Jorge Street*, ed. Evaristo de Morais Filho (Senado Federal, 1981). The rationalizing measures taken by the Vargas government were extensive and systematically encompassed all areas of the state. Beatriz de Souza Wahrlich, "O Governo Provisório de 1930 e a reforma administrativa," *Revista de Administração Pública* (December 1975): 5–68. In my view, Gustavo Capanema gives the best account of public ownership between 1930 and 1945. See his contribution to *O Estado Novo: um auto-retrato*, ed. Simon Schwartzman (Universidade Nacional de Brasília, 1983).

37. See Sílvia Ferraz Petersen's "As greves no RGS (1890–1919)," *RS: economia e política*, ed. J. Dacanal and S. Gonzaga (Porto Alegre: Mercado Aberto, 1979).

38. For a broader overview of the problem, see Robert Rowland's essay "Classe operária e Estado de compromisso: origens estruturais da legislação trabalhista e sindical," in *Estudos Cebrap*, no. 8 (1974): 5–40. (Translator's note: "Salary shall not be determined with regard to any general norm, but rather shall be a function of the collective agreement entered into by the contracting parties.")

39. See "Os positivistas e as greves," in Cruz Costa, *O positivismo na República*, 56–66.

40. For a better understanding of the tactical interactions between positivists and socialist reformists in Brazil, see Evaristo de Morais Filho's essay "Sindicato e sindicalismo no Brasil desde 30," *Tendências do Direito Público* (Rio de Janeiro: Forense, 1976). The author is a scholar of the young Comte and an expert in labor law. See also Ângela de Castro Gomes's *A invenção do trabalhismo* (Rio de Janeiro: IUPERJ, 1988).

41. *Idéias políticas de Júlio de Castilhos*, 478–79.

42. This article was published on October 4, 1887, in the republican newspaper *A Federação*. This newspaper, which Lindolfo Collor would later edit, is an impressive example of the partisan journals that were published during the Old Republic.

43. Miguel Lemos, newly arrived from the meetings that took place on Rue Monsieur-le-Prince, had stated categorically: "Industrialism, when left unregulated, becomes an immoral and disturbing force that over time can lead to a society's decomposition"; apud Ruyter Demaria Boiteux, "A questão social e o positivismo," *Anais da IV Reunião de Positivistas* (Rio de Janeiro: 1981), 101.

44. *Discours sur l'ensemble du positivisme*, p. 165. J. H. Bridges translates Comte's phrase as follows: "In all healthy conditions of Humanity, the citizen, whatever his position, has been regarded as a public functionary" (Auguste Comte, *General View of Positivism*, trans. J. H. Bridges [London: Trübner and Co., 1986 5], 165).

45. P. Arbousse-Bastide, *La doctrine de l'éducation universelle dans la philosophie d'Auguste Comte*, 2 vols. (Paris: PUF, 1957).

46. Leopoldo Zea, *Pensamiento positivista latinoamericano* (Caracas: Ayacucho, 1980).

47. Message to the Assembly, September 1913.

48. Statement by the Budgetary Commission, in response to the executive's message, given November 10, 1908.

49. See *Idéias políticas de João Pinheiro*, a volume edited by Francisco de Assis Barbosa for the Senado Federal (Federal Senate) in 1908.

50. Translator's note: *Coronelismo* refers to an informal system of local rural government in Brazil in which influential landowners from privileged families exercised de facto control over local politics and used coercive power to subvert democratic processes. By tradition, these men were referred to as *coronéis* (colonels), though they held no formal military rank. This system of governance was particularly strong between 1889 and 1930. *Coronelismo* has been compared to feudalism in its decentralization, dependence on local strongmen, and patron-client relationships.

51. Osvaldo Aranha, "Discurso na Assembléia Nacional Constituinte," April 30, 1943, in Moacyr Flores, *Osvaldo Aranha* (Porto Alegre: IEL, 1991), 61–62.

10. Brazilian Culture and Brazilian Cultures

1. "Um testemunho do presente," preface to Carlos Guilherme Mota, *Ideologia da cultura brasileira*, 2nd ed. (São Paulo: Ática, 1977).

Postscript to "Brazilian Culture and Brazilian Cultures" (1992)

1. Translator's note: Bosi is no doubt referring to the Japanese-American political scientist Francis Fukuyama, author of *The End of History and the Last Man* (1992).

2. This song, written by Sérgio Porto in 1968, parodies the historical content of many songs by Rio de Janeiro's famous *escolas de samba* (samba schools). The song's premise is that a samba composer goes crazy and writes a song about Brazilian history, but gets everything wrong—hence, Bosi's reference to "illogical connections and profusion of confused references."

3. Donella H. Meadows, Dennis L. Meadows, Jorgen Randers, and William W. Behrens III, *The Limits to Growth* (New York: Universe Books, 1972).

4. Translator's note: I believe that Bosi might have misattributed this quote, and that it may in fact be from the Marquis of Vauvenargues.

5. I [Bosi] found this quotation in A. Kondratov, *Nombre et pensée* (Moscow: Éditions Mir, 1967), 7; translated from Portuguese by R. Newcomb.

6. Sergio Solmi, preface to *Minima Moralia* (Turin: Einaudi, 1954), xvi–xvii.

7. A good summary of the present situation can be found in Hélio Jaguaribe, ed., *Brasil: reforma ou caos* (Rio de Janeiro: Paz e Terra, 1989). For a wide-ranging

view of the Third and Fourth Worlds, see the final report from the South Commission, *Desafio ao Sul* (Lisbon: Ed. Afrontamento, 1991).

8. Translator's note: I believe that Bosi is referring to the American psychologist B. F. Skinner.

9. Translator's note: This is an apparent reference to Shakespeare's *Julius Caesar*.

A Retrospective Glance

1. Translator's note: This is an uncredited reference to Mark 16:15.

2. I don't think that it is necessary here for me [Bosi] to explain the modernists' visions of Brazil or their playful oscillation between the primitivism and internationalism of *Tupi* and *not Tupi*. I have already addressed these issues in the essays "Moderno e modernista no Brasil" and "Situação de Macunaíma," both included in *Céu, inferno* (Ática, 1989). However, in the interest of adding to our picture, it is worth referring to the modernizing ideology of the Partido Democrático (Democratic Party), which was founded by dissidents from the PRP, intellectuals who revered the Revolution of 1930 but quickly returned to the fold, prompted by the strong pro-*paulista* feeling of 1932.

Epilogue (2001)

1. See *O ser e o tempo da poesia*, 6th ed. (São Paulo: Companhia das Letras, 2000), first edition published by Cultrix in 1977.

Index

Pages in **boldface** indicate primary discussion.

Abreu, Capistrano de, xi, 130, 314
Acosta, Joseph de, 127
Adorno, Theodor W., 274, 278, 306, 312, 339, 342n8
Afro-Brazilian religious practices (*candomblé, calundu, umbanda, macumba*, etc.), 32, 40, 46, 92, 267, 279, 286, 291, 323, 345n47
agregado (informal household member), 12
Aleijadinho, 22–23, 42–44, 345n44
Alencar, José de, **146–62**; *Cartas de Erasmo*, 185; *O demônio familiar*, 211; Romantic nationalism, 210, 287, 330, 334
Alighieri, Dante, 61–62
Alves, Castro, 202, **209–27**, 330, 334, 357n1
Amado, Jorge, 212
Amaral, Amadeu, 37
Ampère, André-Marie, 311
Anchieta, José de, xii, **48–74**; and Amerindians, 20; and Company of Jesus, 124, 327; devotional plays, 32; multilingual literary composition, 18–19
Andrade, Mário de, 364n2; and Aleijadinho, 292, 345n44; and Castro Alves, 226; and cultural mixture, 288; *Macunaíma*, 296; and "popularesque" culture, 280
Andrade, Oswald de, 288, 313
Andreoni, André João (Antonil), **123–45**, 351n7; *Cultura e opulência do Brasil*, 21, 330; and Antônio Vieira, 334, 351n9
Anglo-Brazilian agreement of 1826, 166
Anhanga (Amerindian deity, demonic figure), 50–51, 57
Antônio, João, 296
Aragon, Louis, 308
Aranha, Osvaldo, 252, 264, 361n23
Araripe Júnior, Tristão de Alencar, 82, 313
Arbousse-Bastide, Paul, 259
Arcadismo mineiro (literary movement), 22–23
Arrais, Amador, 82, 101, 103
Arte de Furtar (literary work), 83
Asian tigers (economics), 318
Assis, Joaquim Maria Machado de: and José de Alencar, 149, 156; "Almada," 21; "História de Quinze Dias," 187; and imitation, 313; mixed ancestry, 228; social criticism, 357n73
Azevedo, Miranda, 239

bacharéis (degree holders, generally in law), 13, 189, 239
Bacon, Francis, 6

Bakhtin, Mikhail, 88
bandeirantes (São Paulo–based colonial-era adventurers), 11, 15, 23, 124, 131, 151; *bandeirismo*, 326; conflict with the Jesuits, 17, 19, 113, 327; and Sérgio Buarque de Holanda, 17; term used to describe persons from São Paulo, 206
Barbosa, Adoniran, 296
Barbosa, Rui: disciple of José Bonifácio de Andrada e Silva, 202; monarchism, 263; parliamentarian, 190; reformism, 195, 199, 204, 212, 327; and social inequality, 106; *A queda do Império*, 169
Barreto, Lima, **228–34**, 334; anarchism and socialism, 233; critical intellectual, 210–11; and imitation, 313; mixed ancestry, 335; *República do Kaphet*, 208
Barreto, Manuel Pereira, 80, 239
barroco mineiro (artistic movement), 33, 47
Barros, João de, 344n35
Barros, Moraes, 207
Barthes, Roland, 300
Basque language, 68
Bastide, Roger, 42
Bastos, Pereira, 360n7
Bastos, Tavares, 179, 189–90, 195–96; critical intellectual, 204, 210; economic views, 199; reformism, 327, 353n2; and U.S. Civil War, 201
Bastos, Tocary Assis, 250
Batlle y Ordóñez, José (President of Uruguay), 242, 245, 249
Baudelaire, Charles, 63
Beethoven, Ludwig von, 307
belle époque in Brazil, 211, 229, 314, 335
Benci, Giorgio, 124, 126
Benjamin, Walter, 63, 301, 306, 339, 342n8
Bentham, Jeremy, 180, 355n25
Bento, Antônio, 199, 204
Bernardes, Manuel, 103
Bilac, Olavo, 229
Blake, William, 307
Bloch, Ernest, 306
Boal, Augusto, 296
Boas, Franz, 47
Bocayuva, Quintino: *A crise da lavoura*, 187, 197; and positivism, 239; reformism, 190
Bomfim, Manoel, 211–12, 313
Bopp, Raul, 288
Braganzas (Luso-Brazilian royal house), 172, 186
Brandão, Ambrósio Fernandes, 21
Brecht, Bertolt, 63
Brito, Saturnino de, 252
Brougham, Henry, 172
Buarque, Chico, 296
Burckhardt, Jacob, 6
Burke, Edmund, 178
Byron, Lord George Gordon, 218–19

Cabral, Pedro Álvares, 344n34
Cadogan, Léon, 346n3
caipira (rustic person), 35
Cairu, José da Silva Lisboa, Viscount of, 174, 185, 327
Calado, Manuel, 24
Caminha, Pero Vaz de, 21
Camões, Luís de, 4–5, **24–31**, 87, 330, 337, 344n34–35
Campos, Martinho, 190
Campos Salles, Manuel Ferraz de (president of Brazil): industrial policy, 250–51; presidency, 238; as São Paulo republican, 207
Camus, Albert, 340
Canabrava, Alice, 131
Cancioneiro geral (poetic anthology collected by Garcia de Resende), 72, 344n35
Canudos (messianic movement, civil conflict), 36, 287
Cardim, Fernão, 32
Cardoso, Fernando Henrique, 318
Cardoso, Maurício, 361n23
Cardozo, Jacob Newton, 176
Carlos, Roberto, 292
Carnaval (Brazilian festivity), 284, 291
Carneiro, Édison, 212
Carpeaux, Otto Maria, 235, 238
Carvalho, João Simplício Alves de, 262
Carvalho, José Pedro Dias de, 195
Castilhos, Júlio de, 254; and economic and

budgetary policy, 251–53; labor policy, 256; and positivism, 245, 253; in Rio Grande do Sul, 244, 255, 260, 263; and superorganic character of society, 240
Cato, 1
Cavalcanti, Amaro, 252
Césaire, Aimé, 203–4, 354n11
Chateaubriand, François-René de, 146
Childe, Gordon, 3–4
Clastres, Helène, 346n3
Club of Rome, 307
Cochin, Augustin, 204
Coelho Neto, Henrique Maximiano, 230
Coimbra, University of, 80, 93
Collor, Lindolfo: and journalism, 362n42; as member of "Generation of 1907," 361n23; and Rio Grande do Sul landowners, 247; and taxes, 246; and Getúlio Vargas, 201, 253–55, 263
Colo (Latin term), xi, **1–47**, 143, 337
Companhia das Índias Ocidentais (West Indies Company), 98
Company of Jesus (Jesuits), 22, 329; and Amerindians, 44, 52–53, 286; and Antonil, 124–25, 137, 145; conflict with *bandeirantes*, 17, 19, 113, 327, 334; South American missions, 5, 15, 20, 22, 115, 326–37, 338; and St. Ignatius of Loyola, 66, 68, 137; and Antônio Vieira, 104, 115, 118, 124
Comte, Auguste, 329; and budgeting, 252; and *développement*, 236; influence in Brazil, 200, 237, 240, 255, 259, 265; and political economy, 243; and progress, 248, 319; and "republican dictatorship," 360n19; and Rio Grande do Sul republicans, 242, 245, 249, 251, 336; and slavery, 240, 360nn7–8; and "social engineers," 317; and workers, 260
Condestado War (messianic movement, civil conflict), 36
Conrad, Robert, 165, 205
Consolidação das Leis do Trabalho (CLT, Brazilian Labor Code), 254, 259
Constant, Benjamin: followers of, 238, 241, 252, 262, 328; and moderating power, 171; and positivism, 200–201, 239

Constitution of 1824 (Brazil), 147, 171
Constitution of 1891 (Brazil), 231
Constitution of 1891 (Rio Grande do Sul), 265
Constitution of 1934 (Brazil), 261, 264
Cooper, Thomas, 176
Coronéis (land-owners, local political bosses), 194, 328
Correia, Serzedelo, 252
Cortés, Hernán, 10
Costa, João Cruz, 237–39
Council of Trent, 47, 91
Couto, Diogo do, 344n34
Croce, Benedetto, 63
Culturus (Latin term), **1–47**
Cultus (Latin term), **1–47**, 143, 337

Da Costa, Cláudio Manuel, 24
Da Cunha, Euclides, 210, 212, 287, 334–35, 357n70
Da Cunha, Flores, 361n23
Da Gama, Antonio Pinto Chichorro da, 195
Da Gama, Basílio, 22
Da Gama, Vasco, 25, 27–28, 30
Da Nóbrega, Manuel, 327
Da Veiga, Evaristo, 168, 170, 182–83
Da Vinci, Leonardo, 37, 307, 311
Dantas, Manuel Pinto de Sousa, 174
Darwin, Charles, 239–40, 287
Davis, Jefferson, 178–79
De Gaulle, Charles, 317
Dewey, John, 201–2, 313
Dias, Gonçalves, 151, 154–56, 209–10, 330
Díaz, Porfirio (President/dictator of Mexico), 246
Dostoyevsky, Fyodor, 307
Du Bois, W. E. B., 163, 169
Dupront, Alphonse, 18
Durão, José de Santa Rita, 24

Eco, Umberto, 274, 277–78
Egydio, Paulo, 206
Einstein, Albert, 311
Eliot, T. S., 18
Élis, Bernardo, 296
encadenado (chained) verse, 69

Encina, Juan de, 69
Engels, Friedrich, 105, 163, 349n9
Engenho (Brazilian sugar plantation), 9, 15
Estado Novo (Brazilian government under Getúlio Vargas), 253, 259, 271

Faoro, Raymundo, xi, 167, 239
Feijó, Diogo Antônio, 164, 168–69
Figueira, Andrade, 163
Fonseca, Dutra, 245
Fonseca, Rubem, 296
Fontoura, João Neves da, 251, 360n19, 361n23
fotonovela (form of Brazilian print media), 277, 285
Foucault, Michel, 300
Franco, Bernardo de Souza, 195
Franco, Maria Sylvia Carvalho, 14
Franco, Sérgio da Costa, 238, 244
Frankfurt School, 267, 278, 338
Franklin, John Hope, 176
Freire, Moniz, 252
Freire, Paulo, 294–95
French Artistic Mission of 1816, 43
Freyre, Gilberto: and Franz Boas, 47; *Casa-grande & senzala*, 15, 86; on colonizer-colonized relations, 16; *Sobrados e mucambos*, 15; and the sugar economy and Amerindians, 11
Fukuyama, Francis, 303–4, 363n1
Furtado, Celso, xi, 14, 174, 318
Furtado, Francisco José, 195

Galich, Manuel, 10
Galilei, Galileo, 309, 311
Gama, Luís, 199–200, 204–5, 207, 210; abolitionism, 228
Gândavo, Pero de Magalhães, 52, 286
Garibay, Ángel María, 154
George, Henry, 361n28
Gerschenkron, Alexander, 235–37
Gide, André, 226
Gil, Gilberto, 296
Gladstone, William, 165, 301
Godinho, Magalhães, 79
Goethe, Johann Wolfgang von, 63, 67, 223, 307

Góis e Vasconcelos, Zacarias de, 183, 188, 194–95, 204
Gorender, Jacob, xi, 12, 14, 205
Gracián, Baltasar, 95
Gramsci, Antonio, 7, 21, 81, 289, 336-37
Grotius, Hugo, 127
Guarnieri, Gianfrancesco, 296
Guimarães, Bernardo, 43–44
Gullar, Ferreira, 1

Habermas, Jürgen, xiv, 307
Haeckel, Ernst, 239, 287
Hamilton, Alexander, 174
Hegel, G. W. F., 310
Heine, Heinrich, 212–13, 357n1
Herder, Johann Gottfried, 224
Herskovits, Meville, 42
História trágico-marítima (literary work), 344n35
Hobsbawm, Eric, 172
Holanda, Sérgio Buarque de: on *bandeirantes*, 17; *Caminhos e fronteiras*, 15; on colonizer-colonized relations, 16; *Do Império à República*, 353n2; on positivists, 241; *Raízes do Brasil*, 15
Homem, Francisco de Sales Torres, Viscount of Inhomirim, 183, 186
Homem bom ("good man," gentleman or nobleman), 81, 83
Horkheimer, Max, 278, 306
Hugo, Victor, 188, 209, 226
humanism, 269
Humboldt, Alexander von, 307
Hybris, 30

ideological filtering, 183
independence of Brazil (1822), 166
Indianismo (literary movement), 146, 149–50, 223, 334
Inquisition, 22, 114
Itaboraí, Joaquim José Rodrigues Torres, Viscount of, 167, 178, 184, 194

Jaeger, Werner, 6
Jansenism (Catholic religious movement), 104
Jardim, Silva, 200, 239

Jesus, Clementina de, 296
Jesus, Tomé de, 103
João VI (King of Portugal, resident in Brazil), 43

Kafka, Franz, 63
Kant, Immanuel, 308
Kempis, Thomas à, 68
Kierkegaard, Søren, 307
Klee, Paul, 63
Knight, Franklin, 179

Laffitte, Pierre, 237, 239, 242, 260
Lanson, Gustave, xiii
Las Casas, Bartalomé de, 10, 127
Leal, Victor Nunes, 353n2
Lei Áurea (Golden Law, abolition of slavery, 1888), 198, 205, 228, 240, 243, 328
Lei do Ventre Livre (Law of the Free Womb, 1871), 163, 175, 188, 197, 205, 211
Lei dos Sexagenários (Sexagenarians' Law, 1885), 207
Leibniz, Gottfried Wilhelm, 310
Leite, Serafim, 124
Leixa-pren (poetic term), 102
Lemos, Miguel: and Auguste Comte, 242; and industry, 362n43; orthodox positivist, 201, 239; and slavery, 200, 238, 359–60n7, 360n8; and superorganic character of society, 240
León-Portilla, Miguel, 154
Leroy-Beaulieu, Pierre Paul, 246
Léry, Jean de, 32, 52
Lévi-Strauss, Claude, 288
Lévy-Bruhl, Lucien, 288
Leyenda negra ("black legend" of Spanish colonization), 2
Lima, Araújo, 164, 204
Lima, Barbosa, 252
Lima, Hermes, 169
Lima, Jorge de, 286
Lincoln, Abraham, 201
Língua geral (standardized form of Tupi-Guarani dialects), 48
Lins, Ivan, 237, 252
Lisboa, João Francisco, 186–87
Lisle, Rouget de, 236

List, Friedrich, 237
Literatura de cordel (Brazilian folk narrative form), 14, 55, 291–92, 326, 338
Littré, Émile, 260
Lobo, Edu, 296
Lobo, Francisco Rodrigues, 347–48n1
Loew, Jacques, 290
"lost decade" in Latin America (economics), 322–23
Louverture, Toussaint, 200, 238
Love, Joseph, 238, 244, 361n23
Lukács, Georg, 63
Luso-Tropicalism (ideology), 326
Luther, Martin, 314

Machado, Dyonélio, 296
Machiavelli, Niccolò, 100, 326
Magalhães, Couto de, 287
Magalhães, Gonçalves de, 43
Maistre, Xavier de, 146
Malheiro, Perdigão, 199, 201–2
Mallarmé, Stéphane, 304
Manchester, Alan K., 80
Mannheim, Karl, 7, 342n8
Manzoni, Alessandro, 301
Marco, Plínio, 296
Marcuse, Herbert, 278
Marinho, Saldanha, 190
Marrou, Henri Irénée, 6
Martins, Silveira, 190
Marx, Karl: and Friedrich Engels, 163; and European colonization of the Americas, 9; and exchange, 75; and ideology, 163; and labor, 119, 138; and religion, 17; and slave labor, 11–12
Matos, Gonçalo de, 89
Matos, Gregório de, **75–96**, 101, 334: and Afro-Brazilian customs, 45, 286–87; and foreign merchants, 21; and Francisco Rodrigues Lobo, 347–48n1; and the *máquina mercante*, 14; and multi-racial persons, 21; and Antônio Vieira, 97
Mauro, Frédéric, 79
Mauss, Marcel, 16
Mazzini, Giuseppe, 217
McLuhan, Marshall, 283, 306
Medeiros, Antônio Augusto Borges de:

and agriculture, 247–48; and budgeting, 252; and education, 261–62; and industrial policy, 250; and political economy, 253; political figure, 265; and positivism, 245, 253; and public services, 249–50; in Rio Grande do Sul, 255, 260, 263; and social policy, 254; and taxes, 246
Melo, João Manuel Cardoso de, 193
Melo Neto, João Cabral de, 296
Mendes, Teixeira: and French leadership of positivism, 237; journalism, 255; orthodox positivist, 200–201, 239; and right to property, 241; and slavery, 238; and superorganic character of society, 240
Mendonça, Lúcio de, 210
Mendonça, Ribeiro de, 237
Merleau-Ponty, Maurice, 342n8
Mesquita Filho, Júlio de, 17
Métraux, Alfred, 21, 346n3
Meyer, Augusto, 213, 357n1
Michelet, Jules, 146
Milagre brasileiro ("Brazilian miracle"), 271
Mill, John Stuart, 245
Ministério de Educação e Cultura (Ministry of Education and Culture, Brazil), 275
Miranda, Sá de, 30
Moles, Abraham, 283
Molina, Luís, 127
Molinos, Miguel de, 104
Montaigne, Michel de, 10, 307
Montesquieu, Charles-Louis de Secondat, Baron of Le Brède and, 307
Montoya, Antonio Ruiz de, 327
Moraes, A. J. Mello, 177
Moraes, Prudente de (President of Brazil), 207, 238, 360n15
Morais, Evaristo de, 256, 263
Muller, Gerardo, 245
Murtinho, Joaquim, 251
Myrdal, Gunnar, 178

Nabuco, Joaquim, 334; abolitionism, 198, 204; and Brazilian party politics, 170; critical intellectual, 210; and his father, 190; *Minha Formação*, 198; monarchism, 208, 263; on the *novo liberalismo*, 188, 193, 209, 335; parliamentarian, 190; reformism, 190, 196, 199, 212, 327, 353n2; and São Paulo republicans, 205, 239; "O terreno da luta," 187
Nabuco de Araújo, José Tomás, 185, 190, 194–97
Nascimento, Milton, 296
Nazareth, Agripino, 256
Newton, Isaac, 311
Nietzsche, Friedrich, 308
Nimuendaju, Curt, 346n3, 352n6
Novais, Fernando, 14

Olinda, Pedro de Araújo Lima, Viscount and Marquis of, 178, 204
Ottoni, Teófilo Benedicto, 195–96

Paim Filho, Firmino, 361n23
Pajé (Amerindian shaman), 52–53, 55, 65
Paraguayan War (1864–70), 200
Paraná, Honório Hermeto Carneiro Leão, Marquis of, 164, 167, 178, 183, 185
Paranaguá, João Lustosa da Cunha, 183, 195
Pascal, Blaise, 310
Patrocínio, José do, 199, 204, 228
Paul III (pope), 112
paulistinhas (fired clay religious figures), 39, 326, 338
Pedro I (Emperor of Brazil), 147, 170–71
Pedro II (Emperor of Brazil), 155; and dissolution of Góis cabinet, 188, 196, 211; majority, 172; political views, 202; and positivism, 255; and José Antônio Saraiva, 194
Peixoto, Floriano (President of Brazil), 229–30, 238, 241, 263, 328
Peláez, Severo Martínez, 179
Pena, Martins, 165
Pereira, Nuno Marques, 32, 44–46
Pereyra, Juan de Solorzano, 127
Pesavento, Santa, 245
Petrarch, 87
Pimenta, Joaquim, 256
Pinamonti, Gian Pietro, 128
Pinheiro, João, 252, 261–62

Pinto, Heitor, 103
Pizarro, Francisco, 10
Plato, 224
Plautus, 1, 8
Plebe, Armando, 89
Pompéia, Raul, 200, 210, 229, 239, 313
popular music in Brazil, 291–92, 296
Portinari, Candido, 286
Porto, Sérgio, 305, 363n2
Porto Alegre, Araújo, 43
positivism, **235–65**, 314, 362n40
Pound, Ezra, 24
Prado, Antônio, 205
Prado, Caio, Jr., xi, 14
Prestes, Antônio, 242
Prestes, Luís Carlos, 242
Prosopopoeia, 217, 221
Protestantism: and Brazil, 37, 279; John Calvin and Calvinism, 55, 137, 314; Puritanism, 56

Queirós, Eusébio de, 163, 167, 183–84
Questão servil ("servile" or slave question), 147
Quevedo, Francisco de, 92
Quietism (Catholic religious movement), 104
Quilombo (Afo-Brazilian maroon settlement), 12, 15; Palmares settlement 22, 223
Quintilian, 102

Rabelais, François, 88
Ramalho, João, 19
Ramos, Arthur, 266
Ramos, Graciliano, 36, 296, 313–14
Ravel, Maurice, 224
Rebouças, André: abolitionism, 228; critical intellectual, 211; *democracia rural*, 199, 205; monarchism, 208, 263; reformism, 190, 195, 199, 327, 356–57n69
Recôncavo (coastal region of Bahia, northeastern Brazil), 139
redondilho, redondilla (poetic term), 48, 69
Rego, José Lins do, 296
reinol (native-born Portuguese person), 84

Reis, Aarão, 252
Revolution of 1930 (Brazil), xii, 238, 241, 252–53, 328, 336, 361n23, 364n2
Ribeiro, João, 287
Ricardo, Cassiano, 288
Ricardo, David, 236
Ricardo, Sérgio, 296
Rio Branco, José Paranhos, Viscount of, 183, 190
Rodrigues, José Honório, 353n2
Rodrigues, Nina, 42, 287
Rolland, Jacob, 125
Romero, Sílvio: and Brazilian oral tradition, 37, 287; and Charles Darwin, 240; and positivism and evolutionism, 200, 240; and Herbert Spencer, 201; and Bernardo Pereira de Vasconcelos, 355n25
Rosa, Francisco Octaviano de Almeida, 195–96
Rosa, João Guimarães, 235, 281, 286, 296, 313, 329, 338
Rousseau, Jean-Jacques, 147, 288, 307

Sahagún, Bernardino de, 154
Saia, Luís, 41
Saint-Hilaire, Jules Barthélémy-, 171
Saint-Simon, Claude Henri de Rouvrey, Count of: *développement*, 236; and entrepreneurial discourse, 237; and influence in Brazil, 254; and progress, 319; and socialism, 235; and utopian industrialism, 242, 255
Salazar, Antônio de Oliveira (Portuguese dictator), 305
Saldanha, Gaspar, 246–47
Santo Amaro, Count of, 135–36
Santos, José Maria dos, 205, 353n2
São Vicente, José Antônio Pimenta Bueno, Marquis of, 190
Saraiva, Antônio José, 350n15
Saraiva, José Antônio, 174, 183, 194–95
Sartre, Jean-Paul, 342n8
Say, Jean-Baptiste, 180–82, 243
Schaden, Egon, 346n3
Scheler, Max, 342n8
Schiller, Friedrich, 307
Schoelcher, Victor, 203–4

Schwarz, Roberto, 357n73
Scott, Walter, 146
Sertão (Brazil's northeastern backlands), 267, 285, 291
Siger, Carl, 11
Silva, José Bonifácio Andrada e (father), 172
Silva, José Bonifácio Andrada e (son), 190, 202
Silva, Rodrigo, 205
Simonsen, Roberto, 79, 252
Sinimbu, João Lins Vieira Cansanção de, 183
Smith, Adam, 174–75, 180–81, 243, 327, 329
soccer, 285
Sodré, Nelson Werneck, 14
Solmi, Sergio, 312
Sousa, Cruz e, 334; Afro-Brazilian, 228; critical intellectual, 210; "Emparedado," 232–34, 330, 335
Sousa, Gabriel Soares de, 52, 286
Sousa, Octávio Tarqüínio de, 170
Spanish language, 68
Spencer, Herbert, 329; and São Paulo republicans, 239; and Sílvio Romero, 200–201, 240; and Getúlio Vargas, 250
St. Augustine, 67
St. Bonaventure, 68
St. Ignatius of Loyola: and José de Anchieta, 66, 130, 327; and Antonil, 130, 137; and Company of Jesus, 66, 68, 327; and *Spiritual Exercises*, 66, 68
St. James, 5
St. John of Patmos, 155
St. John the Baptist, 103–4
St. John the Evangelist, 17
St. Maurice, 59–60
St. Paul: letters, 8, 22, 55, 68
St. Roch, 98–99
St. Thomas Aquinas, 358n5
Staden, Hans, 32, 52
Steuart, James, 181
Street, Jorge, 252, 263, 362n36
structuralism (literary-critical method), 268–70
Suárez, Francisco, 127
Suassuna, Ariano, 297
Sue, Eugène, 218–19

Taine, Hippolyte, 82
Tamandaré (legendary Amerindian figure), 162
Tauney, Afonso d'Escragnolle, 124
Teixeira, Bento, 23–24
Thevet, André, 52
Third Estate, 104, 106–7
Tibiriçá, João, 207
Tocqueville, Alexis de, 166, 354n11
Tolstoy, Leo, 307
Torres, Alberto, 231
Torres, Rodrigues, 183
Treaty of Methuen (1703), 80
Trevisan, Dalton, 296
Trotsky, Leon, 312
Trovão, Lopes, 239
Tucker, George, 176
Tupã (Brazilian indigenous deity), 19, 44, 49–53, 154, 346n3
Turgot, Anne-Robert-Jacques, 181

Ungaretti, Giuseppe, 42
Uruguai, Paulino José Soares de Sousa, Viscount of, 167, 183

Vandré, Geraldo, 296
Varela, Fagundes, 210, 218–19
Vargas, Getúlio (President/dictator of Brazil): industrial policy, 252–54, 263; member of "Generation of 1907," 361n23; political career in Rio Grande do Sul, 201, 246–47, 249–50; and positivism, 201, 359n5; presidency, 264, 336, 361n34; and Herbert Spencer, 250
Vargas, Protásio, 242
Varnhagen, Francisco Adolfo de, Viscount of Porto Seguro, 178, 201–2
Vasconcelos, Bernardo Pereira de: economic beliefs, 175, 185; *pai da pátria* (father of the country), 182; in government, 165; political beliefs, 164, 166, 168–70, 183; pro-slavery, 170, 172; and Romantic nationalism, 178
Vasconcelos, Simão de, 327
Vatican II, 35
Veiga, J. J., 296
Veloso, Caetano, 296
Veloso, José Mariano da Conceição, 132

Veríssimo, Érico, 296
Veríssimo, José, 217–18
Vianna, Oliveira, 231, 263
Vianna Filho, Oduvaldo, 296
Vico, Gianbattista, 22, 307, 321, 329–30
Vieira, Antonio, xii, **97–122**, 313, 327, 334; and Antonil, 124–30, 143, 145; and the Baroque, 350n15; on colonizer-colonized relations; defense of Amerindians, 20, 125; defense of Jews, 22; and the Inquisition, 22, 128; millenarianism, 22, 128; on slavery, 23, 330
Vigny, Alfred de, 219, 223
Villa-Lobos, Heitor, 286
Vitoria, Francisco de, 127

Xangô (Afro-Brazilian deity), 40
Xidieh, Oswaldo Elias, 36

Wallon, Henri, 204
Walsh, Robert, 170
Weber, Max, 137, 281, 318–19
Weil, Simone, 36, 307, 340
Wiener, Norbert, 299, 309–10, 315

Yancey, William L., 176
Yrigoyen, Hipólito (President of Argentina), 242, 249

Zea, Leopoldo, 260
Zurara, Gomes Eanes de, 358n5

ALFREDO BOSI is the director of the Institute of Advanced Studies at the University of São Paolo. He is the author of *A Concise History of Brazilian Literature*.

ROBERT PATRICK NEWCOMB is an associate professor of Luso-Brazilian studies at the University of California–Davis.

The University of Illinois Press
is a founding member of the
Association of American University Presses.

Composed in 10.5/13 Minion Pro
with Cronos display
by Jim Proefrock
at the University of Illinois Press
Manufactured by Sheridan Books, Inc.

University of Illinois Press
1325 South Oak Street
Champaign, IL 61820-6903
www.press.uillinois.edu